Detail in Process

Detail in Process

Christine Killory and René Davids, editors

AsBuilt

PRINCETON ARCHITECTURAL PRESS, NEW YORK

AsBuilt

A PRINCETON ARCHITECTURAL PRESS SERIES

AsBuilt features formal and material innovation in architecture, emphasizes structure and function, and explores the development and application of new technologies and materials.

Published by
Princeton Architectural Press
37 East Seventh Street
New York, New York 10003

For a free catalog of books, call 1.800.722.6657.
Visit our website at www.papress.com.

Printed and bound in China
11 10 09 08 4 3 2 1 First edition

Publication of this book has been supported by a grant from the Graham Foundation for Advanced Studies in the Fine Arts.

Editing: Linda Lee
Design: Paul Wagner

Special thanks to: Nettie Aljian, Sara Bader, Dorothy Ball, Nicola Bednarek, Janet Behning, Becca Casbon, Penny (Yuen Pik) Chu, Russell Fernandez, Pete Fitzpatrick, Wendy Fuller, Jan Haux, Clare Jacobson, John King, Aileen Kwun, Nancy Eklund Later, Laurie Manfra, Katharine Myers, Lauren Nelson Packard, Jennifer Thompson, Arnoud Verhaeghe, Joseph Weston, and Deb Wood of Princeton Architectural Press
—Kevin C. Lippert, publisher

Library of Congress
Cataloging-in-Publication Data
Killory, Christine, 1958–
Detail in process / Christine Killory and
René Davids.
p. cm. — (AsBuilt ; 2)
Includes bibliographical references.
ISBN 978-1-56898-718-7 (hardcover : alk. paper)
1. Architecture—United States—21st century.
2. Architecture—Technological innovations—United
States. I. Davids, René, 1949– II. Title.
NA712.7.K55 2008
720.973'090511—dc22
2007034955

Contents

6 Preface

12 **Morimoto New York**, New York, New York · Tadao Ando Architect & Associates · Gotodesigngroup LLC · Guggenheimer Architects

20 **Terrence Donnelly Centre for Cellular and Biomolecular Research**, Toronto, Canada · Behnisch Architekten · architectsAlliance

28 **BRIDGES Center**, Memphis, Tennessee · buildingstudio

38 **Des Moines Public Library**, Des Moines, Iowa · David Chipperfield Architects · Herbert Lewis Kruse Blunck Architecture

44 **Picower Institute for Learning and Memory**, Cambridge, Massachusetts · Charles Correa Associates · Goody Clancy

50 **University of Phoenix Stadium**, Glendale, Arizona · Eisenman Architects · HOK Sport

60 **Hearst Tower**, New York, New York · Foster + Partners · Adamson Associates Architects

68 **Leslie Dan Pharmacy Building**, Toronto, Canada · Foster + Partners · Cannon Design

78 **Floating Box House**, Austin, Texas · Peter L. Gluck & Partners, Architects

84 **Biodesign Institute Building B**, Tempe, Arizona · Gould Evans Associates · Lord, Aeck & Sargent Architecture

90 **La Maison Unique**, New York, New York · Heatherwick Studio · Atmosphere Design Group LLC

100 **de Young Museum**, San Francisco, California · Herzog & de Meuron Architekten · Fong & Chan Architects

112 **Children's Museum of Pittsburgh**, Pittsburgh, Pennsylvania · Koning Eizenberg Architecture · Perkins Eastman

118 **Marsupial Bridge and Urban Plaza**, Milwaukee, Wisconsin · La Dallman Architects, Inc.

126 **Desert House Prototype**, Desert Hot Springs, California · Marmol Radziner Prefab

132 **Pedestrian Bridge**, Austin, Texas · Miró Rivera Architects

136 **University of Cincinnati Campus Recreation Center**, Cincinnati, Ohio · Morphosis · KZF Design

144 **Guthrie Theater**, Minneapolis, Minnesota · Ateliers Jean Nouvel · Architectural Alliance

150 **High Museum of Art**, Atlanta, Georgia · Renzo Piano Building Workshop · Lord, Aeck & Sargent Architecture

158 **Meinel Optical Sciences Building**, Tucson, Arizona · Richärd + Bauer

168 **Gary Comer Youth Center**, Chicago, Illinois · John Ronan Architect

174 **Toledo Museum of Art Glass Pavilion**, Toledo, Ohio · Kazuyo Sejima + Ryue Nishizawa / SANAA · Kendall/Heaton Associates, Inc.

186 **7 World Trade Center**, New York, New York · Skidmore, Owings & Merrill LLP

194 **Library for Manuscripts**, Wellesley, Massachusetts · vir.mueller Architects

198 **House of Sweden (Swedish Embassy)**, Washington, D.C. · Wingårdh Arkitektkontor AB · VOA Associates

204 Acknowledgments

205 Project Credits

208 Illustration Credits

Preface

With engineering being touted as the new architecture, it is worth considering how design and engineering construction technologies are coming together in ways unimaginable forty years ago, when computer-aided design began to replace traditional drafting tools. Technology is changing not just materials, built form, manufacturing processes, fabrication, construction documents, and software, but also professional relationships between architects and engineers. If engineering is revolutionizing the field of architecture with new forms that technically and aesthetically extend its possibilities, architects are beginning to think more like engineers, focusing less on symbolic expression and more on exploiting the design opportunities presented by building type, user needs, climate, and location.

For many centuries, when architecture was a collective act of imitation built by artisans who understood the principles of both architecture and engineering, geometry alone provided the fundamental basis of building science, and individual creativity was regarded with suspicion. Architecture—as the profession is practiced today—began during the thirteenth century, when the introduction of scale drawings that resolved building plans and details in advance of construction began the gradual separation of architecture from building. Architects became the creators and masters of an abstract, symbolic formal language that would eventually provide a substitute for their presence on the building site. During the Renaissance, architecture was defined as a humanistic art, further distinguishing it from building science.

When the first model curriculum for the education of architects was introduced in 1648 at the École des Beaux-Arts in Paris, it emphasized the study and imitation of the classical arts, individual creativity, and the development of multiple original solutions to design problems. A century later, civil engineering became a profession separate from architecture with the establishment, also in Paris, of the École Royale des Ponts et Chaussées, where geometry, algebra, and the applied sciences of mechanics and hydraulics formed the basis of theoretical learning. The civil engineering curriculum focused on a single, most-correct solution for each design problem, resolved through application of the scientific method rather than creativity or aesthetic criteria. In *French Architects and Engineers in the Age of Enlightenment*, historian Antoine Picon describes how the increasing autonomy of science and technology during the eighteenth century provoked tension between advocates of the science embodied in building technology and proponents of the art of architecture.[1]

By century's end, as architects and engineers realized that they no longer shared the same intellectual culture, the professions of architecture and engineering became estranged, with consequences that still reverberate today: architects are inclined to regard engineers as technicians interested only in function, and engineers perceive architects as aesthetes preoccupied mainly with styling building facades and finishes. Engineers limited their specialization to include bridges, roads, and other structures that did not provide human habitation, and everything else was considered architecture. The process of exchange between the professions continued—their work integrated to varying degrees—but the authority of the architect remained absolute regarding matters of aesthetics, function, structure, construction technology, and supervision of the building process until the increasing complexity of structural steel framing in the mid-nineteenth century forced architects to rely on the expertise of civil engineers. The development of sophisticated environmental systems eventually required consultation with mechanical and electrical engineers as well, but because technical services were subservient to aesthetics and structure, mechanical engineers were last to join the design team, usually after schematic design had been completed.

In early twentieth century Europe, many architects, in particular, longed to see the professions of architecture and engineering reunited. Walter Gropius founded the Bauhaus with the aim of unifying architecture and technology, arts and crafts. In *Vers une architecture*, Le Corbusier claimed that the only genuine architecture of the day was to be found among the work of engineers: "The engineer, inspired by the law of economy and governed by mathematical calculation, puts us in accord with universal law. He achieves harmony."[2] As buildings continued to acquire advanced technology and performance specifications, highly specialized engineers became more indispensable and influential. By the end of the twentieth century, a major portion of most building budgets was controlled by the engineering professions.

Architecture and engineering remain disciplines with separate professional identities and two very different ways of looking at the world. Architects are trained to produce a creative synthesis that can be altered or revised throughout the design process in response to new information or changing circumstances. Engineers are taught to systematically analyze available data to produce the single optimum solution using rigorous analysis and engineering principles based on applied science. Reliance on engineering principles alone, however, is insufficient as a response to the challenges of contemporary architectural design practice, a somewhat indeterminate and messy process that involves elements of risk—including the risk of failure—and that demands a balance of technical and aesthetic skills. For engineers, failure is not an option, and they often use their influence on the design team to restrain the irrational exuberance of architects. In retaliation, architects have limited or denied engineers opportunities to influence design during the early project stages, leaving them to figure out how to build what the architects have produced with no technical input.

The proliferation of new materials and technologies now driving the design process requires architects and engineers to work together as equals and is also rapidly expanding the areas of common ground between them. The recent shift in emphasis from static to dynamic form; the transition from plane and solid geometry to an integrated landscape with forms and processes that grow and change; the demand for buildings that are responsive to climate and use, with intelligent facades that automatically control daylighting, ventilation, and more; hybrid building envelopes that combine two or more interactive strategies; and structures with complex assemblies of moving parts have shifted the design focus away from formal expression and the aesthetics of architecture toward materials and technology.

While the dynamic process of exchange between architecture and engineering has been eased by recent advances in 3-D modeling software and imaging technology, such as Building Information Modeling (BIM), structural engineers have used computers in their design processes for decades and were among the first to use 3-D models to communicate complex engineering concepts visually and graphically in a more direct and understandable format without recourse to calculations and data. Using a variety of 3-D modeling techniques, both architects and engineers can now predict and visualize any aspect of a building's performance, including its responsiveness to natural and artificial light, seasonal light and temperature fluctuations, and dynamic loading, with a reasonable degree of accuracy Representational images on the screen behave like objects, active in real time, with physical properties that provide instant feedback indicating the effect a change in one part of the building's design has on the entirety of the building.

Where traditional CAD enabled more efficient design and faster, easier production and alteration of construction documents, new technologies, such as BIM, allow architects to coordinate information at every stage of the design process and develop construction documents for the completed building before it ever breaks ground. They also permit accurate estimates of project costs early in the design process, when adjustments are less expensive. Although the creation of these complex 3-D models is a painstaking, time-consuming, and costly exercise, they allow architects and engineers greater creative freedom coupled with the assurance that a building's performance can be accurately studied and adjusted while still in the conceptual design phase.

Three-dimensional models provide continuity from the initial concept to construction documents for the entire design team and allow for continual movement back and forth between micro and macro scales. The design process is no longer a linear sequence of hand-offs, with the project passed along in successive stages from architects, to engineers, consultants, contractors, and fabricators. To coordinate the complex geometries of the five buildings that make up the University of Cincinnati's Campus Recreation Center, Morphosis created a 3-D model that evolved dynamically as the buildings advanced. When compared with similar models produced by consultants and fabricators, the model eased the process of three-dimensional detailing and made it possible to detect and resolve conflicts in the building systems during the production of construction documents, rather than on the job site. The quality of the information shared among architects, engineers, and those who fabricated and assembled the buildings allowed construction details for the five geometrically complex buildings to be produced with accuracy and precision.

Architectural design continues to advance with materials and technology developed by and for other industries, including aerospace, defense, manufacturing, and automotive. These adaptations are not limited to the use of now-familiar tools such as CAD/CAM, CATIA, CNC systems, 3-D printers, and rapid prototyping, but also include conceptual constructs that affect an architect's basic understanding of their creative process. Among the most significant of those are the notion of buildings as composed of groups of systems rather than thousands of individual parts—a concept borrowed from the physical sciences—and the use of techniques that directly affect design development, such as the experiments with full-sized mockup models used to study and perfect complex building components, a technique first developed by the U.S. Department of Defense to test weapons systems. Images of mockup models of various sizes accompany several of the projects included in *Detail in Process*. Although they are relatively expensive to build, the use of mockups greatly improves the accuracy with which the performance of building systems and assemblies of parts can be predicted.

Unlike structural engineers, who have often exerted significant influence on design decisions in architecture, mechanical engineers have typically been restricted to spaces zoned for building services, a territory willingly ceded to them by architects who have traditionally preferred minimal involvement with mechanical systems. But as issues of environmental responsiveness, energy efficiency, and related concepts derived from mechanical engineering have become more important, the impact of environmental technologies on building design has begun to impact the formal aspects of architecture, making collaboration between architects and mechanical engineers more essential for both professions.

Mechanical engineers use computational fluid dynamics (CFD), a branch of fluid mechanics, with computers performing the millions of calculations required to simulate the interaction of fluids and gases on complex architectural surfaces, then generate computer simulations and 3-D models that give the resulting data visual form. Mechanical and climate engineers applied CFD analysis to develop a variety of ventilation solutions for the transparent double-shell glass facade of the Glass Pavilion at the Toledo Museum of Art. Each of the self-contained glazed spaces inside the monolithic glass envelope and the various indoor and cavity spaces has different thermal challenges: condensation on the glass walls, solar heat gain and glare resulting from natural illumination, humidified exhibition spaces, very cold winter temperatures in Toledo, and increased glass surface temperatures during the hot summers. Diagrammatic drawings produced from complex CFD calculations revealed the effects of the flow of heat through various adjacent building assemblies and components on the building's facade.

At the University of Toronto's Terrence Donnelly Centre for Cellular and Biomolecular Research, the double facade of the south elevation has two-and-a-half-foot-wide air space between the exterior single-glazed skin and an argon-filled, thermally broken, double-glazed interior skin. Motorized dampers and vents on the outer skin, retractable perforated aluminum louvers located between the two skins, and four-inch concave slats programmed to tilt according to the sun's angle prevent direct sunlight from reaching the interior glazing. The building is a successful synthesis of architectural form and structural, mechanical, and environmental engineering.

In these and many similar projects where the design process is necessarily open and collaborative, the architecture of single authorship—with the architect in charge as form-giver and decision maker—is fast becoming a thing of the past as the ability to access complete, updated building information throughout the design process eliminates the traditional barriers between the design and engineering disciplines. Architects no longer have exclusive access to the client during the early project stages; the mostly private interval that used to be devoted to sketching plans and perspectives by hand while exploring the creation of form and space through study models is now commonly mediated by data and shared with the entire design team.

To ensure the viability of their profession in these increasingly challenging design environments, architects must become more technologically and scientifically literate, more familiar with engineering concepts, and knowledgeable about the ways in which they can inform architecture. Unfortunately, in the standard three-year professional-degree program offered at most graduate schools in the United States, there is barely enough time for students to acquire a rudimentary education in architecture, let alone the fundamentals of engineering. At present, most engineers are trained to be service providers rather than creative visionaries. If engineers are to assume some creative responsibility for design, their education should include the design of complex structural and environmental systems in addition to standardized technical knowledge. Engineers and architects are better educated together, as they have been traditionally in Germany and Switzerland, with at least one shared studio course in which to explore new materials, innovative construction methods, and nontraditional structures, utilizing the new technology as both a means to an end and a means of working together.

In his manifesto *Informal: New Structure in Architecture*, renowned Arup engineer Cecil Balmond, who views engineering as a fundamentally creative activity and specializes in the design of buildings with innovative structures, urges his fellow engineers "to release the world of engineering and feel free to enter architecture," as he himself has recently done.[3] With conceptual thought in architecture increasingly influenced by tectonic, material, and construction-related considerations long regarded as belonging to the domain of engineering, the space between design and building construction is closing fast, and soon the separation between the material and intellectual worlds will disappear altogether, along with the architect's traditional role of mediator between them. During the eighteenth century, antagonism between the advocates of architecture as an art form and architecture as the product of applied science provoked a crisis of identity among architects no longer certain about its theoretical foundations. Some time in the future, architects may once again confront similar questions about what it means to be an architect, about what it is that determines the quality of architectural thought and constitutes the proprietary knowledge base of architecture. As they have for many centuries, architects continue to provide the meaning inherent in architecture, but they operate on terrain increasingly more congenial to engineers.

Christine Killory

Notes

1. Antoine Picon, *French Architects and Engineers in the Age of Enlightenment* (Cambridge: Cambridge University Press, 1992).
2. Le Corbusier, *Towards a New Architecture*, trans. Frederic Etchells (Mineola, NY Dover Publications, 1985).
3. Cecil Balmond, *Informal: New Structure in Architecture* (New York: Prestel Publishing, 2002).

AsBuilt

Morimoto New York, New York, New York
Tadao Ando Architect & Associates, Osaka, Japan
Gotodesigngroup LLC, New York
Guggenheimer Architects, New York

Located in the former loading dock of an early twentieth century manufacturing building, Morimoto is a 12,000-square-foot restaurant specializing in contemporary Japanese cuisine with seating for 160 on the main level—including 24 seats at the sushi bar surrounding the 1,500-square-foot open kitchen and an *omakase* (chef's choice) table for 8—and 40 in the lower-level lounge.

The renovation of the existing space included the addition of a reinforced concrete foundation to accommodate the lower level of the new restaurant, as well as reinforcement of the existing structure to create column-free space for the central staircase and clear sightlines from the upper level down to the lounge and bar. At the street entrance are 130-foot-long inset panels of blackened galvanized-steel and an oversized *noren*, a traditional Japanese divided curtain hung in the doorway of a shop or restaurant to indicate that it is open for business, as well as for protection from heat, light, dust, and weather.

The ceiling of the street-level space is covered with panels of white canvas pressed into undulating folds and sprayed with fiberglass to hold their shape. For visual and acoustical privacy, dining tables are separated by glass partitions fritted with white ceramic dots; in the lounge, the dots are larger and spaced closer together for greater opacity and privacy. A concrete stair with a glass balustrade leads down to the lounge and bar, its landing cantilevered over the lower level.

Separating the main stair from the communal dining room is a 20-foot-square two-story-high wall of 17,400 water-filled bottles mounted on both sides of a structural steel frame that acts as a light diffuser for an installation of warm and cool white LEDs inserted lengthwise into both sides of every third row of bottles. A metal grid between the two layers of bottles supports the LEDs and electrical wiring conduits. Behind the bar on the lower level is a floor-to-ceiling, single-layer water-bottle wall, three rows of two bottles stacked vertically with the opening ends joined and an upright top row. Other indirect and concealed lighting sources are located within vertical and horizontal surfaces: in continuous bands at the intersection of the ceiling soffit and perimeter walls, within the seams and inserted through the fiberglass-reinforced ceiling, and embedded within the volume of the transparent resin bar in the lounge.

This page
Entrance on Tenth Avenue

Opposite
Basement lounge

This page
Top: Upper-level plan (left); lower-level plan
Bottom: Section

Opposite
Top: Communal dining
Bottom: Basement bar

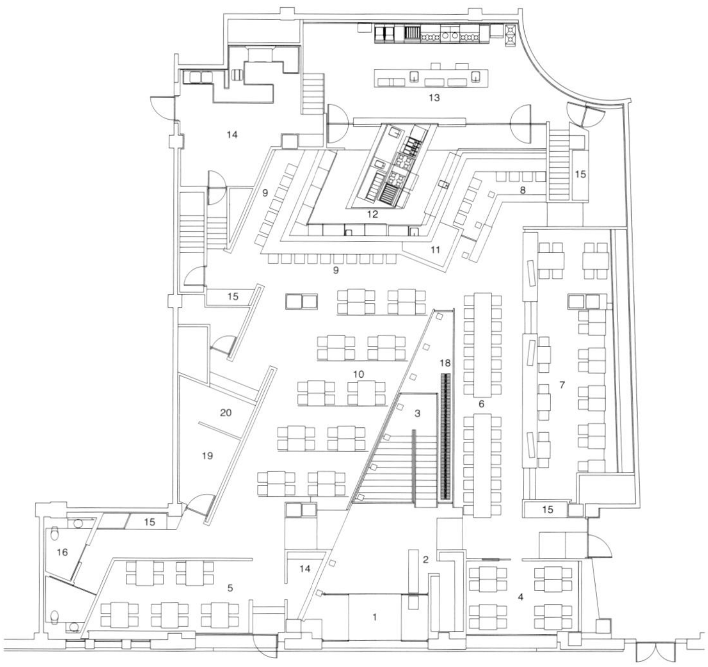

1. ENTRY VESTIBULE
2. HOST STAND
3. MAIN STAIR
4 PRIVATE DINING ROOM A
5. PRIVATE DINING ROOM B
6. COMMUNAL DINING
7. ELEVATED DINING
8. OMAKASE BAR
9. SUSHI BAR
10. DINING ROOM
11. RAW BAR DISPLAY
12. EXPOSITION KITCHEN
13. MAIN KITCHEN
14. DISH WASHING ROOM
15. WAITER STATION
16. BATHROOM
17. BEVERAGE STORAGE
18. BOTTLE WALL
19. BEVERAGE STORAGE
20. SERVICE BAR

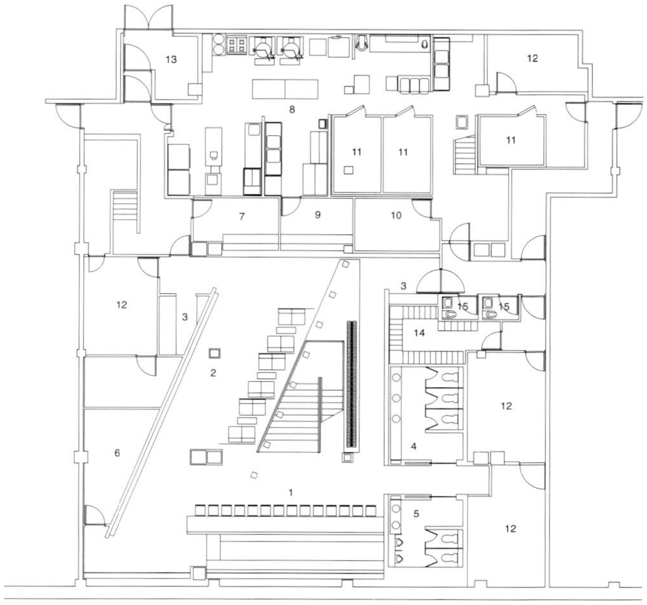

1. BAR
2. LOUNGE
3. WAITER STATION
4. WOMEN'S BATHROOM
5. MEN'S BATHROOM
6. BEVERAGE STORAGE
7. MANAGER'S OFFICE
8. PREP KITCHEN
9. CHEF'S OFFICE
10. DRY STORAGE
11. WALK-IN REFRIGERATION
12. MECHANICAL/ELECTRICAL ROC
13. GARBAGE STORAGE
14. LOCKER ROOM
15. STAFF BATHROOM

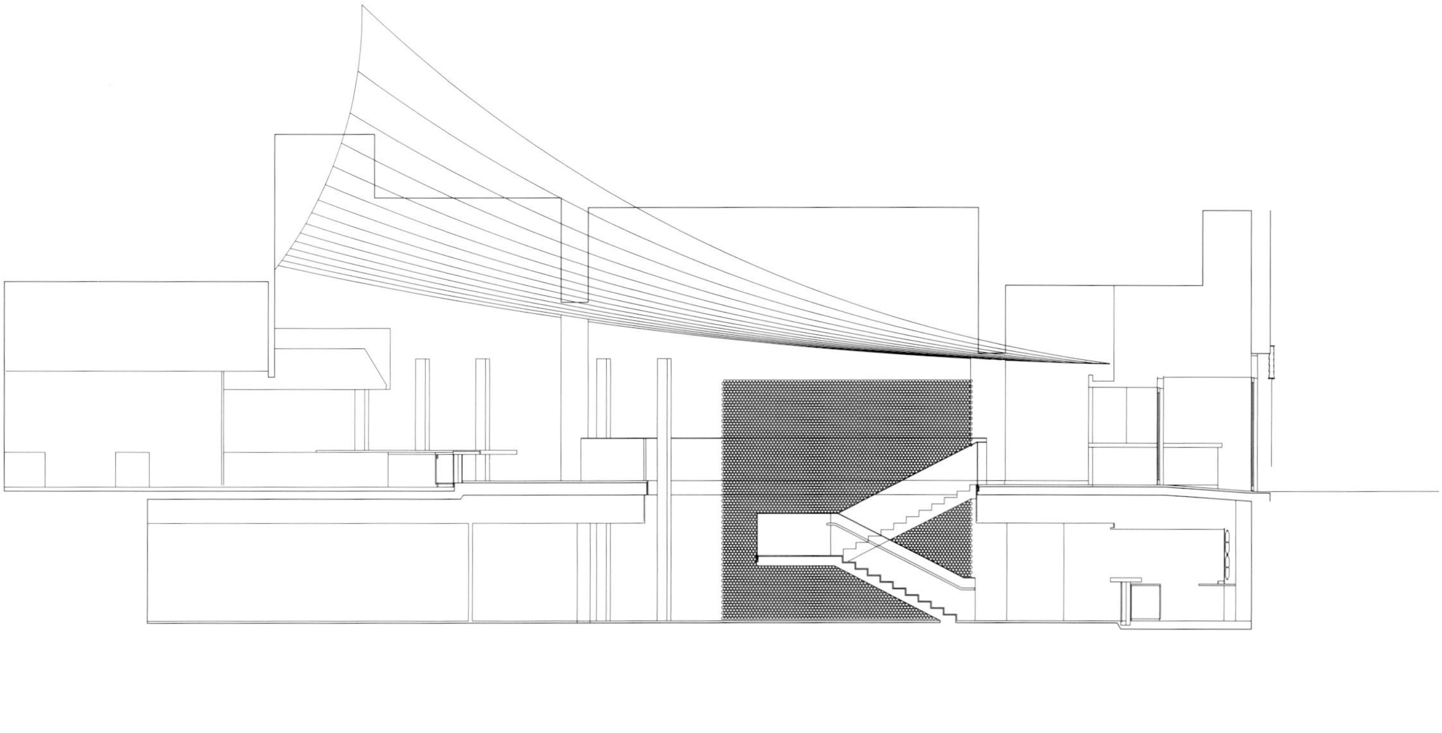

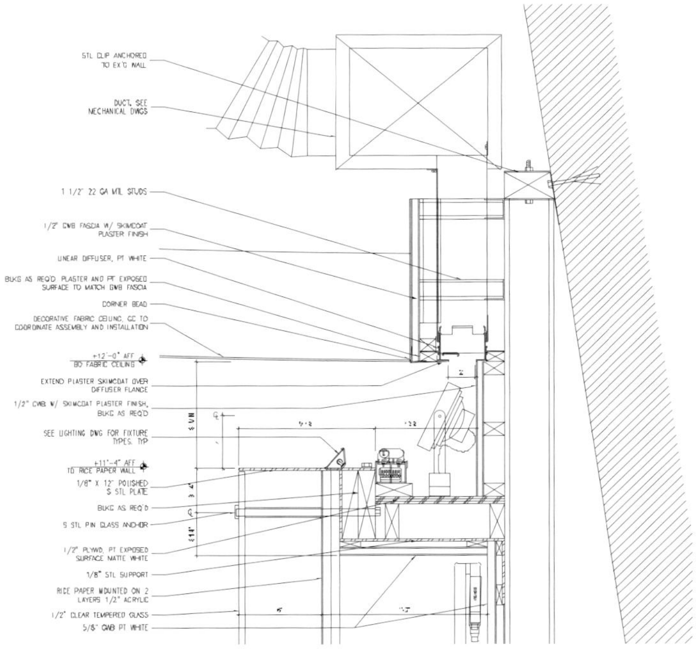

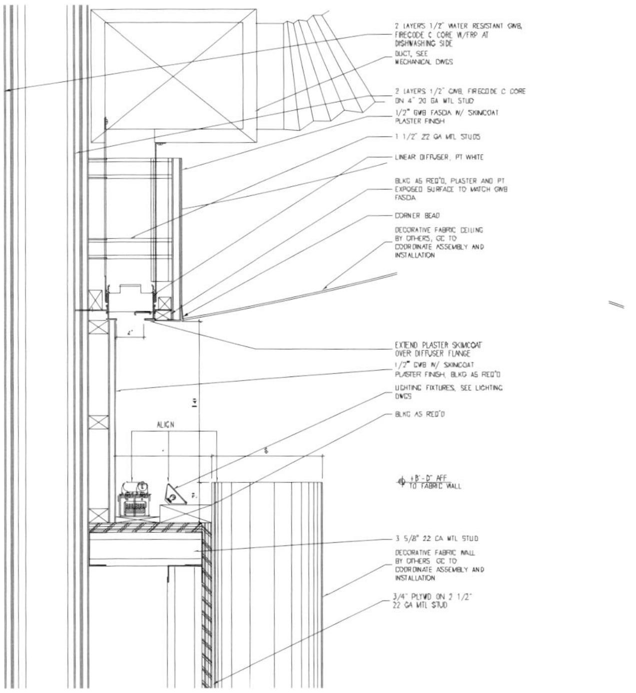

This page
Top: Light-cove detail, rice-paper wall (left); light-cove detail, decorative-fabric wall
Middle: Light-cove detail, decorative-fabric wall
Bottom (left and right): Main stair and bottle wall

Opposite
Top: Section detail, rice-paper wall in elevated dining area (left); section detail, rice-paper wall in private dining area
Bottom: Dining room (left); sushi bar

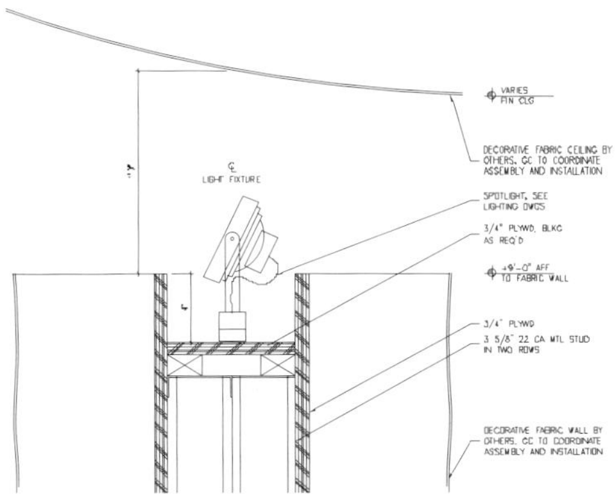

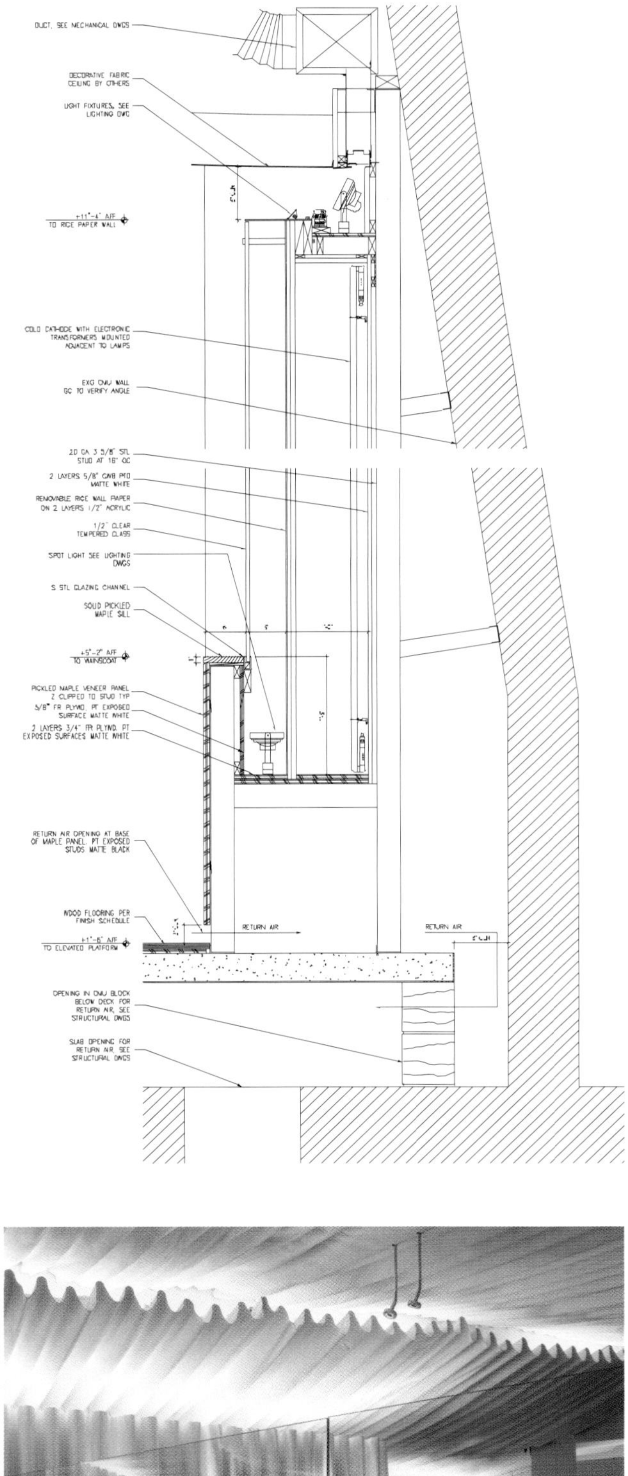
DUCT, SEE MECHANICAL DWGS
DECORATIVE FABRIC CEILING BY OTHERS
LIGHT FIXTURES, SEE LIGHTING DWG
+11'-4" AFF TO RICE PAPER WALL
COLD CATHODE WITH ELECTRONIC TRANSFORMERS MOUNTED ADJACENT TO LAMPS
EXG CMU WALL GC TO VERIFY ANGLE
20 GA 3 5/8" STL STUD AT 16" OC
2 LAYERS 5/8" GWB PTD MATTE WHITE
REMOVABLE RICE WALL PAPER ON 2 LAYERS 1/2" ACRYLIC
1/2" CLEAR TEMPERED GLASS
SPOT LIGHT SEE LIGHTING DWGS
S STL GLAZING CHANNEL
SOLID PICKLED MAPLE SILL
+5'-2" AFF TO WAINSCOAT
PICKLED MAPLE VENEER PANEL Z CLIPPED TO STUD TYP
5/8" FR PLYWD. PT EXPOSED SURFACE MATTE WHITE
2 LAYERS 3/4" FR PLYWD. PT EXPOSED SURFACES MATTE WHITE
RETURN AIR OPENING AT BASE OF MAPLE PANEL. PT EXPOSED STUDS MATTE BLACK
WOOD FLOORING PER FINISH SCHEDULE
+1'-6" AFF TO ELEVATED PLATFORM
RETURN AIR
RETURN AIR
OPENING IN CMU BLOCK BELOW DECK FOR RETURN AIR, SEE STRUCTURAL DWGS
SLAB OPENING FOR RETURN AIR, SEE STRUCTURAL DWGS

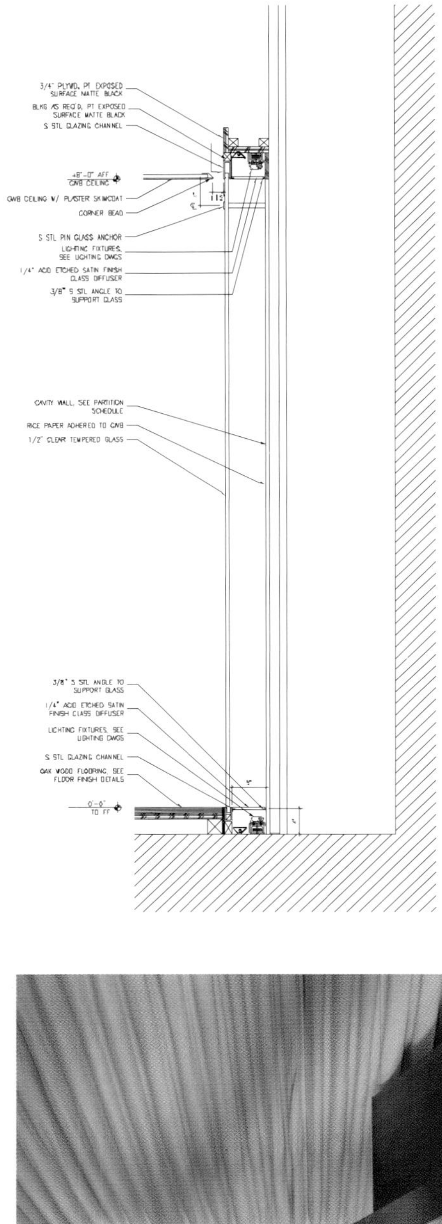
3/4" PLYWD. PT EXPOSED SURFACE MATTE BLACK
BLKG AS REQ'D, PT EXPOSED SURFACE MATTE BLACK
S STL GLAZING CHANNEL
+8'-0" AFF GWB CEILING
GWB CEILING W/ PLASTER SKIMCOAT
CORNER BEAD
S STL PIN GLASS ANCHOR
LIGHTING FIXTURES, SEE LIGHTING DWGS
1/4" ACID ETCHED SATIN FINISH GLASS DIFFUSER
3/8" S STL ANGLE TO SUPPORT GLASS
CAVITY WALL, SEE PARTITION SCHEDULE
RICE PAPER ADHERED TO GWB
1/2" CLEAR TEMPERED GLASS
3/8" S STL ANGLE TO SUPPORT GLASS
1/4" ACID ETCHED SATIN FINISH GLASS DIFFUSER
LIGHTING FIXTURES, SEE LIGHTING DWGS
S STL GLAZING CHANNEL
OAK WOOD FLOORING, SEE FLOOR FINISH DETAILS
0'-0" TO FF

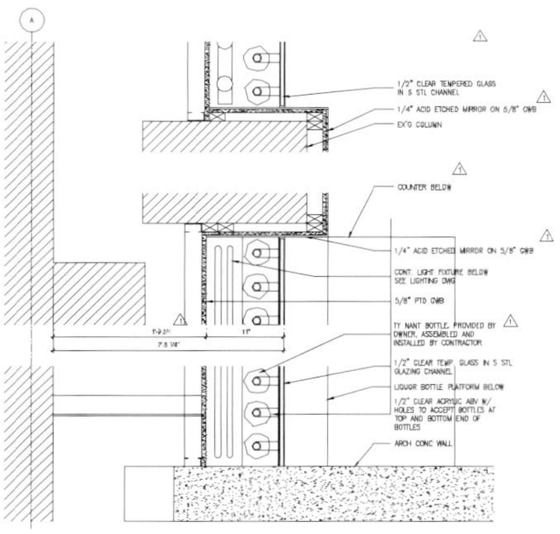

1/2" CLEAR TEMPERED GLASS IN S STL CHANNEL
1/4" ACID ETCHED MIRROR ON 5/8" GWB
EX'G COLUMN
COUNTER BELOW
1/4" ACID ETCHED MIRROR ON 5/8" GWB
CONT LIGHT FIXTURE BELOW SEE LIGHTING DWGS
5/8" PTD GWB
TY NANT BOTTLE, PROVIDED BY OWNER, ASSEMBLED AND INSTALLED BY CONTRACTOR
1/2" CLEAR TEMP GLASS IN S STL GLAZING CHANNEL
LIQUOR BOTTLE PLATFORM BELOW
1/2" CLEAR ACRYLIC ARV W/ HOLES TO ACCEPT BOTTLES AT TOP AND BOTTOM END OF BOTTLES
ARCH CONC WALL

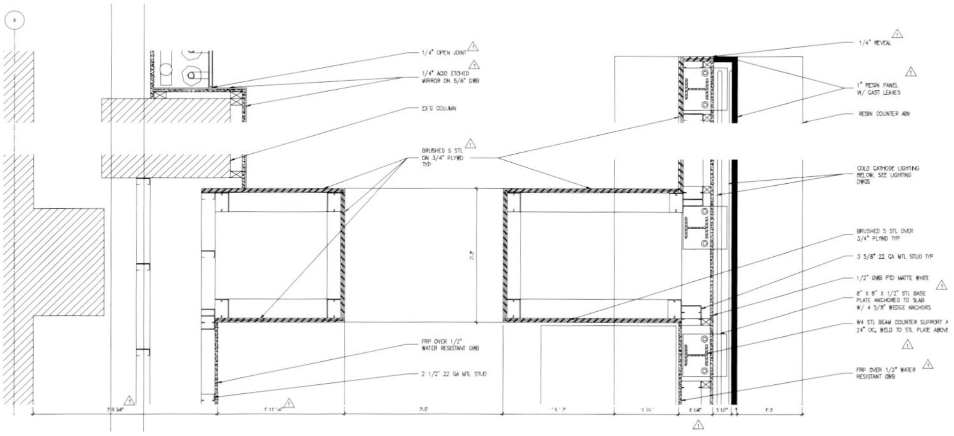

1/4" OPEN JOINT
1/4" ACID ETCHED MIRROR ON 5/8" GWB
EX'G COLUMN
BRUSHED S STL ON 3/4" PLYWD TYP
FRP OVER 1/2" WATER RESISTANT GWB
2 1/2" 22 GA MTL STUD
1/4" REVEAL
1" RESIN PANEL W/ CAST LEAVES
RESIN COUNTER ABV
COLD CATHODE LIGHTING BELOW, SEE LIGHTING DWGS
BRUSHED S STL OVER 3/4" PLYWD TYP
3 5/8" 22 GA MTL STUD TYP
1/2" GWB PTD MATTE WHITE
8" X 8" X 1/2" STL BASE PLATE ANCHORED TO SLAB W/ 4 5/8" WEDGE ANCHORS
W4 STL BEAM COUNTER SUPPORT A 24" OC, WELD TO STL PLATE ABOVE
FRP OVER 1/2" WATER RESISTANT GWB

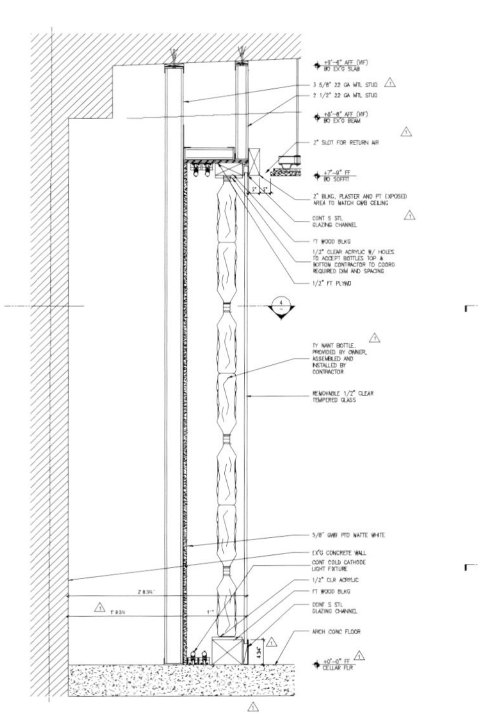

BO EX'G SLAB
3 5/8" 22 GA MTL STUD
3 1/2" 22 GA MTL STUD
BO EX'G BEAM
2" SLOT FOR RETURN AIR
BO SOFFIT
2" BLKG, PLASTER AND PT EXPOSED AREA TO MATCH GWB CEILING
CONT S STL GLAZING CHANNEL
FT WOOD BLKG
1/2" CLEAR ACRYLIC W/ HOLES TO ACCEPT BOTTLES TOP & BOTTOM CONTRACTOR TO COORD REQUIRED DIM AND SPACING
1/2" FT PLYWD
TY NANT BOTTLE PROVIDED BY OWNER, ASSEMBLED AND INSTALLED BY CONTRACTOR
REMOVABLE 1/2" CLEAR TEMPERED GLASS
5/8" GWB PTD MATTE WHITE
EX'G CONCRETE WALL
CONT COLD CATHODE LIGHT FIXTURE
1/2" CLR ACRYLIC
FT WOOD BLKG
CONT S STL GLAZING CHANNEL
ARCH CONC FLOOR
CELLAR FLR

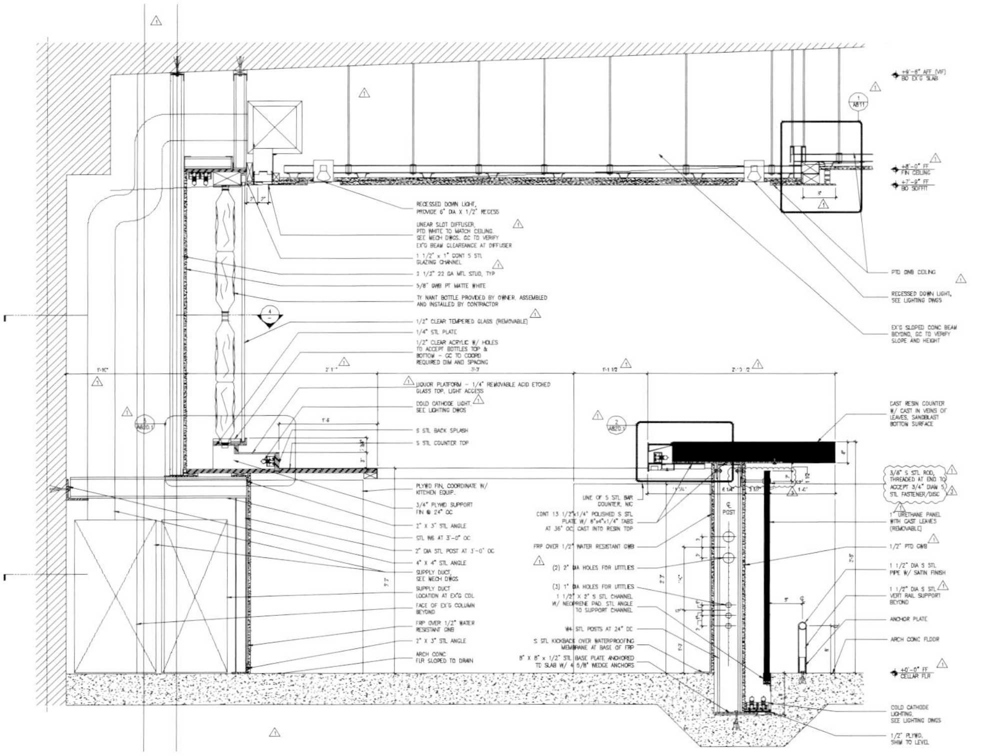

BO EX'G SLAB
FIN CEILING
BO SOFFIT
RECESSED DOWN LIGHT, PROVIDE 6" DIA X 1/2" RECESS
LINEAR SLOT DIFFUSER PTD WHITE TO MATCH CEILING SEE MECH DWGS, GC TO VERIFY EX'G BEAM CLEARANCE AT DIFFUSER
1 1/2" x 1" CONT S STL GLAZING CHANNEL
3 1/2" 22 GA MTL STUD, TYP
5/8" GWB PT MATTE WHITE
TY NANT BOTTLE PROVIDED BY OWNER, ASSEMBLED AND INSTALLED BY CONTRACTOR
1/2" CLEAR TEMPERED GLASS (REMOVABLE)
1/4" STL PLATE
1/2" CLEAR ACRYLIC W/ HOLES TO ACCEPT BOTTLES TOP & BOTTOM - GC TO COORD REQUIRED DIM AND SPACING
LIQUOR PLATFORM - 1/4" REMOVABLE ACID ETCHED GLASS TOP, LIGHT ACCESS
COLD CATHODE LIGHT SEE LIGHTING DWGS
S STL BACK SPLASH
S STL COUNTER TOP
PLYWD FIN, COORDINATE W/ KITCHEN EQUIP.
3/4" PLYWD SUPPORT FIN @ 24" OC
2" X 3" STL ANGLE
STL RIB AT 3'-0" OC
2" DIA STL POST AT 3'-0" OC
4" X 4" STL ANGLE
SUPPLY DUCT, SEE MECH DWGS
SUPPLY DUCT LOCATION AT EX'G COL
FACE OF EX'G COLUMN BEYOND
FRP OVER 1/2" WATER RESISTANT GWB
3" X 3" STL ANGLE
ARCH CONC FLR SLOPED TO DRAIN
PTD GWB CEILING
RECESSED DOWN LIGHT, SEE LIGHTING DWGS
EX'G SLOPED CONC BEAM BEYOND, GC TO VERIFY SLOPE AND HEIGHT
CAST RESIN COUNTER W/ CAST IN VEINS OF LEAVES, SANDBLAST BOTTOM SURFACE
3/8" S STL ROD, THREADED AT END TO ACCEPT 3/4" DIAM S STL FASTENER/DISC
1" URETHANE PANEL WITH CAST LEAVES (REMOVABLE)
1/2" PTD GWB
1 1/2" DIA S STL PIPE W/ SATIN FINISH
1 1/2" DIA S STL VERT RAIL SUPPORT BEYOND
ANCHOR PLATE
ARCH CONC FLOOR
CELLAR FLR
LINE OF S STL BAR COUNTER, NIC
CONT 1.5 1/2"x1/4" POLISHED S STL PLATE W/ 6"x4"x1/4" TABS AT 36" OC CAST INTO RESIN TOP
FRP OVER 1/2" WATER RESISTANT GWB
(2) 2" DIA HOLES FOR UTILITIES
(3) 1" DIA HOLES FOR UTILITIES
1 1/2" X 3" S STL CHANNEL W/ NEOPRENE PAD, STL ANGLE TO SUPPORT CHANNEL
W4 STL POSTS AT 24" OC
S STL KICKBACK OVER WATERPROOFING MEMBRANE AT BASE OF FRP
8" X 8" X 1/2" STL BASE PLATE ANCHORED TO SLAB W/ 4 5/8" WEDGE ANCHORS
COLD CATHODE LIGHTING SEE LIGHTING DWGS
1/2" PLYWD, SHIM TO LEVEL

Opposite
Top: Plan detail, cellar-lounge bottle wall (left);
plan detail, cellar-lounge bar
Middle: Section detail, cellar-lounge bottle wall (left);
section detail, cellar-lounge bar
Bottom: Three-quarter view of bottle-wall mockup with LEDs (left);
bottle-wall mockup, double-socket detail

This page
Right: Bottle wall from main stair
Bottom (left to right): Bottle-wall prototype; bottle wall, side view; bottle-wall detail with warm and cool LEDs

Terrence Donnelly Centre for Cellular and Biomolecular Research, Toronto, Canada
Behnisch Architekten, Los Angeles, California
architectsAlliance, Toronto

The University of Toronto's Terrence Donnelly Centre for Cellular and Biomolecular Research (TDCCBR) is a collaborative and interdisciplinary research center for four hundred specialists who perform groundbreaking research on genetics and disease. The location of the TDCCBR, at the southeast corner of the University of Toronto's St. George Campus, establishes physical and symbolic links with the university community to the north and the medical center to the south.

On the narrow building site, formerly a parking and service area, Behnisch Architekten and architectsAlliance designed a rectangular structure twelve stories high distinguished by its environmental responsiveness, connections to the surrounding urban context, transparency, and informal spaces that promote interdisciplinary collaboration. In contrast to neighboring brick buildings, the TDCCBR is a slender tower with a crisp, light, and colorful facade that rises gracefully over neighboring structures.

Designed as a north-south thoroughfare, the TDCCBR is entered through an exterior granite-paved forecourt surrounded by gardens and neighboring buildings. The granite pavement continues into the concourse atrium—an indoor-outdoor environment with multicolored skylights, lush plantings, a cafeteria, lounges, offices, and seminar rooms—that provides public passage through the building. The subdued materials and planting palette of the atrium contrast with the building's complex colors and forms.

The TDCCBR is linked to the Medical Sciences Building by ground-level walkways and a glass bridge on the sixth level; an upper-level connection leads to the Rosebrugh Building, which was restored during the construction. To better adapt to the scale of surrounding buildings, the TDCCBR is broken into two vertically stacked volumes divided by an intermediate sixth level that houses mechanical systems for lower floors. Laboratory space is organized below on floors 2 through 5 and above on floors 7 through 12. The smaller floor area of the sixth level divides the building form into two volumes, allowing the laboratory floors below to remain flexible, open spaces. Mechanical systems serving the upper levels and six of the seven air-handling units are located on the rooftop in an oval stainless-steel clad penthouse; a seventh unit is located on the ground floor and serves the basement.

The cladding on each of the four elevations is designed to enrich the building's mass and meet occupants' needs for privacy and shading. Color is used extensively throughout: shades of yellow, blue, and orange animate the laminated glass on the eastern and western facades. Colored interior walls are visible through the patterned ceramic frit glass, used to mitigate solar gain on the west elevation, which is further articulated with bay-window volumes that house lounges, cafes, and stairways. The richly textured, transparent south facade, the building's main elevation, is double walled and double glazed for maximum acoustic and solar control.

Qualities of transparency, flexibility, connectivity, and functionality inform the design of the interior spaces. Airy spaces and extended floor-to-ceiling heights were achieved by omitting suspended ceilings and exposing services and the superstructure. Shallow floor plates and glass walls allow for high levels of transparency and natural light throughout the labs, while

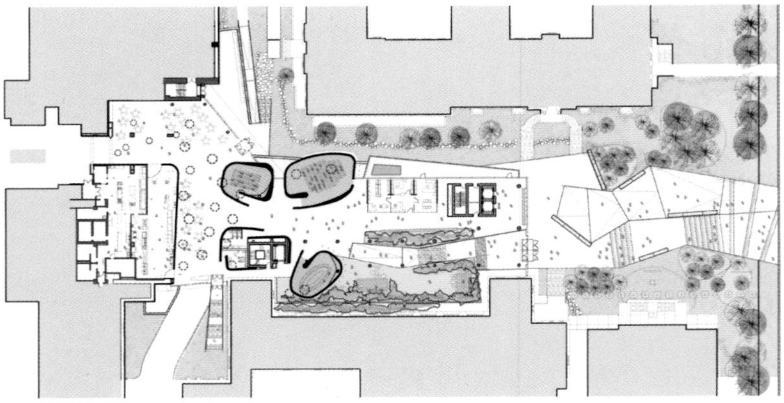

This page
Site plan

Opposite
Top: Rosebrugh Court, view north
Bottom: West elevation

720° 4730905 DET

This page
Lab floor plan (left); east elevation

Opposite
Top: Diagram of east-west section airflow
Bottom: Entrance with seminar rooms and winter garden (left); Rosebrugh Court, view south

color, lighting, and materials differentiate work zones. Wet and dry laboratories are located in the central service spine, which runs north and south through the middle of each floor. The laboratories are designed for easy conversion: wet labs can be altered to accommodate biology, chemistry, or bioinformatics usage, and dry labs can be converted to wet labs with the addition of fume hoods and laboratory casework.

Spacious circulation corridors on the west side of the building provide entry to the labs and research-associate stations beyond. Connected by staircases, the corridors on levels 2 through 5 overlook the atrium and provide informal spaces for employee interaction. On levels 7 through 12, bay-window volumes contain interconnecting stairways, lounges, and cafes, and there are three double- and triple-height indoor gardens around the perimeter.

The TDCCBR incorporates both passive and active environmental design features to increase energy efficiency and promote employee quality of life. Two energy zones minimize the building's overall requirements, with labs and offices separated from common areas that can sustain higher mean temperatures. The architects also challenged traditional ventilation standards for laboratory spaces by reducing air changes per hour to between ten and twelve from more than twenty.

Low-E, high-performance glazing limits solar gain, and the polymide thermal breaks on the aluminum extrusions have superior insulating properties. The double facade of the south elevation has 2.5 feet of air space between the exterior single-glazed skin and a second interior thermal skin of argon-filled, thermally broken double glazing. Sunblinds on the interior side of the single-glazed skin reduce heat loss and gain and provide wind protection and acoustic buffering. Motorized dampers and vents on the outer skin and retractable perforated aluminum louvers located between the skins further reduce heat gain, redirect daylight into the building, and modulate the natural stack effect to heat and vent the interstitial space, compartmentalized from floor to floor. The retractable louvers have 4-inch concave slats programmed to tilt according to the sun's angle, blocking direct sun from contact with the interior glazing. Glass floors within the cavity allow for maintenance without compromising the facade's transparency. The principal researchers' offices on the southern side have operable windows and sunblinds, which can be controlled by individual users but are also connected to the computerized building management system, ensuring override control. When users open their windows, programmable heating and cooling units in the ceiling switch off.

The circulation corridors, garden, and lounges are powered by a mechanically assisted natural ventilation system, and the atrium's automated operable windows connected to the building management system naturally ventilate the corridors on laboratory floors 2 through 5. The double- and triple-height gardens on the upper levels that filter air and provide oxygen and humidity to the common areas are irrigated and drained as part of the building's stormwater reclamation system.

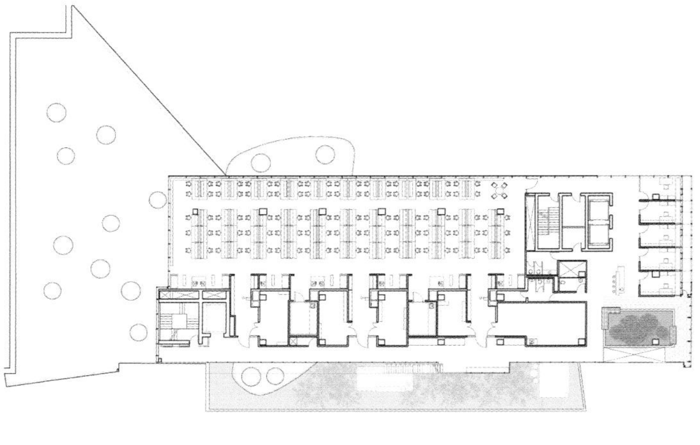

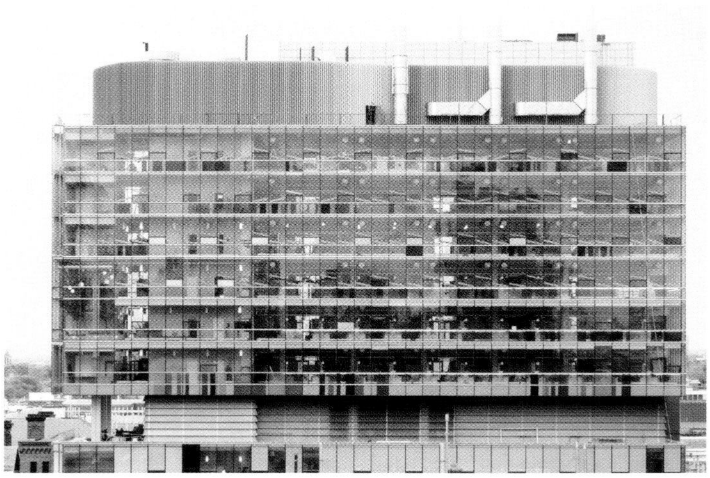

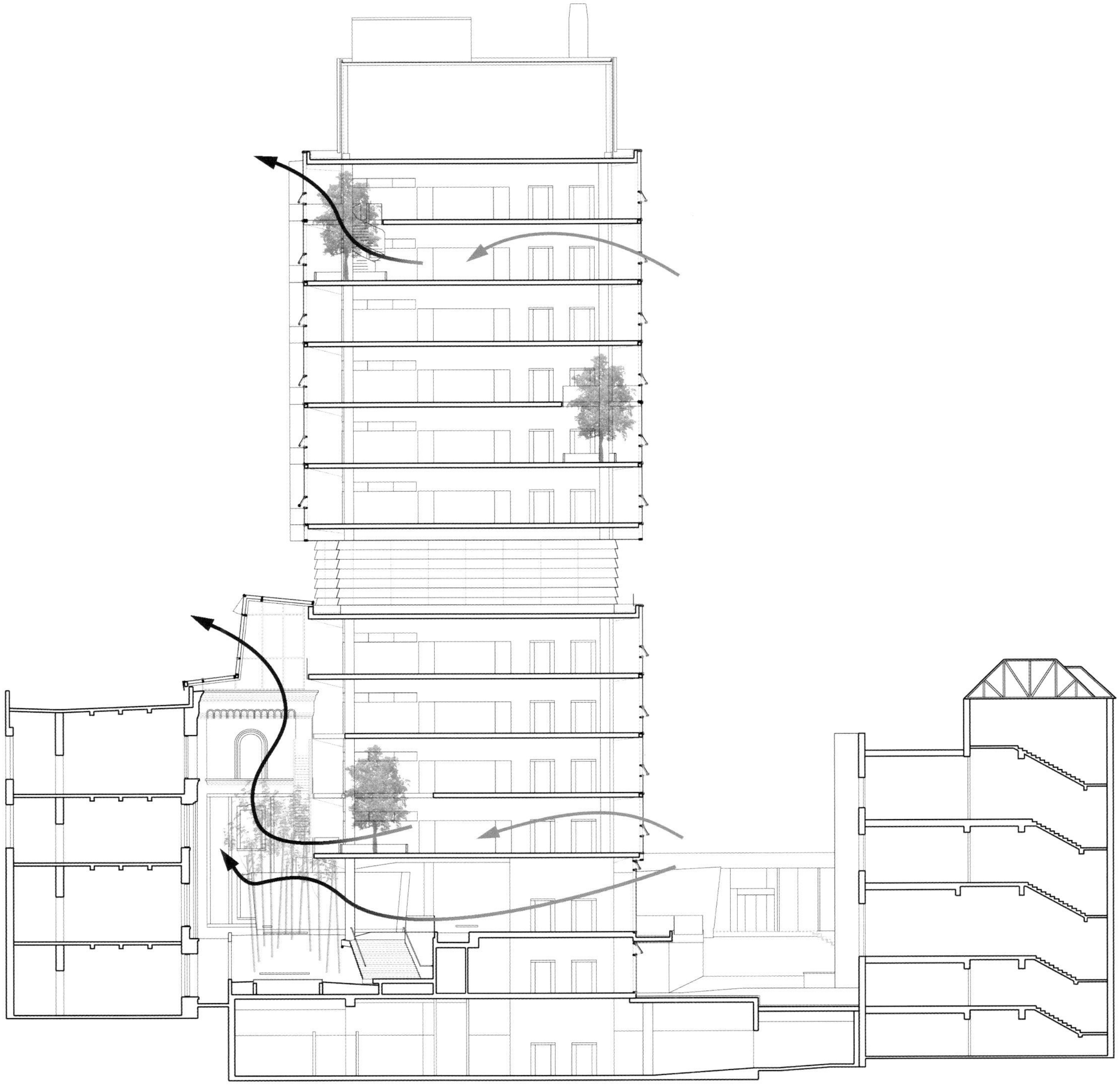

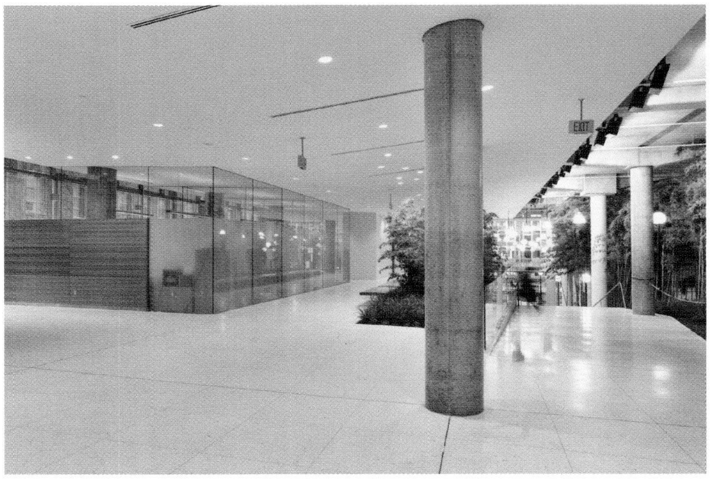
EXIT

This page
Lab section

Opposite
Top: West elevation
Bottom: Rosebrugh Court, night view (left); south elevation

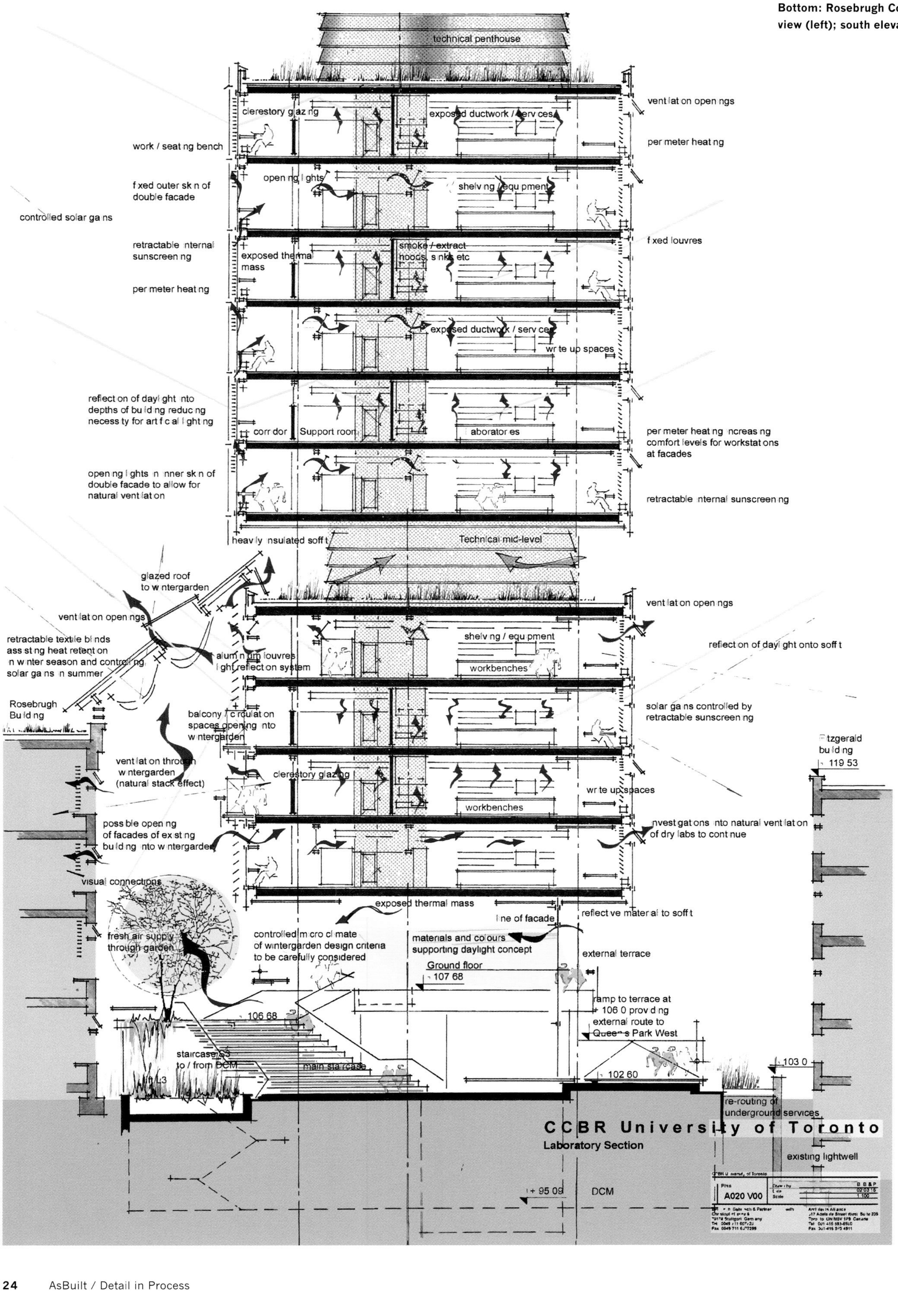

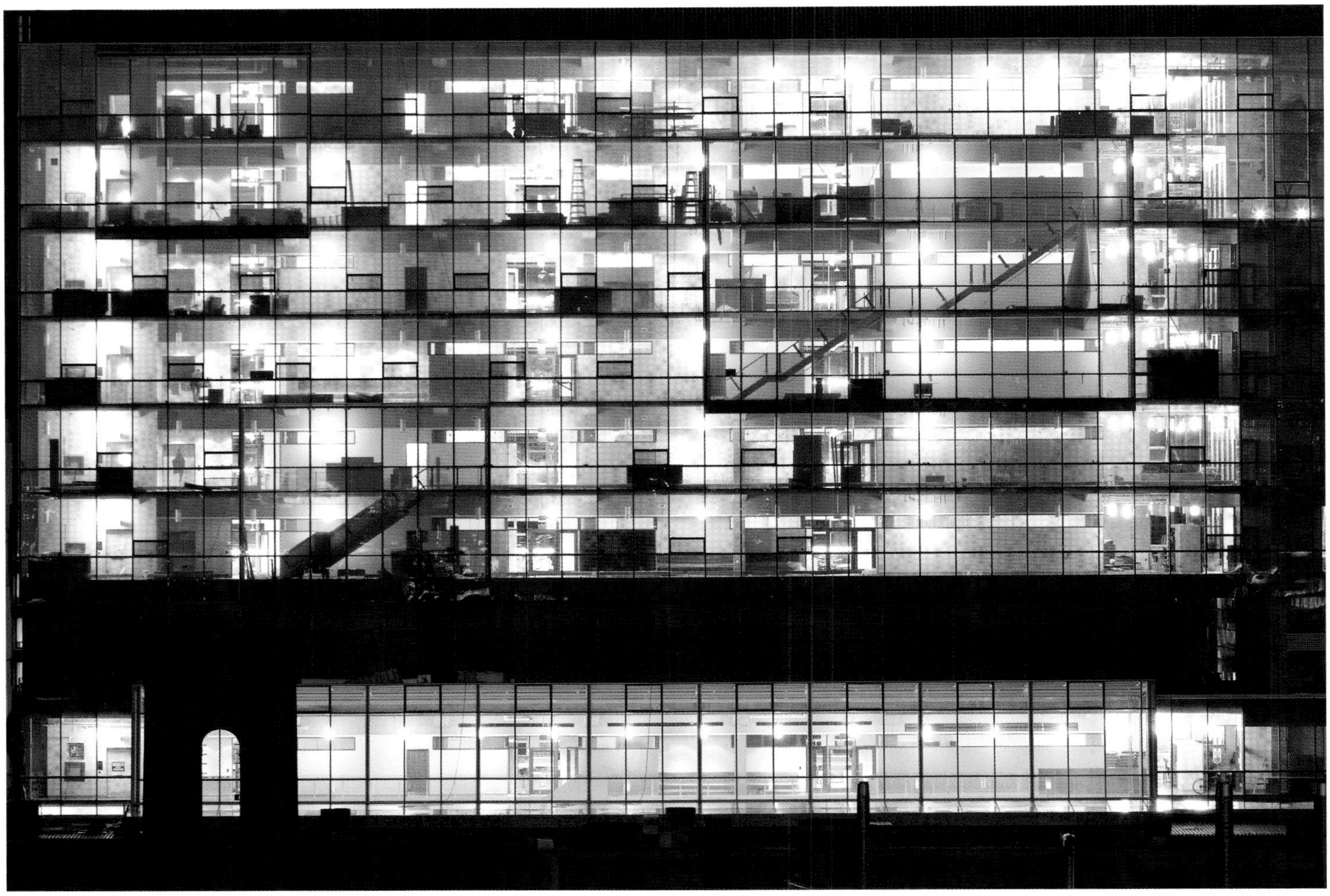

This page
Top: South elevation, soffit
Middle: South elevation, outer wall (left); south elevation, outer-wall detail
Bottom: South elevation, double-wall interior space

Opposite
South elevation, double-wall section

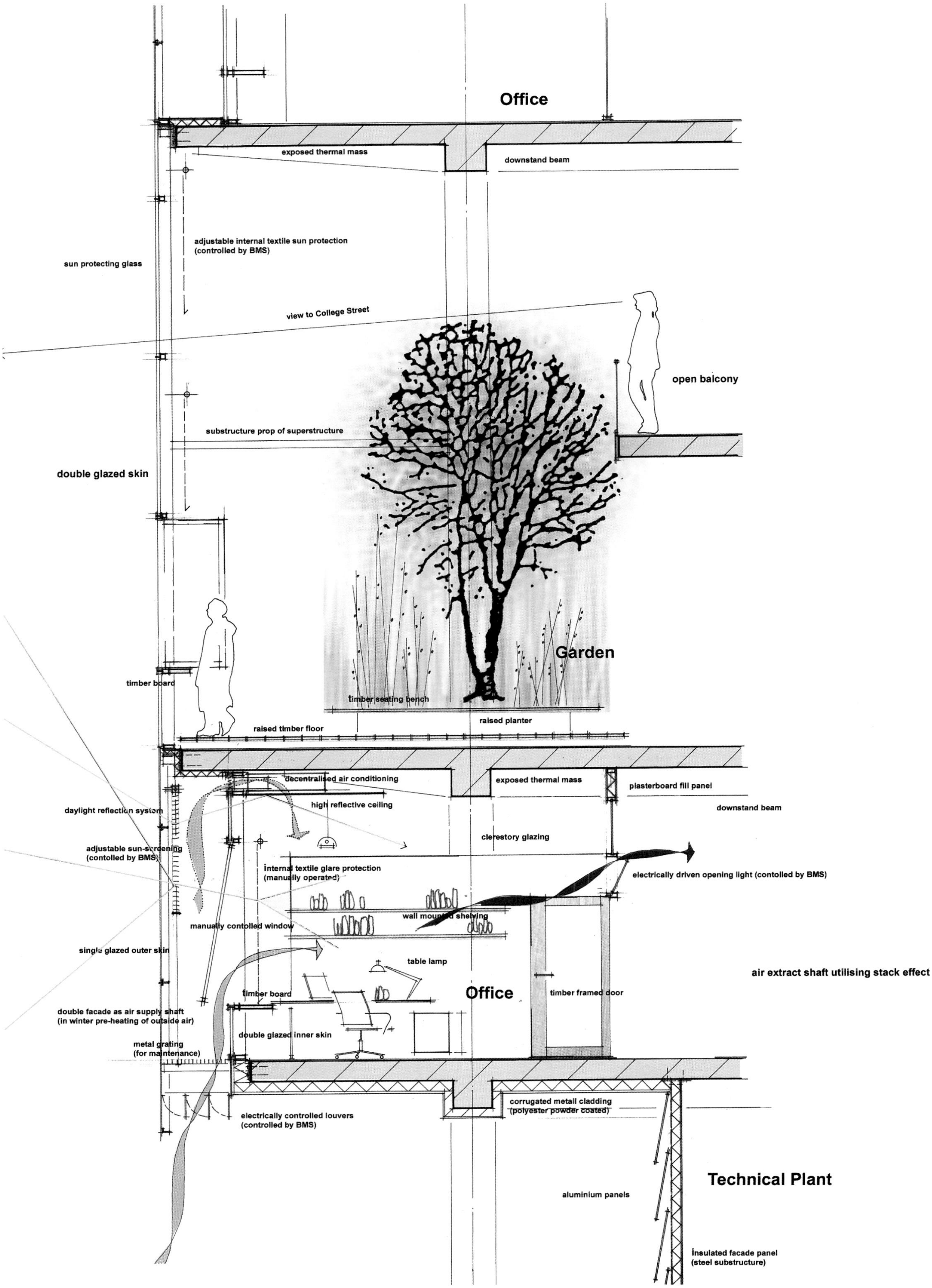
Office
exposed thermal mass
downstand beam
adjustable internal textile sun protection
(controlled by BMS)
sun protecting glass
view to College Street
open balcony
substructure prop of superstructure
double glazed skin
Garden
timber board
timber seating bench
raised timber floor
raised planter
decentralised air conditioning
exposed thermal mass
plasterboard fill panel
downstand beam
daylight reflection system
high reflective ceiling
clerestory glazing
adjustable sun-screening
(contolled by BMS)
internal textile glare protection
(manually operated)
electrically driven opening light (contolled by BMS)
wall mounted shelving
manually contolled window
single glazed outer skin
table lamp
air extract shaft utilising stack effect
timber board
Office
timber framed door
double facade as air supply shaft
(in winter pre-heating of outside air)
double glazed inner skin
metal grating
(for maintenance)
corrugated metall cladding
(polyester powder coated)
electrically controlled louvers
(controlled by BMS)
Technical Plant
aluminium panels
insulated facade panel
(steel substructure)

BRIDGES Center, Memphis, Tennessee
buildingstudio, Memphis

BRIDGES Center in Memphis brings together white high-school students, mostly from private schools, and African American high-school students, mostly from public schools, for a variety of activities; offers educational programs for adults without high-school diplomas; sponsors an afternoon art program, Arts Bridge, for inner-city children; and also helps public-school students with reading problems.

The new 53,000-square-foot headquarters facility on the northern edge of downtown is part of the revitalization of Greenlaw, the city's oldest neighborhood. The 2.7-acre site has approximately 325 feet of frontage on the surrounding streets. The design brief called for a distinctive urban building that would stimulate public interest in BRIDGES programs and fit into the existing neighborhood without overpowering it.

The building was designed to act as a teaching tool, a structure that expresses its tectonics and that includes environmental features: retention areas for stormwater, photovoltaic arrays to produce electricity, and a solar water heater. There are operable windows throughout and high ceilings with wide overhangs, especially critical on the south elevation. Both fixed and operable window walls are of insulated glass, while other walls are made of exposed concrete and painted gypsum wallboard and are covered with translucent plastic panels so that the wall framing is visible. To reveal the building's operation as an active structure, ceilings are mostly exposed throughout, as are the structural, mechanical, and electrical systems. The building's didactic function accounts for its most prominent feature, the hinged truss on the south wing. Engineers Guy Nordenson and Associates designed an open steel frame along each elevation that is counterbalanced on a single fulcrum point. The cast-in-place concrete floor and roof slabs are supported by an exposed steel column system in one-story areas and a cantilevered steel truss system in the multistory space.

To accommodate the requested number of parking spaces—a total of 120 for staff and guests on-grade—more than half the property would have been covered by asphalt. As an alternative, the single-story roof is used for parking and the building given its form by the inclined access ramp; the other wing is sloped at the opposite end to accommodate the climbing wall and high-ropes course. Roof parking also provides controlled access and greater security, as well as a better relationship with the streets on the site's perimeter and the smaller shotgun houses in the surrounding neighborhood.

Guy Nordenson and Associates contributed to this text.

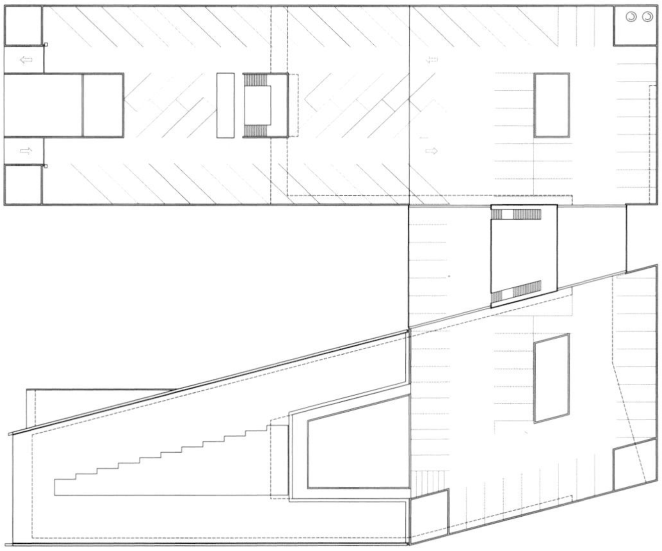

This page
Roof plan

Opposite
Top: North elevation
Bottom: South elevation

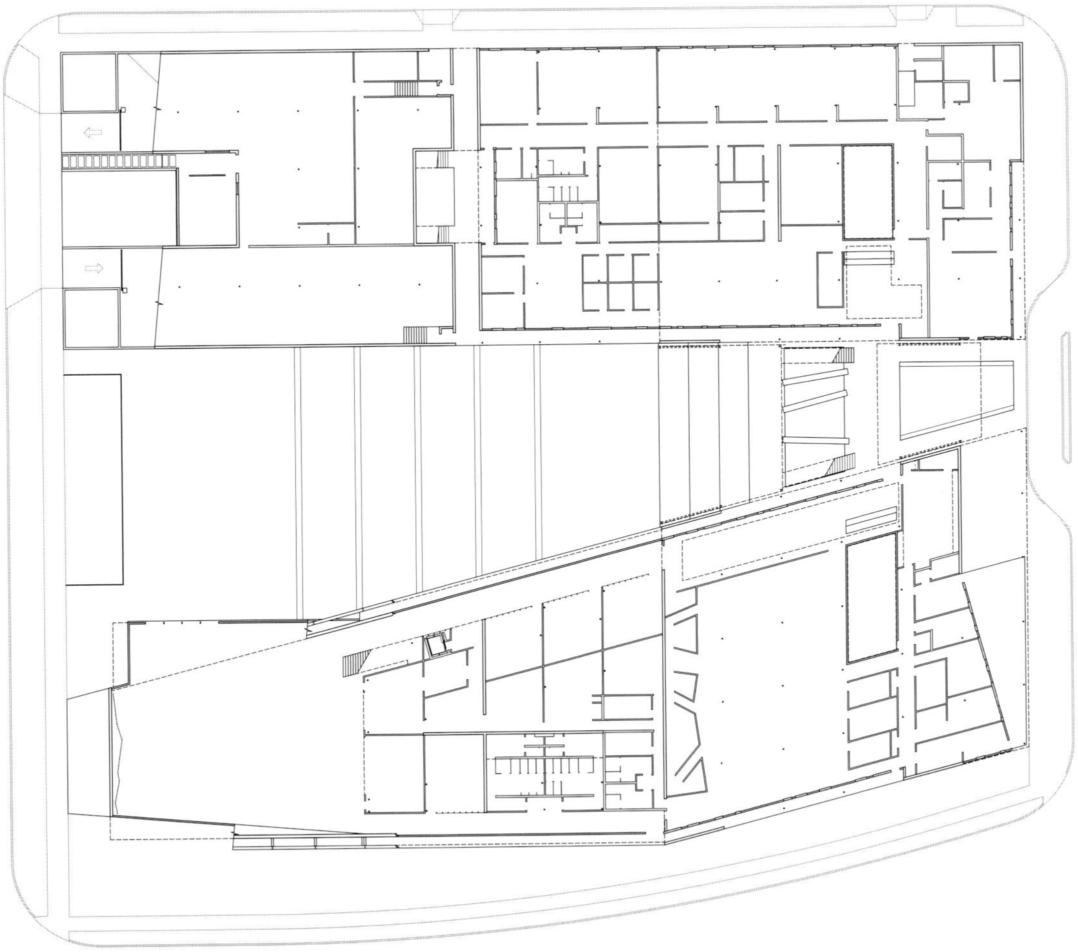

This page
Top: First-floor plan
Below (top to bottom): Section one; section two; section three

Opposite
Top: South elevation, truss
Bottom: Courtyard, view west

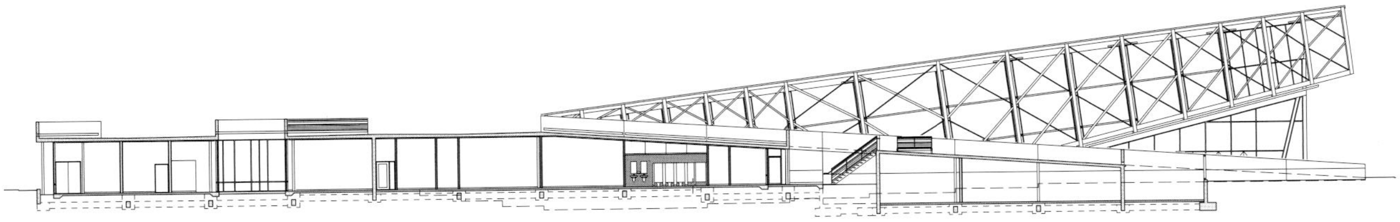

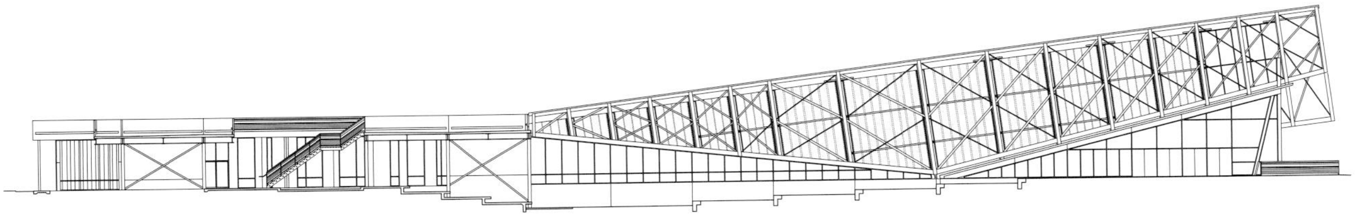

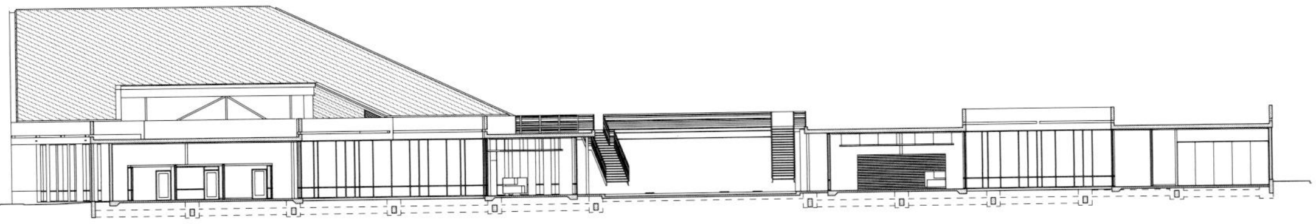

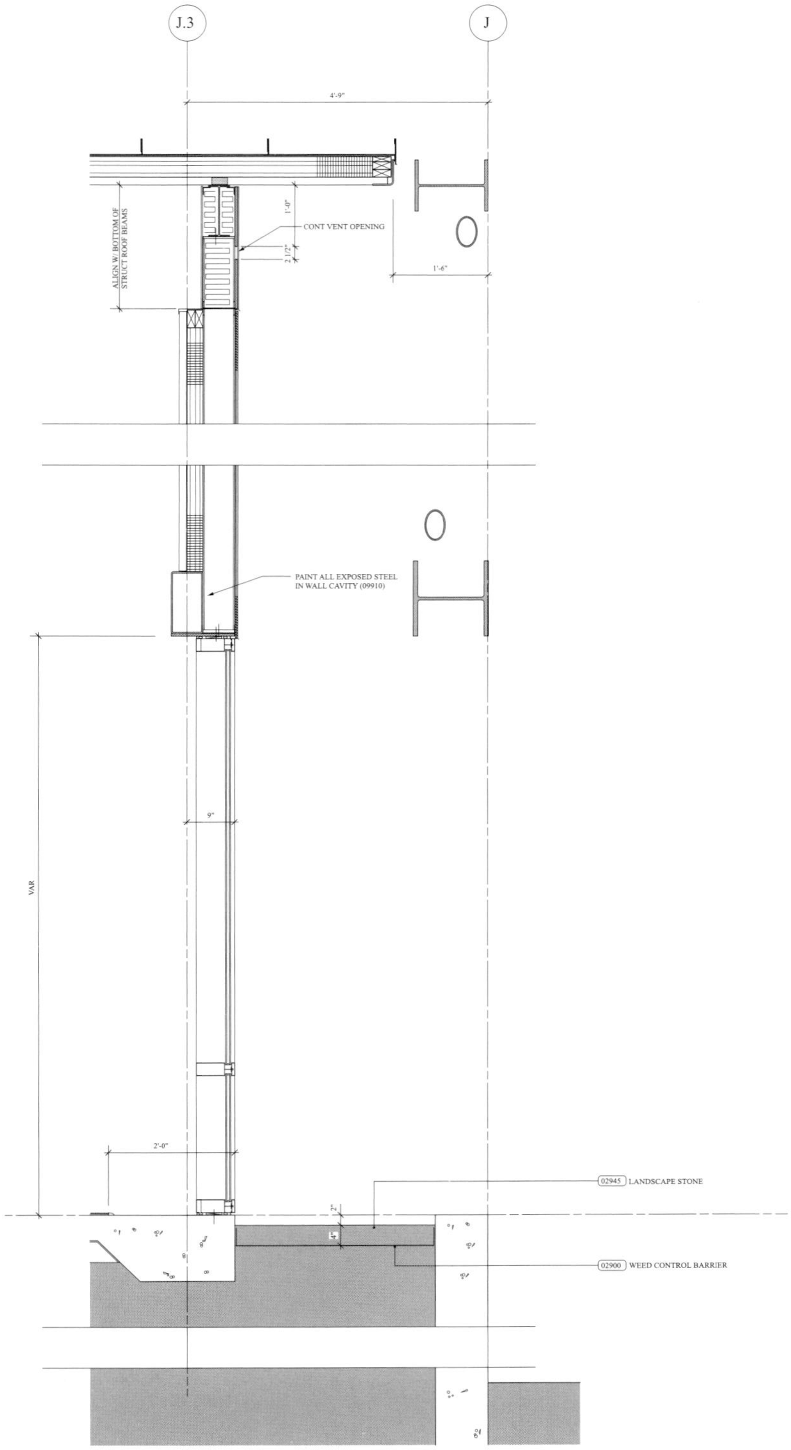
J.3
J
4'-9"
CONT VENT OPENING
1'-0"
2 1/2"
1'-6"
ALIGN W/ BOTTOM OF STRUCT ROOF BEAMS
PAINT ALL EXPOSED STEEL IN WALL CAVITY (09910)
9"
VAR
2'-0"
02945 LANDSCAPE STONE
02900 WEED CONTROL BARRIER

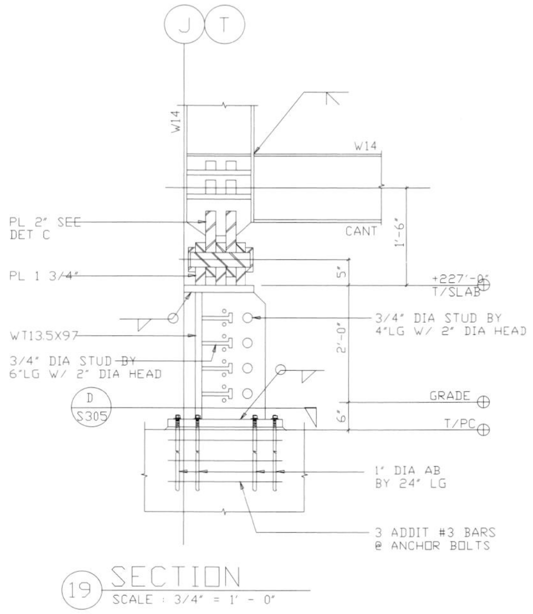
J
T
W14
W14
PL 2" SEE DET C
CANT
1'-6"
PL 1 3/4"
5"
+227'-0"
T/SLAB
WT13.5X97
3/4" DIA STUD BY 4"LG W/ 2" DIA HEAD
3/4" DIA STUD BY 6"LG W/ 2" DIA HEAD
2'-0"
D
S305
GRADE
6"
T/PC
1" DIA AB BY 24" LG
3 ADDIT #3 BARS @ ANCHOR BOLTS
19 SECTION
SCALE : 3/4" = 1' - 0"

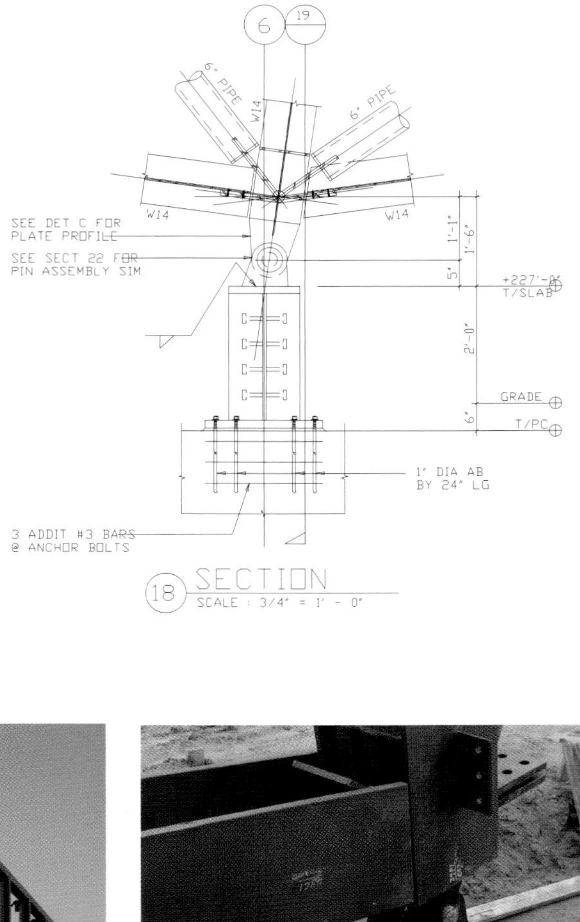
6
19
6" PIPE
W14
6" PIPE
W14
W14
SEE DET C FOR PLATE PROFILE
SEE SECT 22 FOR PIN ASSEMBLY SIM
1'-1"
1'-6"
5"
+227'-0"
T/SLAB
2'-0"
GRADE
6"
T/PC
1" DIA AB BY 24" LG
3 ADDIT #3 BARS @ ANCHOR BOLTS
18 SECTION
SCALE : 3/4" = 1' - 0"

Opposite
Top: Typical truss-wall section
Top and middle right: Structural details at truss base
Bottom (left to right): Pouring concrete for parking ramp; truss detail; articulated truss bearing

This page
Top: Typical truss wall at shear roof
Bottom (left to right): Roof-ramp framing; truss framing; south truss wall

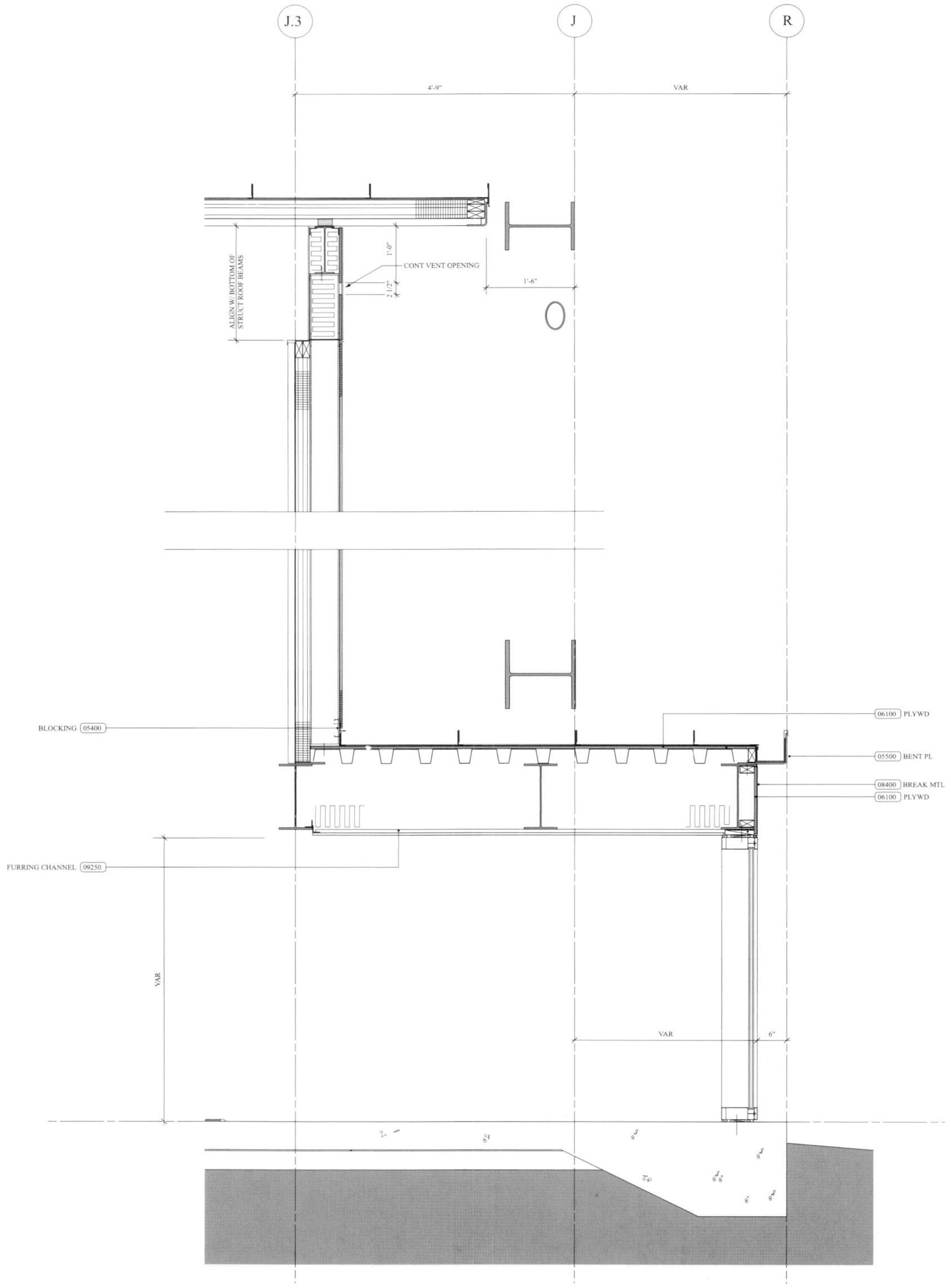

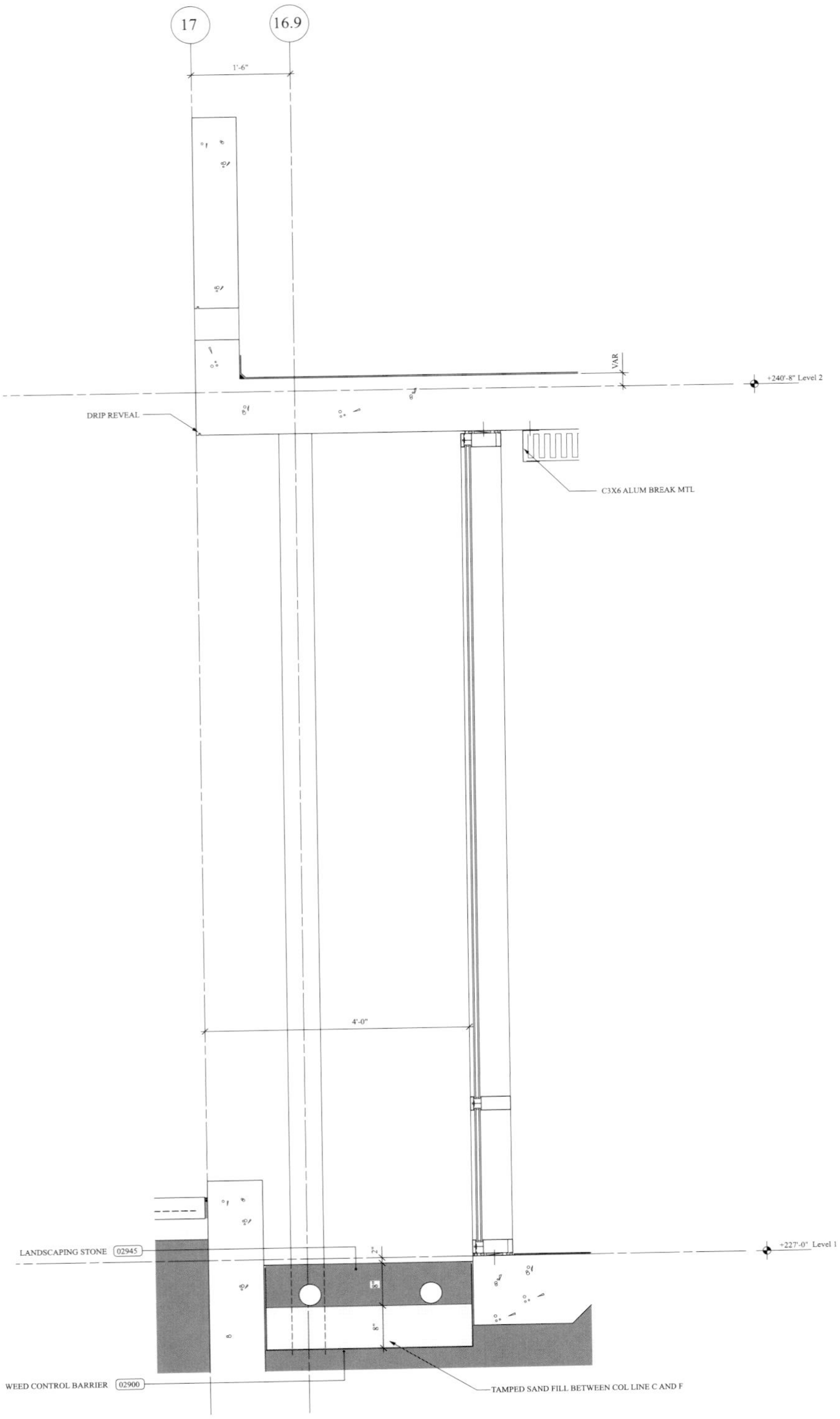

This page
Top: Typical parking-deck section
Bottom: Bridges center, roof view

Opposite
Top: South truss (left); courtyard, view east
Middle: Gathering area (left); front courtyard
Bottom: Truss roof, view southwest

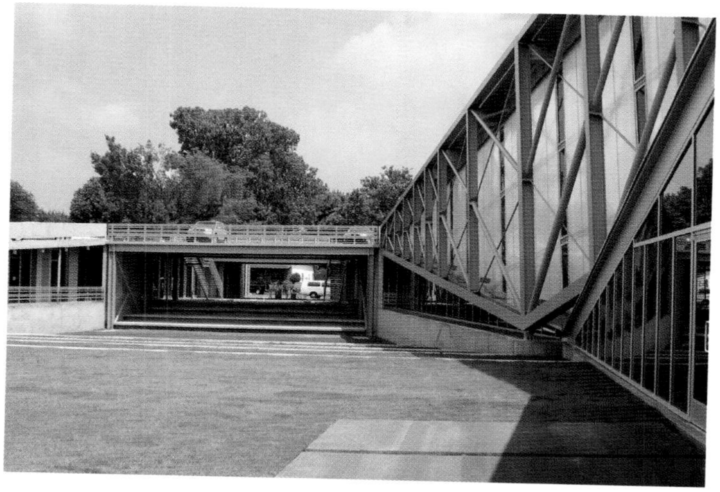

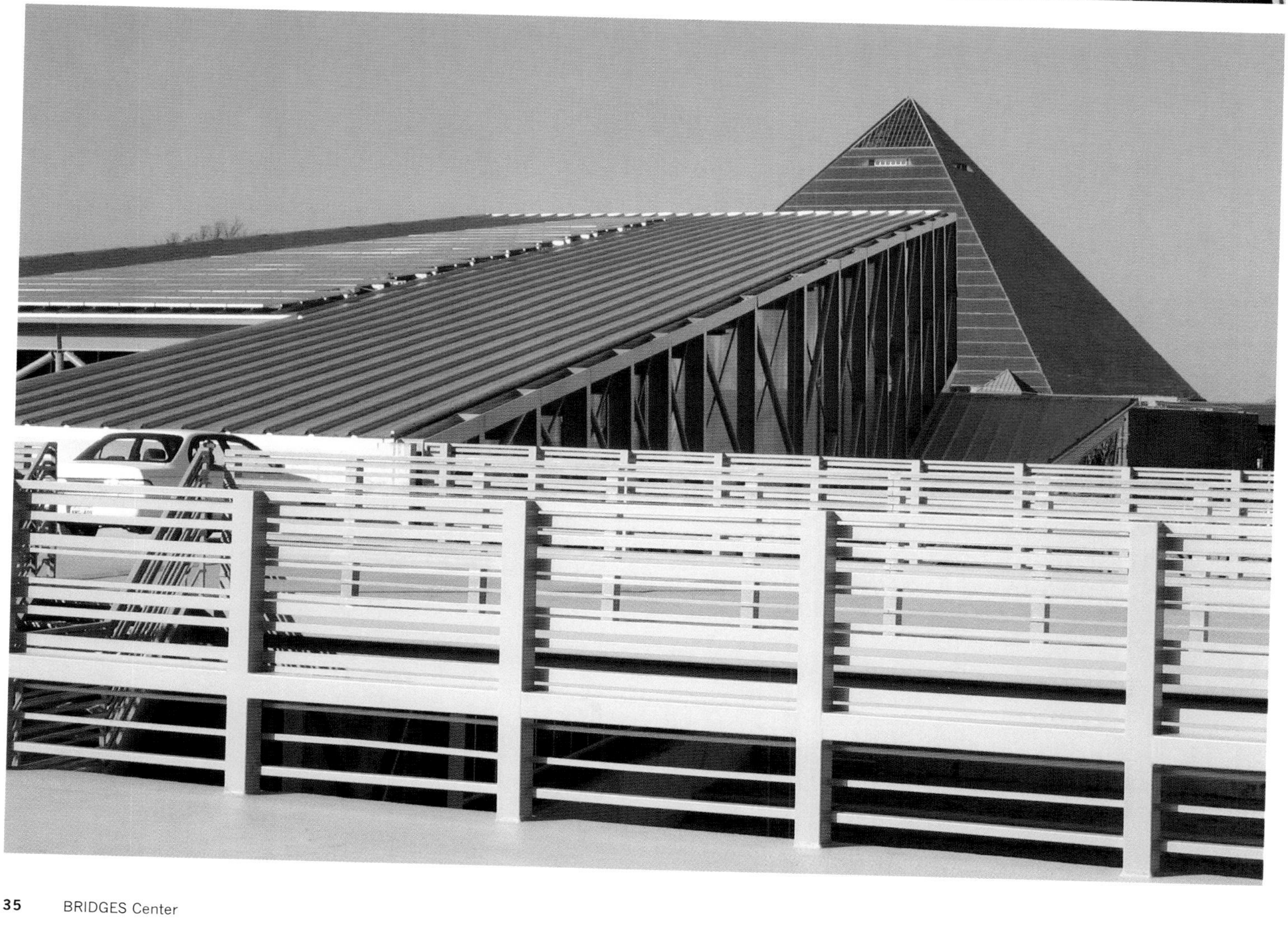

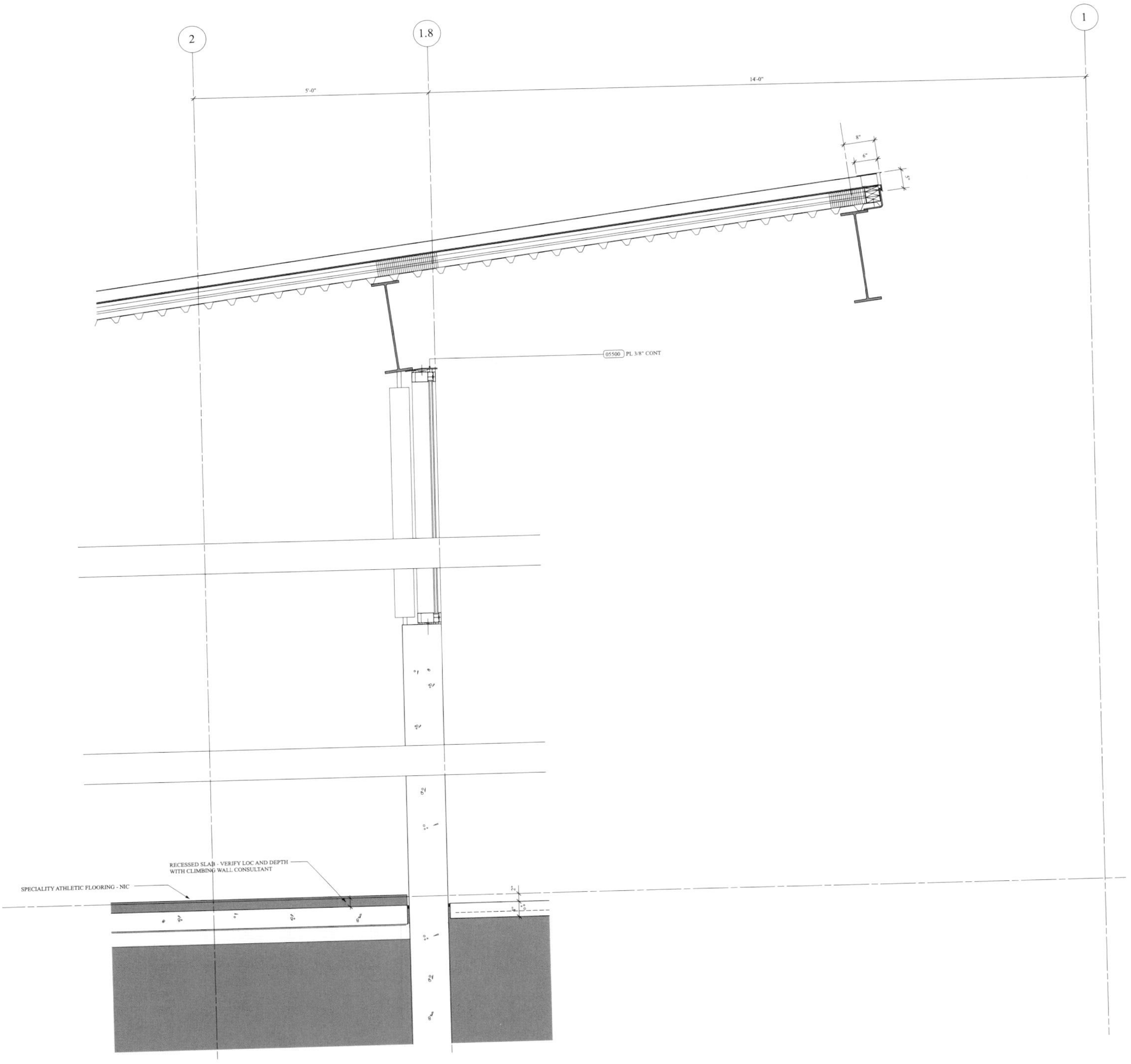

This page
Top: Typical climbing-wall section
Right: Climbing wall

Opposite
High-ropes course

Des Moines Public Library, Des Moines, Iowa
David Chipperfield Architects, London, United Kingdom
Herbert Lewis Kruse Blunck Architecture, Des Moines

In an area of the city currently undergoing extensive redevelopment, the Des Moines Public Library forms an integral part of the new Western Gateway Park and links it with downtown Des Moines. The library stacks are arranged so that the park is always visible, creating a sense of openness and transparency to convey the experience of reading in an outdoor setting. The building's green roof provides visual continuity with the surrounding park and increases the structure's thermal mass, reducing temperature extremes and heating and cooling loads.

A composite energy-efficient glass and metal skin of Okatech—made by the German manufacturer Okalux—wraps the two-story structure. Okatech is a triple-glazed insulating panel unit, with a metal mesh layer sandwiched between the external and middle sheets of glass, that admits rays of winter sunlight deep into the interior of the building and blocks heat and the strong light of the high summer sun. The views to the outside remain unobstructed.

The Okatech system is flexible; the material composition of the metal mesh layer and the distances between the three sheets of glass can vary according to the application. At the Des Moines Public Library, the Okatech system comprises, from the outside in, a 5/16-inch layer of low-iron glass, a 5/64-inch cavity filled with an expanded copper mesh, a 5/16-inch glass sheet with a low-E coating, a 5/8-inch cavity, and two 13/64-inch laminated-glass sheets. The expanded copper-mesh interlayer blocks 69 percent of the sunlight and admits just 7 to 22 percent of the sun's heat, depending on the sun's angle, which significantly reduces the cost of purchasing and operating HVAC equipment. Because the expanded copper-mesh interlayer is the only sun-shading device required, views from the inside to the park are maintained at all times during daylight hours. From the outside, the skin appears opaque, the view to the inside blocked by the combined effects of reflection and glare from the copper mesh and the triple layers of glass. The mesh also mitigates the intensity of the sunlight, reducing the need for artificial light to balance disparities in levels of interior and exterior illumination and giving the glazed facade a warm, metallic glow. At night the effect is reversed: the imbalance between levels of illumination in the brightly lit library interior and the surrounding darkness of the park causes most of the facade to appear transparent from the outside. Forty percent of the facade panels are backed with insulation and aluminum, in areas where it is necessary or desirable to shield mechanical and library support spaces from public view, but they retain an appearance almost identical to that of the transparent panels. Slight variations in the expanded copper-mesh interlayer provide the building with a differentiated yet uniform skin, which emphasizes its irregular plan. The height of the panels was determined by differentials in the thermal expansion rates of the glazing, the expanded copper mesh, and the dimensions of the sealed aluminum frame units; their width was determined by the maximum dimension of copper sheets available: 4 feet. The sealed 4-foot-wide by 14-foot-high cladding panels arrived on site already fixed into two-story-high units with an overall height of 28 feet.

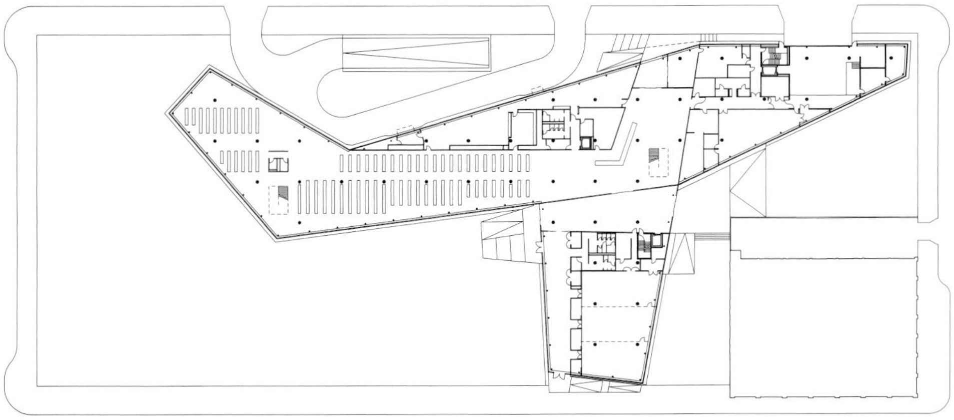

This page
First-floor plan

Opposite
Top: West elevation
Bottom: West elevation, night view

This page
Top to bottom: East elevation, south elevation; west elevation; north elevation; cross section

Opposite
First-floor reading area

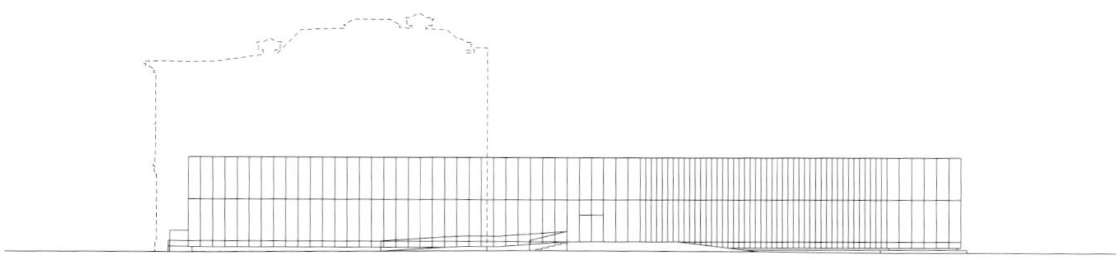

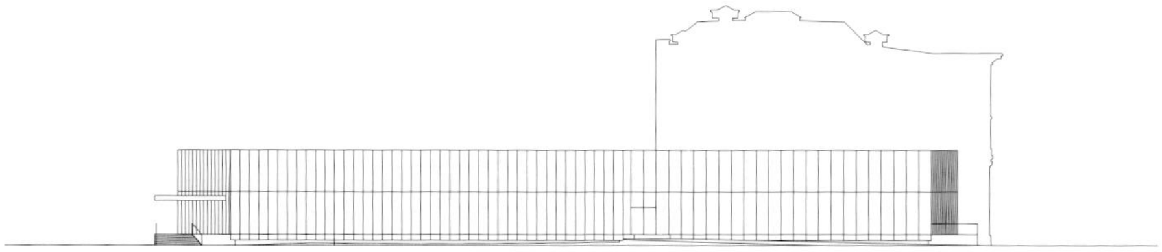

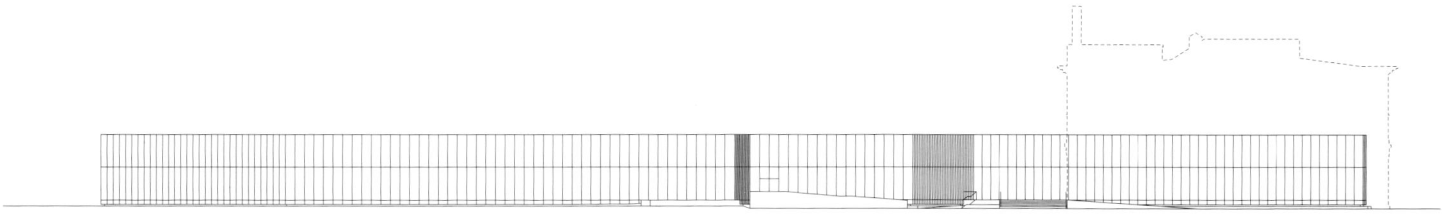

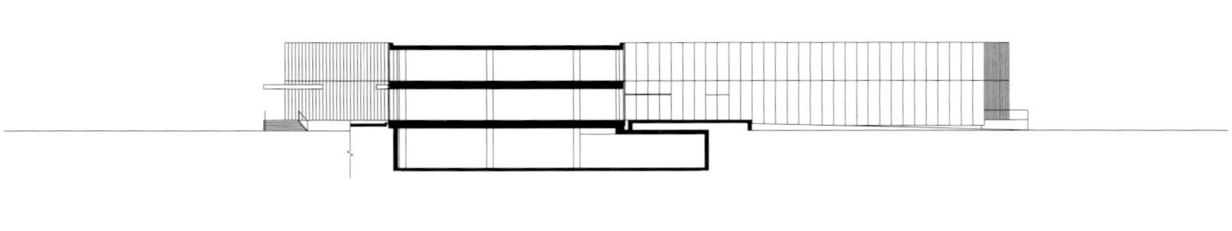

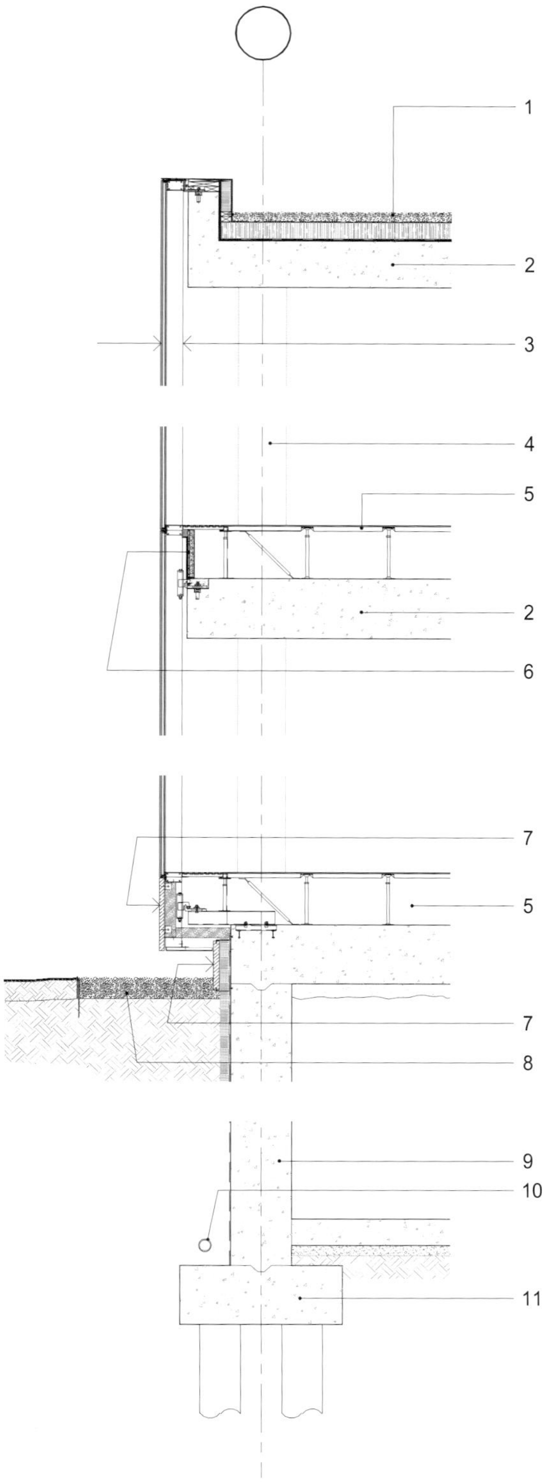

1 - GREEN ROOF SYSTEM

2 - CAST-IN-PLACE CONCRETE ROOF STRUCTURE

3 - ALUMINUM CURTAIN WALL WITH COPPER MESH OKALUX GLAZING PANELS

4 - PERIMETER CONCRETE COLUMNS

5 - RAISED ACCESS FLOOR AND MECHANICAL PLENUM

6 - METAL FACED PLENUM CLOSURE PANEL

7 - GRAPHITE REINFORCED CONCRETE PANEL

8 - PERIMETER CRUSHED ROCK DRAINAGE BAND

9 - CONCRETE FOUNDATION WALL

10 - AUGER CAST FOUNDATION AND GRADE BEAM

This page
Top: Wall section
Bottom: Delivery of glazing units (left); installation of glazing units

Opposite
Top (left to right): Okatech view from outside in; Okatech view from inside out; Okatech sample with copper interlayer
Bottom: Interior, view south

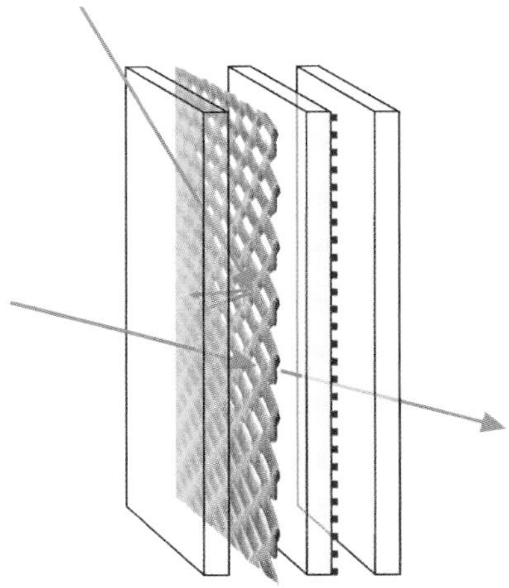

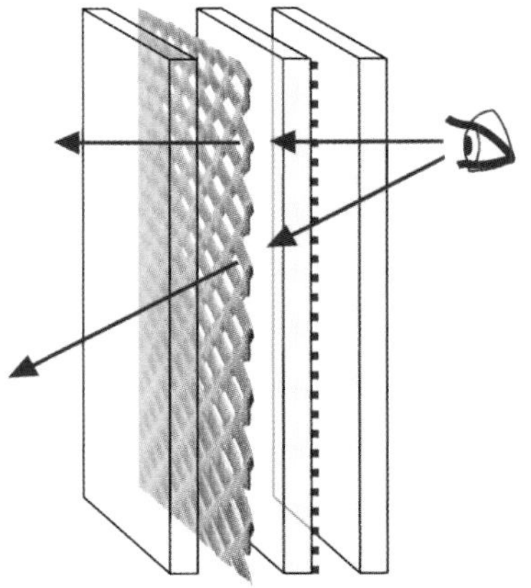

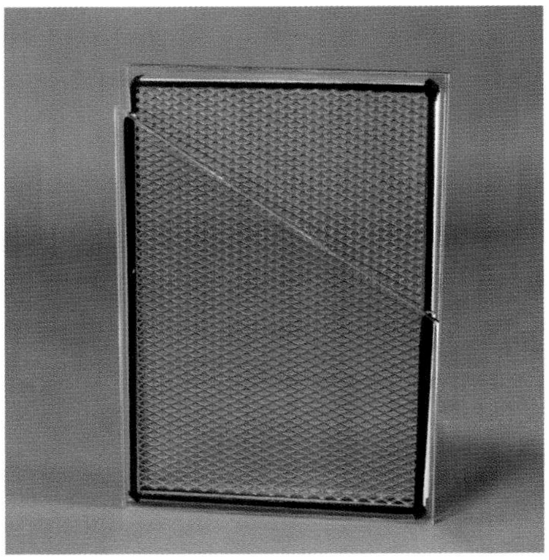

Picower Institute for Learning and Memory,
Massachusetts Institute of Technology, Cambridge, Massachusetts
Charles Correa Associates, Mumbai, India
Goody Clancy, Boston, Massachusetts

The Picower Institute for Learning and Memory is a new research and teaching complex at the Massachusetts Institute of Technology (MIT) devoted to the study of cellular, molecular, behavioral, cognitive, and computational neuroscience. The complex comprises a mix of research laboratory types, faculty offices, teaching labs, animal facilities, a conference center, and a cafe. The site is bounded by three streets and three neighboring buildings and split in two by an active freight rail line, constraints that posed a set of design and technical challenges for a research institute intended to perform as a single unified entity.

The building conforms to its irregular site by reinforcing the street edges while forming distinctive entry plazas on the two principal streets. The north-south orthogonal grid of the main campus extends through the building and is intersected by the diagonal of Main Street. Its facade responds to the irregular geometry with a composition of solids and voids that brings daylight into the labs and offices on the perimeter. A skylit atrium with sculptural walls at the building's center is the social heart of the complex; clustered around it are shared tearooms and seminar rooms, bringing colleagues together.

Laboratories adjacent to the atrium are suffused with daylight, direct and indirect, and windows illuminate internal corridors. Color is used sparingly but purposefully to aid in wayfinding and to subtly demarcate territories of the major research groups. An integrated network of secure vertical and horizontal circulation routes for researchers and research animals ensures infection control and security throughout the building.

Unified by a simple materials palette, the exterior skin employs subtle variations in window type and detailing to express the separate identities of the three research entities within the complex while maintaining an overall visual coherence. Several sophisticated glazing systems distinguish portions of the exterior envelope. A shallow-pitched gabled skylight measuring 90 feet by 63 feet surmounts the central five-story atrium at the heart of the building, constructed of stainless-steel cables and steel king posts and supported by an innovative tension-net truss nearly 16 feet deep. The skylight's Viracon glass units are 1 5/16-inch thick, with three layers of insulated low-E laminated glass, which inhibits the transmission of radiant heat while allowing abundant daylight to pass through, plus a clear interlayer.

In order to make the atrium feel as much as possible like an outdoor urban courtyard, a low-E coating on the glazing was used instead of a ceramic frit or other forms of built-in sun control that would have compromised its transparency. The result is an atrium space that is bright and luminous even on cloudy days, enlivened by the changing quality of light during the day and the dramatic shadows of the cable trusses at night. As a custom-designed system, the skylight could not be factory fabricated in its entirety. Instead, it was constructed in place from a temporary platform erected on scaffolding that filled the atrium. The final tensioning of the cables was accomplished in part via jacks built into the king posts. Once the jacks were in their final position with the cables at their design tension, workers welded the jacks in place and sealed them permanently and invisibly into the king posts.

The three reading rooms and entrance facade have full-height exterior glass walls; each is at least two stories tall, built using a point-supported glazing system, with the insulated-glass curtain wall stabilized by interior glass fins perpendicular to the outside wall. The fins provide lateral wind-load

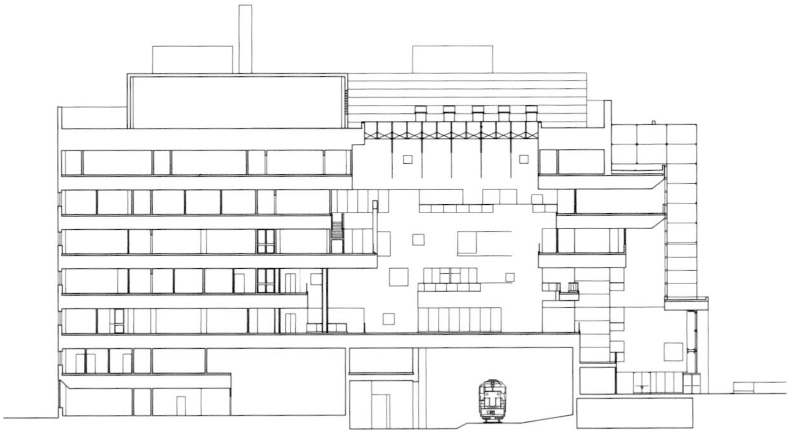

This page
Section

Opposite
Top: Skylight detail
Bottom: Vassar Avenue elevation

This page
Section

Opposite
Top: Plan level 7 (left) and 6
Middle: Site plan
Bottom: Main Street elevation (left); tunnel detail

support and allow for seismic and thermal movement. (All the glass in these systems was fabricated by Pilkington in the United Kingdom.) The south-facing conservatory is a sun-filled space enclosed on three sides and utilizes the same glazing system, as does a portion of the ceiling, where the glazing is suspended from the roof structure above. The glass wall rises to 43 feet, between two and three stories high, with typical fins built of multiple glass layers laminated together in an assembly 1.56 inches thick and 36 inches deep.

The southwest corner of the conservatory is one of the tallest column-free glass corners in the world, braced by a 50-inch-wide laminated-glass fin placed on a diagonal, in combination with horizontal stainless-steel support rods along the short end walls of the space. The outer wall is made of low-E-coated, 1.6-inch-thick insulated glazed units 10 1/2 feet wide by 7 1/4 feet high, among the largest units possible to manufacture. Like the atrium, the conservatory glass has no sun screening other than the low-E coating to admit the maximum amount of daylight into the space and maintain a suitable environment for the trees and plants. Motorized interior shades shield the seating areas from direct sunlight.

An active freight rail line and transit corridor bisects the site. As required by the rail system, the building preserves a no-build zone 22 1/2 feet high over the track area and adjacent spaces, which the transit authority may use for future light-rail alignments. The building was required to cover the entire area, and the designers created a tunnel with two-story-high steel trusses, visible through the windows on the west side of the building and spanning more than 80 feet at the upper levels. Level 3 immediately above the tracks is the most public floor, with a cafe, auditorium, and two large seminar rooms. To maintain the temperature of the floor surface over the tunnel, the floor structure is supported by 6-foot-deep multilayered plate girders with integral hot-water radiant heating and insulation.

The trains generate a low-frequency vibration when they pass through the building twice a day, which would disturb sensitive research equipment if not mitigated. Extensive engineering modeling of the soils, the track, and various train configurations was conducted and alternate engineering strategies considered, including placement of the entire building on 5-foot-high springs at every column point. Ultimately, the design team and the owner determined that the most efficient and cost-effective solution was to place the building on steel piles extending down to the bedrock—more than 100 feet deep—to compensate for the poor bearing capacity of the soil and diminish vibration. There is more steel underground—nearly 3,800 tons—than above ground in the building. To protect the imaging magnets in the functional MRI adjacent to the train tracks at ground level from vibration generated by trains passing through, a special structure was created from large concrete inertia blocks. Post-construction measurements of vibration levels in the building have confirmed that the design successfully mitigates the vibration.

Roger N. Goldstein, FAIA, of Goody Clancy contributed to this text.

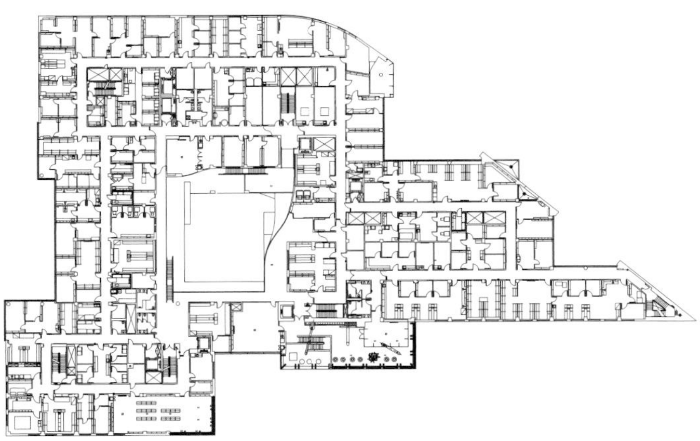

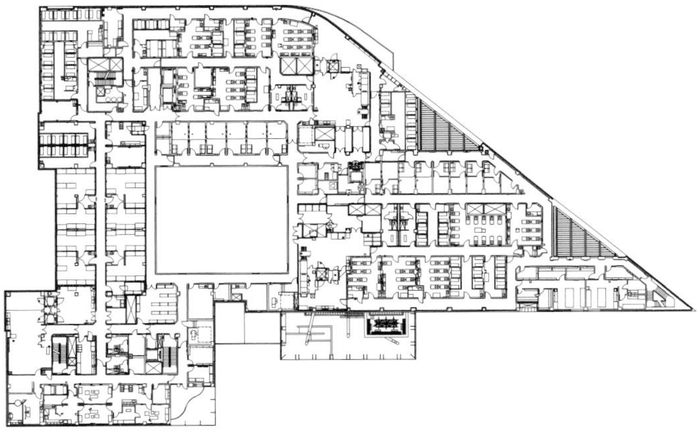

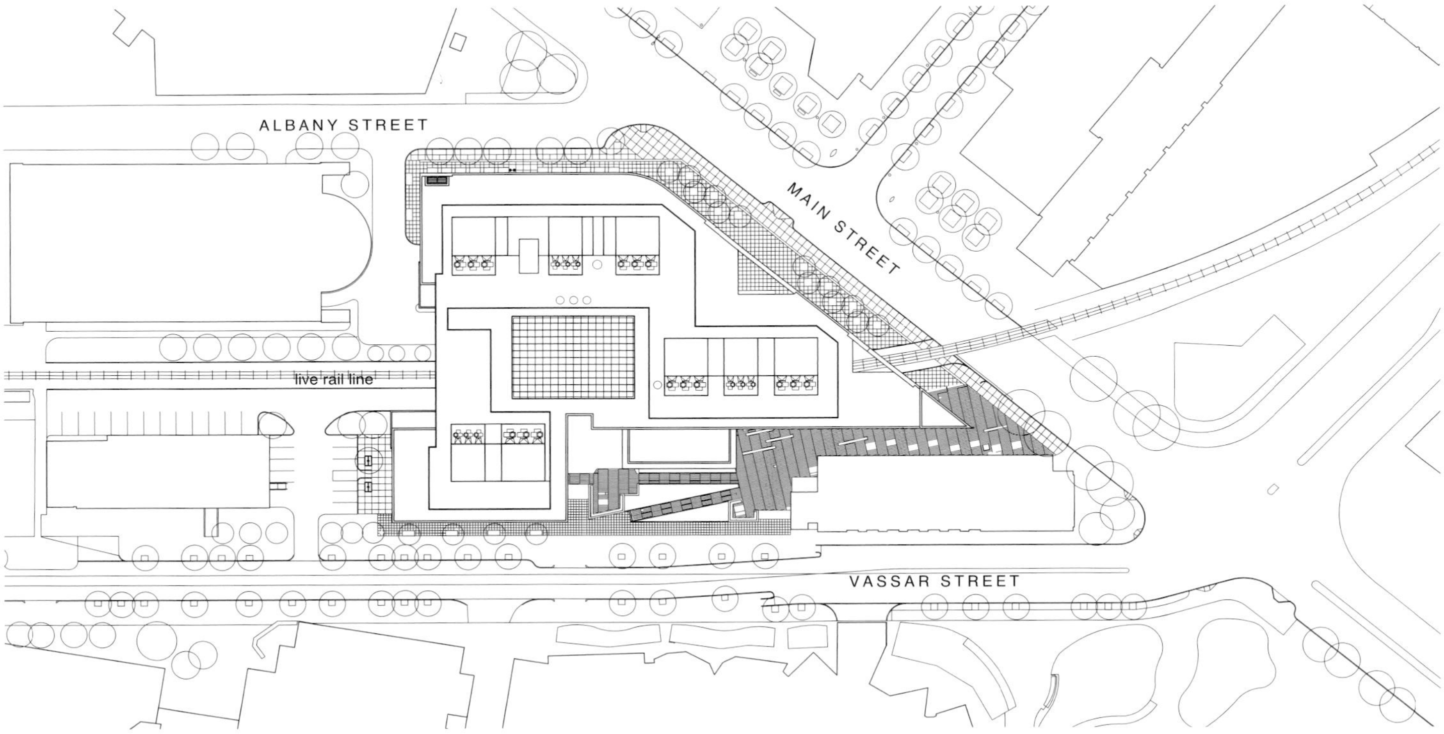
ALBANY STREET
MAIN STREET
live rail line
VASSAR STREET

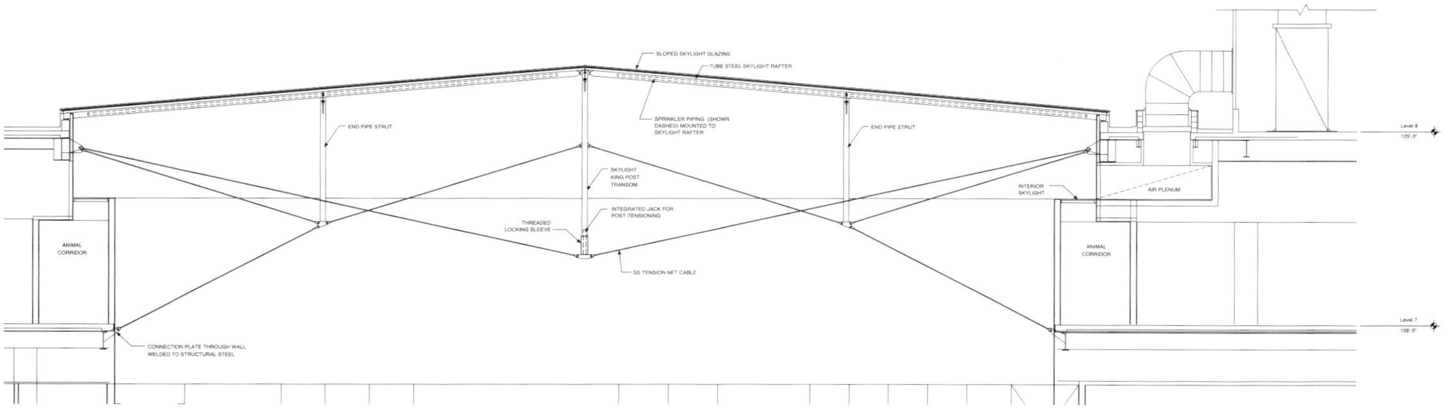

Atrium Skylight East/West Section
1/8" = 1'-0"

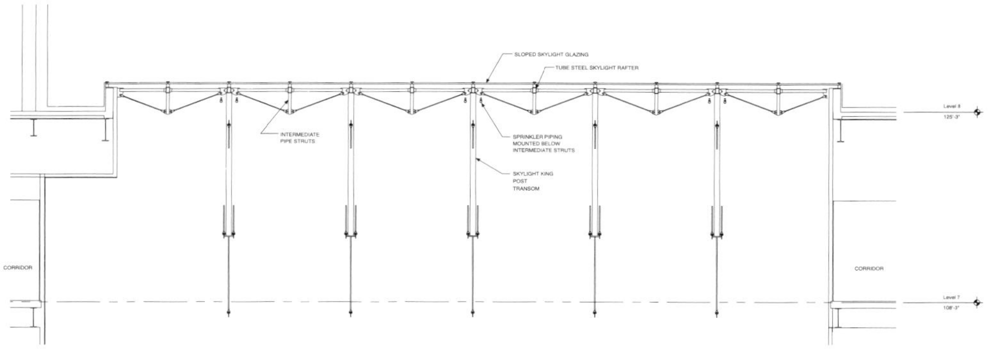

Atrium Skylight North/South Section
1/8" = 1'-0"

This page
Top and middle: Truss sections
Bottom: Skylight installation platform (left); skylight glazing

Opposite
Top (left and right): Strut jack adjustor
Bottom (left and right): Skylight-bracket details

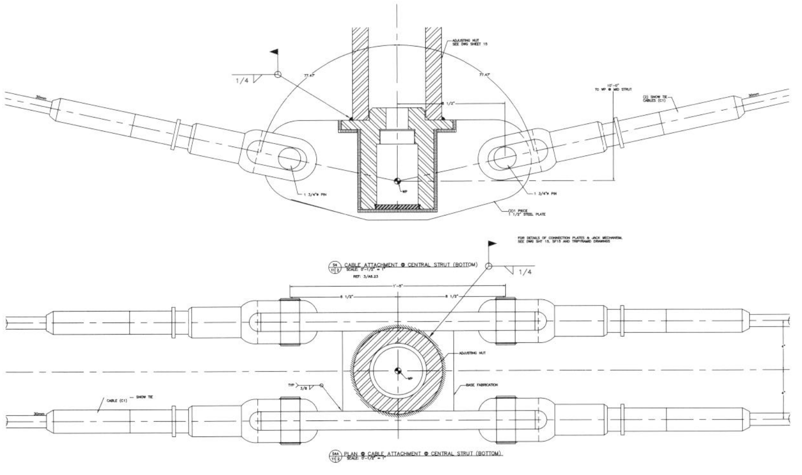

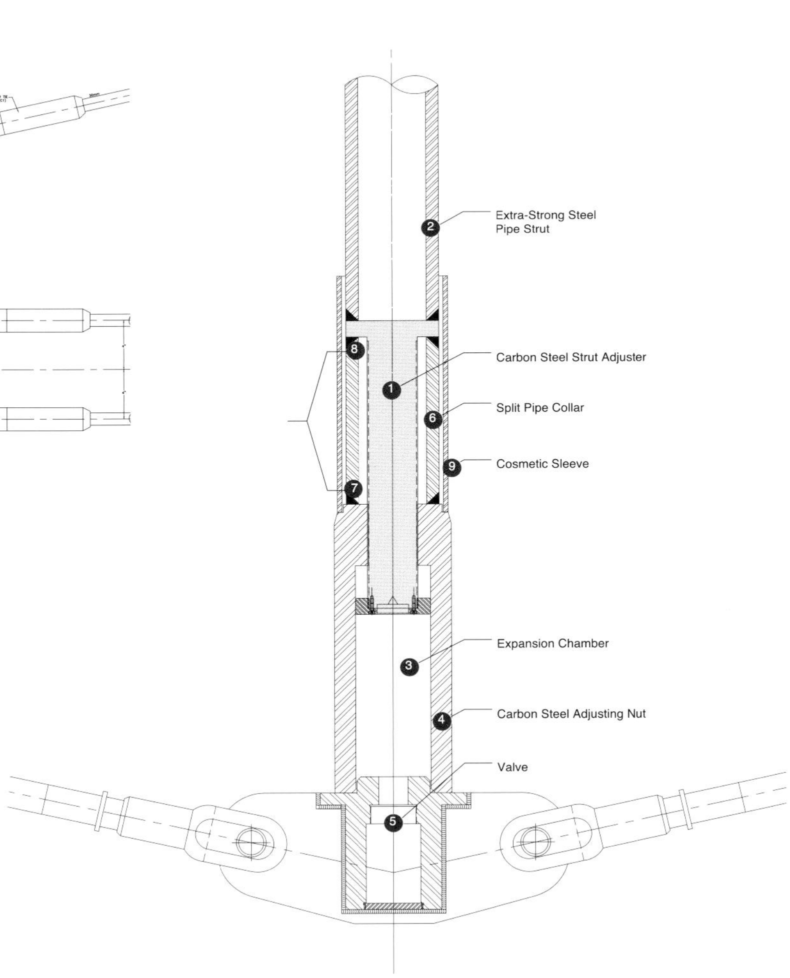
Extra-Strong Steel
Pipe Strut
Carbon Steel Strut Adjuster
Split Pipe Collar
Cosmetic Sleeve
Expansion Chamber
Carbon Steel Adjusting Nut
Valve

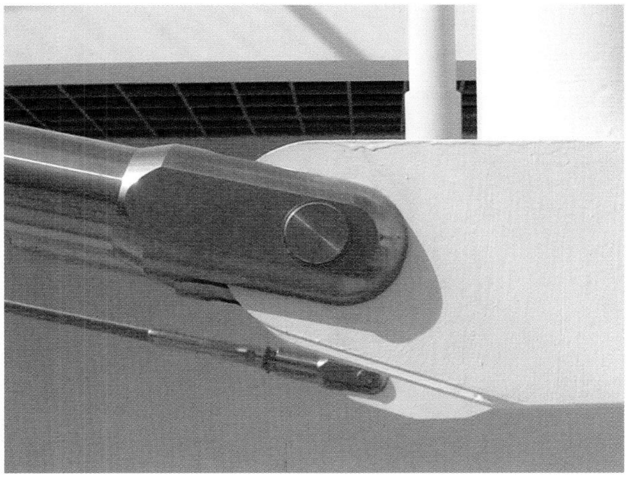

University of Phoenix Stadium, Glendale, Arizona
Eisenman Architects, New York, New York
HOK Sport, Kansas City, Missouri

The new football stadium for the Arizona Cardinals is a multipurpose facility, configurable for any type of event at any time of the year, whose design is intended as a challenge to the conventions of traditional stadium architecture. The form of the building was inspired by the light, color, and textures of the Arizona landscape, its alternating smooth panels and vertical slots by the shape of the indigenous barrel cactus. Rather than making a statement through mass and weight, the stadium's principal formal ambition is to achieve a maximum degree of transparency: vertical slots of glass provide clear views of the surrounding landscape from one side through to the other. The original plan to open the south end with retractable glazing was abandoned because of conflicts with the physical requirements of the end-zone scoreboards, but the retractable roof and field were retained. The two large retractable panels that make up the roof can be deployed to provide shading for 63,000 fans, or opened to expose the playing field. With the roof closed, the stadium can be air-conditioned during the hot months.

The 500,000-square-foot steel-framed roof structure consists of two systems: a fixed roof with a central opening, supported on two 87-foot-deep structural steel trusses that span 700 feet between concrete supercolumns located at the corners of the stadium, and a 100,000-square-foot operable roof consisting of two panels that part to create a 240-foot-wide by 360-foot-long opening. The operable roof is clad in Birdair, a translucent PTFE-coated fiberglass fabric. When closed during the day, the tensioned membrane structure provides a soft, diffuse translucence that appears opaque when viewed from the exterior. At night interior lighting transforms it into a luminescent structure on the desert landscape.

Two giant lenticular trusses—taking the form of a double convex lens—provide primary support to the roof structure and are its dominant architectural elements. (The lenticular trusses are described by the engineers as "Brunel trusses" after the renowned British engineer Isambard Kingdom Brunel, who first pioneered the structural form in 1859 at the Royal Albert Bridge in Saltash, England.) The two retractable roof panels are the first in the United States to operate on an inclined arc along the top roof profile of a building and meet directly over the 50 yard line when in the closed position and roll downhill to reside over each end zone when opened. This innovation allows for a smooth roof surface with minimal weatherproofing elements, but the presence of wind uplift forces and the necessity for braking controls required the engineers to develop an innovative design for the mechanization of the 1.2-acre, 800-ton roof panels.

Each panel traverses an incline varying from 0 degrees at the 50 yard line to 14 degrees over the end zones as it moves from the closed to open position along the curved top chord of the Brunel trusses. During the approximately eleven-minute period needed to fully open or close the roof, the panels are supported by transporters that ride on forged-steel wheels to open and close the roof. Half of the transporters are equipped with cable drums, nestled at the ends of each panel, that spool and unspool the cables, which are anchored to the fixed roof high above the 50 yard line, allowing the weight of the roof to do the work of opening it. The drums lay the cables down and pick them up as they spool and unspool, rather than dragging the cables across the roof steel. This nontraditional arrangement, in which the cable drums travel with the roof panels, puts the drive system in close proximity to the encoders that monitor roof movement and dramatically simplifies the control system; it also allows the large cable drums to be positioned along the roof panels, eliminating the need to make space for all sixteen drums at the center of the fixed roof structure. A fully redundant control system ensures that the retractable roof remains completely under control throughout start-up and operation. Each cable drum is powered by electric-induction motors with fail-safe DC electric brakes that automatically engage when roof movement stops. Should the roof ever move above the maximum permissible speed, a redundant overspeed-sensing system, operating independently of the control system, automatically engages and stops roof movement in seconds.

The roof was built in two phases. The central 240-foot-wide section, consisting of the Brunel trusses, operable roof, and north and south fixed roofs, was preassembled on the floor of the stadium. Once complete, the 6,000-ton roof was lifted 120 feet into place atop the supercolumns using eight strand

Opposite
Top: East elevation, night view
Bottom: Interior view on game day

RED ZONE Budweiser RED ZONE
REDZONE
ARIZONA
CARDINALS

This page
Left: Club-level plan
Right: Main-level plan

Opposite
Top: East elevation
Middle: South elevation
Bottom: Aerial view, roof closed

jacks, believed to be the largest roof lift ever accomplished. The remaining portion of the fixed roof, from the Brunel trusses out to the edge of the stadium, was built in a traditional manner using cranes positioned outside the stadium.

The stadium is the first in North America and one of only a handful of similar facilities in Europe and Japan with a retractable grass playing field. At the touch of a button, the 2.1-acre field moves along a 741-foot travel path into or out of the stadium in approximately one hour, over thirteen steel rails, each 1/5 mile long, that sit nearly flush with the stadium floor. Engineers designed the field for dynamic live load as well as weight so that it would react like a traditional grass playing surface, with ideal conditions for football activities. Weighing 9,371 tons, the composite field includes all components required for healthy grass, including irrigation, drainage, and an optimized growing surface, all contained in a planting tray 18 inches deep. The first layer is a waterproof membrane, followed by a drainage mat, then root-zone mix, an 11-inch layer of sand with fiber filaments to supply roots with air, water, and nutrients, and grass plugs that propagate by stolons, or above-ground runners. The soil/sod system is supported by a 5-inch-thick composite decking system and an 18-inch W-beam structural framing grid. The massive support structure provides the playing field with considerable stiffness and superior vibration characteristics.

When not in use for football or soccer games, the field stays outside the stadium, where the grass can soak up sunshine, rain, and nutrients. For proper water drainage, the playing field is cambered so that the centerline—perpendicular to the 50 yard line—is 2 inches higher than the sidelines, approximately 40 3/8 inches above the finished floor. A maintenance trench similar to those at automotive oil-changing facilities is installed outside the stadium so that any wheel or other drive-system component can be positioned directly above it, giving maintenance workers access from a comfortable workspace with room for tools and other items.

Not only is it more economical to move the field outside than to design the roof to retract to expose the entire field, but keeping the field tray outside also eliminates humidity problems inside the stadium and provides unrestricted access to a clean, flat, well-positioned floor for events other than football or soccer. A utility grid embedded in the concrete floor facilitates access to electrical and service hookups wherever they are required.

Uni-Systems and Mark Waggoner, P.E., of Walter P. Moore and Associates contributed to this text.

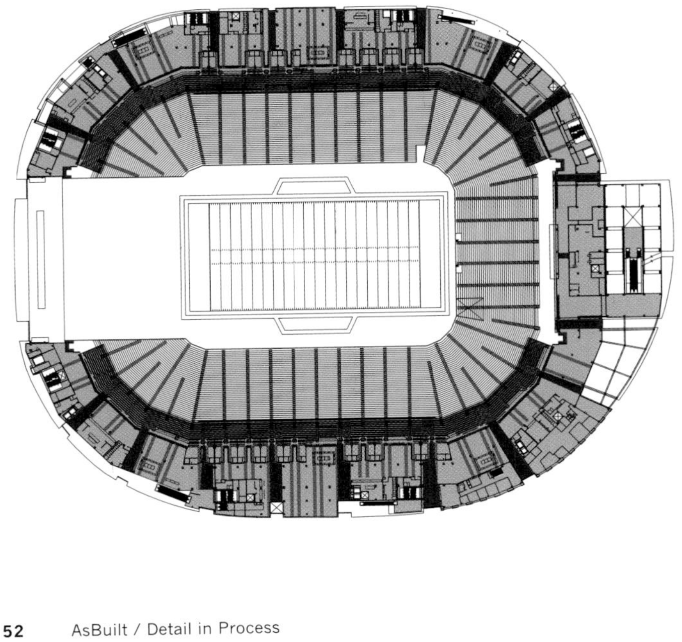

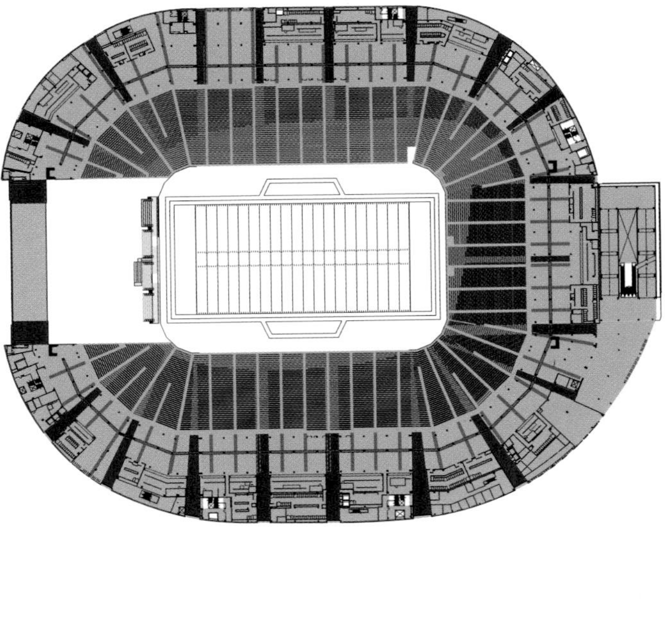

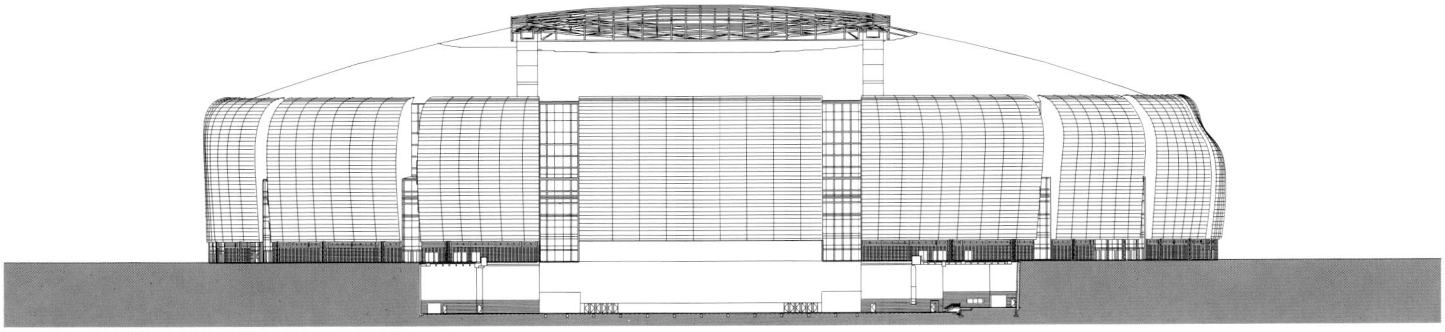

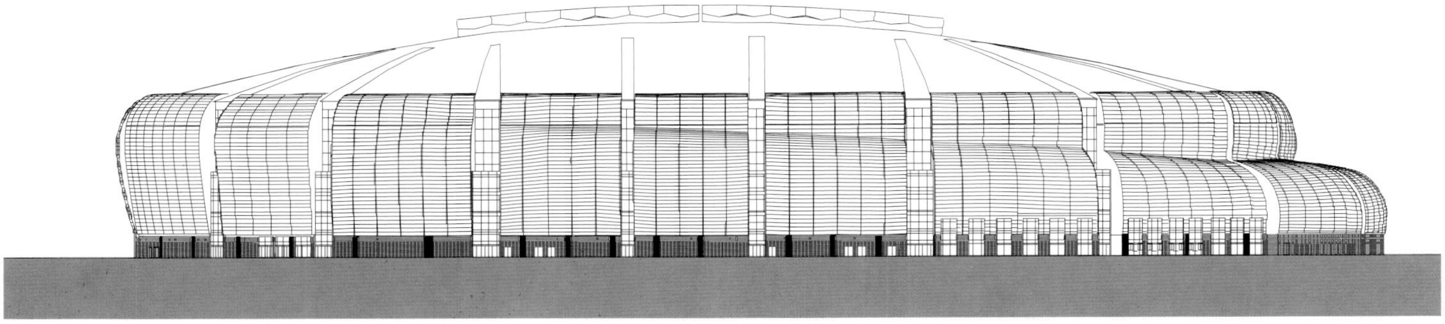

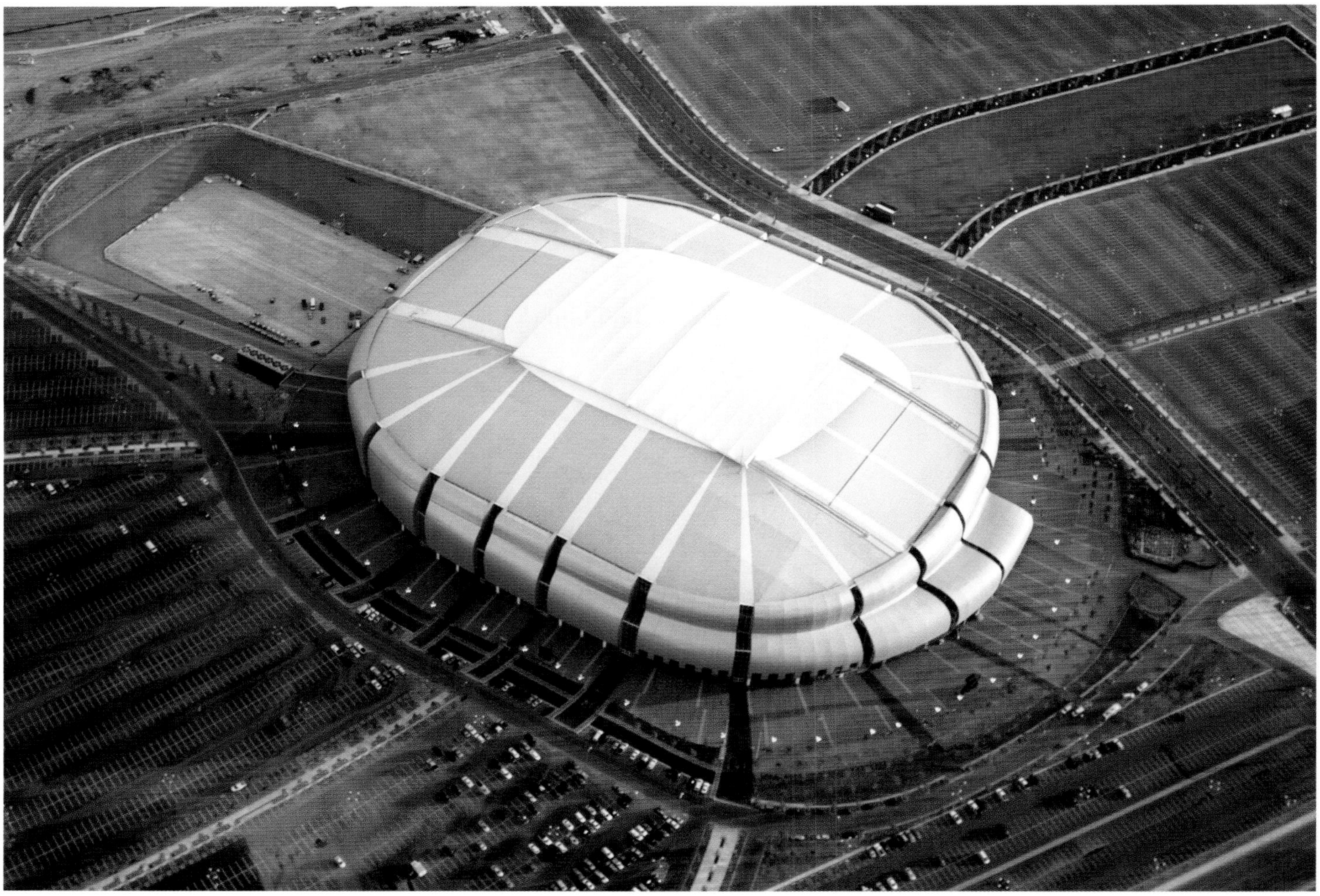

This page
Top: Roof carrier (left); linear bearing diagram
Bottom: Northwest elevation

Opposite
Top: 3-D structural models
Middle: Field moving out, with roof closed
Bottom: Roof, half open (left); roof, open

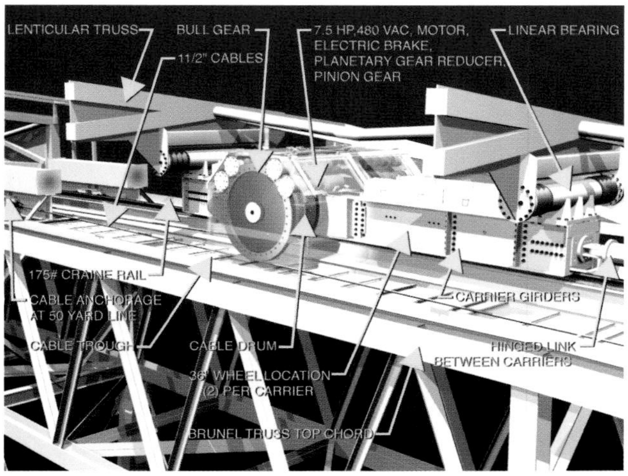

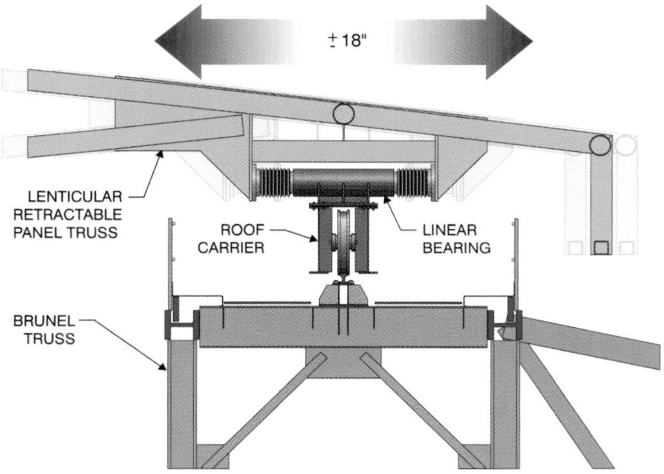

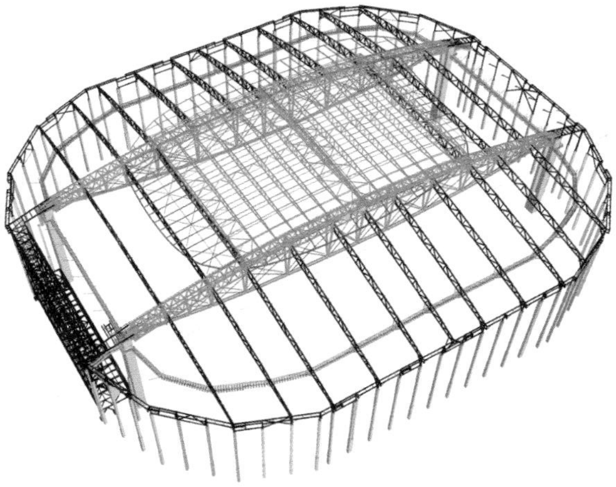

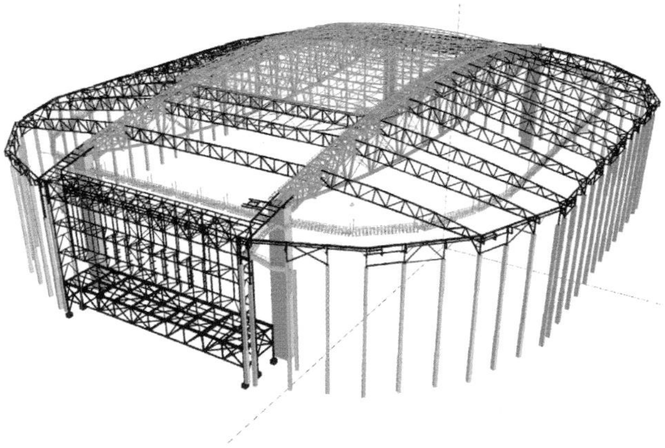

ARIZONA CARDINALS

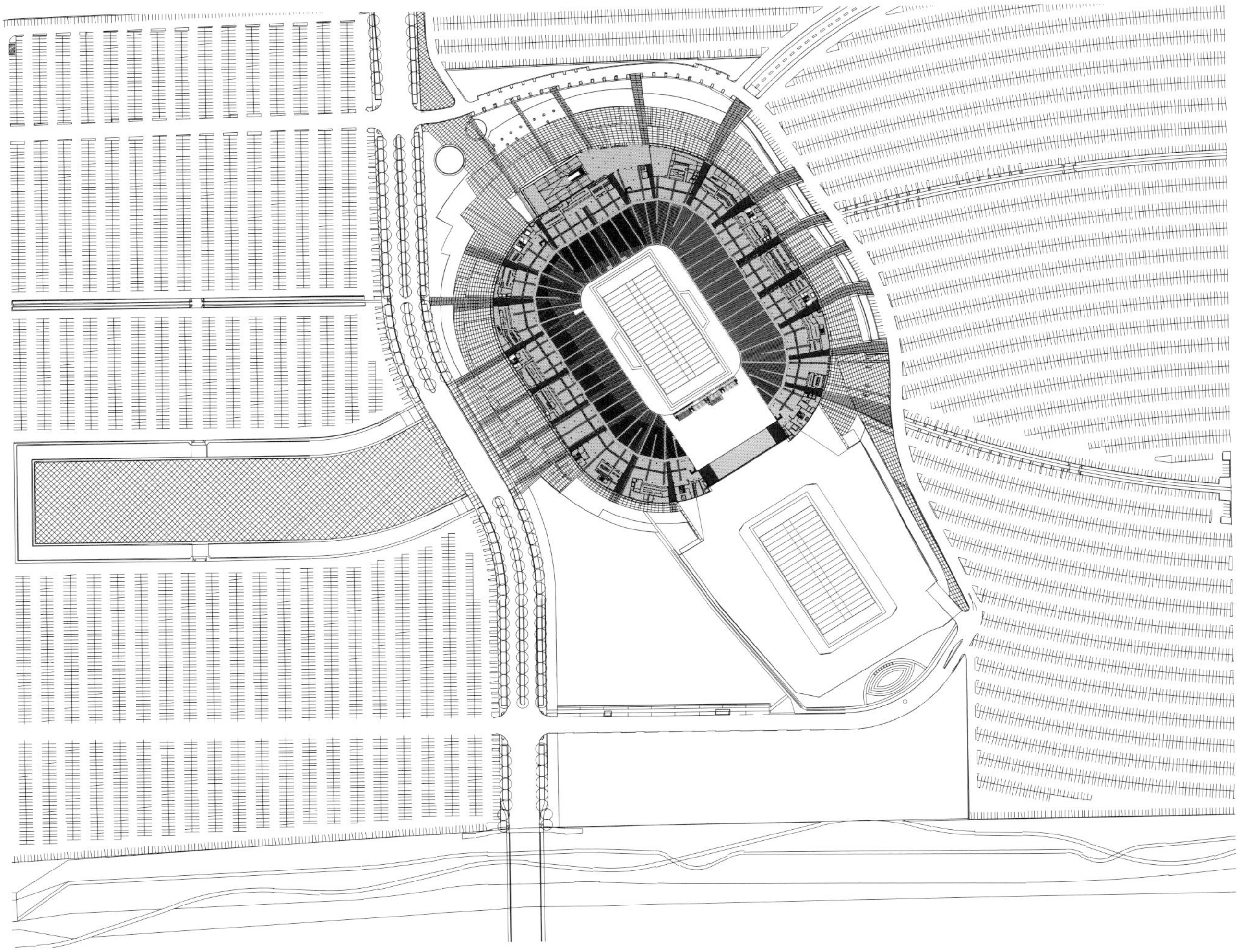

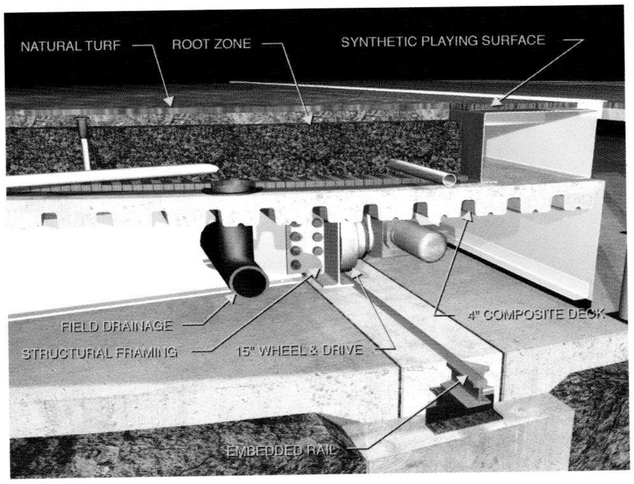
NATURAL TURF
ROOT ZONE
SYNTHETIC PLAYING SURFACE
FIELD DRAINAGE
STRUCTURAL FRAMING
15" WHEEL & DRIVE
4" COMPOSITE DECK
EMBEDDED RAIL

Opposite
Top: Site plan
Middle: Field moving in under field door (left); field-wheel-box alignments
Bottom: Center guide rail with extruded covers installed (left); field cutaway section

This page
Top: Field out
Middle: Field from roof (left); field moving under door
Bottom: Field moving out

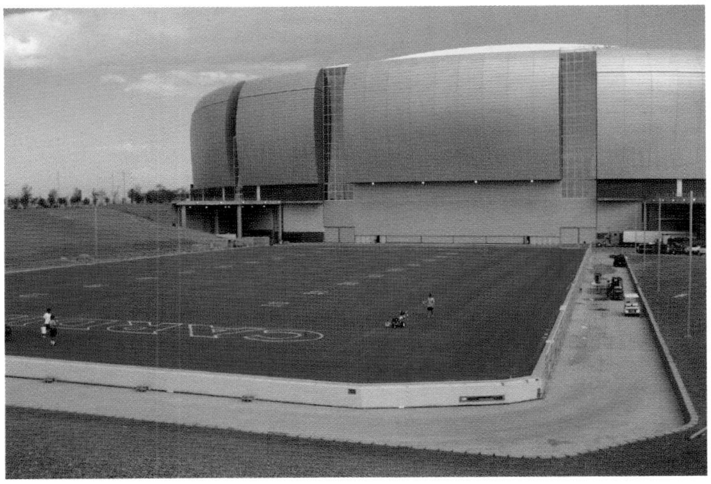

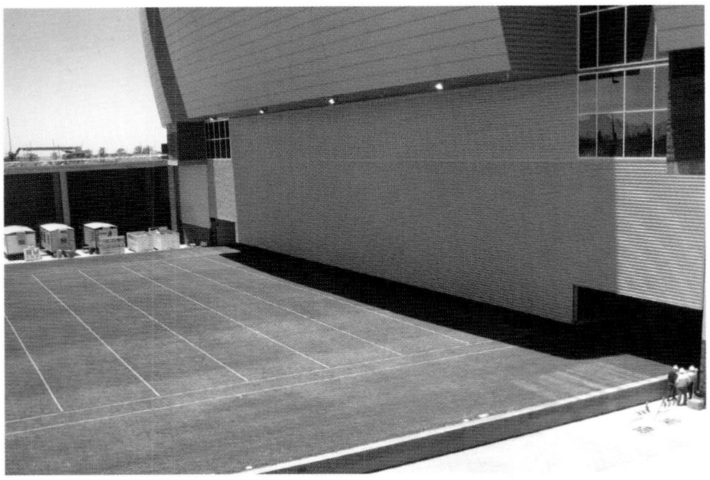

This page
Top: Partial section
Bottom: Shell interior (left); shell detail

Opposite
Top: North elevation
Bottom: Interior, roof closed

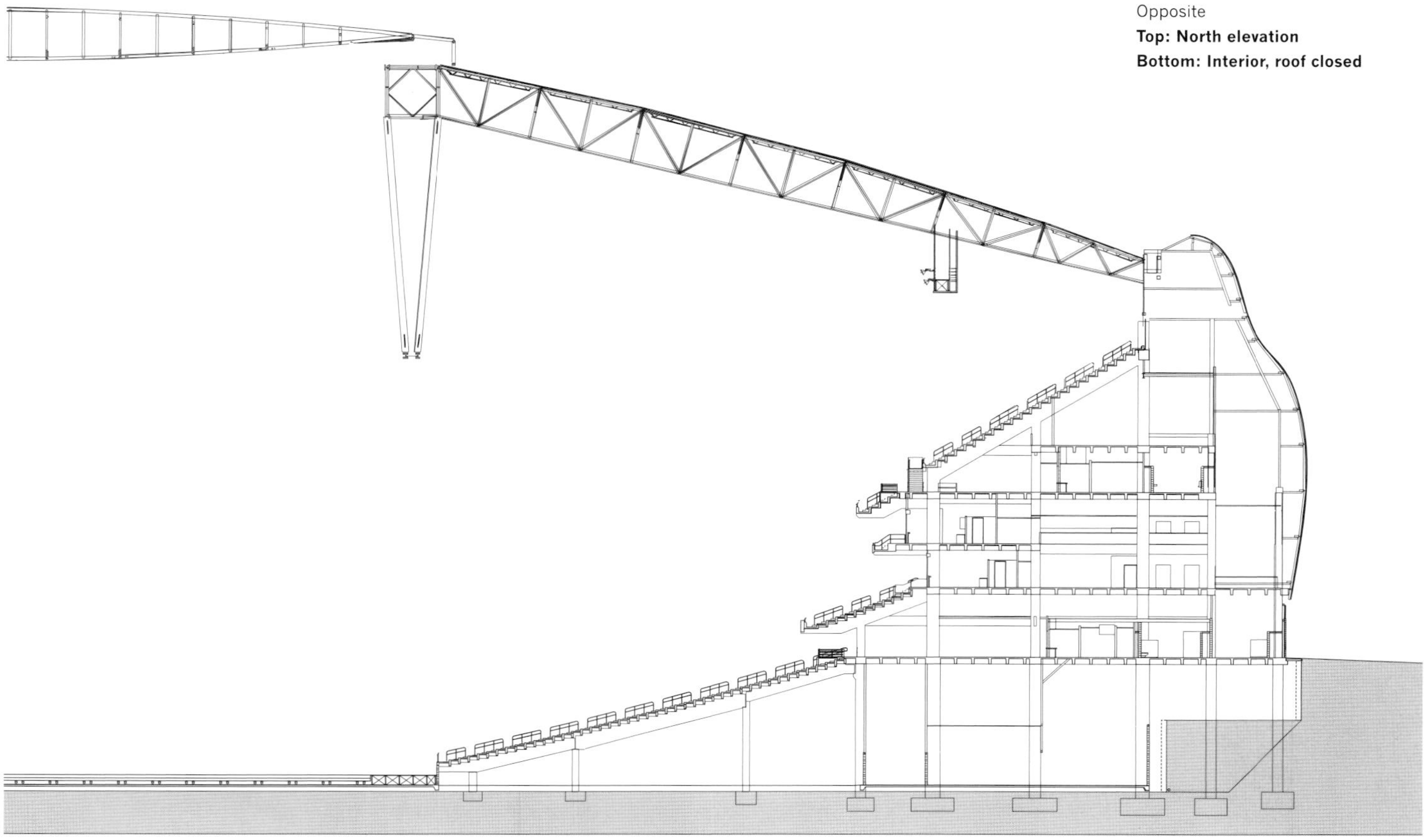

CARDINALS

Hearst Tower, New York, New York
Foster + Partners, London, United Kingdom
Adamson Associates Architects, New York

The Hearst Tower is an expansion of 959 Eighth Avenue in New York, designed in 1926 by Joseph Urban and George B. Post & Sons for William Randolph Hearst, with a tower that was never built. The new design by Foster + Partners reunites the Hearst Corporation's multiple media interests under one roof while preserving the landmark's original facade and street-level entrance lobby, which is constrained on three sides by ground-floor retail spaces. Filled with natural light, the five-story-high upper lobby spans the whole length and width of the building to reveal portions of the original facade, a clerestory above the parapet, and a glass skylight that bridges the original building and the new tower emerging from it. The interval between the entrance lobby and upper lobby thirty feet above is traversed diagonally by an inclined plane with escalators.

To animate the transitional space, Foster + Partners, James Carpenter Design Associates, and Fluidity Design Consultants transformed it into a 75-foot-wide by 30-foot-high field of stepped cast-glass prisms that suffuses the space with light and sound. Light from the clerestory and skylights is refracted as water cascades over the cast-glass prisms, whose profiles are designed to create an even and controlled flow of water. Located at every third row of the prism grid are solid cast-glass blocks whose geometry replicates that of the building's diagrid steel framing—the only elements to emerge above the water; their polished mirror-like surfaces capture and reflect ambient light. The installation's recirculated water is chilled to a temperature lower than that of the surrounding air so that condensation accumulates on its exposed surfaces, providing passive cooling and a more comfortable interior environment.

James Carpenter Design Associates and Fluidity Design Consultants contributed to this text.

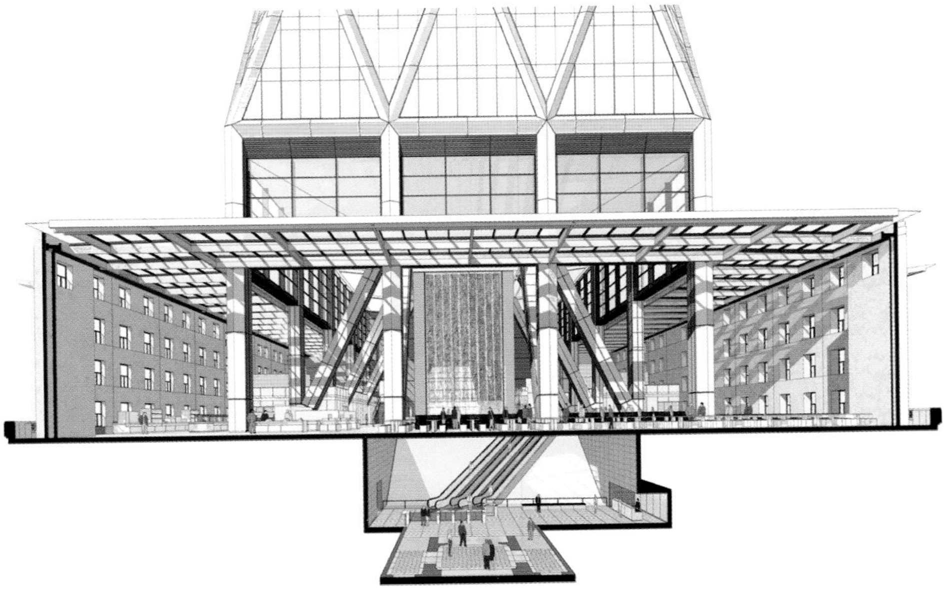

This page
Lobby, perspective

Opposite
Top: Cascade elevation
Bottom: Lower lobby

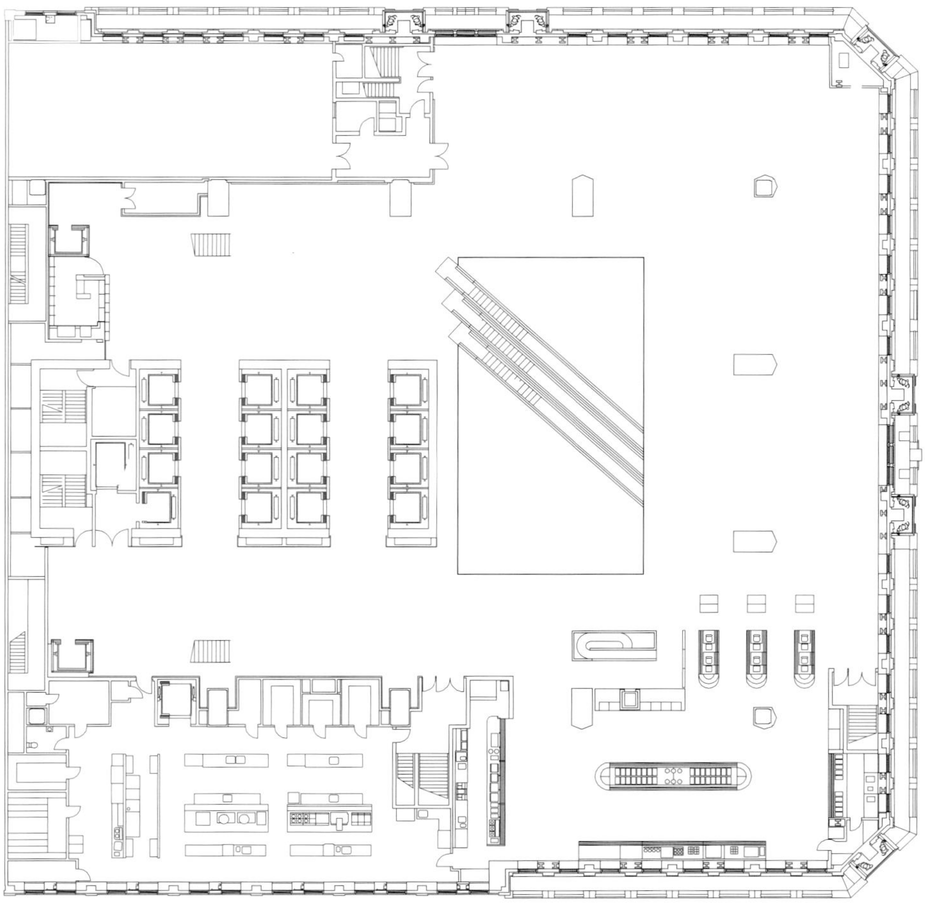

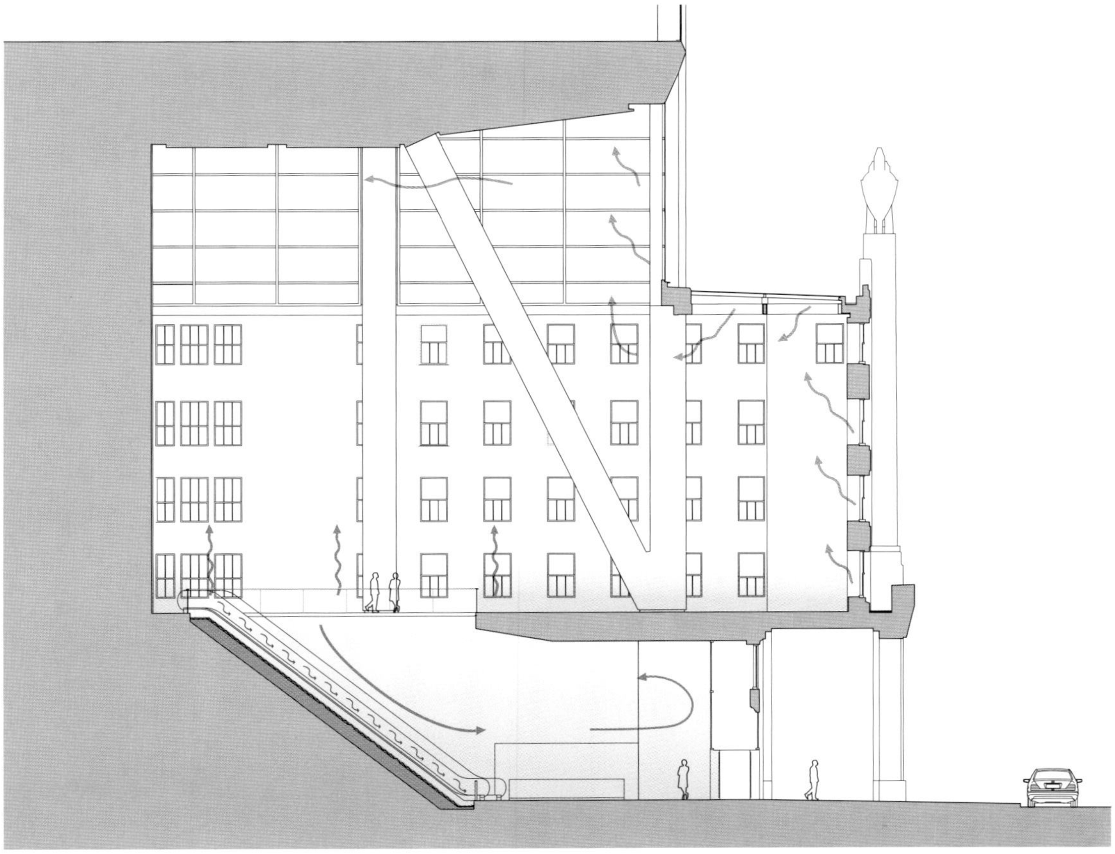

This page
Top: Upper-lobby plan
Bottom: Lobby microclimate

Opposite
Top: Lobby, upper level
Bottom: Lobby escalators

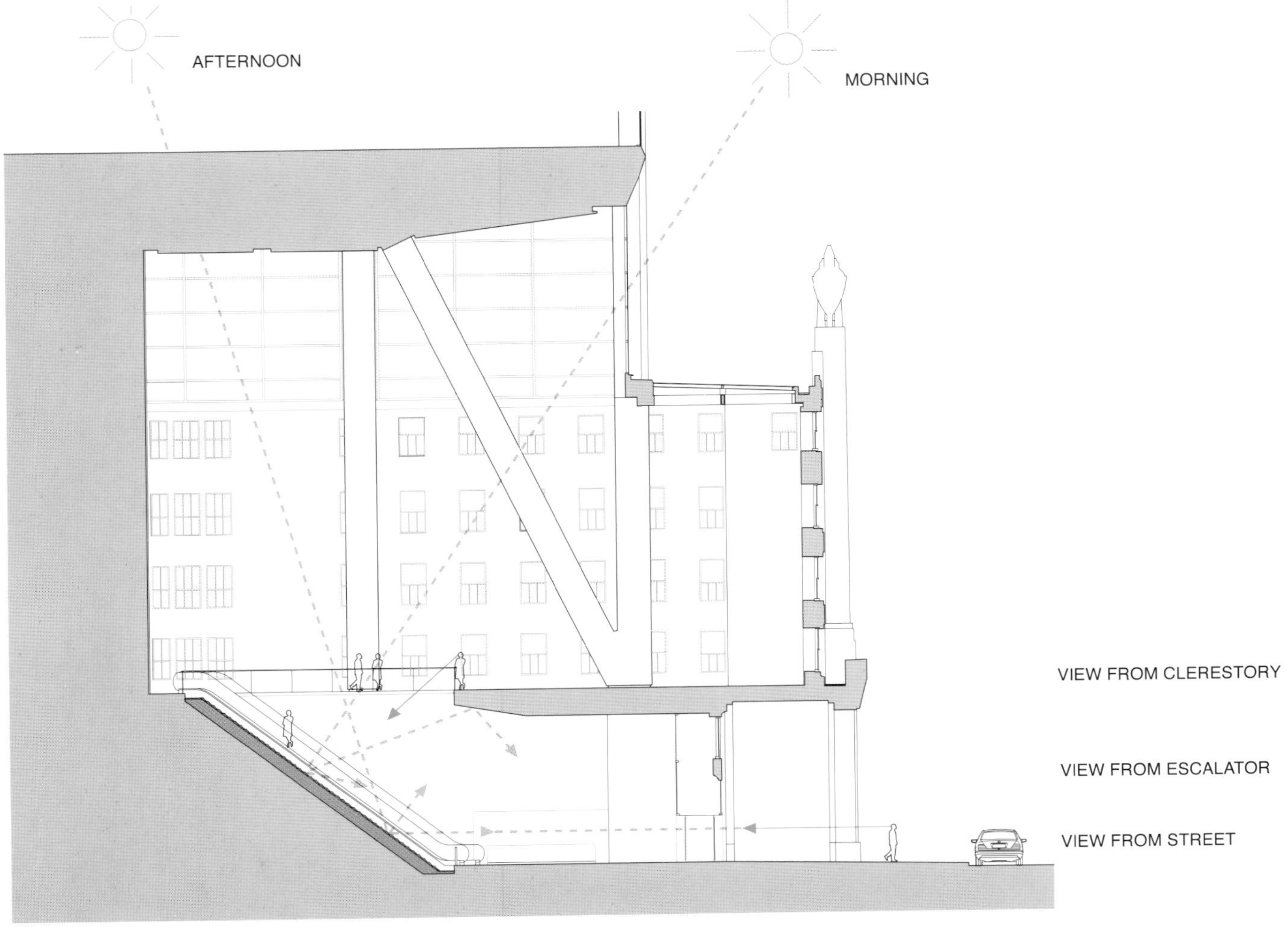
AFTERNOON
MORNING
VIEW FROM CLERESTORY
VIEW FROM ESCALATOR
VIEW FROM STREET

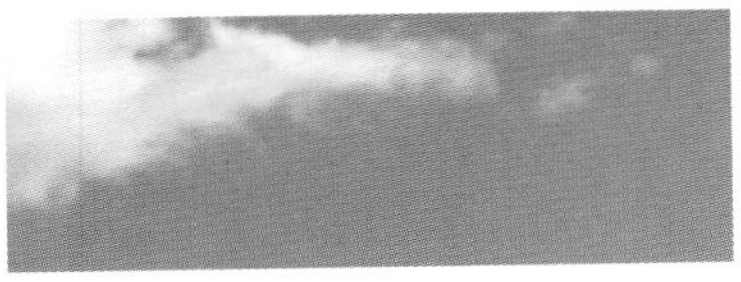

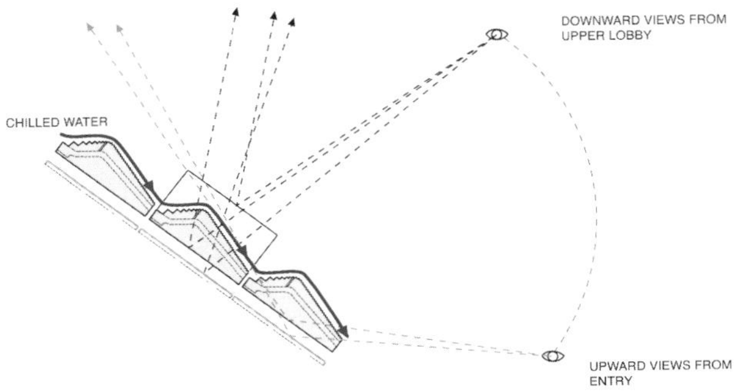
DOWNWARD VIEWS FROM UPPER LOBBY
CHILLED WATER
UPWARD VIEWS FROM ENTRY

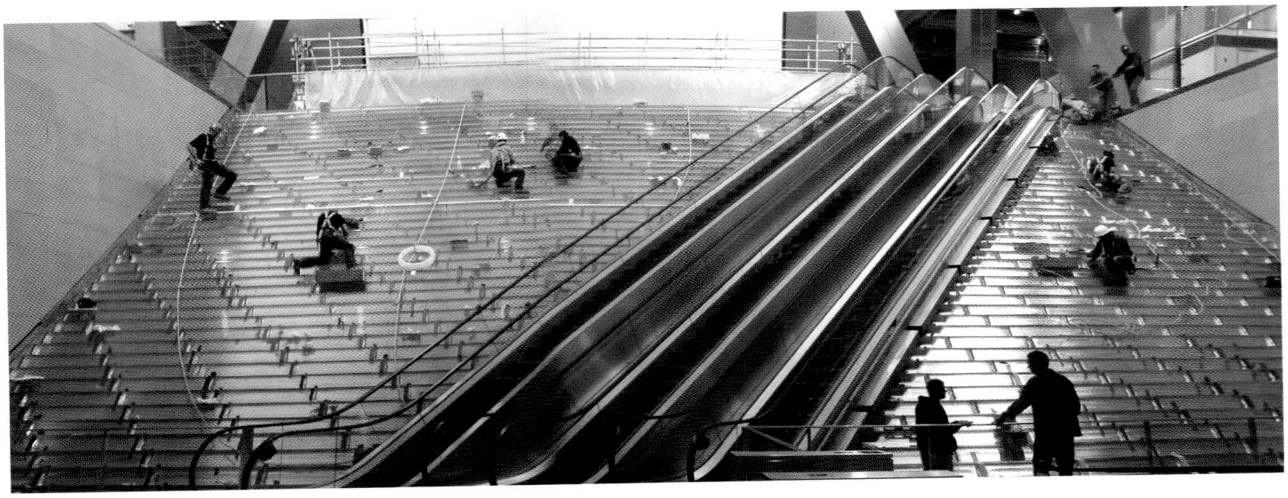

Opposite
Top: Lobby, daylight diagram
Middle: Installation on site (left); viewing angle of reflection
Bottom: Installation on site

This page
Top: Section
Bottom: Cascade plan

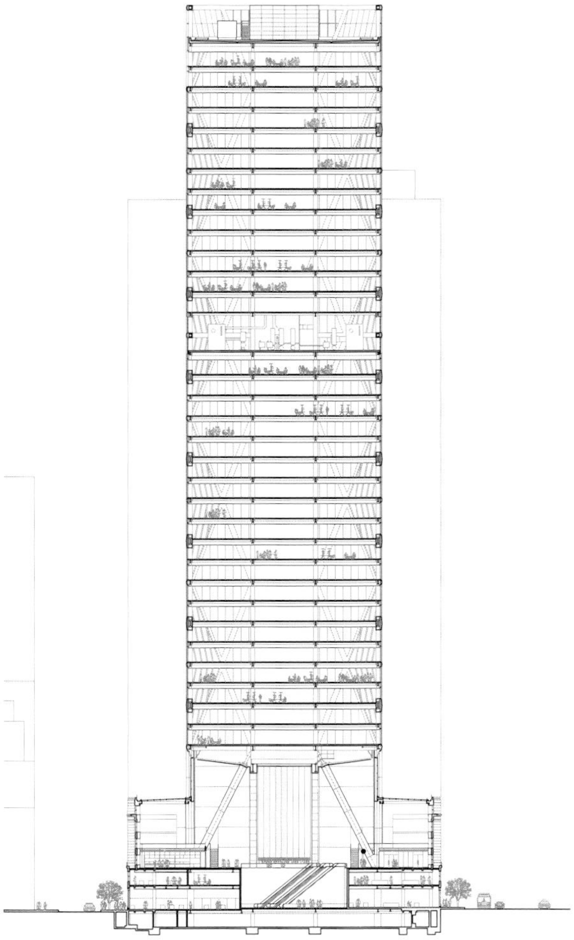

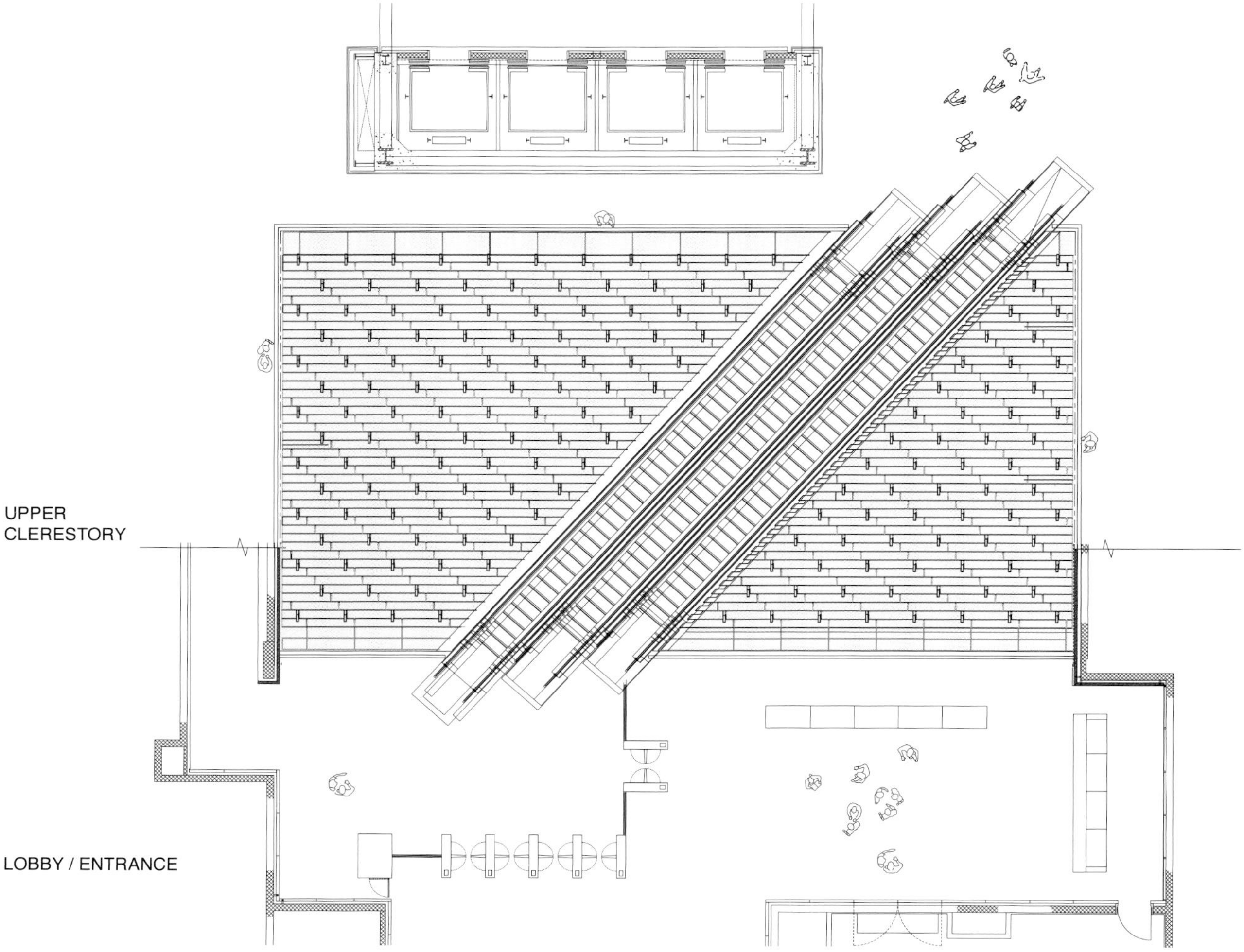

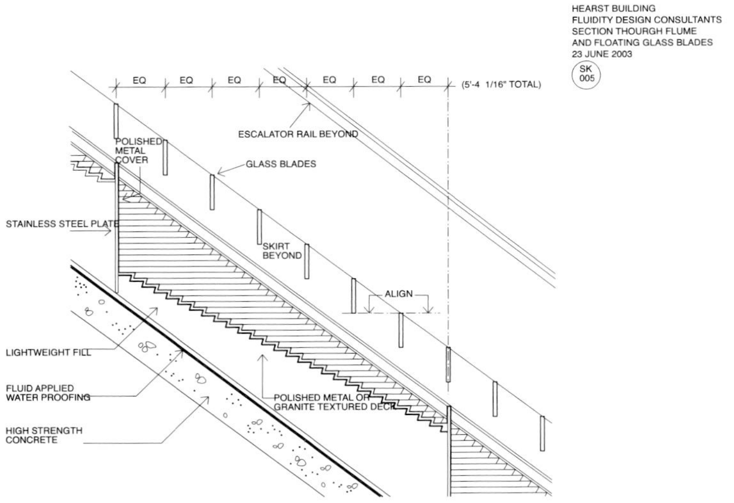
HEARST BUILDING
FLUIDITY DESIGN CONSULTANTS
SECTION THOURGH FLUME
AND FLOATING GLASS BLADES
23 JUNE 2003
SK
005
EQ
EQ
EQ
EQ
EQ
EQ
EQ
(5'-4 1/16" TOTAL)
ESCALATOR RAIL BEYOND
POLISHED METAL COVER
GLASS BLADES
STAINLESS STEEL PLATE
SKIRT BEYOND
ALIGN
LIGHTWEIGHT FILL
FLUID APPLIED WATER PROOFING
POLISHED METAL OR GRANITE TEXTURED DECK
HIGH STRENGTH CONCRETE

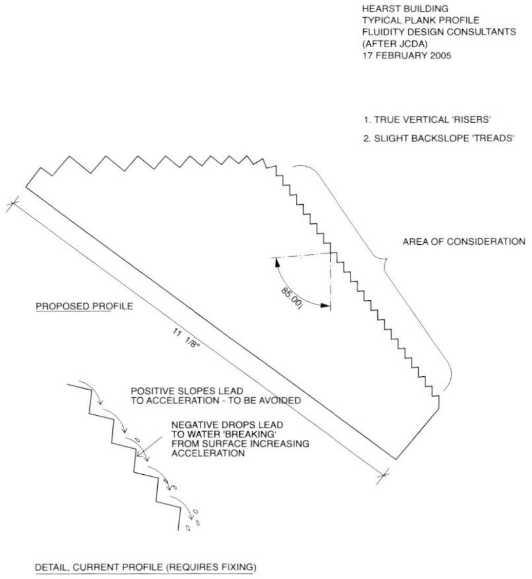
HEARST BUILDING
TYPICAL PLANK PROFILE
FLUIDITY DESIGN CONSULTANTS
(AFTER JCDA)
17 FEBRUARY 2005
1. TRUE VERTICAL 'RISERS'
2. SLIGHT BACKSLOPE 'TREADS'
AREA OF CONSIDERATION
65.00)
PROPOSED PROFILE
11 1/8"
POSITIVE SLOPES LEAD TO ACCELERATION - TO BE AVOIDED
NEGATIVE DROPS LEAD TO WATER 'BREAKING' FROM SURFACE INCREASING ACCELERATION
DETAIL, CURRENT PROFILE (REQUIRES FIXING)

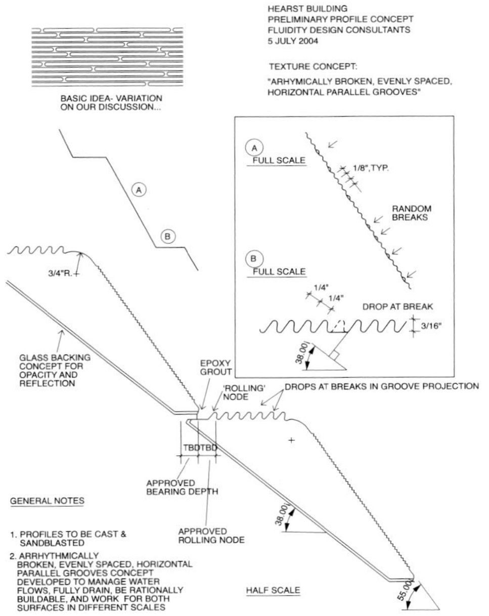
HEARST BUILDING
PRELIMINARY PROFILE CONCEPT
FLUIDITY DESIGN CONSULTANTS
5 JULY 2004
TEXTURE CONCEPT:
"ARHYMICALLY BROKEN, EVENLY SPACED, HORIZONTAL PARALLEL GROOVES"
BASIC IDEA- VARIATION ON OUR DISCUSSION...
A
FULL SCALE
1/8",TYP.
RANDOM BREAKS
B
FULL SCALE
1/4"
1/4"
DROP AT BREAK
3/16"
38.00)
A
B
3/4"R.
GLASS BACKING CONCEPT FOR OPACITY AND REFLECTION
EPOXY GROUT
'ROLLING' NODE
DROPS AT BREAKS IN GROOVE PROJECTION
TBDTBD
APPROVED BEARING DEPTH
APPROVED ROLLING NODE
38.00)
55.00)
GENERAL NOTES
1. PROFILES TO BE CAST & SANDBLASTED
2. ARRHYTHMICALLY BROKEN, EVENLY SPACED, HORIZONTAL PARALLEL GROOVES CONCEPT DEVELOPED TO MANAGE WATER FLOWS, FULLY DRAIN, BE RATIONALLY BUILDABLE, AND WORK FOR BOTH SURFACES IN DIFFERENT SCALES
HALF SCALE

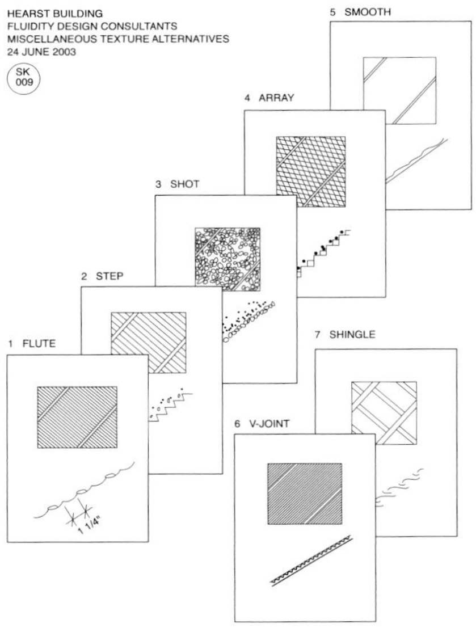
HEARST BUILDING
FLUIDITY DESIGN CONSULTANTS
MISCELLANEOUS TEXTURE ALTERNATIVES
24 JUNE 2003
SK
009
5 SMOOTH
4 ARRAY
3 SHOT
2 STEP
1 FLUTE
7 SHINGLE
6 V-JOINT
1 1/4"

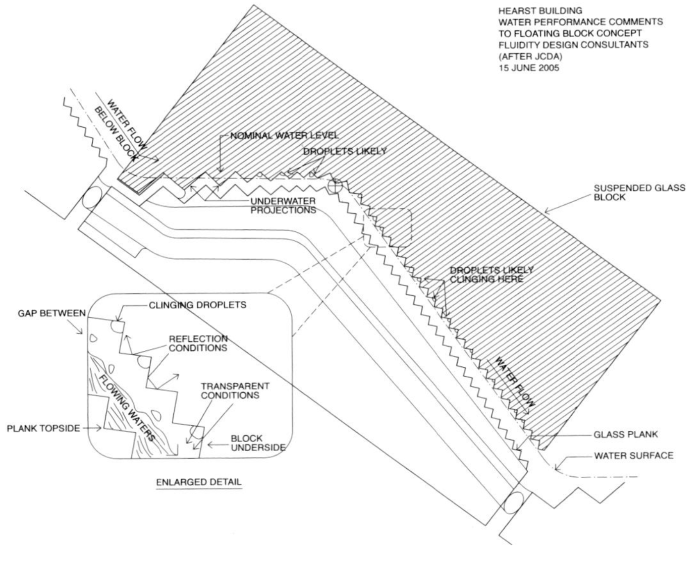
HEARST BUILDING
WATER PERFORMANCE COMMENTS
TO FLOATING BLOCK CONCEPT
FLUIDITY DESIGN CONSULTANTS
(AFTER JCDA)
15 JUNE 2005
WATER FLOW BELOW BLOCK
NOMINAL WATER LEVEL
DROPLETS LIKELY
SUSPENDED GLASS BLOCK
UNDERWATER PROJECTIONS
DROPLETS LIKELY CLINGING HERE
GAP BETWEEN
CLINGING DROPLETS
REFLECTION CONDITIONS
TRANSPARENT CONDITIONS
FLOWING WATERS
PLANK TOPSIDE
BLOCK UNDERSIDE
WATER FLOW
GLASS PLANK
WATER SURFACE
ENLARGED DETAIL

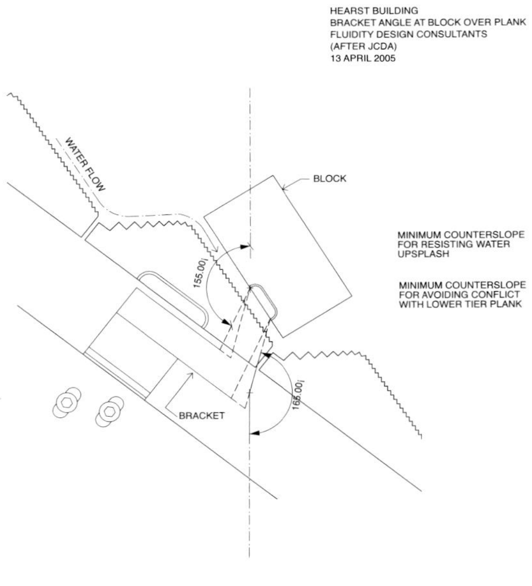
HEARST BUILDING
BRACKET ANGLE AT BLOCK OVER PLANK
FLUIDITY DESIGN CONSULTANTS
(AFTER JCDA)
13 APRIL 2005
WATER FLOW
BLOCK
MINIMUM COUNTERSLOPE FOR RESISTING WATER UPSPLASH
MINIMUM COUNTERSLOPE FOR AVOIDING CONFLICT WITH LOWER TIER PLANK
155.00)
165.00)
BRACKET

Opposite
Cascade details
Top: Section through flume (left); typical plank profile
Middle: Concept (left); texture alternatives
Bottom: Water performance (left); section

This page
Top: Cascade top (left); glass blocks from above
Bottom: Elevation detail

Leslie Dan Pharmacy Building, Toronto, Canada
Foster + Partners, London, United Kingdom
Cannon Design, Toronto

Located on one of the most prominent sites in Toronto, the Leslie Dan Pharmacy Building for the Faculty of Pharmacy at the University of Toronto provides expanded research, teaching, and administrative facilities for an enrollment of twelve hundred undergraduate and postgraduate pharmacy students. The new building also accommodates a substantial increase in research activities in spaces previously dispersed but now consolidated within a single structure.

The building is divided into three parts: undergraduate lecture theaters at the lower level, a five-story colonnaded study area at ground level, and seven stories of postgraduate research space above. To minimize circulation requirements, highly trafficked public and teaching areas are concentrated on the lower floors; the upper floors contain the more private postgraduate research areas and offices that derive the greatest benefit from natural light. To respond to its immediate surroundings, the soffit of the five-story colonnaded main mass of the building space is lifted 65 feet above ground-floor level, aligning with the cornices of two neighboring listed buildings.

Transparent and flooded with daylight, this space is a window into the Faculty of Pharmacy for the rest of the campus and, because of its proximity to the basement lecture theaters, laboratories, and the library, the hub of undergraduate activity. An atrium running through the building functions as a light slot, bringing daylight deep into the laboratory support spaces in the building's interior and providing visual connections among floors.

The building skin is oriented to maximize daylight where needed and minimize unwanted solar gain, reinforcing its clear and logical diagram. Two steel-framed pods appear to float within the atrium space: the larger contains a sixty-seat lecture theater and reading room, the smaller a twenty-four-seat classroom and the faculty lounge. Suspended by solid steel bars and wrapped in smooth white plaster, the atrium pods are illuminated at night in slowing changing shades of red, green, and blue by computer-controlled theatrical spotlights attached to structural columns in the lobby, their images visible through the darkened atrium.

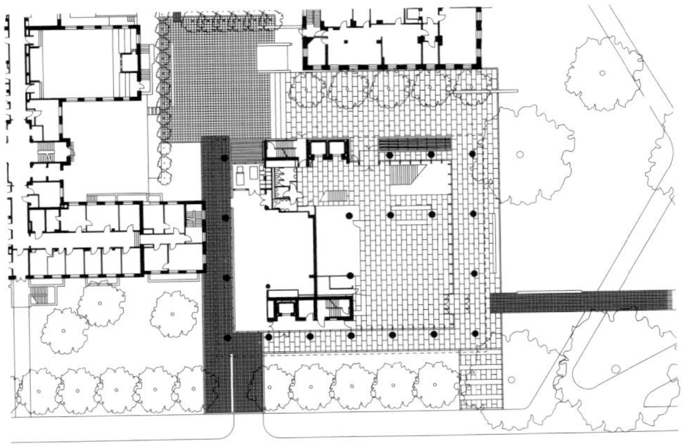

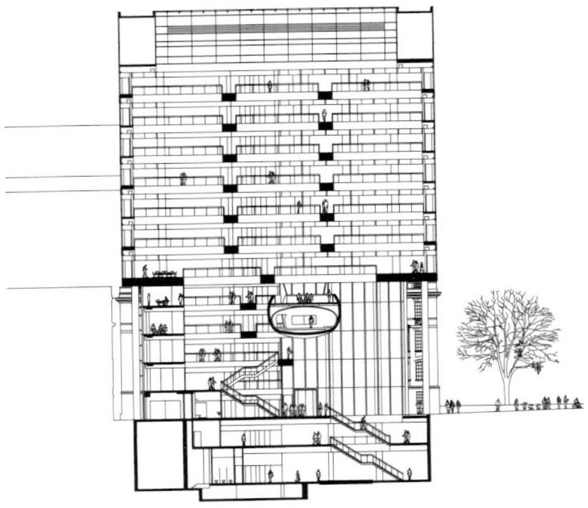

This page
Left: Ground-level site plan
Right: Section

Opposite
Top: Atrium
Bottom: Pods

Apotex

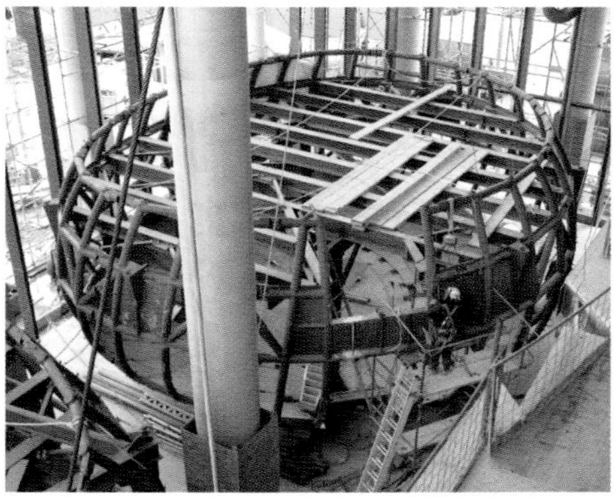

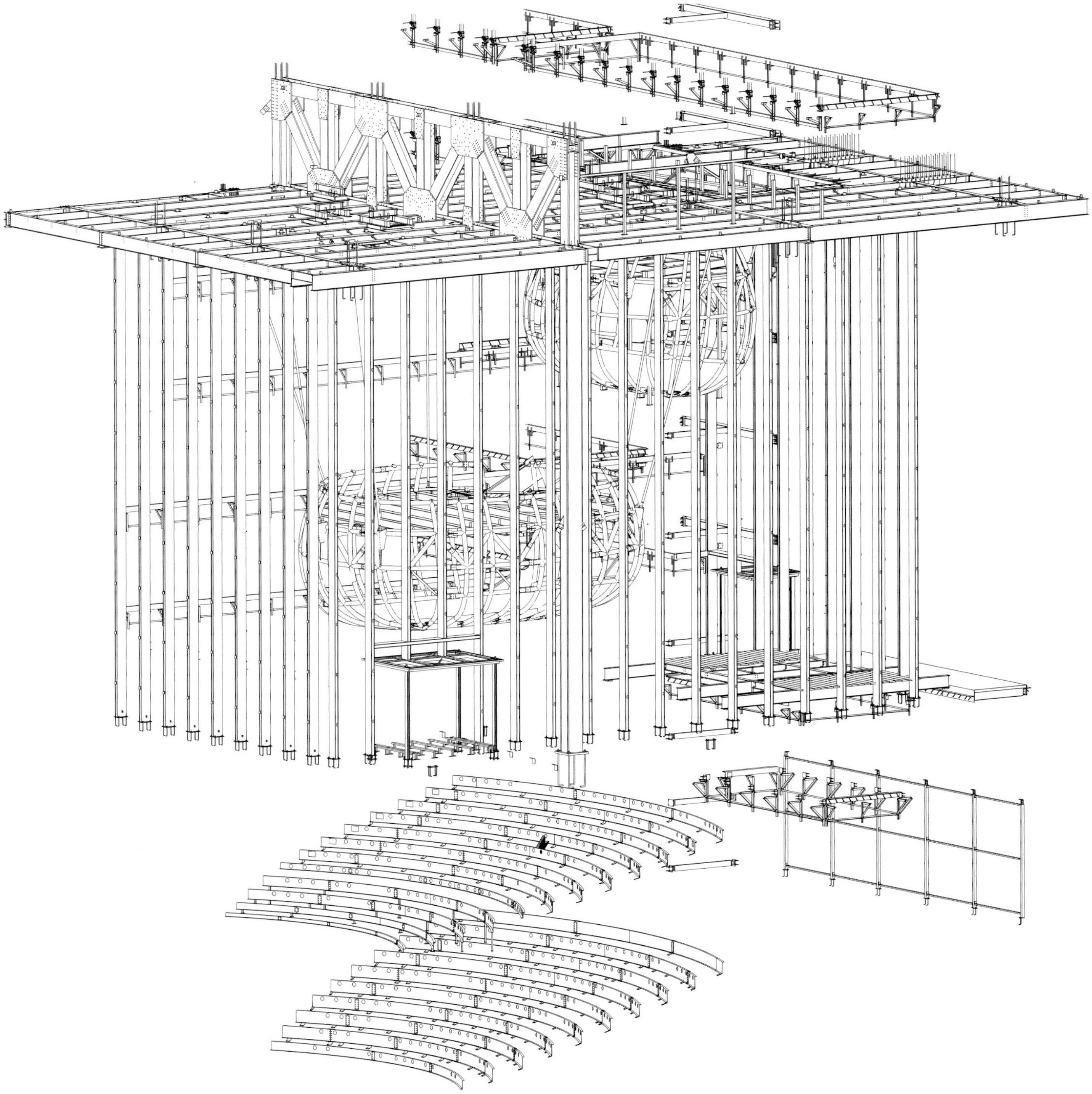

Opposite
On-site fabrication and installation

This page
Level 1 to level 6 steel framing

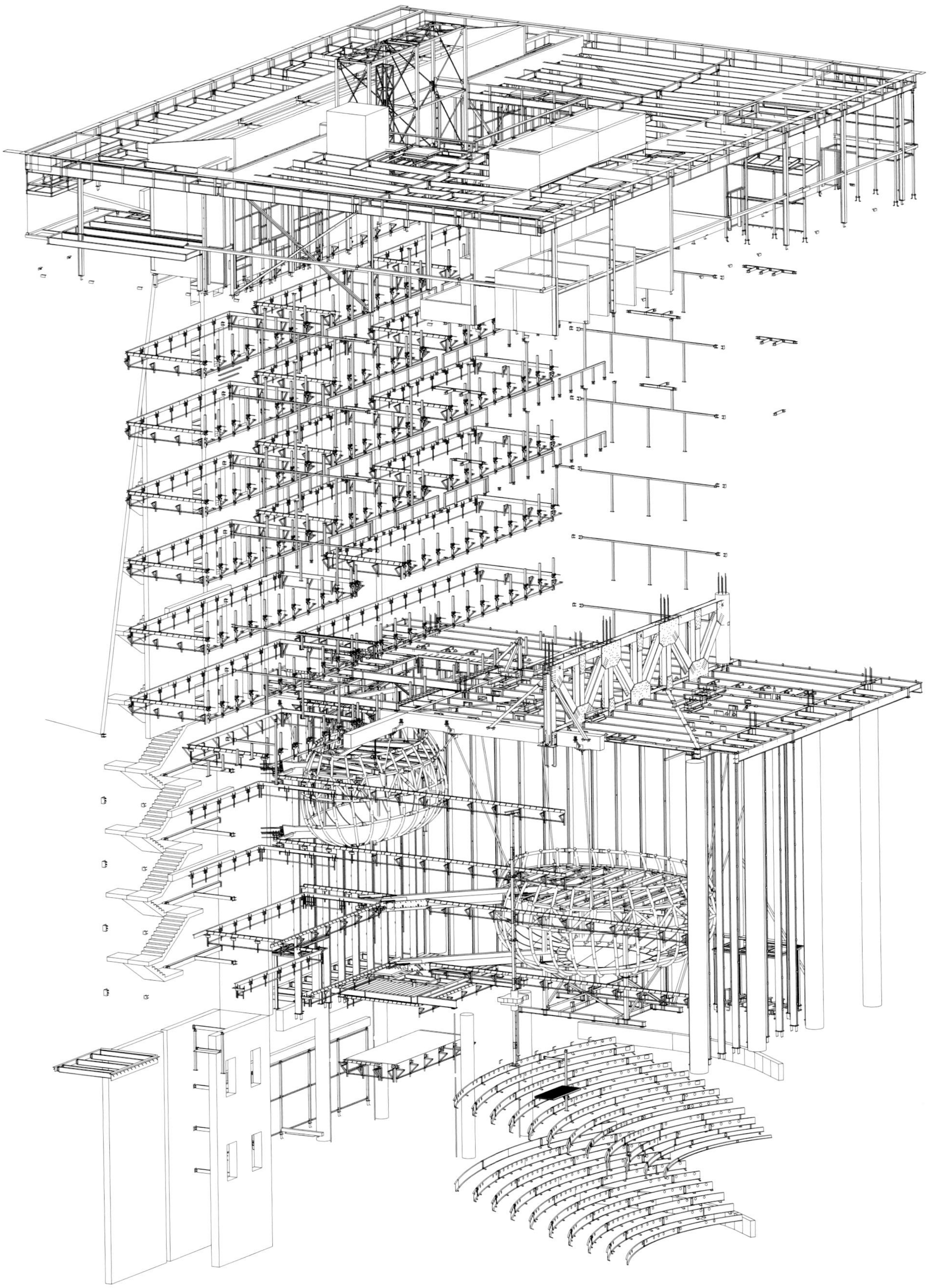

This page
Steel framing

Opposite
Atrium from above

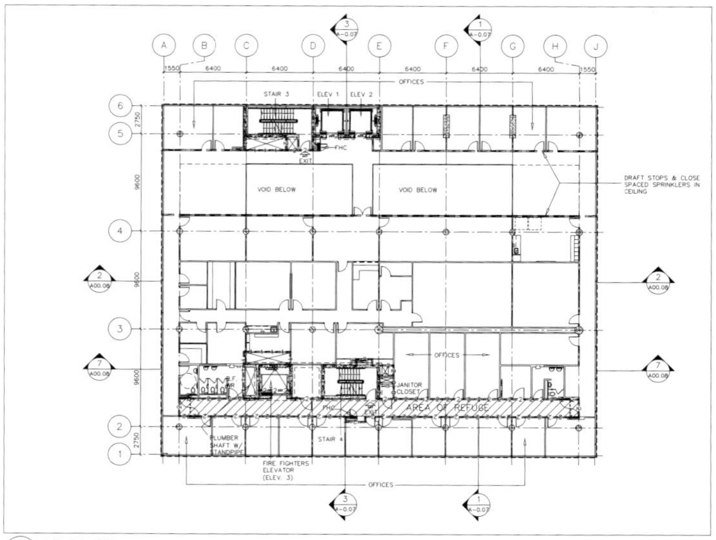

9 LEVEL 06
A00.05 SCALE 1:200

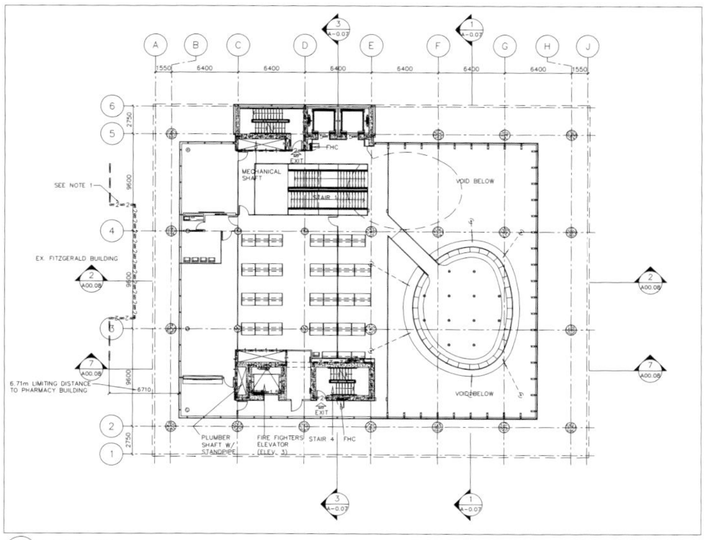

6 LEVEL 03
A00.05 SCALE 1:200

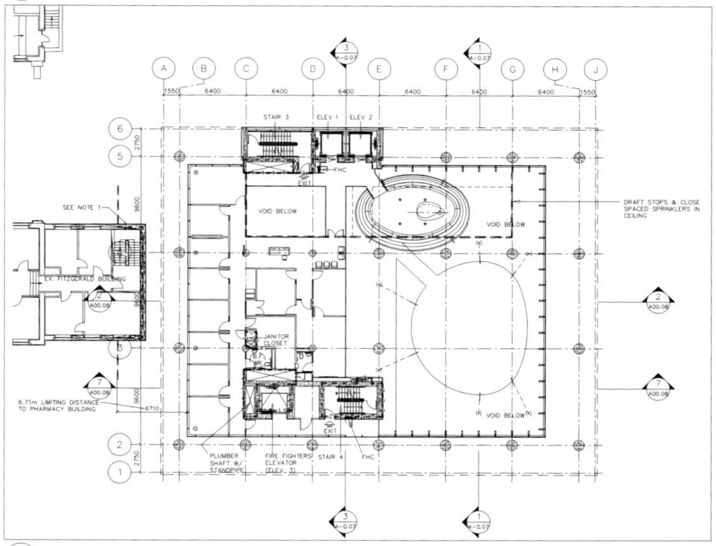

8 LEVEL 05
A00.05 SCALE 1:200

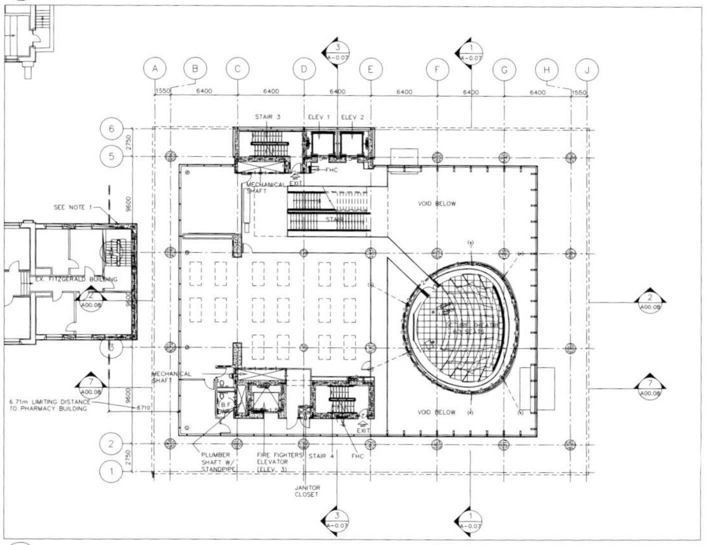

5 LEVEL 02
A00.05 SCALE 1:200

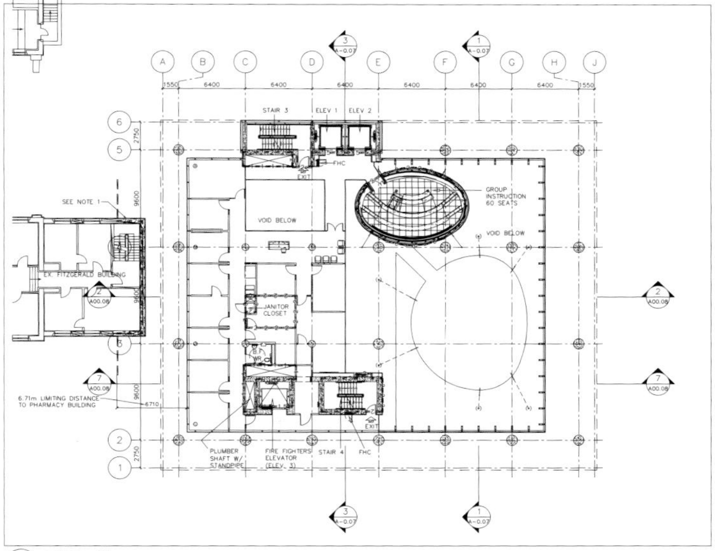

7 LEVEL 04
A00.05 SCALE 1:200

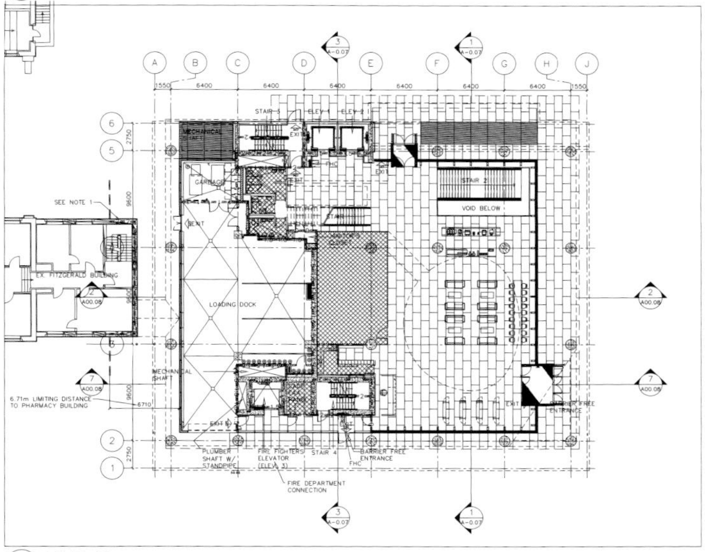

4 LEVEL 01
A00.05 SCALE 1:200

Opposite
Pod plans

This page
Top left: Lecture-pod plan
Top right and middle:
Bridge-section details
Bottom: Pods from above (left); lecture-pod entrance

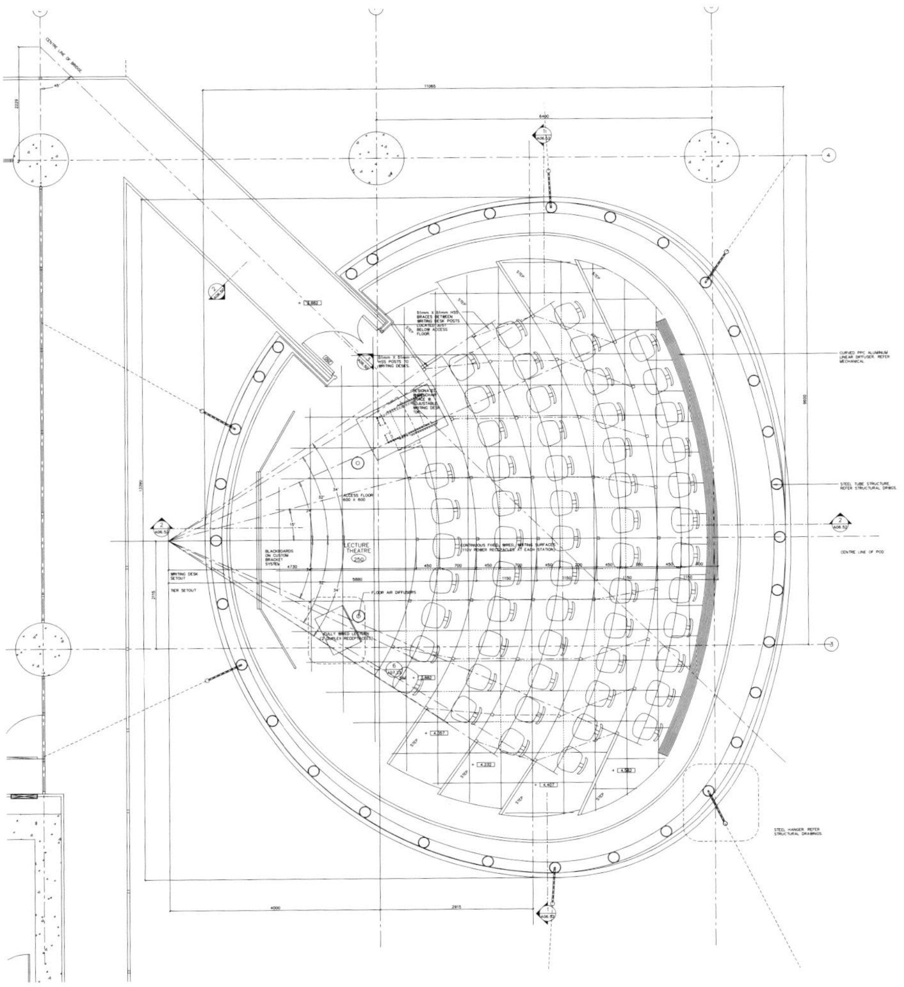

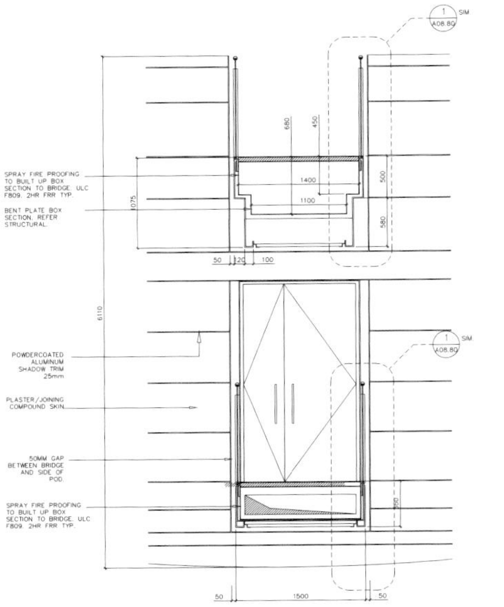

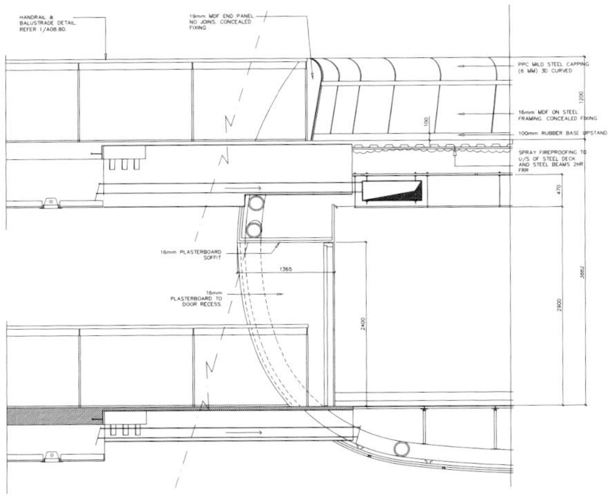

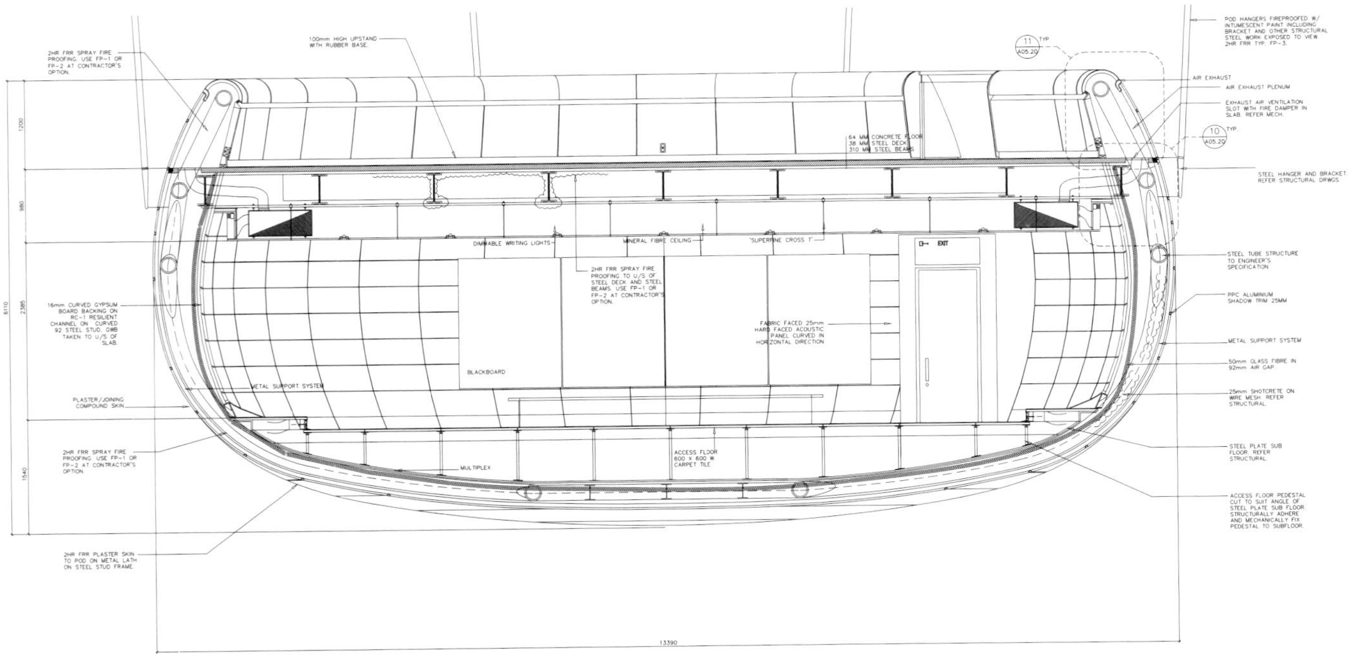
2HR FRR SPRAY FIRE PROOFING. USE FP-1 OR FP-2 AT CONTRACTOR'S OPTION.
100mm HIGH UPSTAND WITH RUBBER BASE.
POD HANGERS FIREPROOFED W/ INTUMESCENT PAINT INCLUDING BRACKET AND OTHER STRUCTURAL STEEL WORK EXPOSED TO VIEW. 2HR FRR TYP. FP-3.
AIR EXHAUST
AIR EXHAUST PLENUM
EXHAUST AIR VENTILATION SLOT WITH FIRE DAMPER IN SLAB. REFER MECH.
64 MM CONCRETE FLOOR 38 MM STEEL DECK 310 MM STEEL BEAMS
STEEL HANGER AND BRACKET. REFER STRUCTURAL DRWGS.
DIMMABLE WRITING LIGHTS
MINERAL FIBRE CEILING
'SUPERFINE CROSS T'
EXIT
STEEL TUBE STRUCTURE TO ENGINEER'S SPECIFICATION
2HR FRR SPRAY FIRE PROOFING TO U/S OF STEEL DECK AND STEEL BEAMS. USE FP-1 OR FP-2 AT CONTRACTOR'S OPTION.
16mm CURVED GYPSUM BOARD BACKING ON RC-1 RESILIENT CHANNEL ON CURVED 92 STEEL STUD. GWB TAKEN TO U/S OF SLAB.
PPC ALUMINIUM SHADOW TRIM 25MM
FABRIC FACED 25mm HARD FACED ACOUSTIC PANEL CURVED IN HORIZONTAL DIRECTION
METAL SUPPORT SYSTEM
50mm GLASS FIBRE IN 92mm AIR GAP
BLACKBOARD
PLASTER/JOINING COMPOUND SKIN
25mm SHOTCRETE ON WIRE MESH. REFER STRUCTURAL
2HR FRR SPRAY FIRE PROOFING. USE FP-1 OR FP-2 AT CONTRACTOR'S OPTION.
ACCESS FLOOR 600 X 600 W CARPET TILE
STEEL PLATE SUB FLOOR. REFER STRUCTURAL.
MULTIPLEX
ACCESS FLOOR PEDESTAL CUT TO SUIT ANGLE OF STEEL PLATE SUB FLOOR. STRUCTURALLY ADHERE AND MECHANICALLY FIX PEDESTAL TO SUBFLOOR.
2HR FRR PLASTER SKIN TO POD ON METAL LATH ON STEEL STUD FRAME.
13390

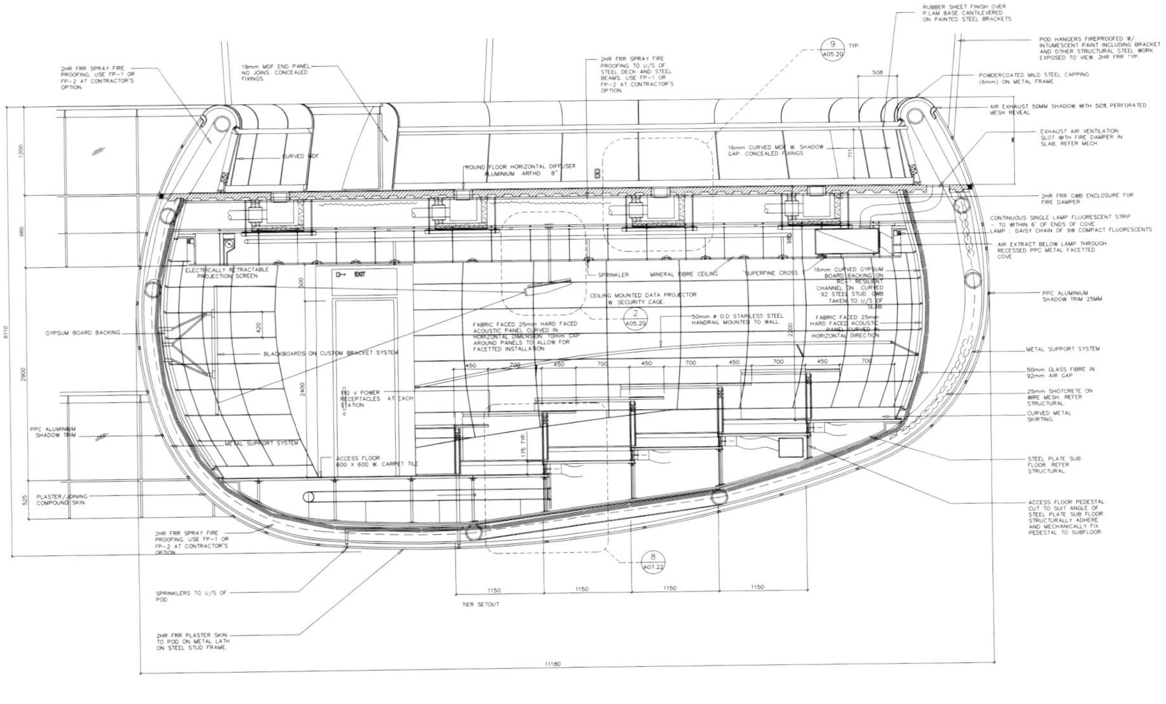
RUBBER SHEET FINISH OVER P.LAM BASE CANTILEVERED ON PAINTED STEEL BRACKETS
POD HANGERS FIREPROOFED W/ INTUMESCENT PAINT INCLUDING BRACKET AND OTHER STRUCTURAL STEEL WORK EXPOSED TO VIEW. 2HR FRR TYP.
2HR FRR SPRAY FIRE PROOFING. USE FP-1 OR FP-2 AT CONTRACTOR'S OPTION.
19mm MDF END PANEL NO JOINS. CONCEALED FIXINGS.
2HR FRR SPRAY FIRE PROOFING TO U/S OF STEEL DECK AND STEEL BEAMS. USE FP-1 OR FP-2 AT CONTRACTOR'S OPTION.
POWDERCOATED MILD STEEL CAPPING (6mm) ON METAL FRAME.
AIR EXHAUST 50MM SHADOW WITH 50% PERFORATED MESH REVEAL
EXHAUST AIR VENTILATION SLOT WITH FIRE DAMPER IN SLAB. REFER MECH.
CURVED MDF
ROUND FLOOR HORIZONTAL DIFFUSER ALUMINIUM ARFHD 8"
16mm CURVED MDF W. SHADOW GAP. CONCEALED FIXINGS
2HR FRR GWB ENCLOSURE FOR FIRE DAMPER
CONTINUOUS SINGLE LAMP FLUORESCENT STRIP - TO WITHIN 6" OF ENDS OF COVE
LAMP : DAISY CHAIN OF 9W COMPACT FLUORESCENTS
AIR EXTRACT BELOW LAMP THROUGH RECESSED PPC METAL FACETTED COVE
ELECTRICALLY RETRACTABLE PROJECTION SCREEN
SPRINKLER
MINERAL FIBRE CEILING
'SUPERFINE CROSS'
16mm CURVED GYPSUM BOARD BACKING ON RC-1 RESILIENT CHANNEL ON CURVED 92 STEEL STUD. GWB TAKEN TO U/S OF SLAB.
CEILING MOUNTED DATA PROJECTOR W. SECURITY CAGE.
PPC ALUMINIUM SHADOW TRIM 25MM
GYPSUM BOARD BACKING
FABRIC FACED 25mm HARD FACED ACOUSTIC PANEL CURVED IN HORIZONTAL DIMENSION. 10mm GAP AROUND PANELS TO ALLOW FOR FACETTED INSTALLATION
50mm Ø O.D STAINLESS STEEL HANDRAIL MOUNTED TO WALL.
FABRIC FACED 25mm HARD FACED ACOUSTIC PANEL CURVED HORIZONTAL DIRECTION
BLACKBOARDS ON CUSTOM BRACKET SYSTEM
METAL SUPPORT SYSTEM
50mm GLASS FIBRE IN 92mm AIR GAP
110 V POWER RECEPTACLES AT EACH STATION
25mm SHOTCRETE ON WIRE MESH. REFER STRUCTURAL
CURVED METAL SKIRTING
PPC ALUMINIUM SHADOW TRIM
ACCESS FLOOR 600 X 600 W. CARPET TILE
STEEL PLATE SUB FLOOR. REFER STRUCTURAL.
PLASTER/JOINING COMPOUND SKIN
ACCESS FLOOR PEDESTAL CUT TO SUIT ANGLE OF STEEL PLATE SUB FLOOR. STRUCTURALLY ADHERE AND MECHANICALLY FIX PEDESTAL TO SUBFLOOR.
2HR FRR SPRAY FIRE PROOFING. USE FP-1 OR FP-2 AT CONTRACTOR'S OPTION.
SPRINKLERS TO U/S OF POD.
TIER SETOUT
2HR FRR PLASTER SKIN TO POD ON METAL LATH ON STEEL STUD FRAME.
11180

Opposite
Top: Lecture theater, cross section
Middle: Lecture theater, longitudinal section
Bottom (left and right): Lecture-theater interior

This page
Top: Group instruction/faculty lounge, longitudinal section
Bottom: Atrium, night view

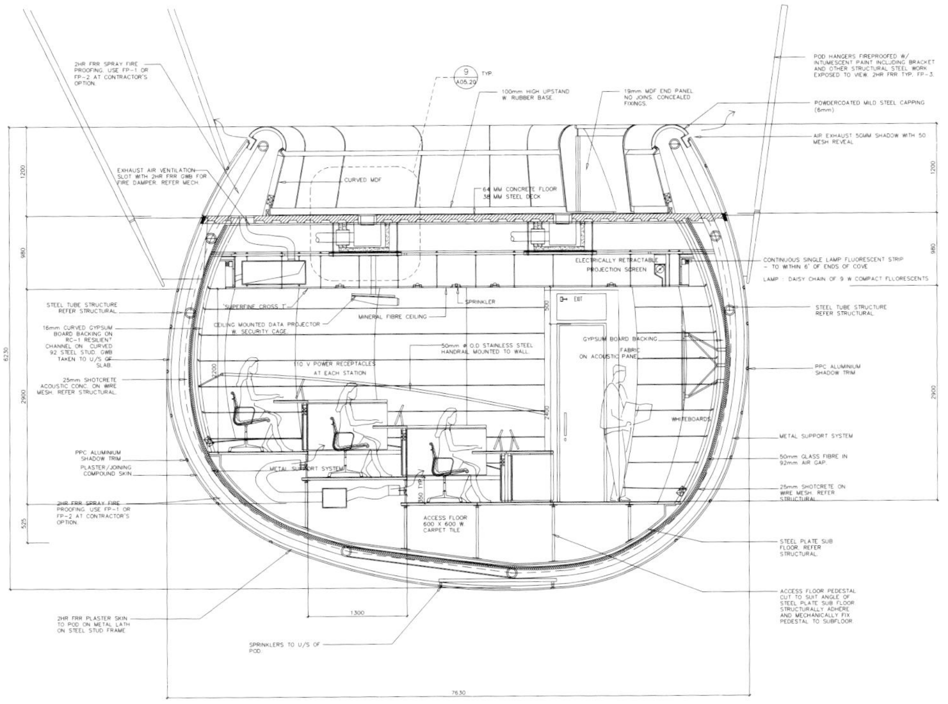

Floating Box House, Austin, Texas
Peter L. Gluck & Partners, Architects, New York, New York

Located outside of Austin in a grove of more than two hundred landmarked live oaks, the Floating Box House was situated carefully to preserve its surroundings. The form of the house—consisting of a rectangular box, the stainless-steel structure on which the box is balanced, a transparent glass volume, and a plinth—is simple, but a journey through the house reveals its sectional complexity. Significant portions of the program, including the guest bedrooms, media room, and gallery, are located below grade to minimize disruption of the landscape. The garage is also located within the buried plinth, so that the grove of trees remains free of cars and paving. The rectangular structure balanced on the plinth creates the illusion of a box floating above the landscape and contains the family bedrooms.

Between the ground plane and the floating box, glazed walls provide an unobstructed view of the live oaks on one side and the Austin skyline on the other from the living room, dining room, and kitchen. The sunken courtyard is connected to the main level by a grass ramp. This ramp becomes the roof of the plinth, with skylights emerging through the grass to provide natural light for the garage and the underground gallery.

The stainless-steel structure contains all of the mechanical equipment for the house so that the living space and the views remain uncluttered. Other materials used in the house include prefinished wood panels, stainless-steel rain-screen panels, zinc metal panels, a stainless-steel glazing system, and a custom mahogany window system.

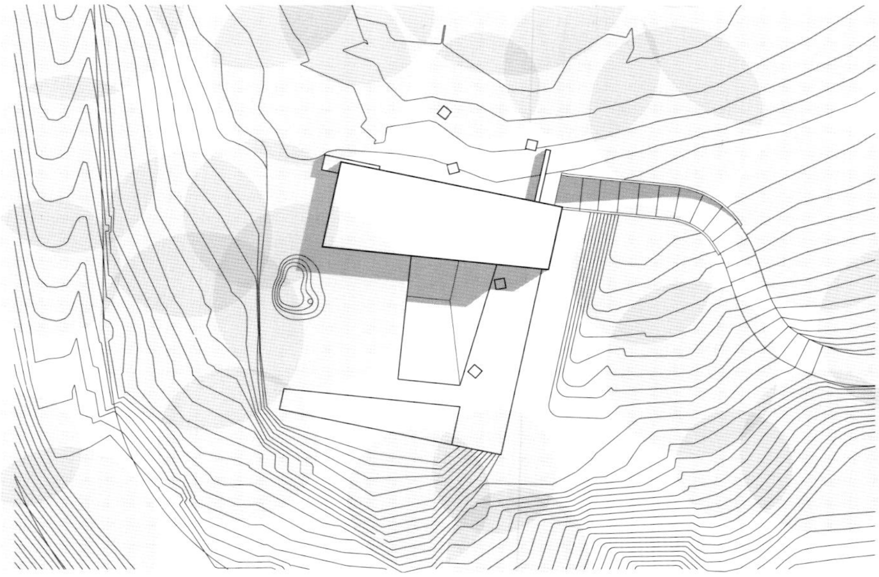

This page
Site plan

Opposite
Top: East elevation
Bottom: North and west elevations

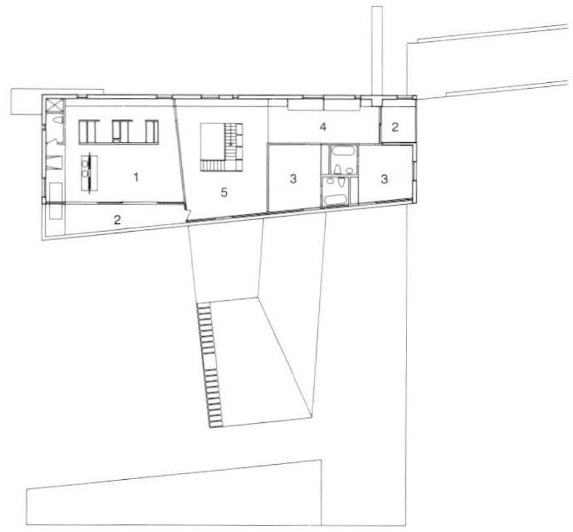
1
2
3
4
5

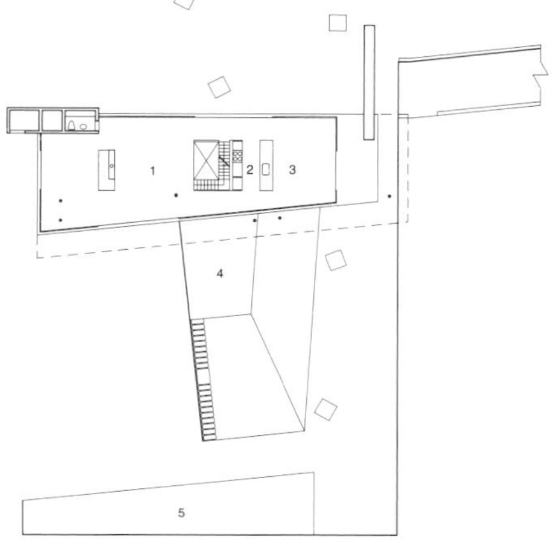
1
2
3
4
5

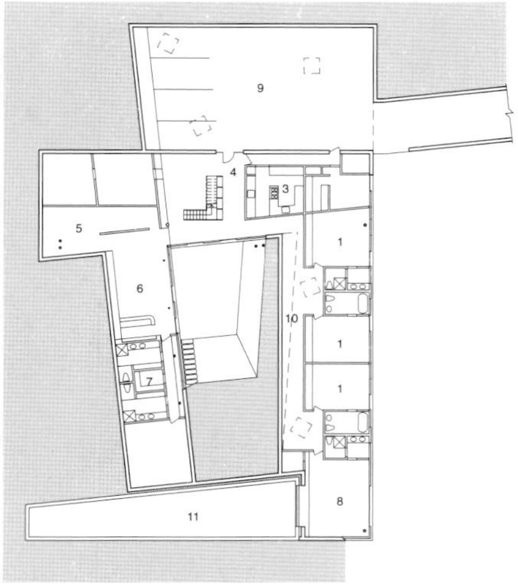
1
3
4
5
6
7
8
9
10
11

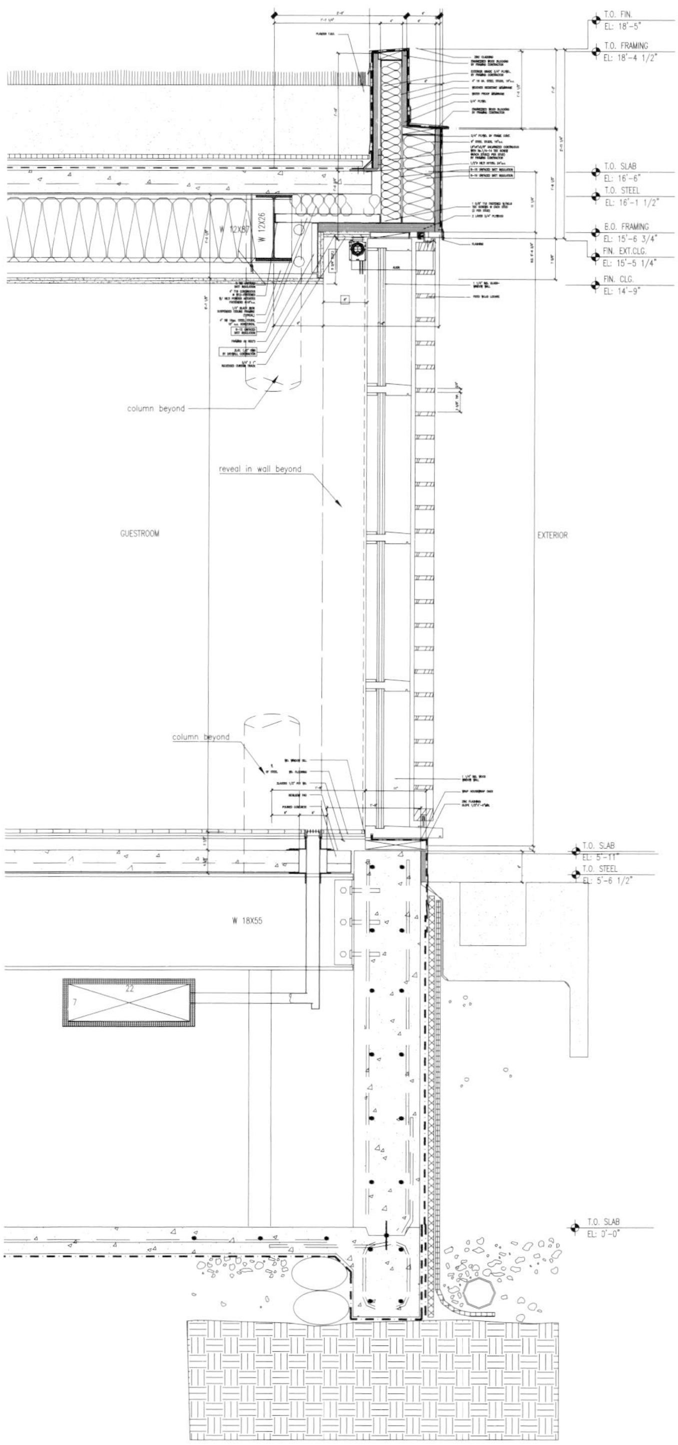
T.O. FIN.
EL: 18'-5"
T.O. FRAMING
EL: 18'-4 1/2"
T.O. SLAB
EL: 16'-6"
T.O. STEEL
EL: 16'-1 1/2"
E.O. FRAMING
EL: 15'-6 3/4"
FIN. EXT.CLG.
EL: 15'-5 1/4"
FIN. CLG.
EL: 14'-9"
W 12X87
W 12X26
column beyond
reveal in wall beyond
GUESTROOM
EXTERIOR
column beyond
T.O. SLAB
EL: 5'-11"
T.O. STEEL
EL: 5'-6 1/2"
W 18X55
T.O. SLAB
EL: 0'-0"

Opposite
Top left: Second-floor plan (top); first-floor plan; lower-floor plan
Top right: Wooden-screen detail
Bottom: West elevation

This page
Right (top to bottom): North elevation; section, view south; section, view west
Bottom: Upper-south and lower-east elevations

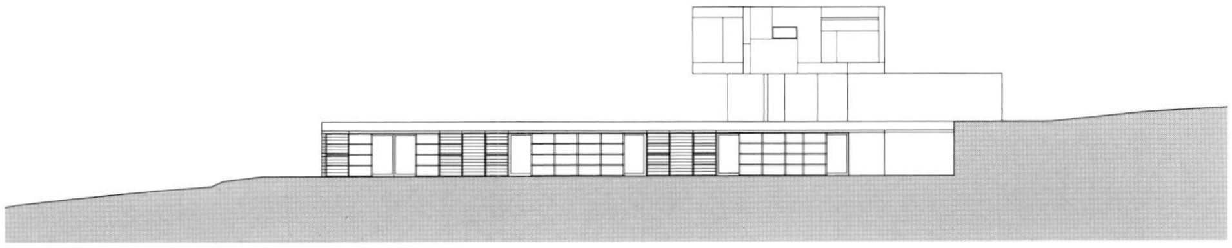

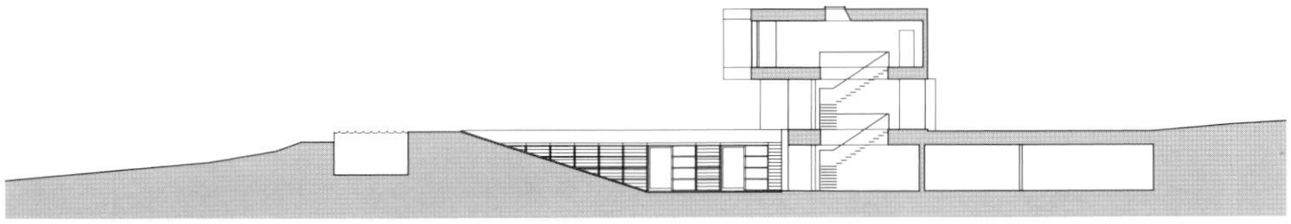

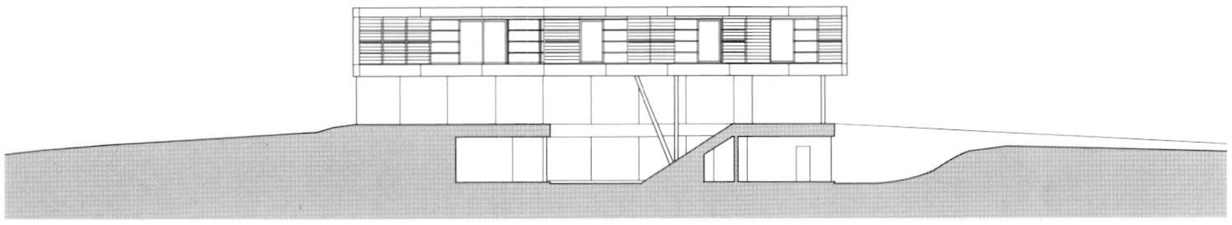

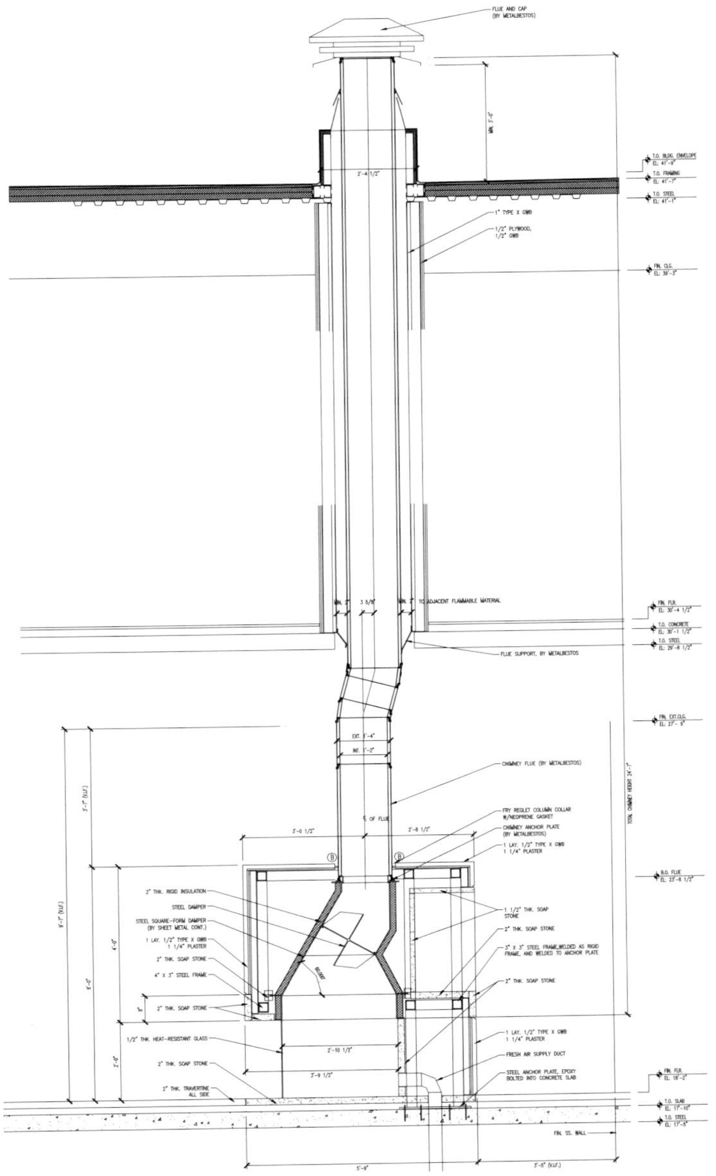
FLUE AND CAP (BY METALBESTOS)
T.O. BLDG. ENVELOPE EL. 47'-9"
T.O. FRAMING EL. 47'-7"
T.O. STEEL EL. 47'-1"
1" TYPE X GWB
1/2" PLYWOOD, 1/2" GWB
FIN. CLG. EL. 39'-3"
TO ADJACENT FLAMMABLE MATERIAL
FIN. FLR. EL. 30'-4 1/2"
T.O. CONCRETE EL. 30'-1 1/2"
T.O. STEEL EL. 29'-8 1/2"
FLUE SUPPORT, BY METALBESTOS
FIN. EXT.CLG. EL. 27'-9"
CHIMNEY FLUE (BY METALBESTOS)
FRY REGLET COLUMN COLLAR W/NEOPRENE GASKET
CHIMNEY ANCHOR PLATE (BY METALBESTOS)
1 LAY. 1/2" TYPE X GWB 1 1/4" PLASTER
B.O. FLUE EL. 23'-6 1/2"
2" THK. RIGID INSULATION
STEEL DAMPER
STEEL SQUARE-FORM DAMPER (BY SHEET METAL CONT.)
1 1/2" THK. SOAP STONE
2" THK. SOAP STONE
2" X 3" STEEL FRAME,WELDED AS RIGID FRAME, AND WELDED TO ANCHOR PLATE
4" X 3" STEEL FRAME
1/2" THK. HEAT-RESISTANT GLASS
FRESH AIR SUPPLY DUCT
STEEL ANCHOR PLATE, EPOXY BOLTED INTO CONCRETE SLAB
2" THK. TRAVERTINE ALL SIDE
FIN. FLR. EL. 18'-2"
T.O. SLAB EL. 17'-10"
T.O. STEEL EL. 17'-8"
FIN. SS. WALL

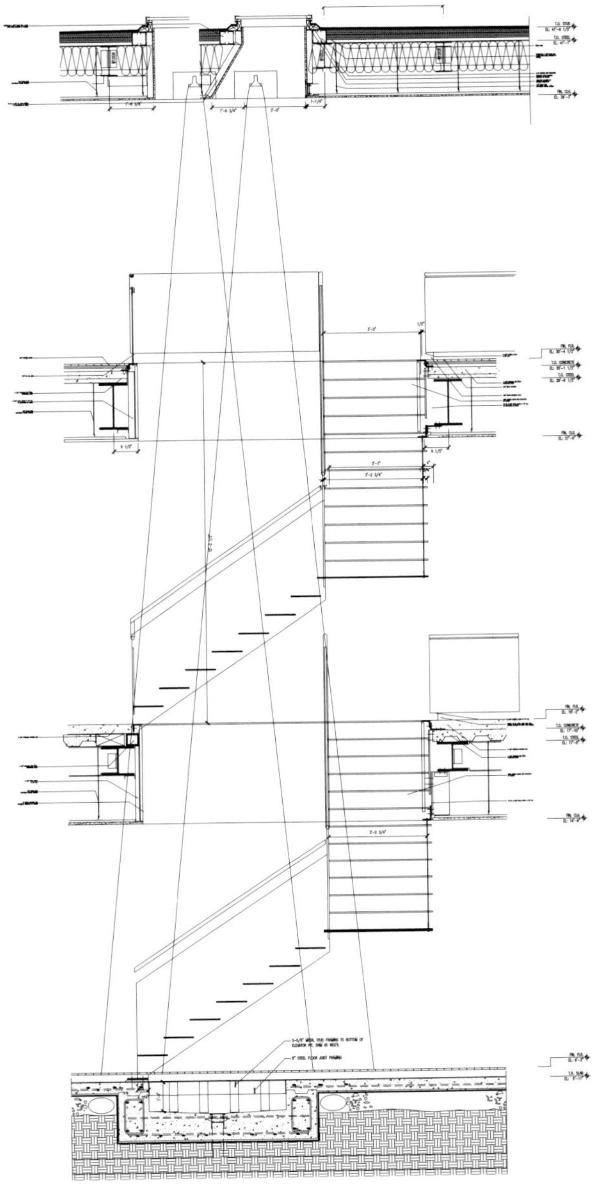

Opposite
Top: Fireplace details (left); stair detail
Bottom: First-floor interior (left); stair details

This page
Top: Lawn-and-lower-floor details (left); steel-window details
Bottom: View east

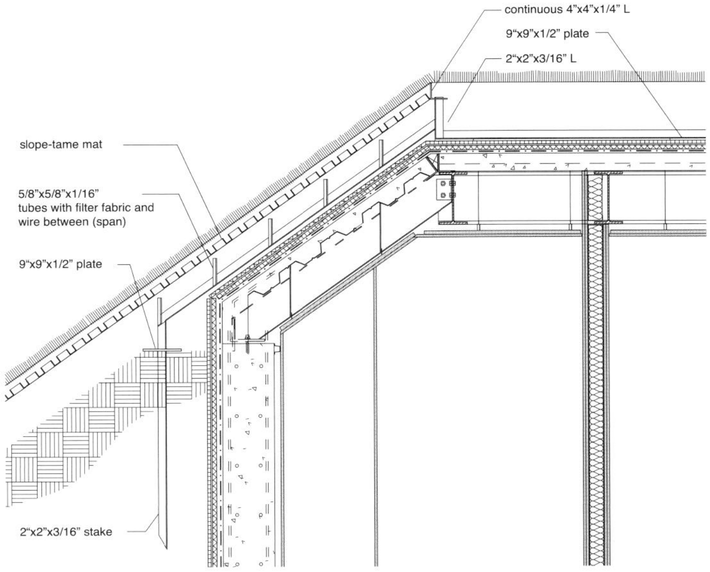

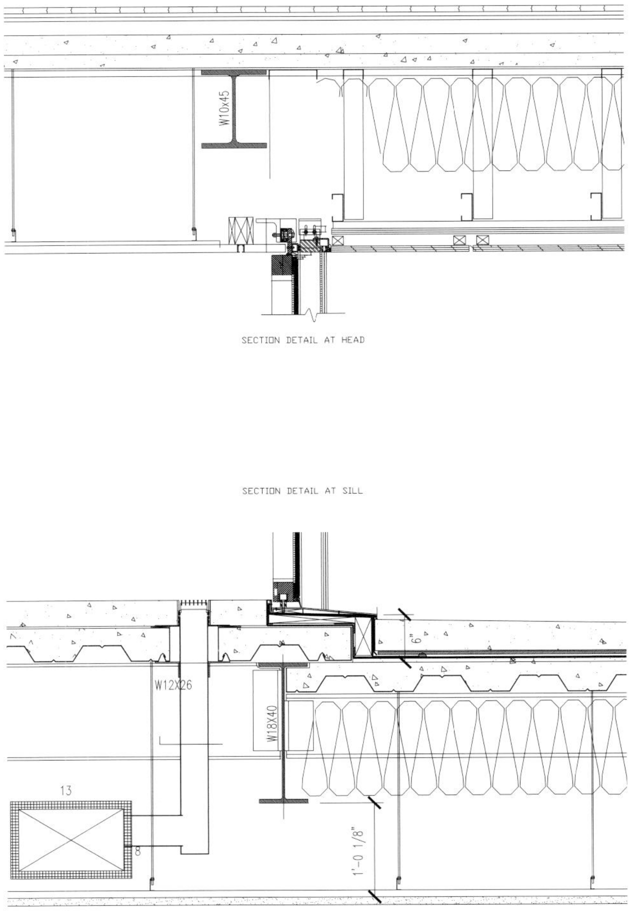

Biodesign Institute Building B, Tempe, Arizona
Gould Evans Associates, Phoenix, Arizona
Lord, Aeck & Sargent Architecture, Atlanta, Georgia

Located on the campus of Arizona State University, Biodesign Institute Building B is dedicated to interdisciplinary research and the collaborative partnerships of biotechnology, nanotechnology, and information technology, which serve as the inspiration for its design. This strategy encourages interaction between buildings, floors, and researchers, as well as the university and the community. The lab, office, and conference spaces converge around an open atrium that links people visually, vertically and horizontally. The four-story building is composed of one opaque mass and one transparent mass: the opaque volume of striated brick echoes the masonry vocabulary of other buildings on campus; the transparency of the glass volume symbolizes the outreach of science to the community.

A partially operable shading system functions as a sunscreen and gives a highly technical and sophisticated image to the exterior. Composed of 4-inch aluminum airfoil shapes within an aluminum frame, the sunscreen shades the west-facing areas of the curtain wall, including conference rooms, administrative areas, private offices, and the main auditorium. The sunscreen assembly is also deployed along the top of the curtain wall on the east facade to connect Building B visually with Building A, the first phase of the Biodesign Institute, completed in 2002.

The offices and labs, located adjacent to the curtain wall, overlook a terraced garden. Interior motorized louvers with 5-inch-wide airfoil sections span the entire width of the private office area's 11-foot-wide curtain-wall bays. The lower portion of the louvers can be adjusted by the office occupants; the upper portion is controlled by a sun sensor so that researchers deep in the building have views above the offices to the outdoors. Vertical wood louvers on the north side shade the main entrance, a two-story atrium space accessed from one of the principal pedestrian thoroughfares of the campus.

Although the sun never strikes the north elevation at an angle higher than 30 degrees, some form of solar shading was required to counter the effects of early summer morning glare. The 30-foot-high louver sections are mounted internally and have an airfoil section formed by plywood sheets bent around a light-gauge steel armature. Each louver is 30 inches deep and divided vertically into four sections, which can be operated independently by individuals who work in the building. Adjustment of these louvers, for shading or privacy, creates random band patterns that represent abstracted protein gel arrays—one of the tools used in genetic study—and continually changes the building's exterior appearance.

Jay Silverberg, AIA, of Gould Evans Associates contributed to this text.

This page
Longitudinal section

Opposite
Top: East elevation
Bottom: East elevation, night view

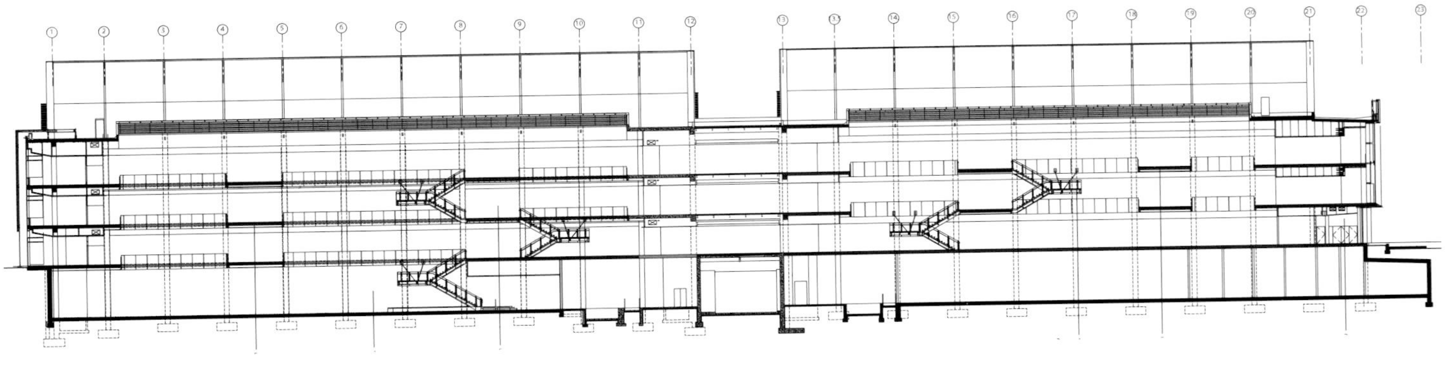

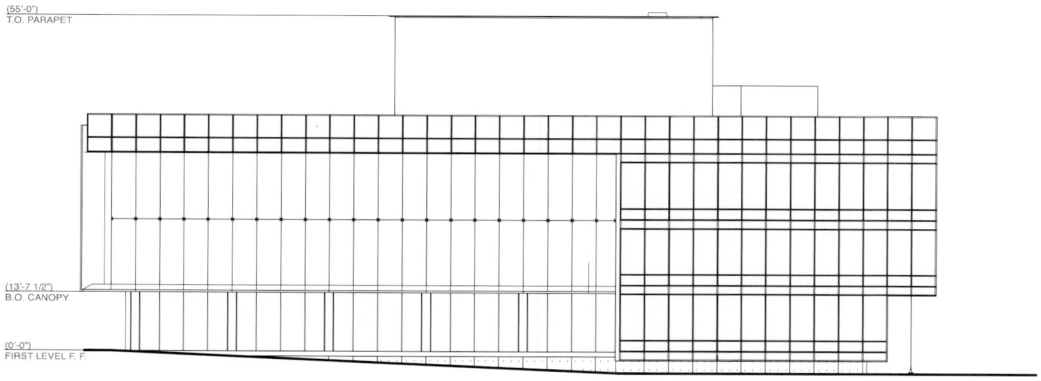
(55'-0")
T.O. PARAPET
(13'-7 1/2")
B.O. CANOPY
(0'-0")
FIRST LEVEL F. F.

Opposite
Top: North elevation
Bottom: North elevation, night view

This page
Top: First-floor plan
Bottom left: North-elevation details
Bottom right: North elevation, vertical section

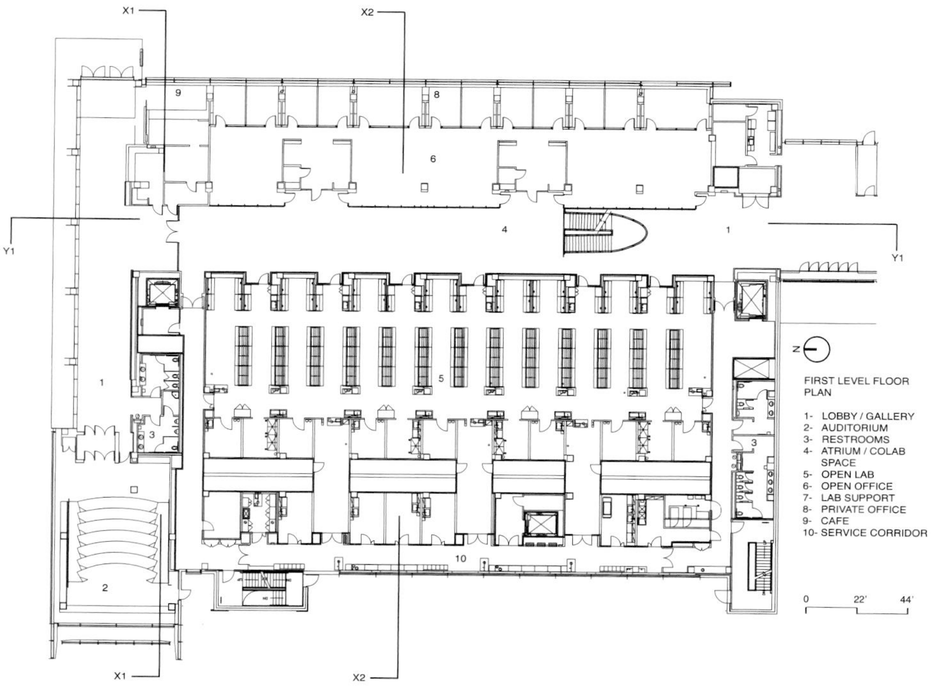

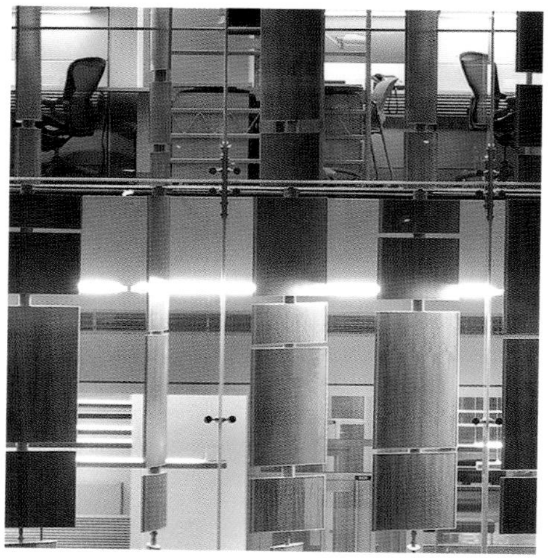

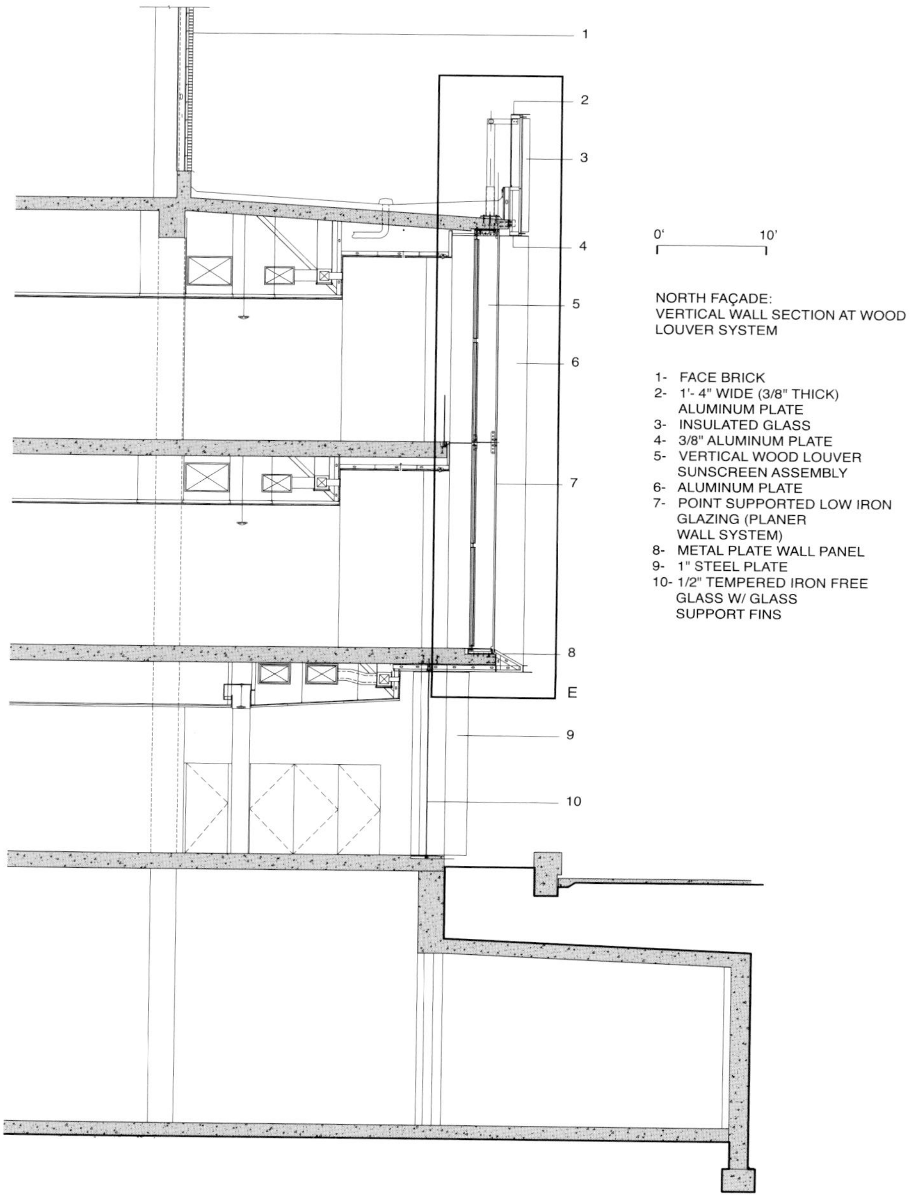

DETAIL D:
WOOD LOUVER PLAN AT THIRD LEVEL

1- TIE BACK SUPPORT ROD
2- VERTICAL WOOD LOUVER SUNSCREEN ASSEMBLY
3- GLASS SUPPORT FIN
4- POINT SUPPORTED LOW IRON GLAZING (PLANER WALL SYSTEM)
5- GLASS HANDRAIL
6- CONCRETE COLUMN

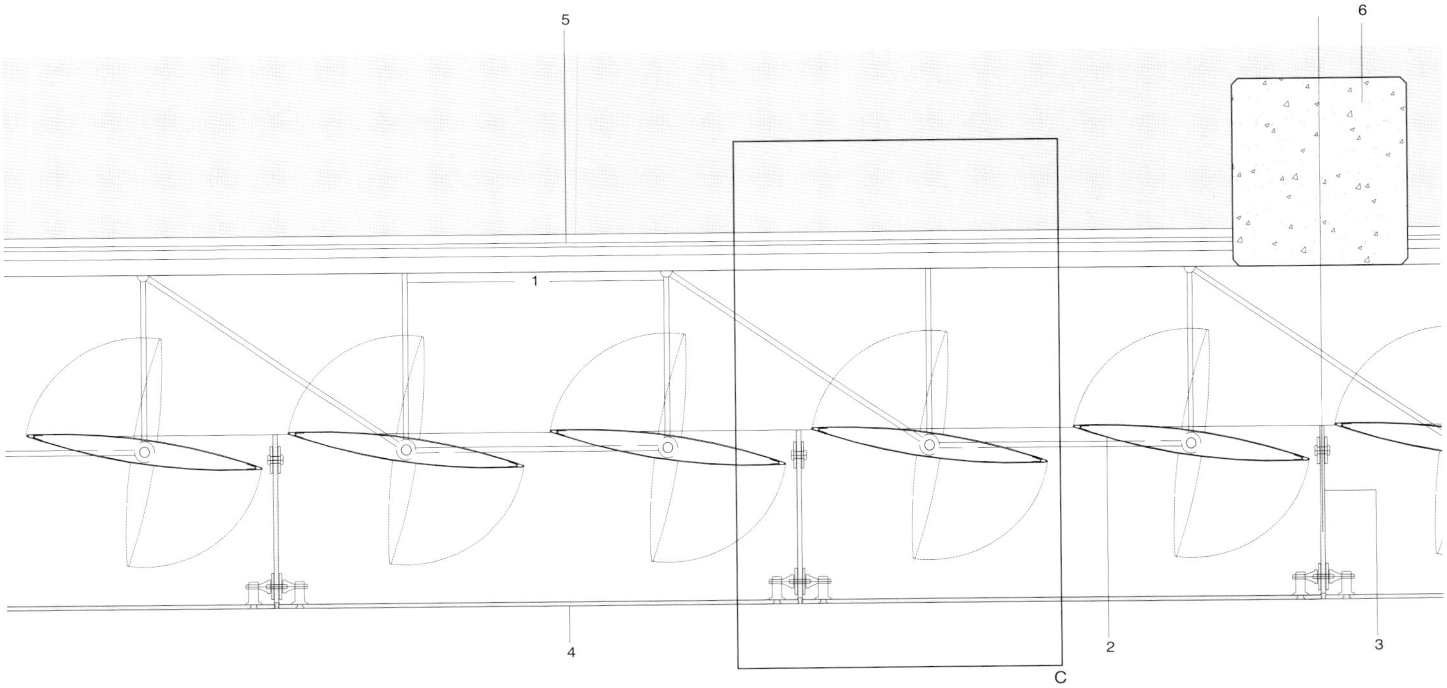

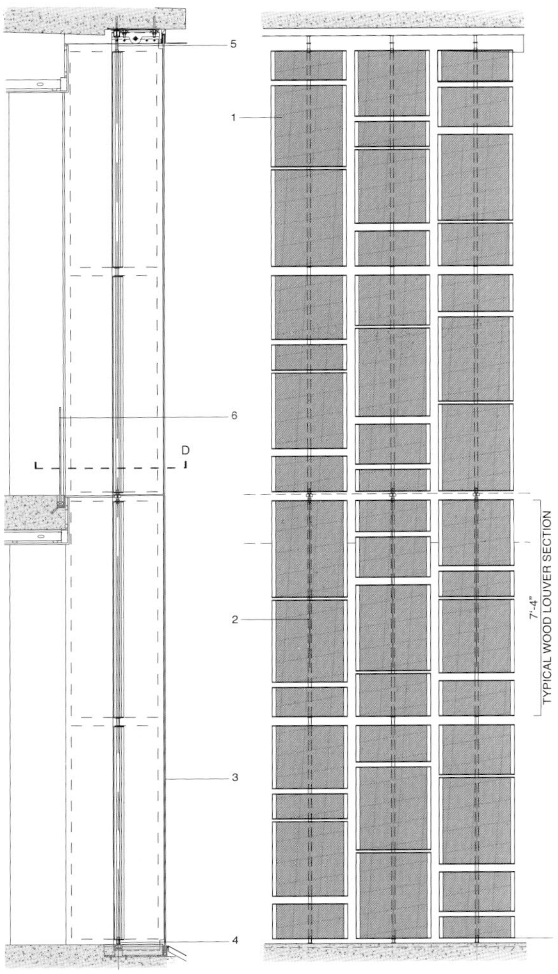

DETAIL E:
SECTION / ELEVATION
OPERABLE WOOD LOUVER

1- VERTICAL WOOD LOUVER SUNSCREEN ASSEMBLY
2- STEEL PIPE LOUVER SUPPORT
3- POINT SUPPORTED LOW IRON GLAZING (PLANER WALL SYSTEM)
4- BOTTOM RAIL SUPPORT SYSTEM
5- TOP RAIL SUPPORT SYSTEM
6- GLASS HANDRAIL

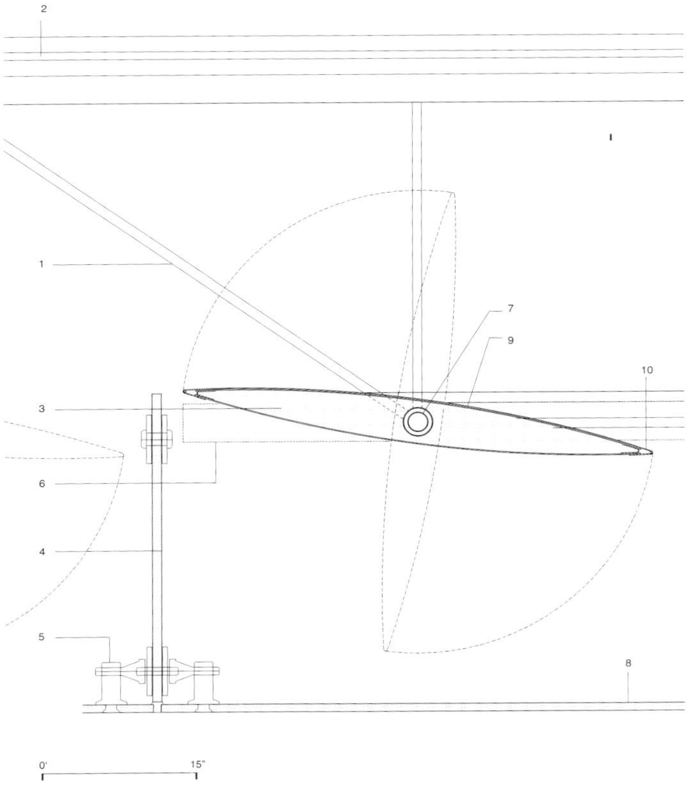

DETAIL C:
PLAN SECTION AT VERTICAL WOOD LOUVER

1- STEEL TIE ROD
2- GLASS HANDRAIL
3- 1/4" ALUMINUM PLATE SUPPORT
4- STRUCTURAL GLASS FIN
5- STAINLESS STEEL STRUCTURAL FIN SUPPORT
6- ALUMINUM TRACK
7- STEEL PIPE LOUVER SUPPORT
8- POINT SUPPORTED LOW IRON GLAZING (PLANER WALL SYSTEM)
9- VERTICAL WOOD LOUVER
10- STEEL END CAP TIP

Opposite
Top: Third-floor wood-louver plan
Bottom: Wood-louver detail

This page
Top: Wood-louver section and elevation (left); wood-louver plan
Right: Wood louvers from above

La Maison Unique, New York, New York
Heatherwick Studio, London, England
Atmosphere Design Group LLC, Mount Kisco, New York

On the dark side of the street in a landmark iron-front conservation area in SoHo is the first contemporary flagship store for Longchamp, the French luxury accessory brand, La Maison Unique, comprising retail space, a showroom, offices, and a roof terrace over three floors. The 1,500-square-foot ground-floor space serves as an entry and display area; the 4,500-square-foot second floor is the main retail area.

Merchandise on the ground floor is for display only; a receptionist directs visitors up to the second level to view the collection and make purchases. Its modest presence on the street gives little indication of the store's actual size. This presented the designers with the challenge of devising a means to draw shoppers up from the street to the second floor and an opportunity to play on consumers' expectations by concealing a spectacular construction project behind an unassuming facade. The solution involved an extensive remodel of the entire building, the construction of a new third story, and major structural reinforcements.

To make space for a larger entrance, the elevator and fire stairs were relocated to a new rear enclosure and a large shaft punched through the entire building. This column of space topped by a glass skylight draws people up through the building to the second floor over undulating steel stairs described by the designers as a "landscape." The ribbonlike forms cascade down through the light shaft, making a topography of steps, landings, and balustrades. An extraordinary piece of craftsmanship, the steel stair took six months to fabricate and required a new foundation in the middle of the building to support its massive 55-ton weight. Thirty rubber-coated bands of steel plate, each 11 inches wide and 1 inch thick, form flat stairs and two landings, also edged in rubber. Overall, the cascading stair measures 60 feet by 46 feet by 17 feet. A panel of steel ribbons extends up the back wall, providing another visual link between the upper and lower levels and further emphasizing the light shaft's verticality.

To fabricate the transparent balustrade, forty-six glasslike polycarbonate panels were cut to size, fitted into frames, and heated to the melting point so that they would drape like fabric into unique fluid forms.

In the main retail space, manipulation of the architectural elements eliminated the need to introduce any extraneous shop-fitting elements. The wood ceiling was sliced open, exposing the building's structure and mechanical systems, and its laminated layers folded downward and separated to form display surfaces for handbags and other merchandise. Maple floor planks, laid parallel to the stair to emphasize the linear geometry of the interior, have been modified to form freestanding displays. For the ground-floor window and entrance-display systems, movable lights and stands are attached to the steel stair with super-strength magnets on horizontal armatures, allowing groups of handbags to be displayed any point on its surface. At the front of the store, magnets support merchandise on display in the storefront window so that when viewed from the street the bags appear to float within the space.

This page
Left to right: Thomas Heatherwick leather and canvas expandable bag for Longchamp; concept sketch; Longchamp exterior

Opposite
Stair

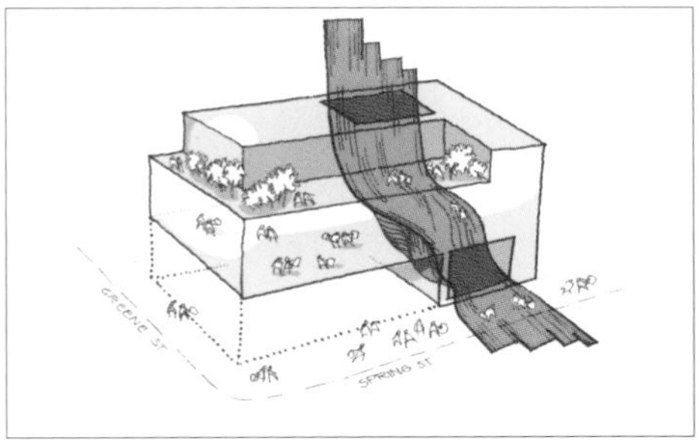

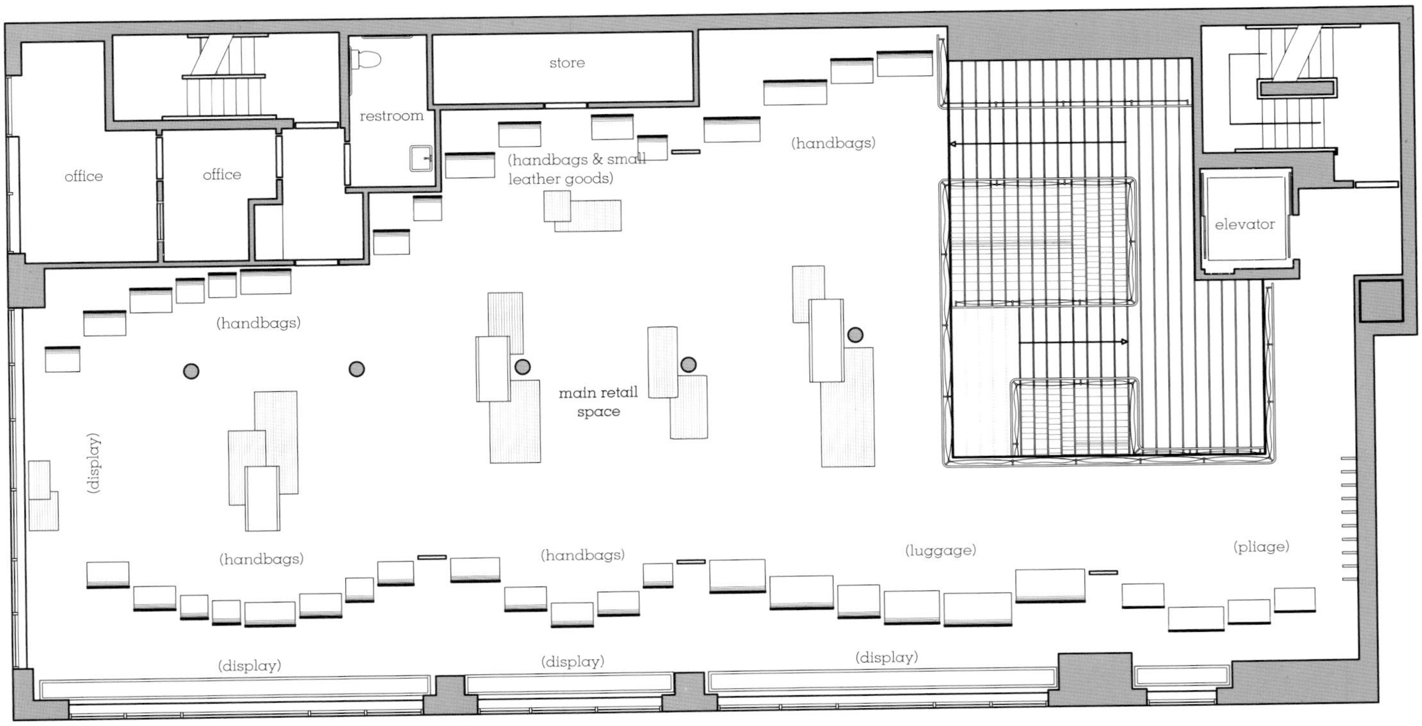
store
restroom
office
office
(handbags & small
leather goods)
(handbags)
elevator
(handbags)
main retail
space
(display)
(handbags)
(handbags)
(luggage)
(pliage)
(display)
(display)
(display)

LONGCHAMP
LONGCHAMP

Opposite
Top: Upper-level plan
Bottom: Stair and skylight (left); landing

This page
Top: Section
Bottom: Display and windows (left); balustrade detail

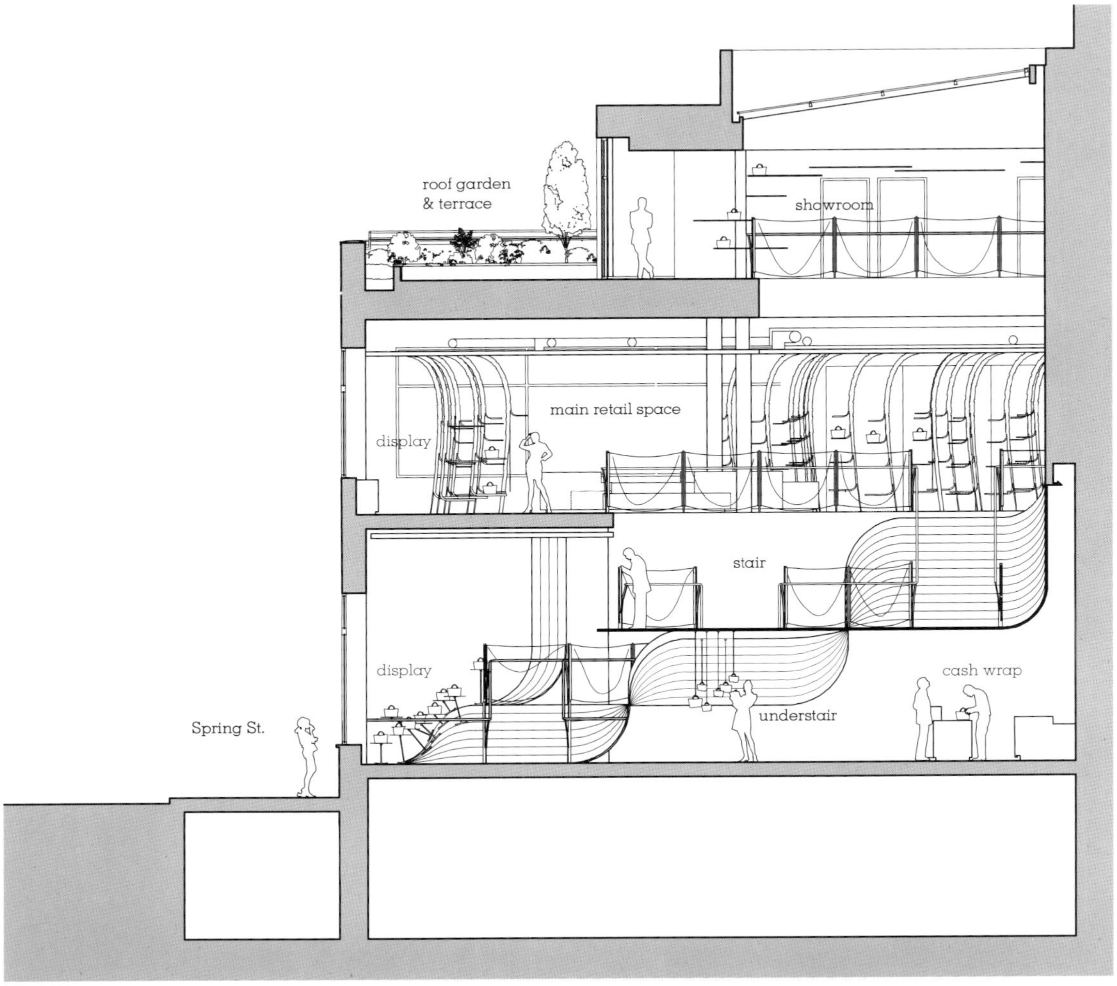

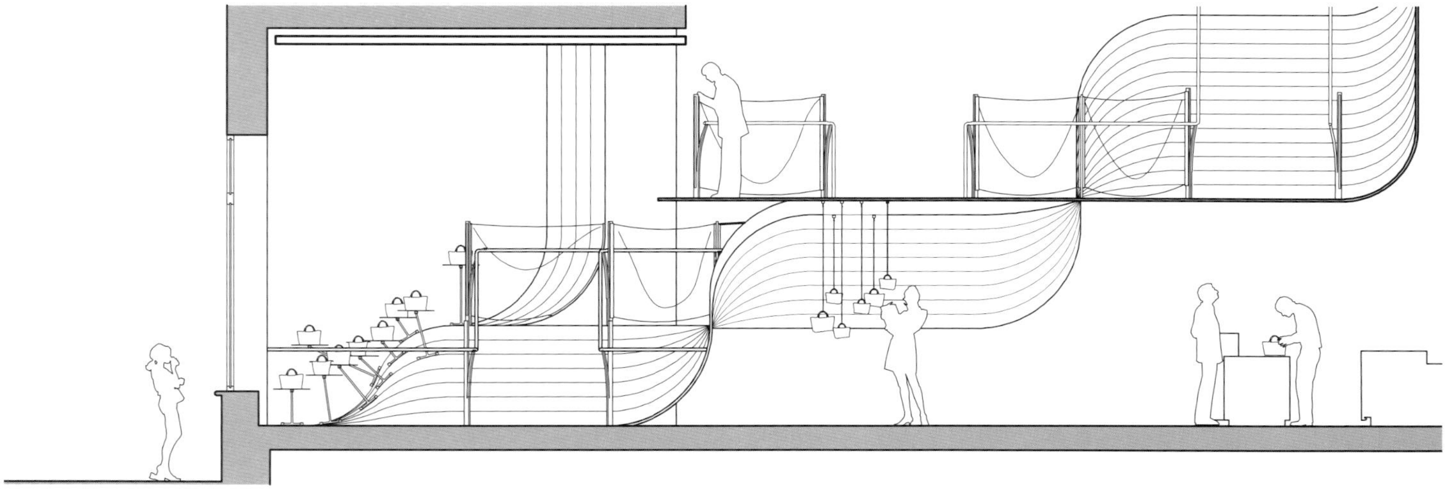

This page
Top: Section detail
Bottom: Lower-level entrance (left); shop window

Opposite
Left (top to bottom): Sections, plates 1 through 5
Right (top to bottom): Plan detail, plates 1 through 5; shop window display with entrance; stair and soffit

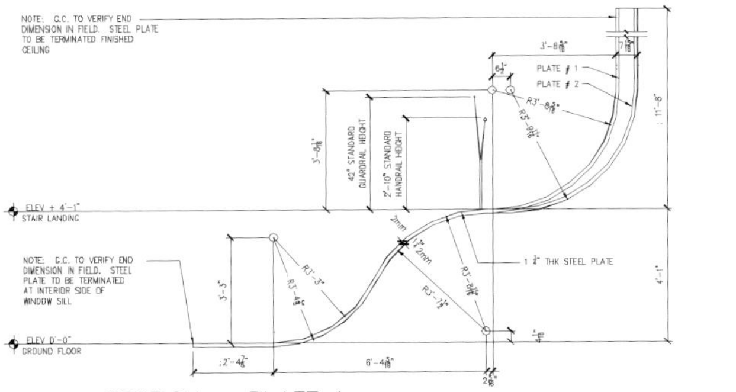

SECTION – PLATE 1

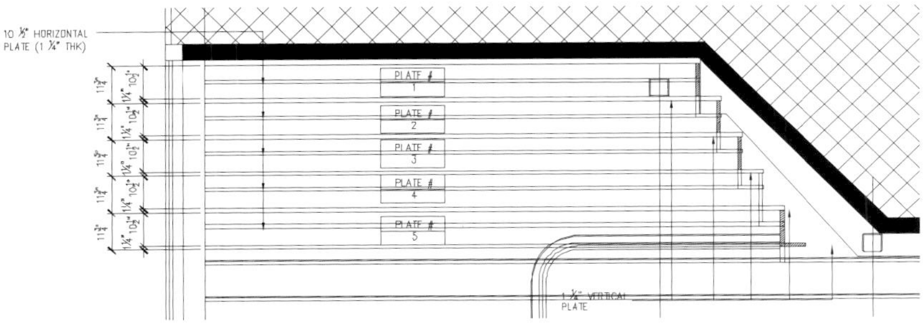

PLAN DETAIL – PLATES 1 TO 5

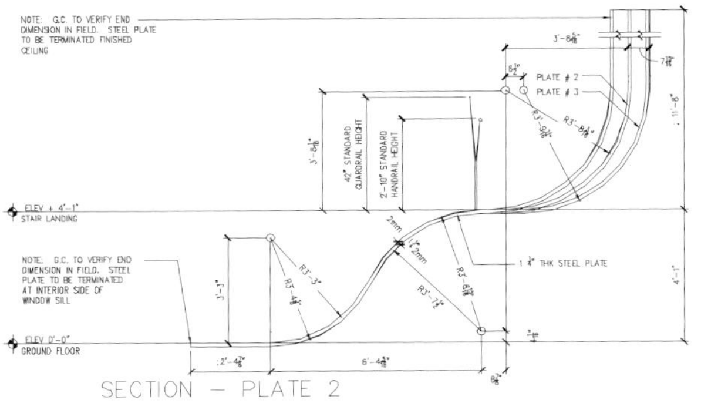

SECTION – PLATE 2

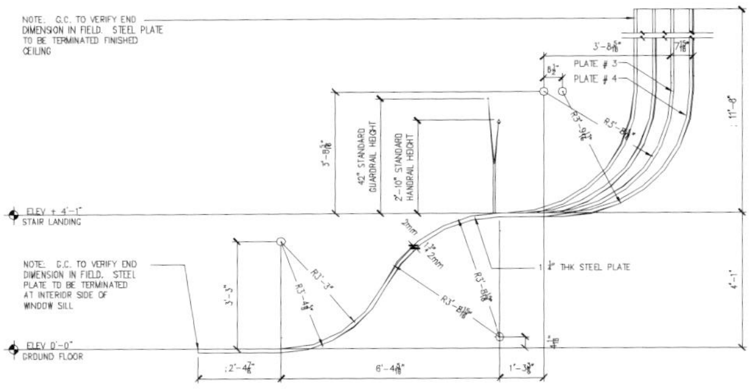

SECTION – PLATE 3

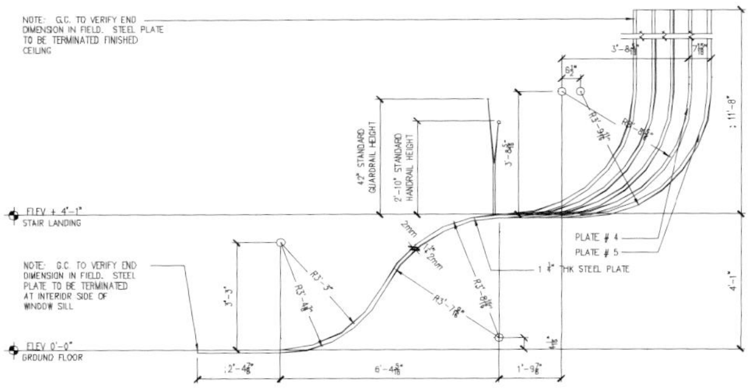

SECTION – PLATE 4

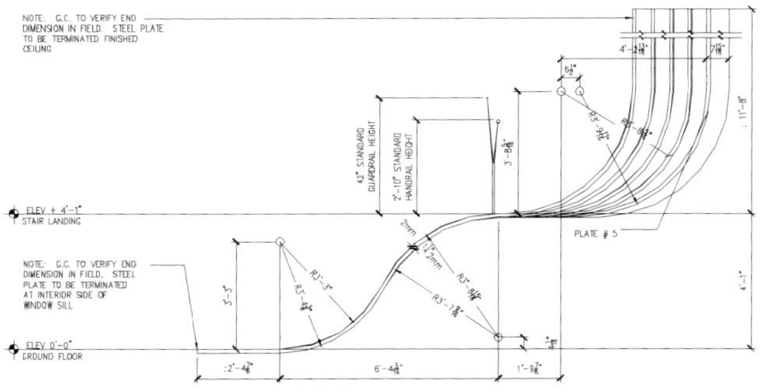

SECTION – PLATE 5

This page
Plan detail and sections, plates 6 through 8

Opposite
Top: Landing
Bottom (left and right): Balustrade details

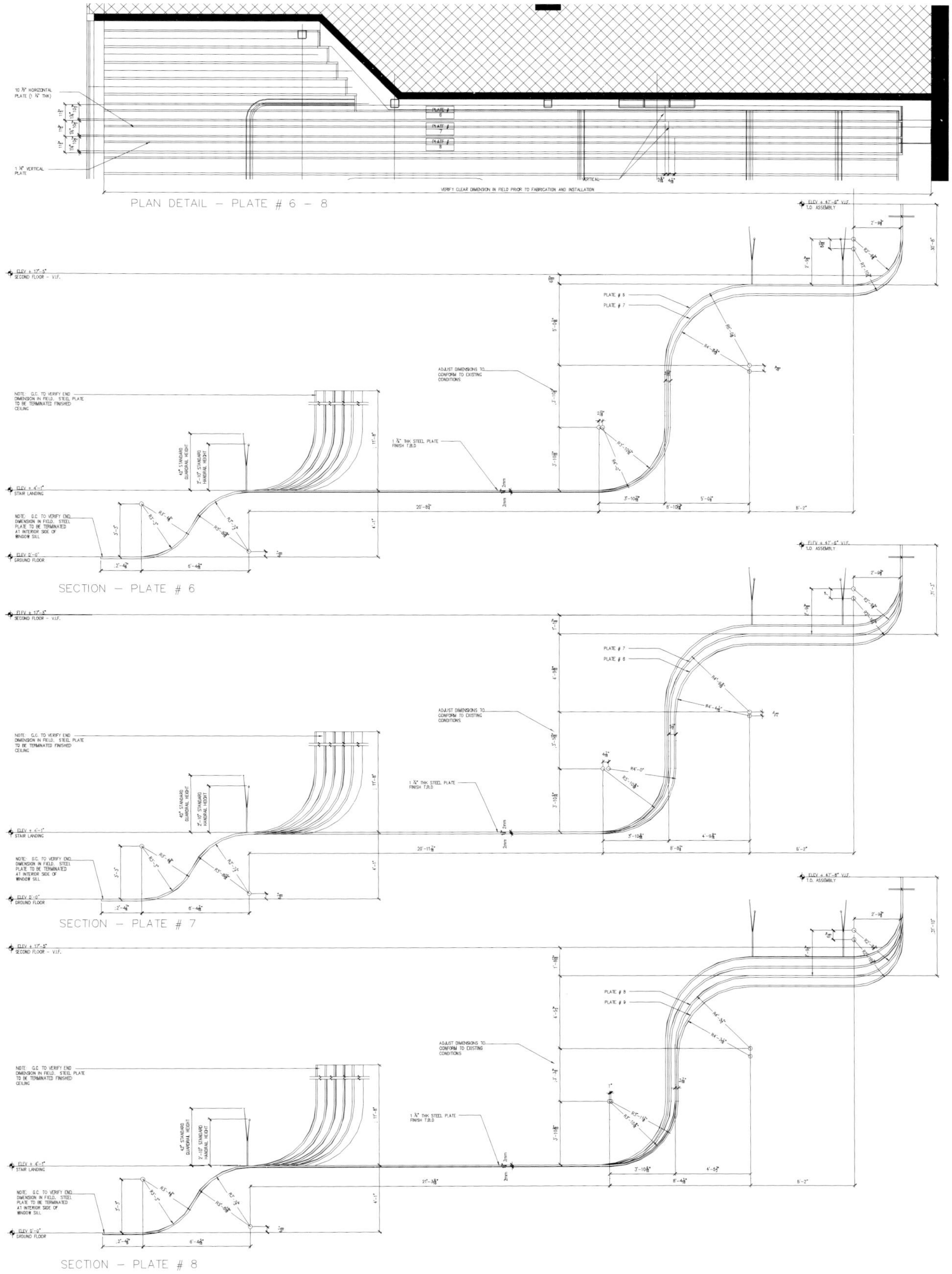

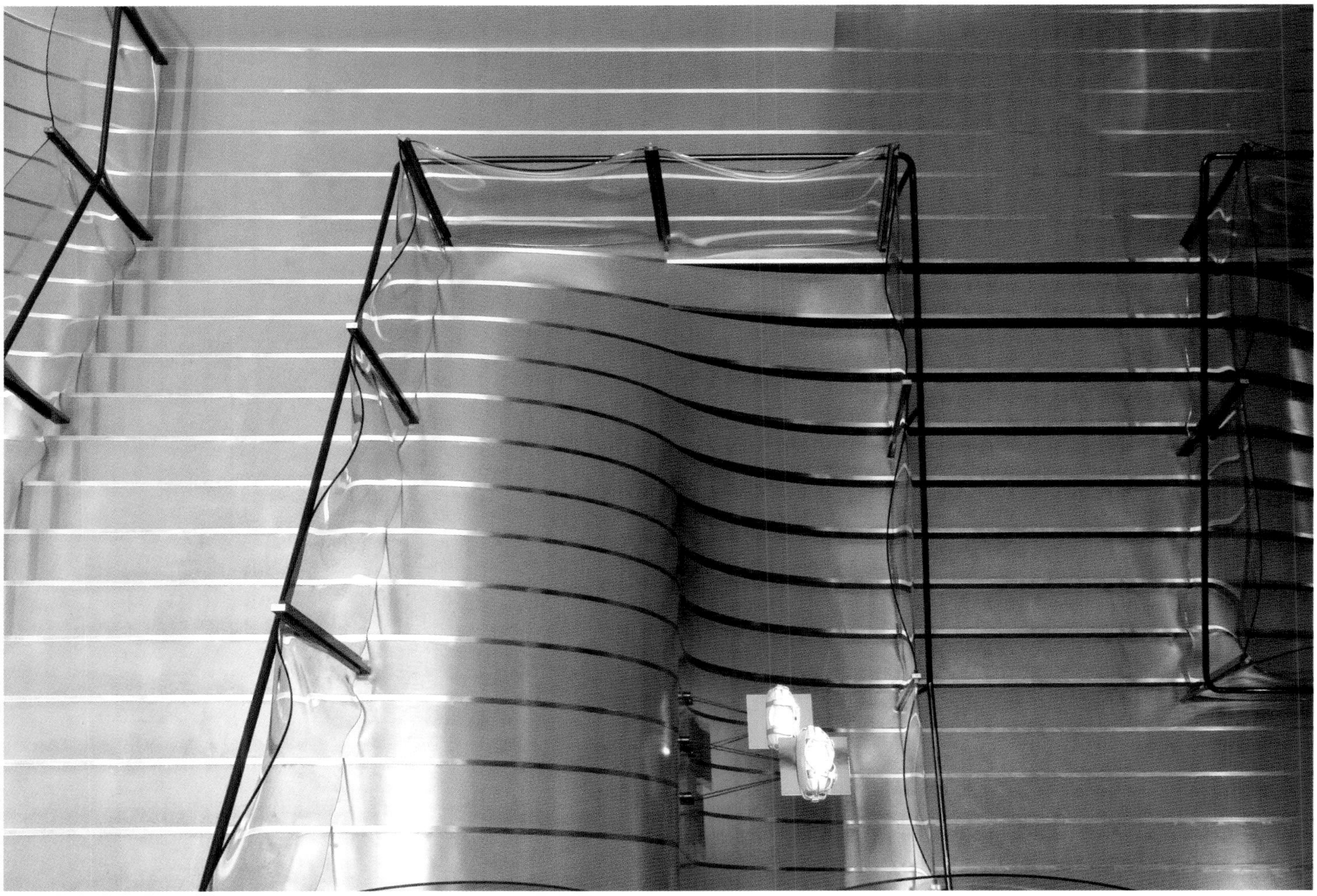

This page

Top: Sections, plates 15 through 17

Bottom: Elevation

Opposite

Top: Stair detail (left); view from landing to upper floor

Bottom: View down from upper level

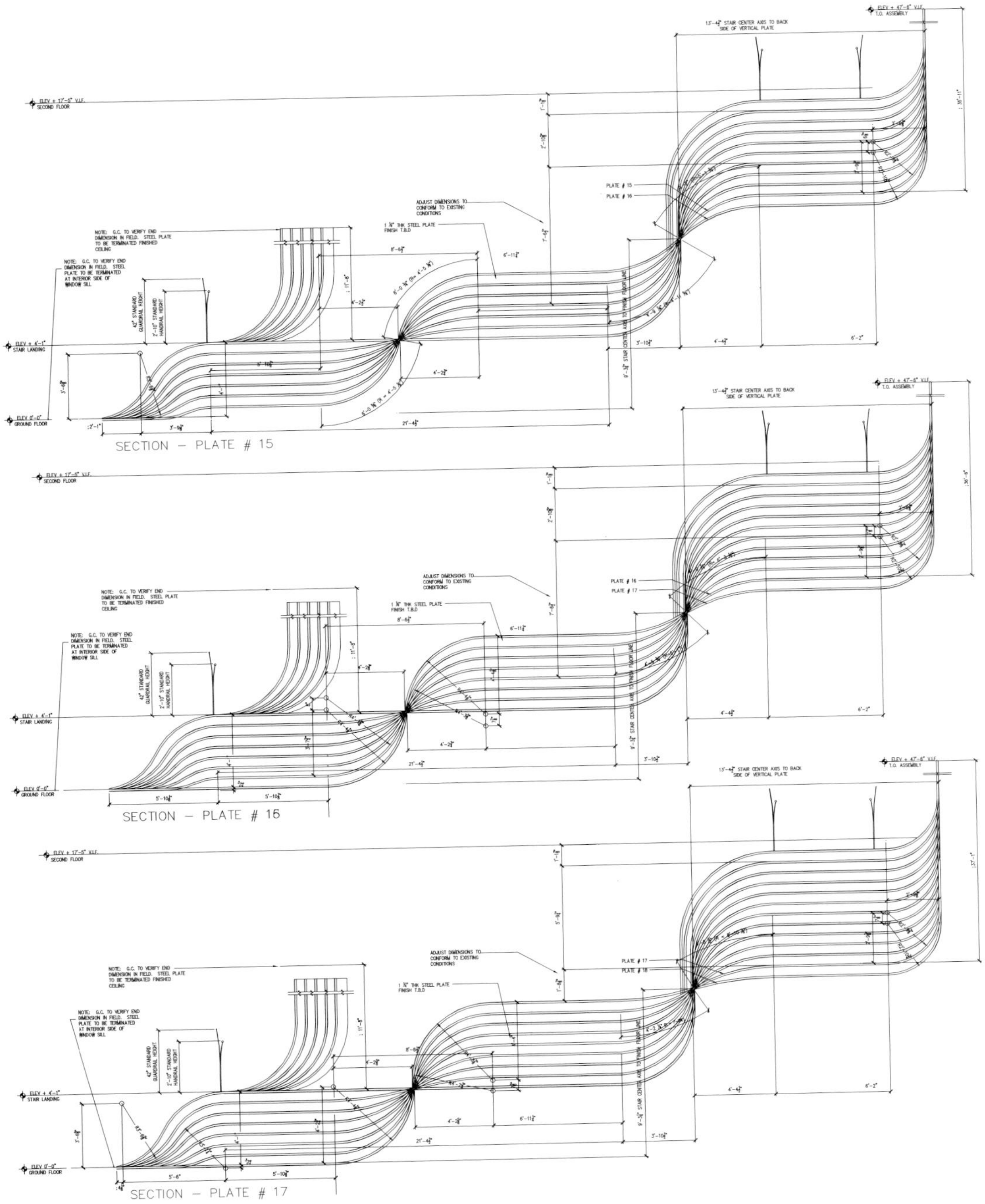

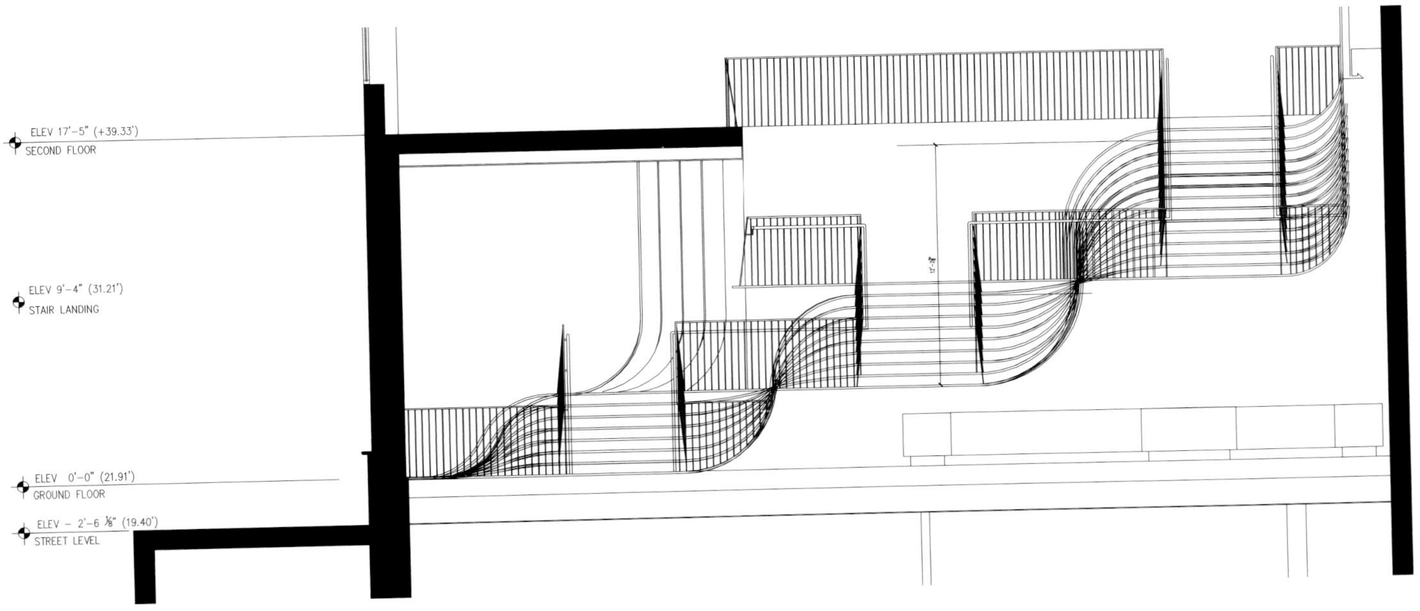

de Young Museum, San Francisco, California
Herzog & de Meuron Architekten, Basel, Switzerland
Fong & Chan Architects, San Francisco

After sustaining extensive damage during the 1989 Loma Prieta earthquake, the de Young Museum in San Francisco's Golden Gate Park was eventually closed in 2000, and construction of a seismically stable home for its art collections began two years later. The new three-level, 293,000-square-foot building reduces the de Young's footprint by 37 percent, returning two acres of open space to Golden Gate Park. Encircled by ribbons of windows, the building's exterior offers park visitors glimpses of the art within the museum and provides museum visitors with panoramic views of the park. The steel-and-concrete structure features a sophisticated seismic base-isolation system, roof trusses cantilevered 50 feet over an outdoor terrace, and a vertically post-tensioned tower on the west side of the building rotated to form a parallelogram as it rises 144 feet to align at the top with the inflected grid formed by the streets of San Francisco.

The museum's unique copper facade is perforated to simulate dappled light filtering through a canopy of trees, creating an abstract pattern that complements the de Young's parkland setting. Over the course of seven to ten years, as the untreated copper is exposed to the weathering effects of salt-laden winds from the nearby Pacific Ocean, the building's facade will continue its transformation from bright copper to a verdigris patina that will harmonize with the surrounding vegetation.

To create the perforation design for the facade, architects Herzog & de Meuron superimposed abstracted digitized photographs of tree canopies onto each elevation of the de Young and its four-sided tower. Facade bump and perforation patterns were then derived from the digital images. The 7,600 unique exterior panels on the main building and tower contain approximately 1.5 million bumps and more than 1.7 million perforations. Kansas City–based A. Zahner Company designed, engineered, fabricated, and installed the entire exterior envelope as a single contract package, including the copper facade, all exterior glazing, the structural glazing frames, waterproofing, both glass and copper-clad doors, the roll-up gate, and the single-ply-membrane and copper roof. The unusually comprehensive scope of work enabled Zahner to work in close collaboration with Herzog & de Meuron to fully integrate all detailing of the copper and glass elements.

After Herzog & de Meuron created small mockups of different bump shapes in plastic, the mockups were sent to Zahner for review and coffer samples made by modifying existing tooling to create the bumps. Some of the variables considered were depth of bump (there were eleven different sizes for varying material thicknesses, temper, and hardness), bump diameter and shape (there were six different sizes), the number of intermediate sizes to the maximum bump depth, the different sizes of panel, the bump direction (a combination of concave and convex), and the layout of bumps on grids of various sizes, made necessary by restrictions on Zahner's tooling. The hydraulic punch used to form each bump clamped material around it to limit stress; the space required for the punch to function determined the minimum spacing on the bump grid.

Initially, the panels warped when the bumps were punched; folding the panel edges helped to straighten out and flatten them. Computer modeling was used to produce files for fabrication, but full-scale mockups proved essential. A 40-foot-by-30-foot performance-mockup section of the building that included both copper and glass, with all of the actual materials and details, was subjected to static and dynamic pressure tests, as well as the stress of lateral-forces.

To develop an efficient layout method for fabricating the facade panels, Herzog & de Meuron produced a master fold-out elevation including all penetrations of the facade and assigned digital tree-canopy images to each of the individual elevations. Zahner then developed a process that extracted data from the digital images and mapped it onto the panel layout by transferring the pixels to a rectilinear grid and determining bump depths based on their relative size. On any given panel, the diameter of the bumps was constant, the depth variable. Though an efficient mapping technique, the process was cumbersome for the architects because any modifications had to be made manually, at the risk of inadvertently altering the fabrication files.

To streamline the manufacturing process, Zahner developed software that automated the system. Herzog & de Meuron submitted image and panel-layout files to a web server that would then be processed to produce a drawing uploaded to the Zahner FTP site. Image-modification tools were programmed

Opposite
Top: West elevation
Bottom: Aerial view

This page
Top: Facade concept
Bottom: Site plan

Opposite
Top to bottom: Longitudinal section; longitudinal section; southwest elevation; southeast elevation

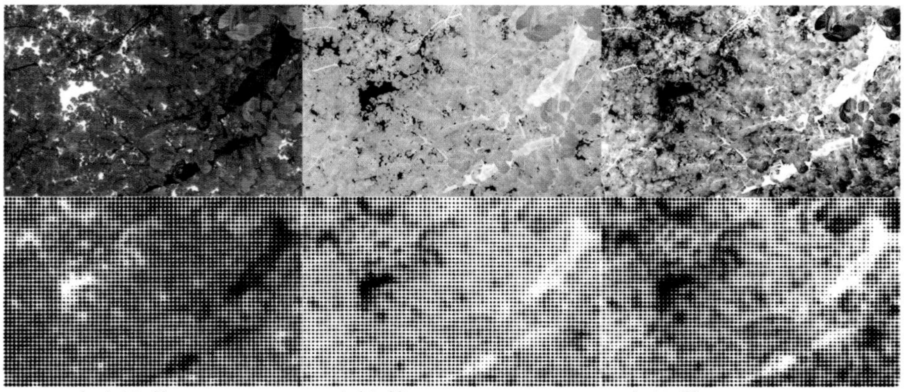

to allow Herzog & de Meuron to alter the appearance of the facade by adjusting the pixel density in an image source file. Changes were then saved in a CAD file used to manufacture the panel. Should any of the 7,600 panels ever need to be replaced, there is a file for each one and a number punched into each one that precisely identifies its location on the building.

A computer model of the tower was produced to determine the relationship of the structure and panels and to generate flattened panel layouts. Herzog & de Meuron provided the basic geometric criteria—overall height, angle of twist, twist start and stop elevations—and Zahner built the model and generated the skin surface. Working from the outside in, panel structure locations and slab-edge boundaries were determined, and a custom structural glazing system was developed and fabricated out of steel pipe and channel to integrate with the facade. Because of schedule constraints and the large number of panels—some were being fabricated as others were installed—precise adherence to the panel layout diagrams was critical so they would fit together as designed.

Paul Martin, P.E., of A. Zahner Company contributed to this text.

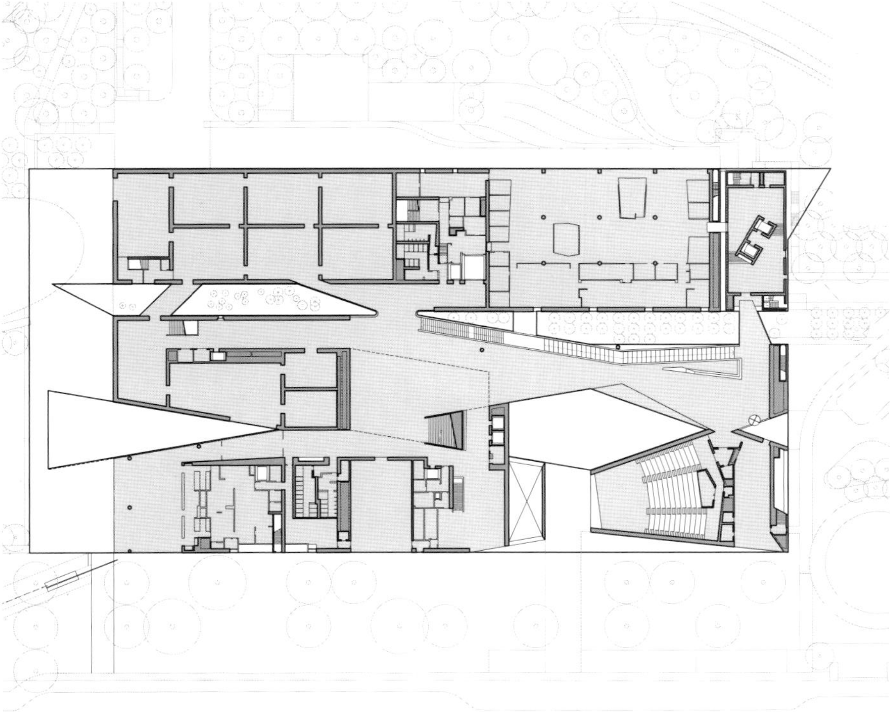

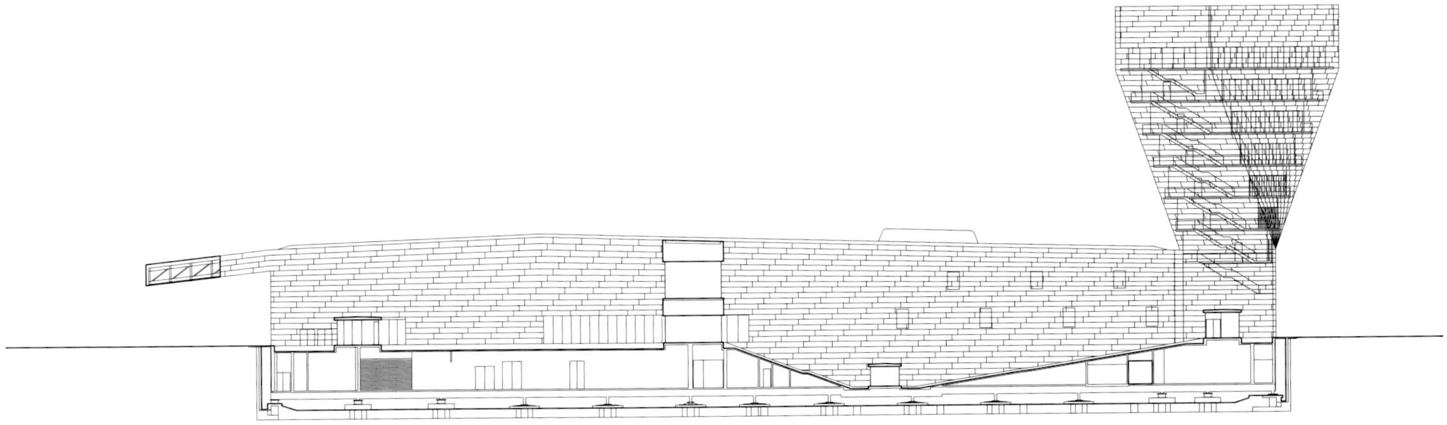

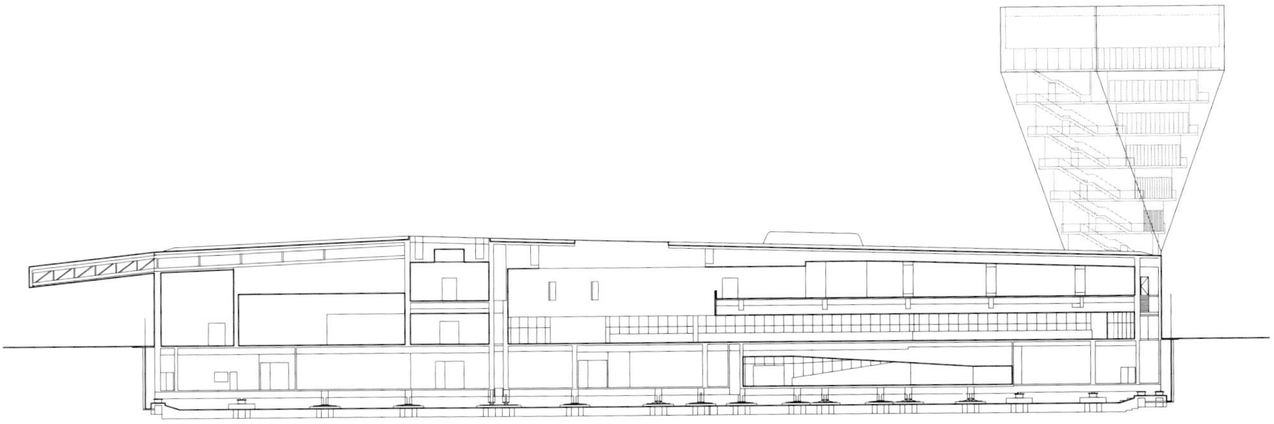

This page
Top (left and right): Tower-wall sections
Middle (left to right): Entrance; view northwest; northeast elevation detail
Bottom (left to right): East-elevation detail; west-elevation detail; west copper curve

Opposite
Top and middle: Plans
Bottom: Northeast elevation (left); south elevation

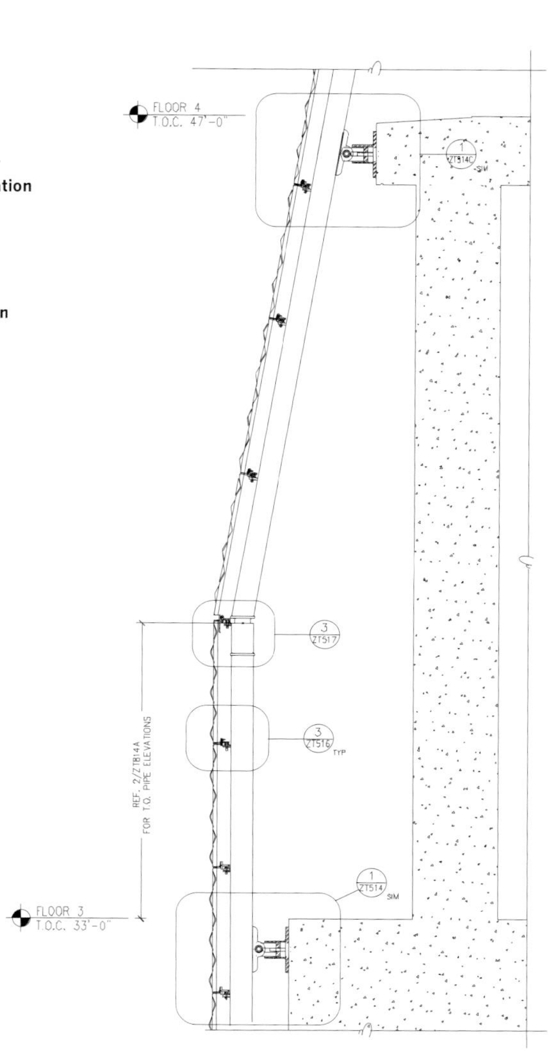

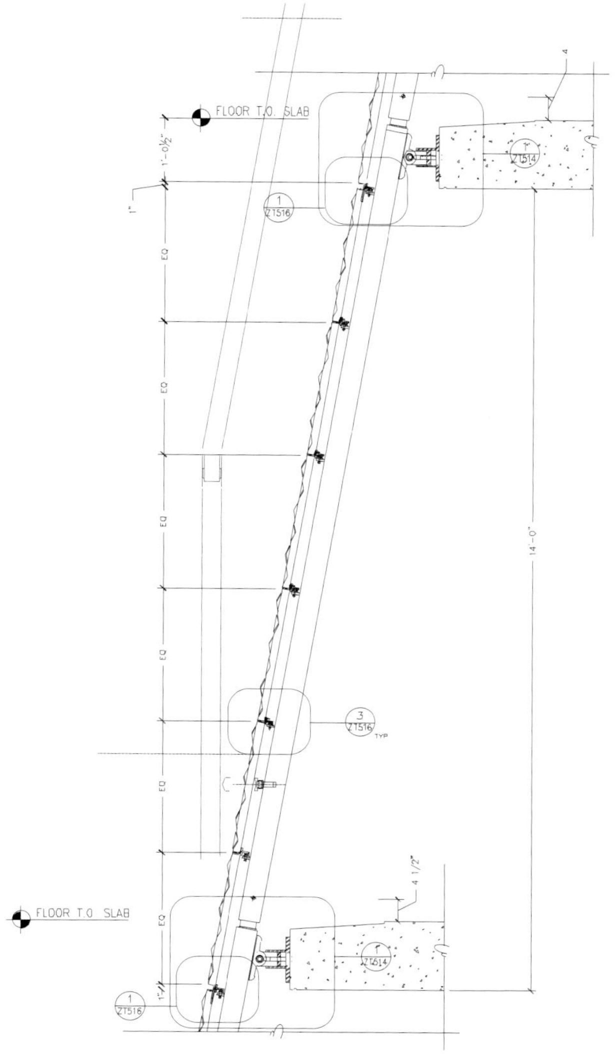

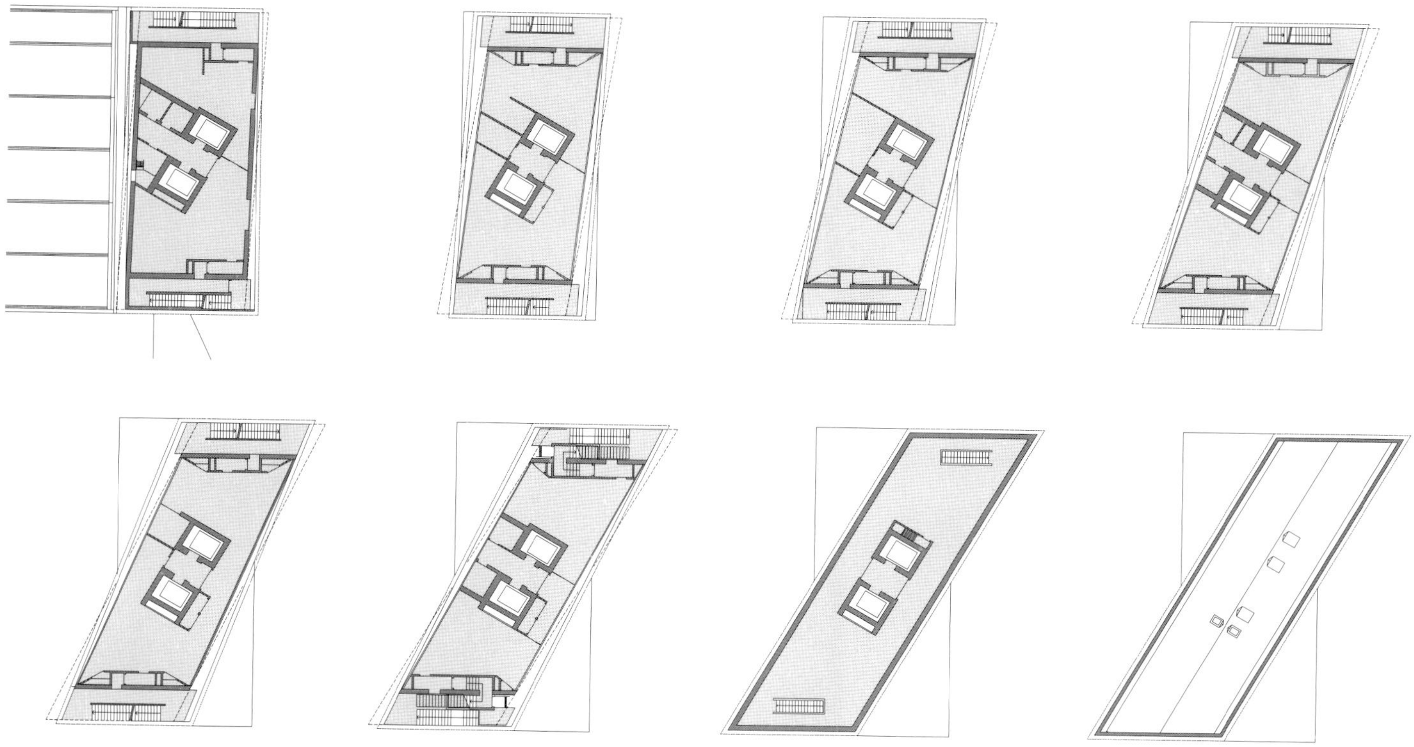

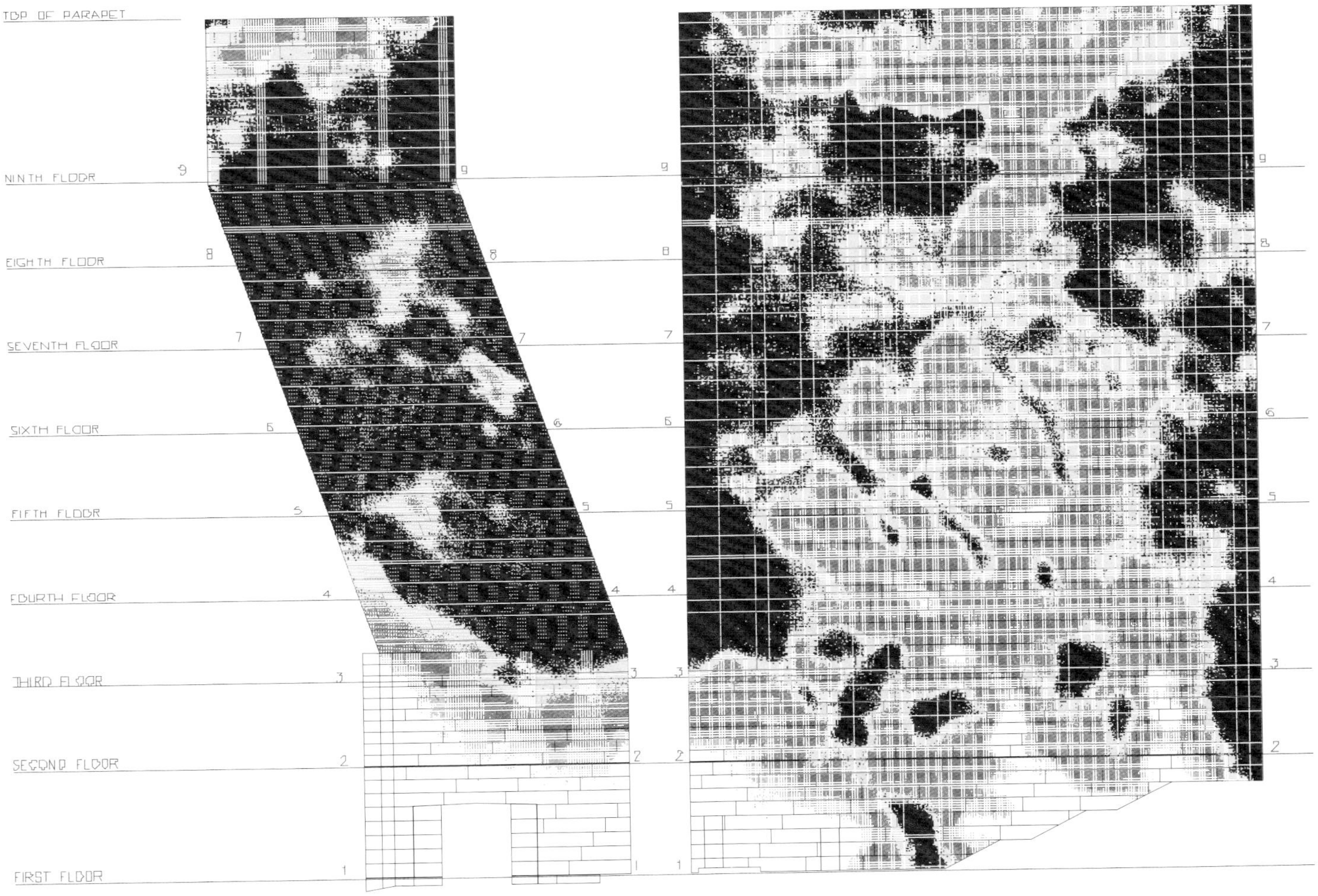
TOP OF PARAPET
NINTH FLOOR
EIGHTH FLOOR
SEVENTH FLOOR
SIXTH FLOOR
FIFTH FLOOR
FOURTH FLOOR
THIRD FLOOR
SECOND FLOOR
FIRST FLOOR

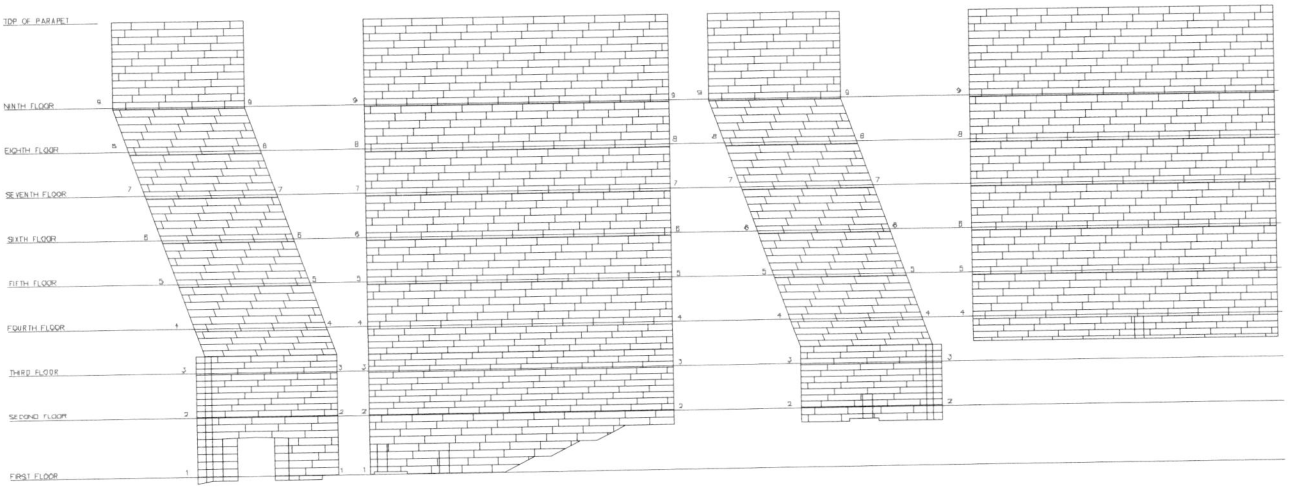
TOP OF PARAPET
NINTH FLOOR
EIGHTH FLOOR
SEVENTH FLOOR
SIXTH FLOOR
FIFTH FLOOR
FOURTH FLOOR
THIRD FLOOR
SECOND FLOOR
FIRST FLOOR

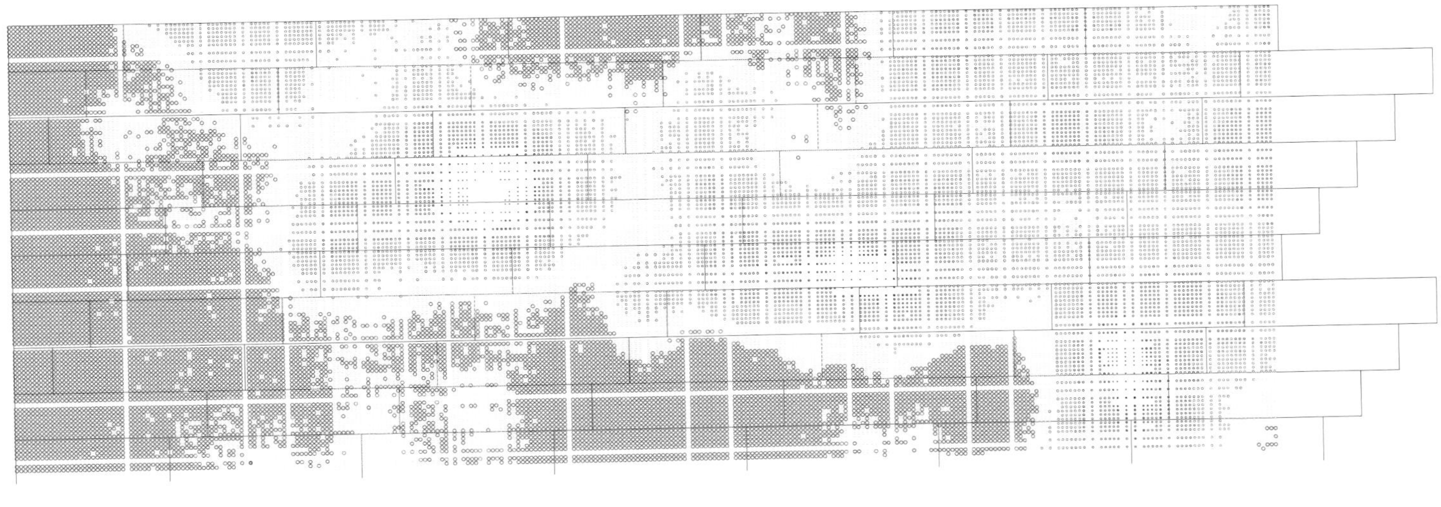

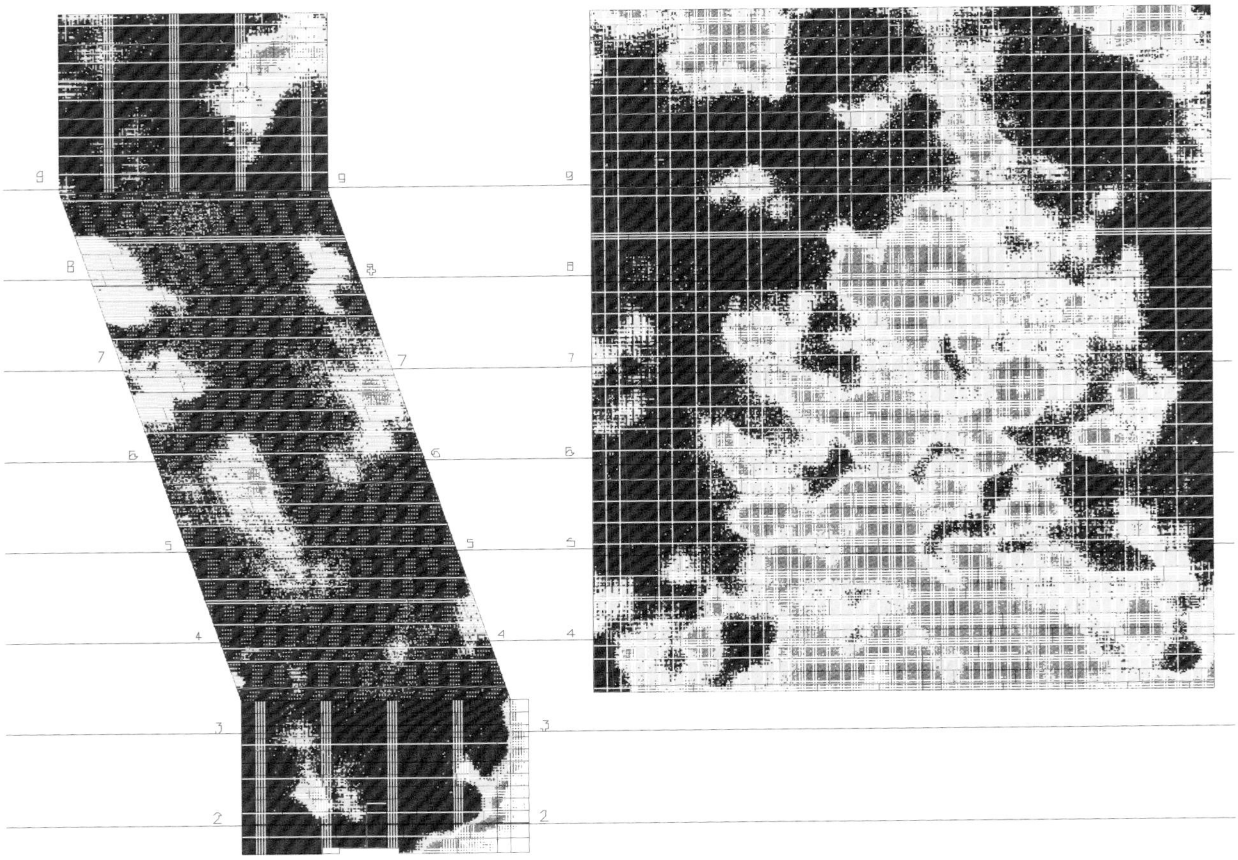

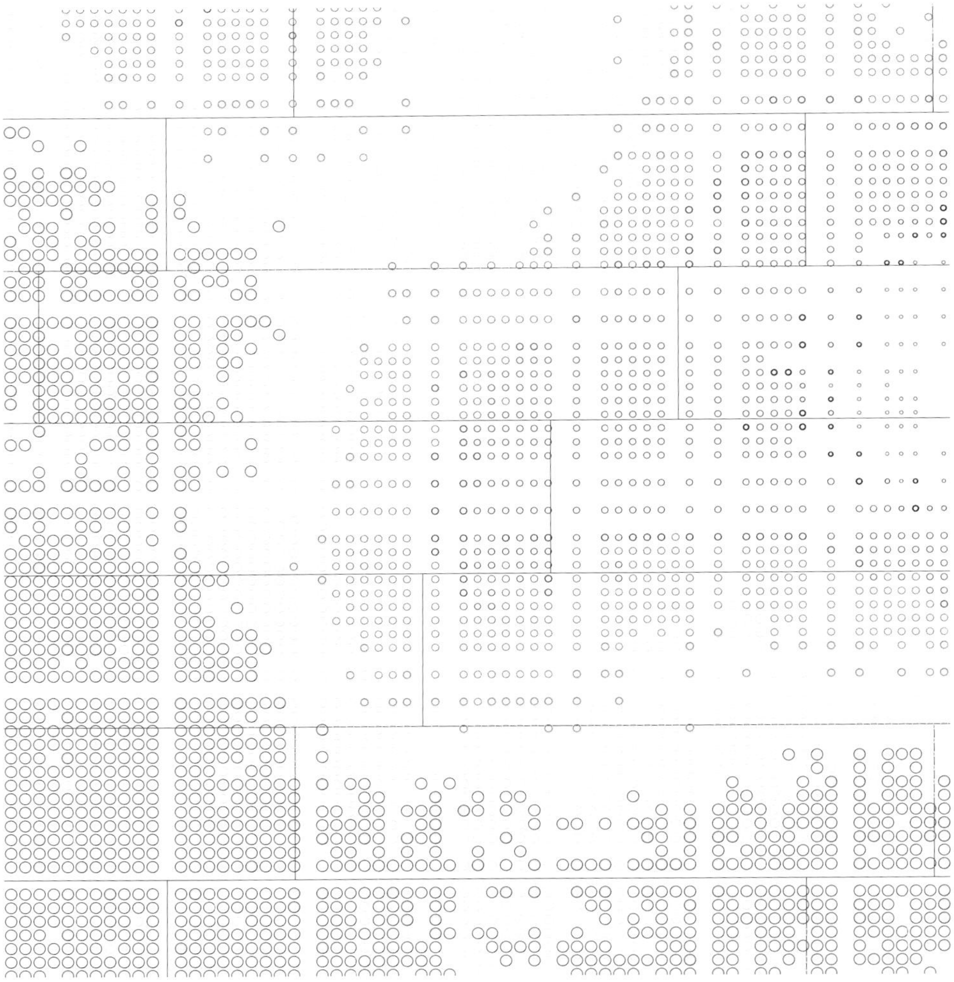

This page
Top: North elevation (left); west elevation
Bottom: Tower-perforations detail, enlarged

Opposite
Top: Tower-perforations layouts
Middle: Tower-panel layouts
Bottom: Tower-perforations detail

This page
Top: Cantilever interior (top left), cantilever-soffit detail (middle left), cantilever detail (top right)
Bottom: Cantilever, southwest elevation

Opposite
Top: Cantilever details
Bottom: Cantilever soffit

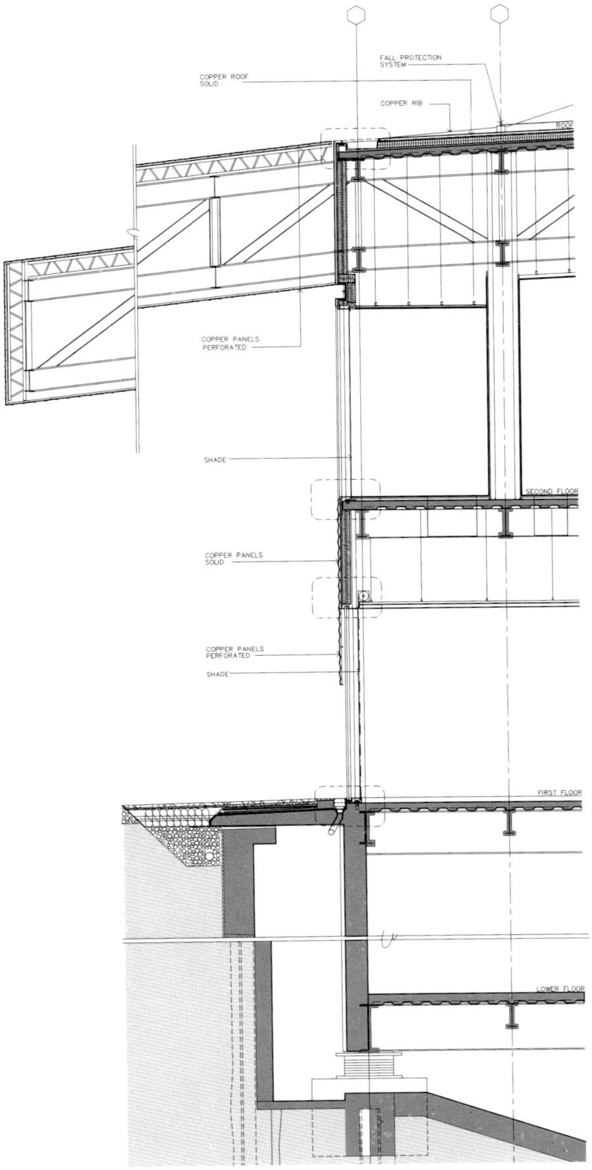

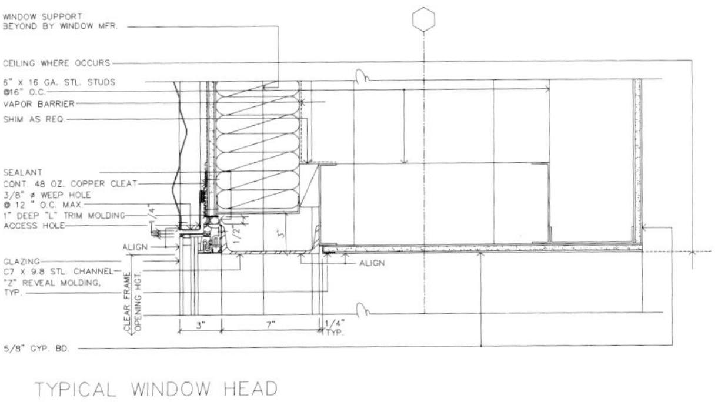

TYPICAL WINDOW HEAD

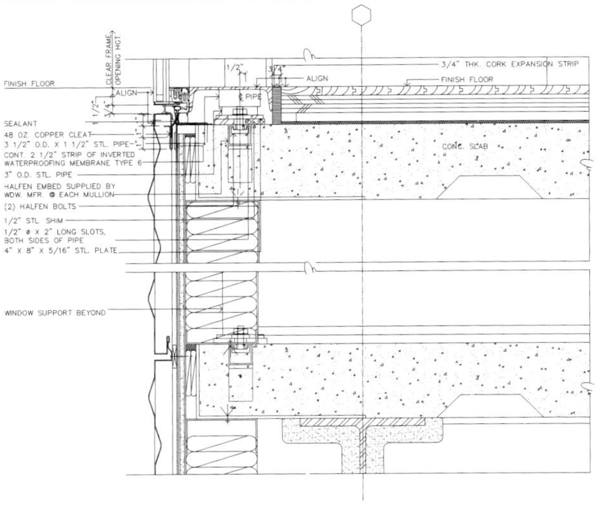

TYPICAL WINDOW SILL ABOVE GRADE

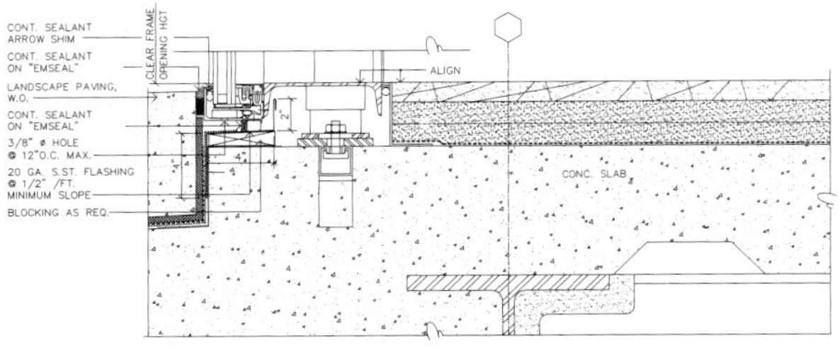

TYP. WINDOW SILL @ GRADE

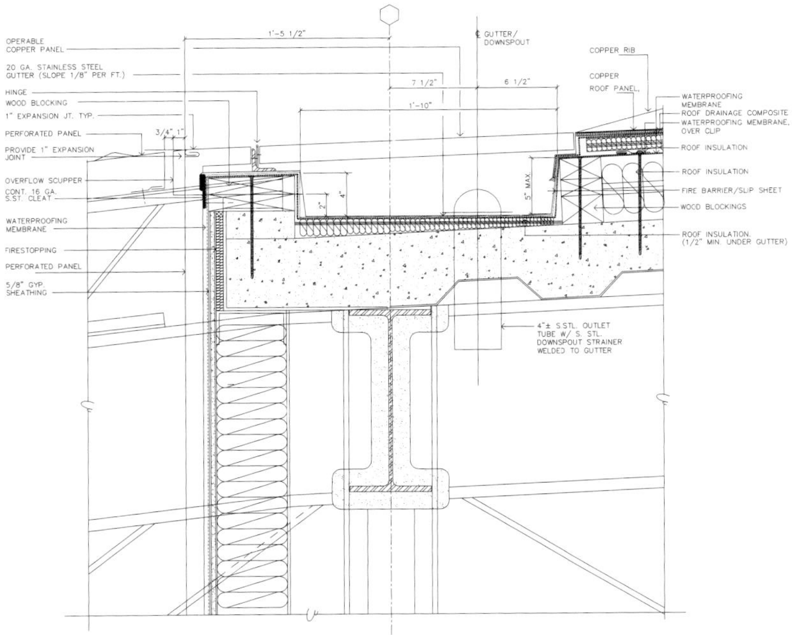

GUTTER DETAIL

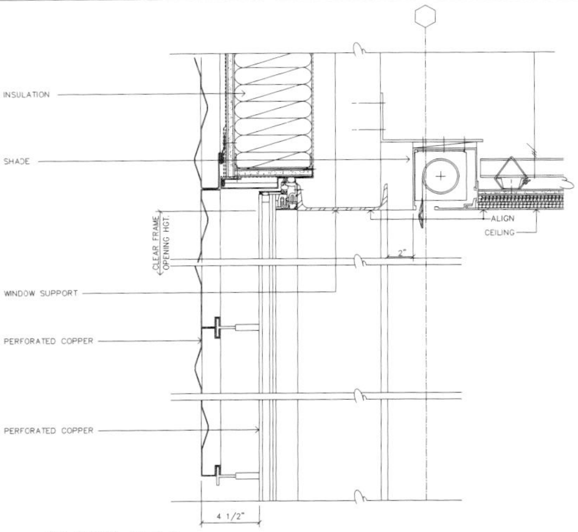

WINDOW HEAD

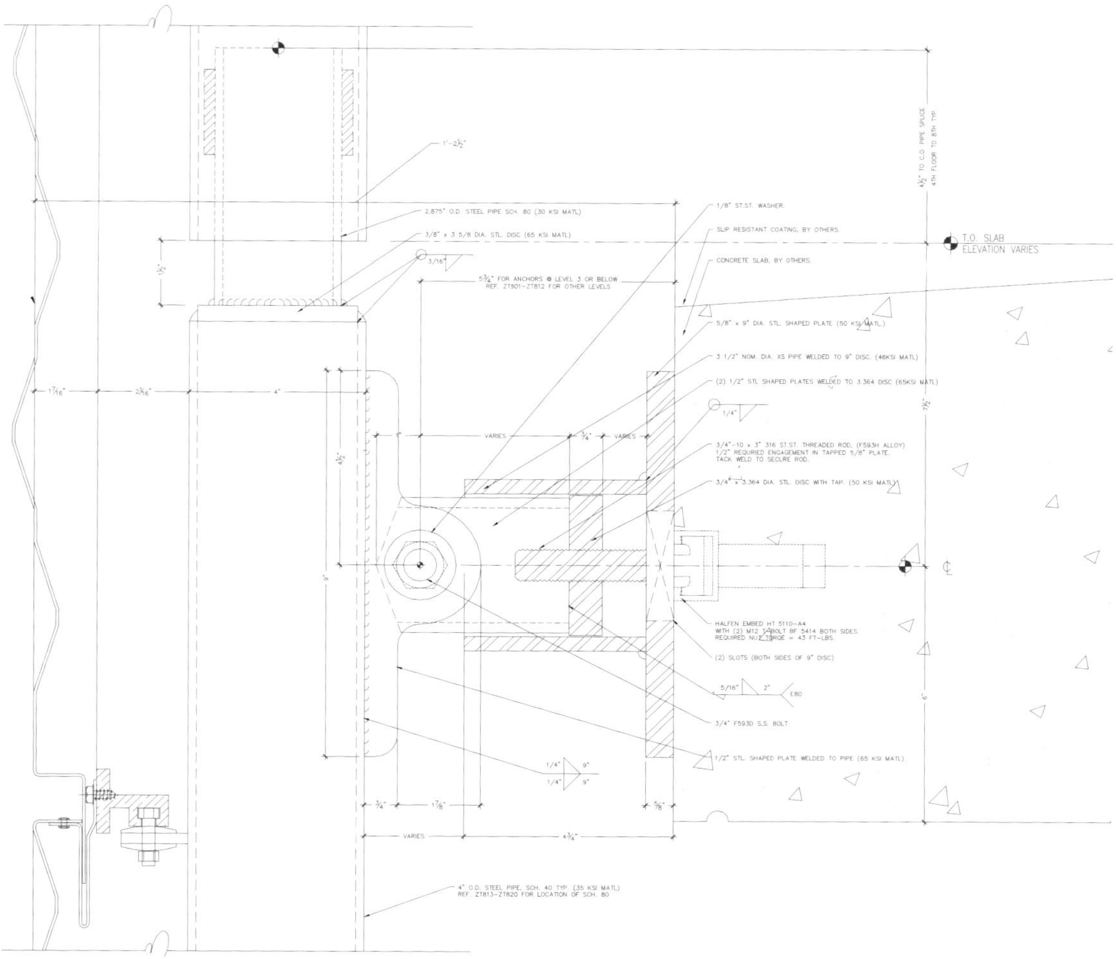

This page

Top: Tower, partial section at ninth floor

Bottom (clockwise from upper left): Tower, west elevation; tower wall assembly, interior view up; tower fourth-floor wall-assembly, interior, view through west elevation; tower seventh-floor wall-assembly, interior, view through west elevation; tower, west-elevation detail

Opposite

Top: Tower, west elevation, panel-perforations detail

Middle: Typical pipe anchor (left); horizontal-panel joints

Bottom: Tower, west elevation

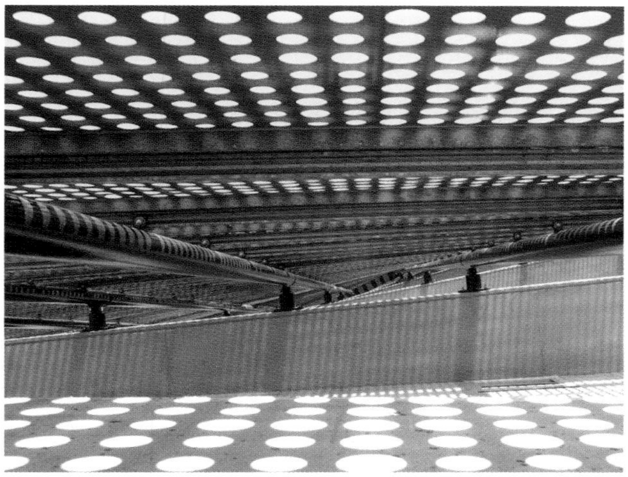

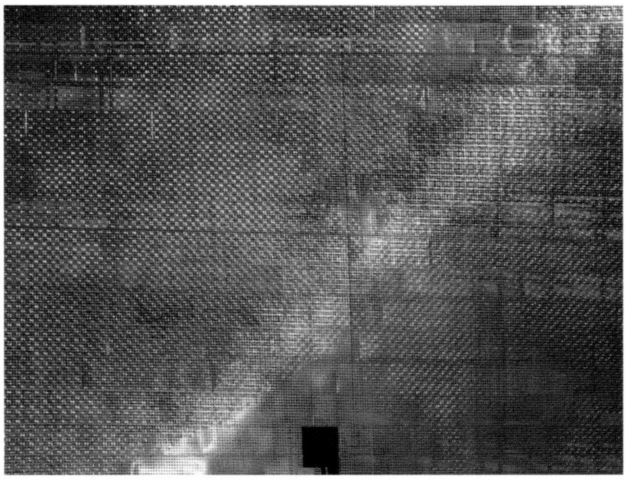

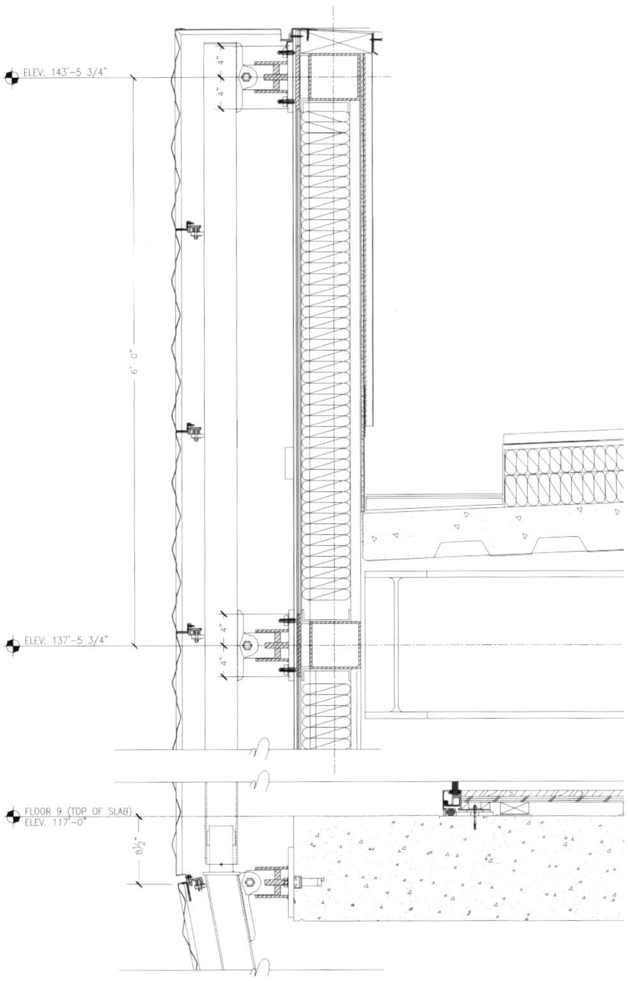
ELEV: 143'-5 3/4"
ELEV: 137'-5 3/4"
FLOOR 9 (TOP OF SLAB)
ELEV. 117'-0"
6'-0"

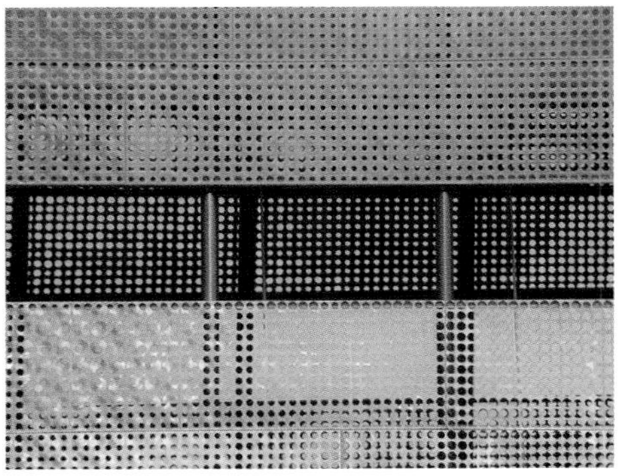

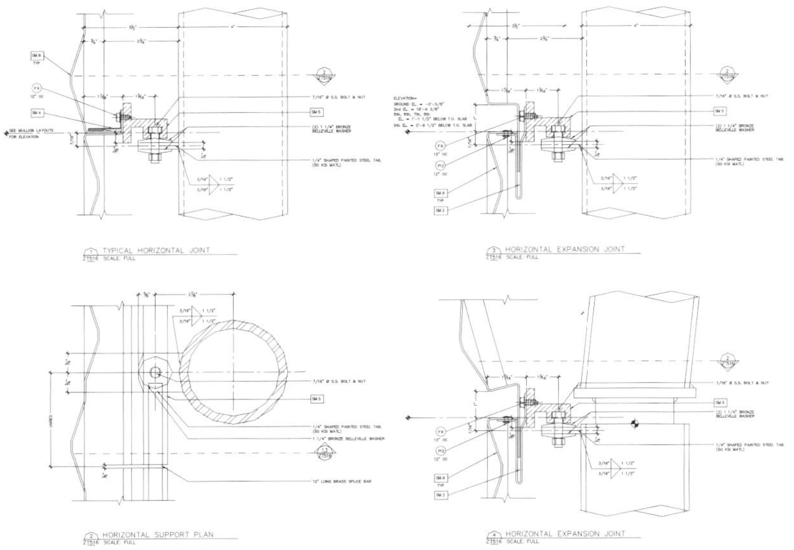
TYPICAL HORIZONTAL JOINT
SCALE: FULL
HORIZONTAL EXPANSION JOINT
SCALE: FULL
HORIZONTAL SUPPORT PLAN
SCALE: FULL
HORIZONTAL EXPANSION JOINT
SCALE: FULL

Children's Museum of Pittsburgh, Pittsburgh, Pennsylvania
Koning Eizenberg Architecture, Santa Monica, California
Perkins Eastman, Pittsburgh

The new Children's Museum of Pittsburgh is an expansion of its premises in the old post office building that leads into the adjacent Buhl Planetarium. The two landmarks are joined together by a third building, a three-story steel-and-glass structure surrounded by a kinetic screen of tens of thousands of 5 1/2-inch translucent white acrylic panels that flutter in the wind, creating a dynamic surface that responds to air movement in beautiful and unpredictable ways. Named the "Articulated Cloud," the screen is intended to suggest that a digitized cloud has enveloped the building, its appearance changing dramatically with variations in light conditions, weather, and time of day. When the wind passes over the acrylic panels, they ripple like clouds moving across the sky. Each panel hangs on a stainless-steel rod attached to an aluminum space frame that appears to float in front of the building. The skin acts as a protective outer layer to reduce heat gain on the glass facade and is visible throughout the interior of the new museum building.

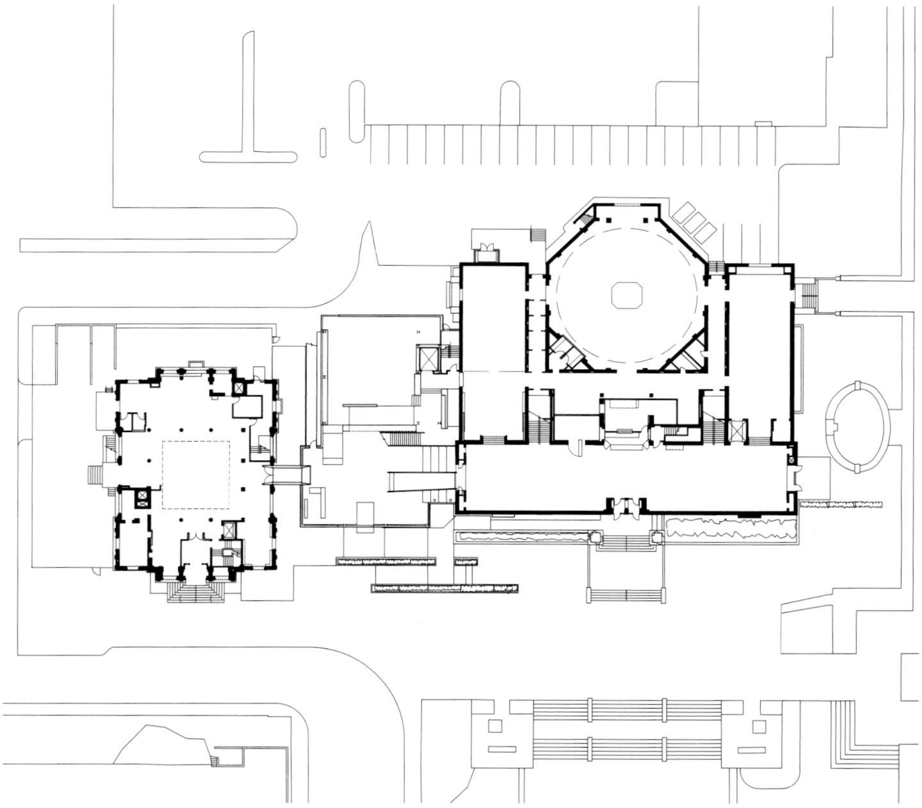

This page
Top: Site plan
Bottom: Section

Opposite
Top: View southeast
Bottom: West elevation

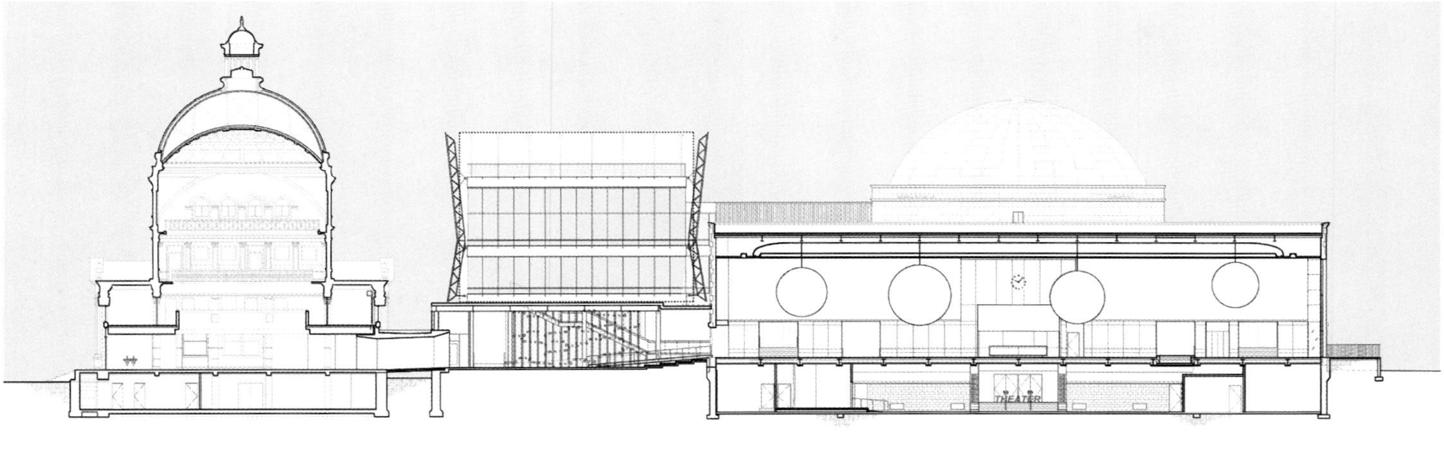

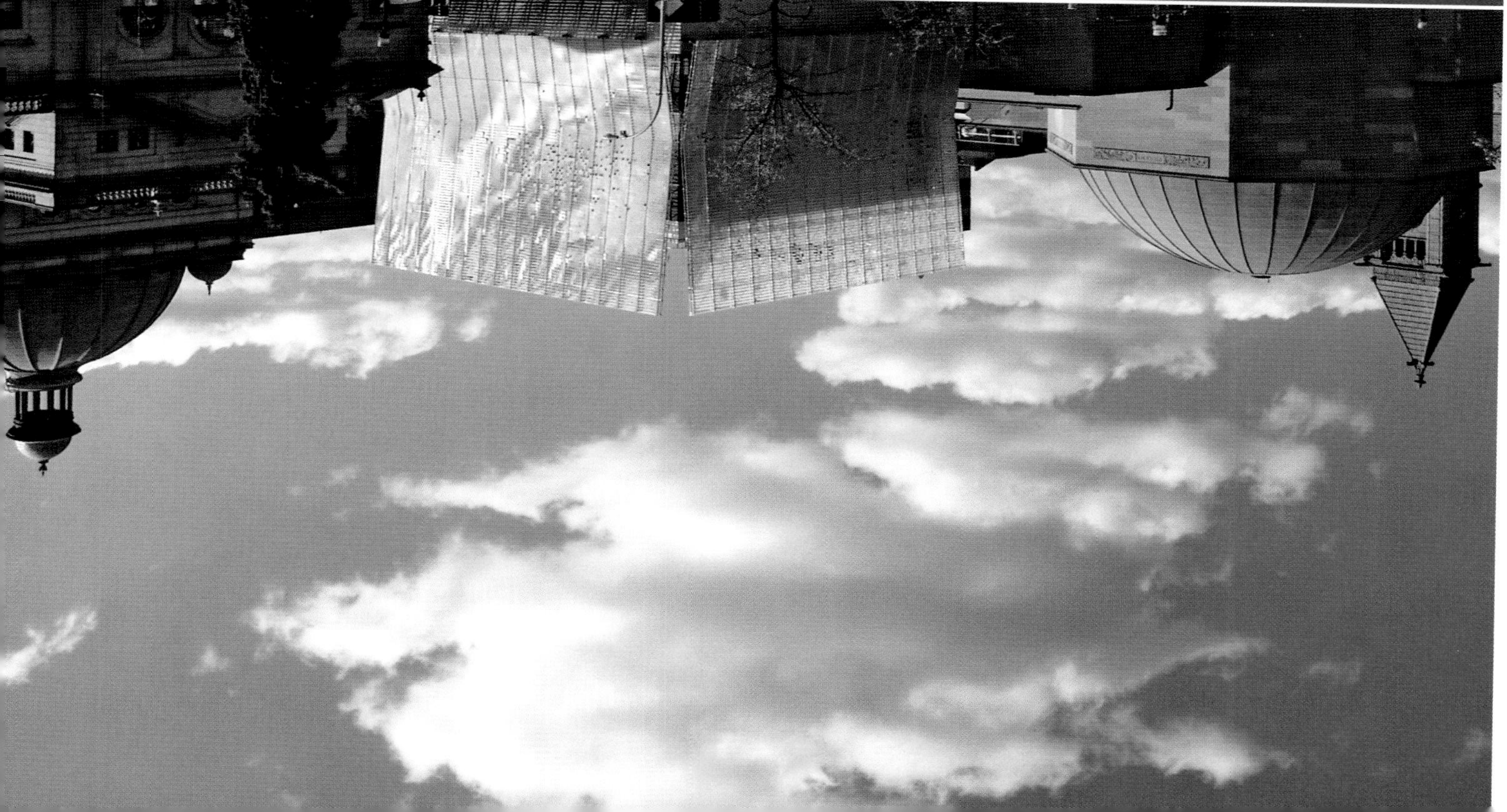

This page
Top: West elevation
Bottom: West-elevation detail

Opposite
Top: Elevation detail
Bottom: Space-frame detail

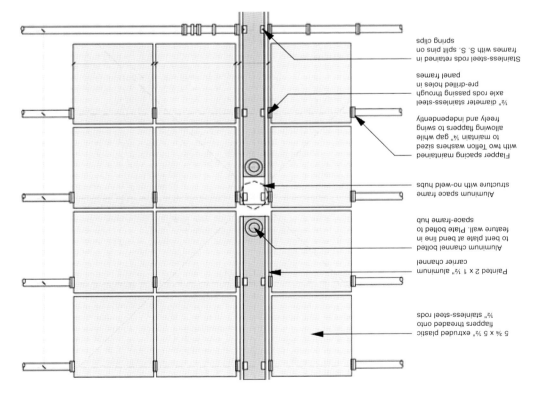

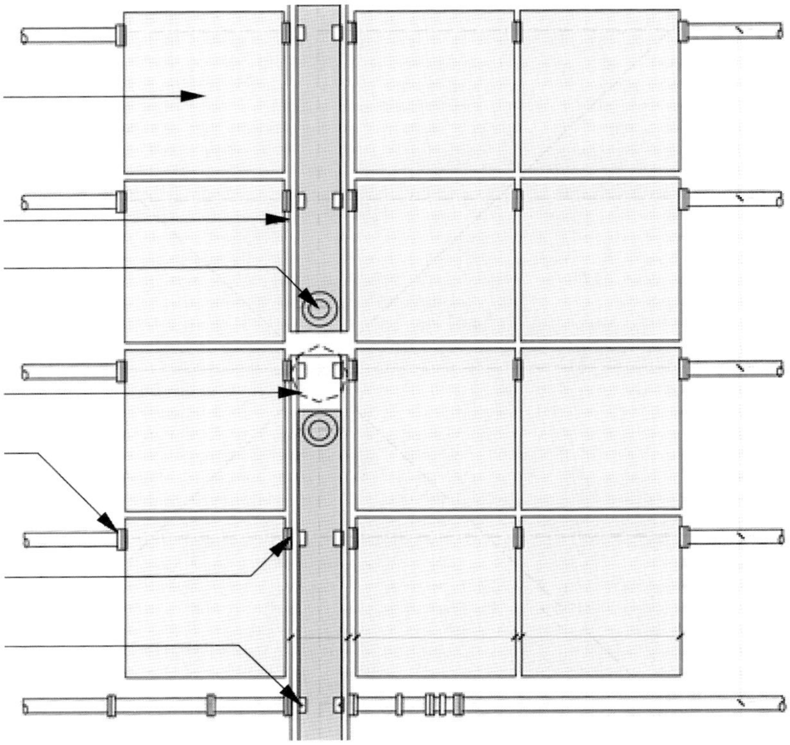
5 ¾ x 5 ½" extruded plastic flappers threaded onto ½" stainless-steel rods
Painted 2 x 1 ½" aluminum carrier channel
Aluminum channel bolted to bent plate at bend line in feature wall. Plate bolted to space-frame hub
Aluminum space frame structure with no-weld hubs
Flapper spacing maintained with two Teflon washers sized to maintain ¼" gap while allowing flappers to swing freely and independently
½" diameter stainless-steel axle rods passing through pre-drilled holes in panel frames
Stainless-steel rods retained in frames with S. S. split pins on spring clips

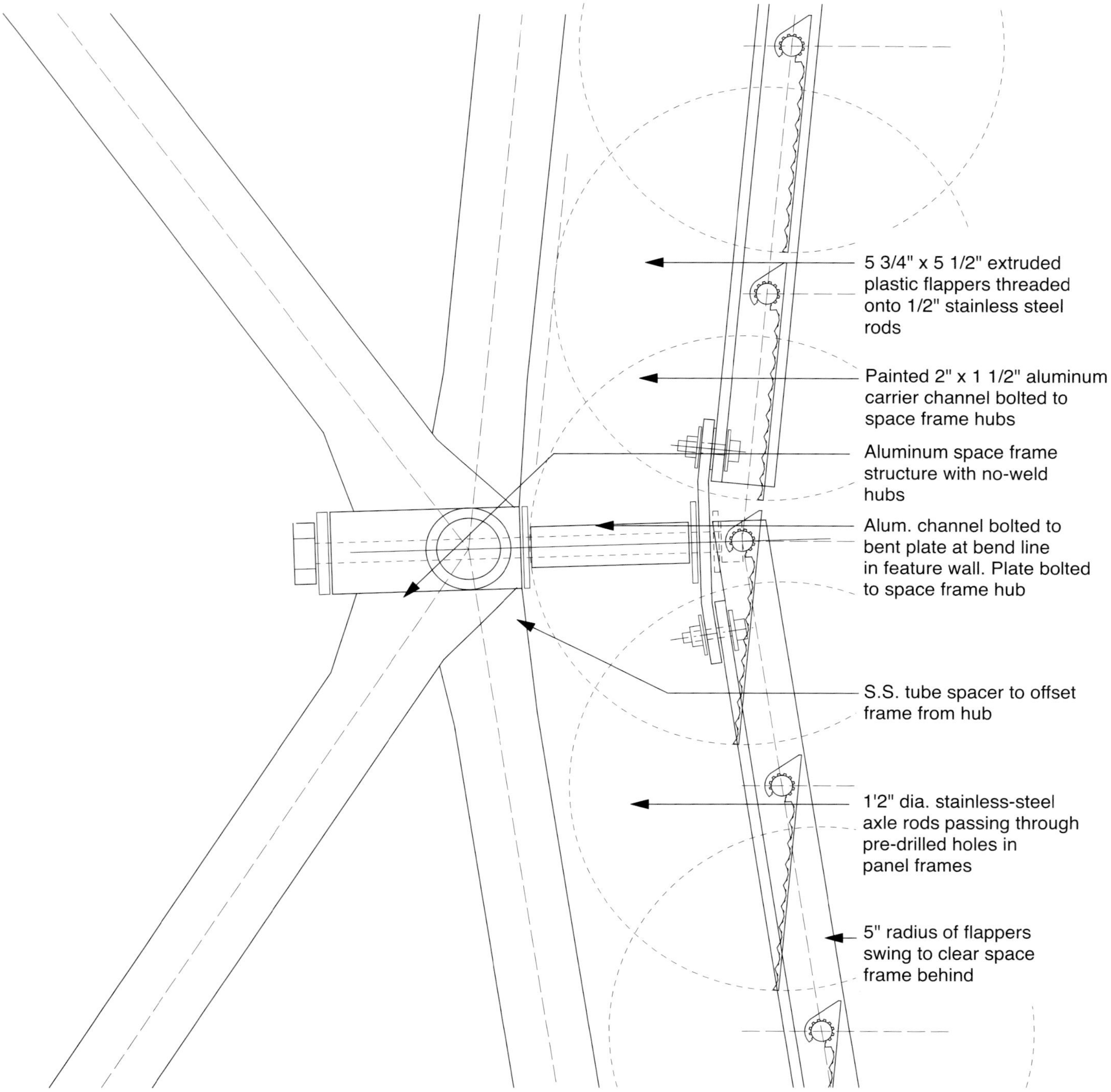
5 3/4" x 5 1/2" extruded plastic flappers threaded onto 1/2" stainless steel rods
Painted 2" x 1 1/2" aluminum carrier channel bolted to space frame hubs
Aluminum space frame structure with no-weld hubs
Alum. channel bolted to bent plate at bend line in feature wall. Plate bolted to space frame hub
S.S. tube spacer to offset frame from hub
1'2" dia. stainless-steel axle rods passing through pre-drilled holes in panel frames
5" radius of flappers swing to clear space frame behind

Opposite
Top: Section detail
Bottom: Space frame, side elevation (left); installation

This page
Top: Space-frame soffit (left); side elevation
Bottom: Interior detail

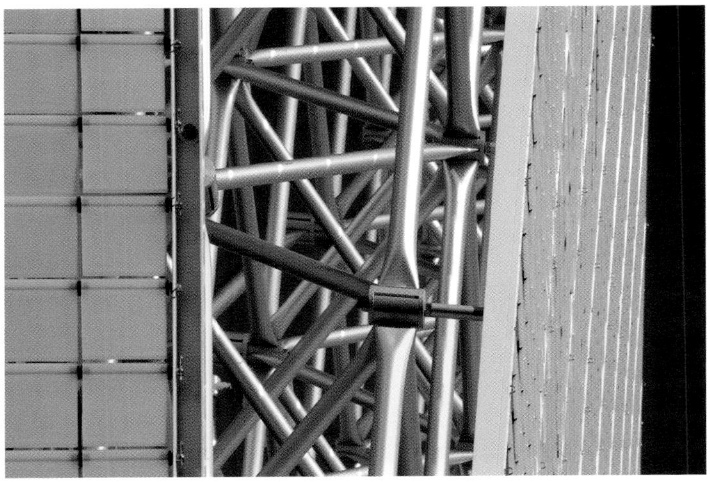

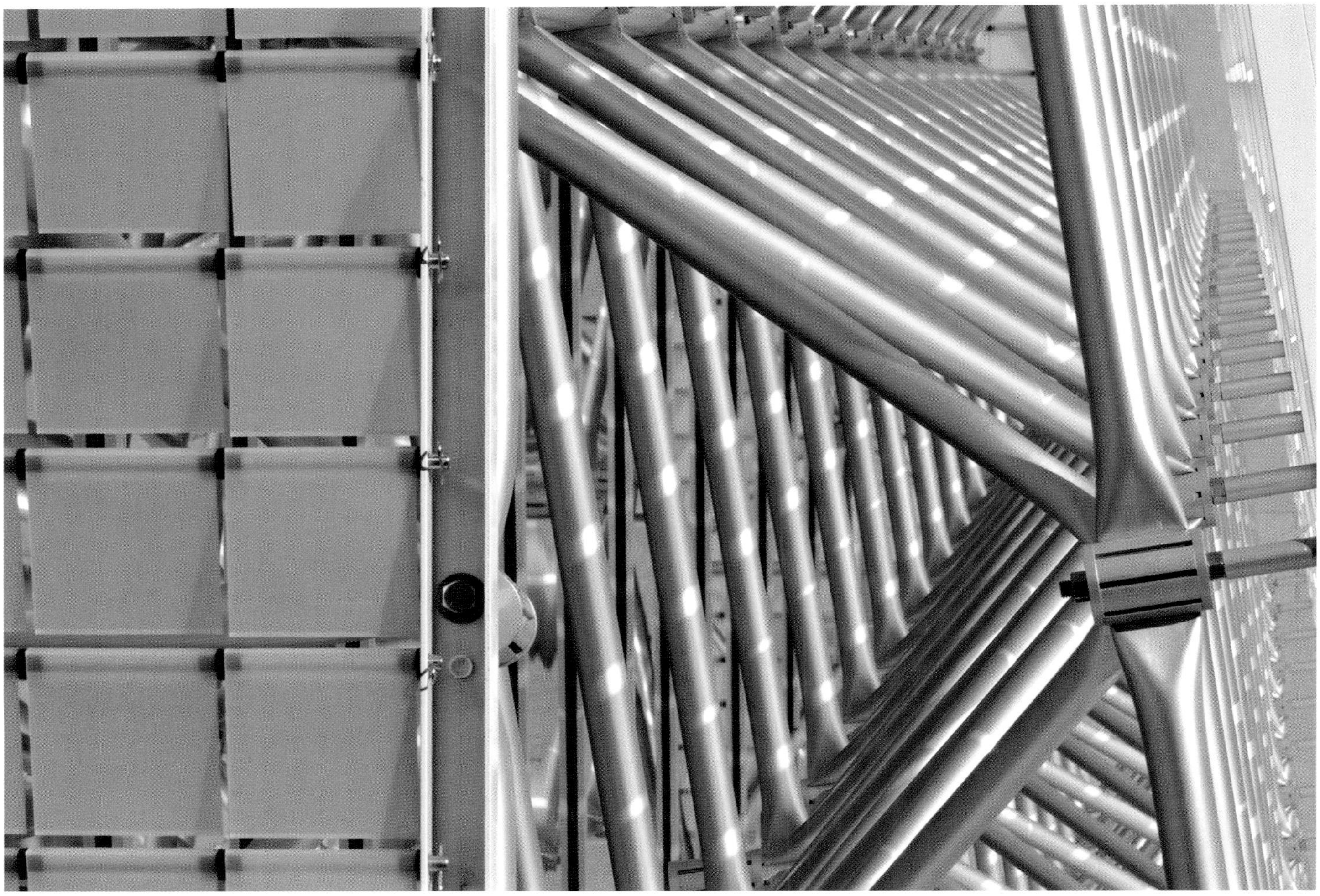

Marsupial Bridge and Urban Plaza, Milwaukee, Wisconsin
La Dallman Architects, Inc., Milwaukee

Like many North American cities with an industrial past, Milwaukee contains many leftover spaces that are the byproducts of an urban infrastructure built without regard for its context. The Marsupial Bridge and Urban Plaza are parts of a multiphase project for the regeneration of the area surrounding the Holton Street Viaduct (1925) that crosses the Milwaukee River. The project consists of a bus shelter that serves as its gateway, an urban plaza with a media garden, and the Marsupial Bridge, which offers a new pedestrian and bicycle route across the river. The existing viaduct is located in the heart of the most densely built up neighborhood in a city that has experienced dramatic population loss since the middle of the twentieth century and has recently become the focus of regeneration projects.

Inspired by civic optimism, a coalition of neighborhood groups sought a transformative intervention to reinvigorate this underused zone, which was surrounded by neglected spaces, empty storefronts, abandoned industrial sites, and streets with poorly planned traffic-circulation patterns. In progress for six years, the project was supported by a coalition of public and private partnerships, as well as government officials and public and private organizations. The Brady Street bus shelter serves as a waiting station for city bus passengers, bicyclists, and pedestrians and marks the gateway between lively Brady Street and the new Urban Plaza and Marsupial Bridge. Completed in early 2006, the Urban Plaza transformed a previously unsafe area under the bridge into a civic gathering space for film festivals and a place to view regattas and other river events. The position of the Urban Plaza within the existing viaduct presented an unusual challenge due to the lack of sufficient natural daylight to support plant growth. Because the plaza could not be defined through landscape design in the traditional sense, concrete benches are set amidst a moonscape of gravel and seating boulders that provide a respite for pedestrians and bicyclists as they make their way across the Marsupial Bridge. By night the benches are lit from within, transforming the illuminated plaza into a beacon for the neighborhood. This strategy provides an urban alternative to traditional public spaces, such as town squares and village greens, and a site-specific program for the under-bridge zone.

Also completed in early 2006, the Marsupial Bridge uses the existing structure of the Holton Street Viaduct as its host. The viaduct was originally engineered to support trolley cars, a transportation system abandoned with increased automobile use in the early 1900s. The Marsupial Bridge hangs opportunistically from the middle third of the viaduct, responding to the city's need for a greater number of pedestrian and bicycle routes. The bridge appropriates the unused space beneath the viaduct, encourages the use of alternative forms of transportation, and connects residential neighborhoods on either side of it to the river, downtown Milwaukee, and the Brady Street commercial district. Inspired by the notion of weaving a new spine through the existing structure, the Marsupial Bridge's undulating concrete deck offers a dynamic counterpoint to the steel frame of the viaduct. Recalling the wood docks along the Milwaukee River, formerly an industrial corridor linking the northern territories with the Great Lakes, the concrete deck is overlaid with a wood-deck surface, handrails, stainless-steel stanchions, and a diaphanous apron with floor lighting. Precision theatrical fixtures are mounted above the deck to create a localized ribbon of illumination, with minimal spillover into the riparian landscape below.

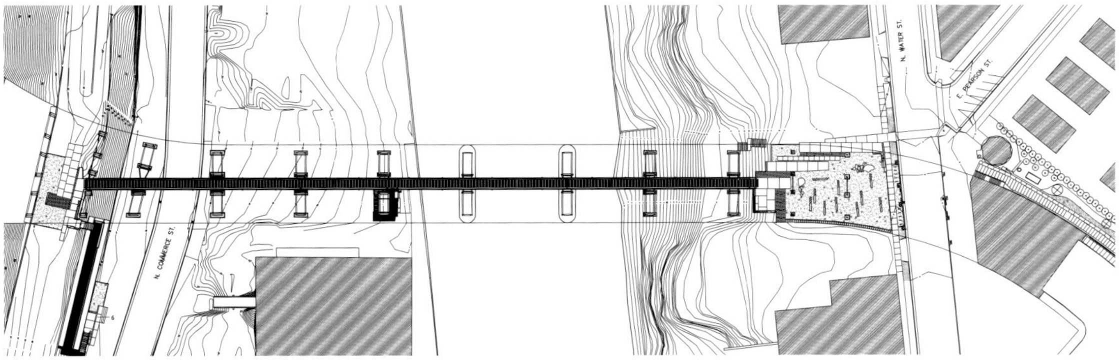

This page
Site plan

Opposite
Top: View northeast
Bottom: View northwest

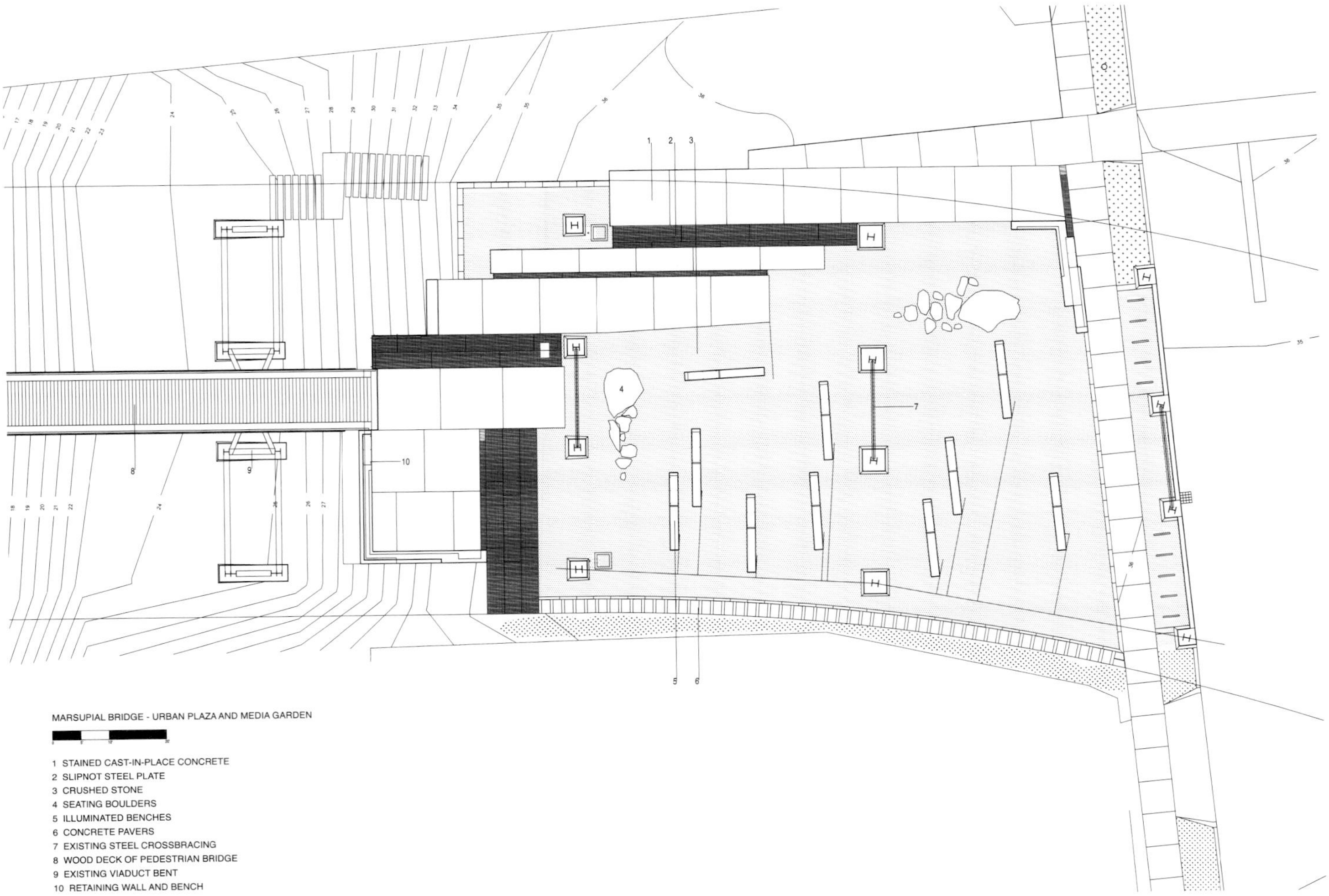

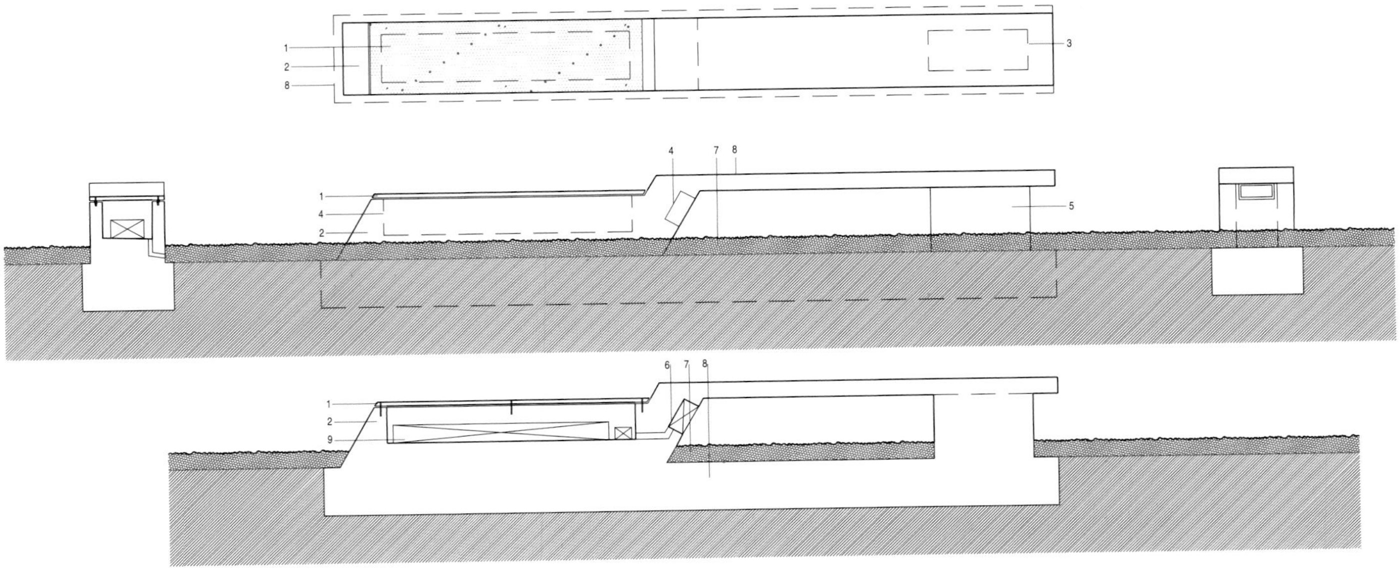

This page
Top: Media Garden plan
Bottom: Illuminated bench details

Opposite
Top: Media Garden, night view northwest
Middle: Media Garden, night view north
Bottom: Cinema

This page
Top: Section
Middle: Bridge, view to North Water Street (left); bridge deck views from above
Bottom: Bridge deck, night view (left); bridge deck, lighting detail

Opposite
Top: Handrail at expansion joint, exterior elevation (left); typical handrail, interior elevation
Middle: Handrail at expansion joint, interior elevation (left); typical handrail, exterior elevation
Bottom: Steel and wood handrail, section (left); steel and wood handrail, plan sections

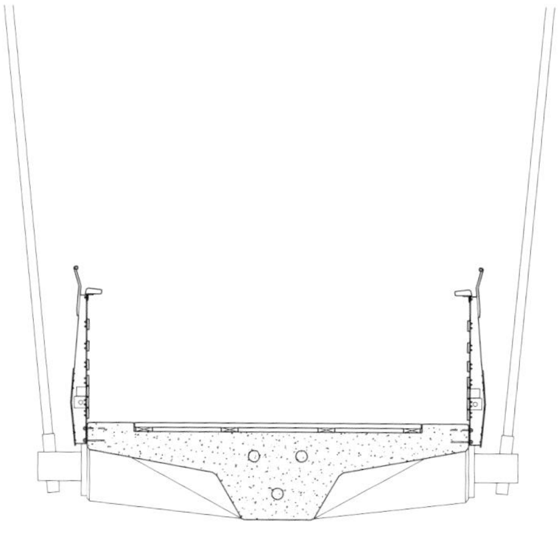

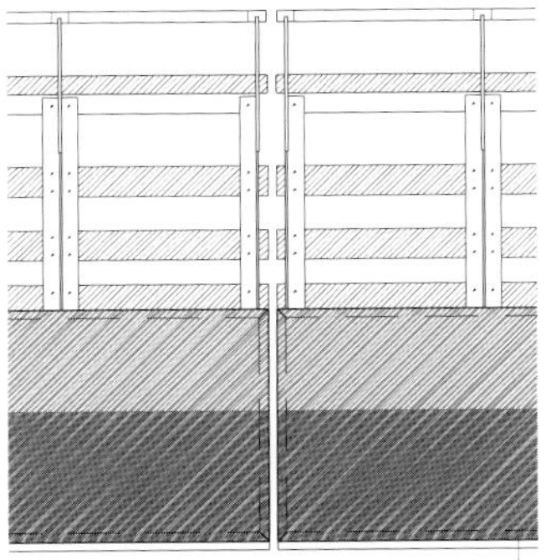

HANDRAIL @ EXPANSION JOINT - EXTERIOR ELEVATION

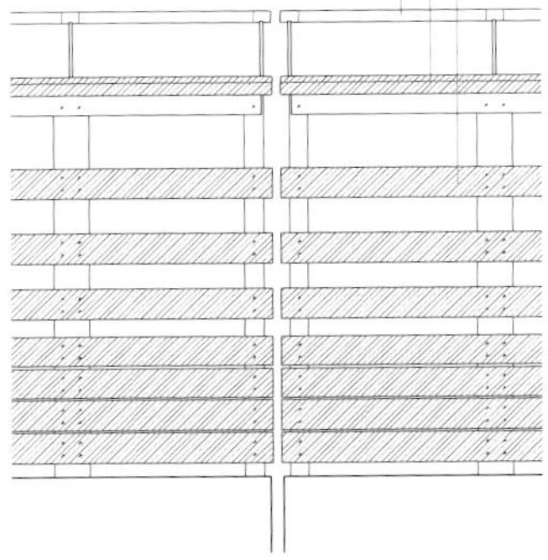

HANDRAIL @ EXPANSION JOINT - INTERIOR ELEVATION

1 STAINLESS-STEEL PERFORATED METAL PANEL
2 STAINLESS-STEEL TUBE
3 MAHOGANY HANDRAIL
4 MAHOGANY SIDING

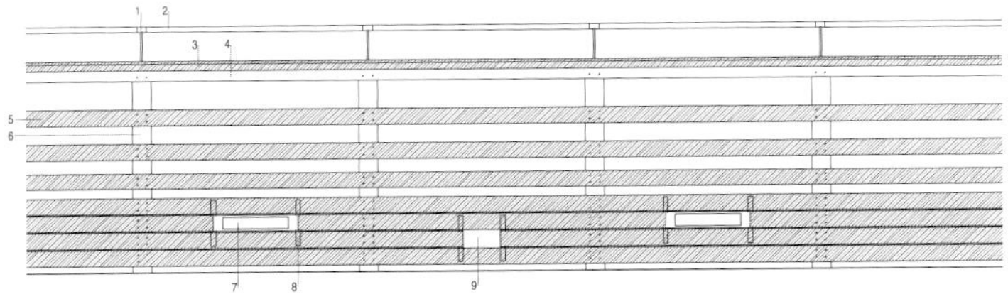

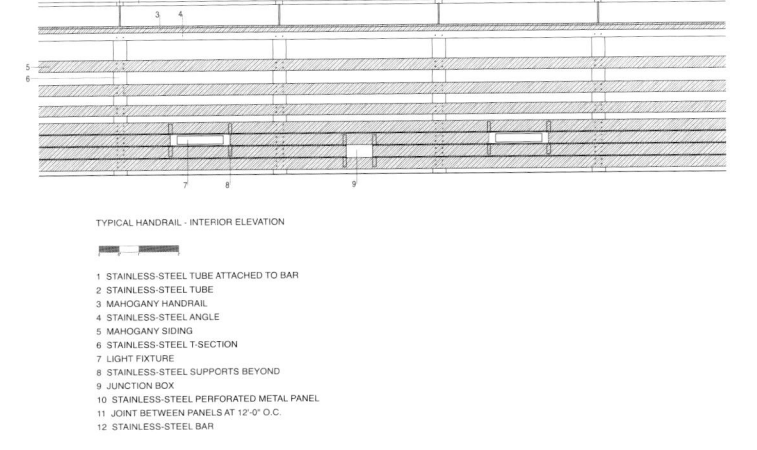

TYPICAL HANDRAIL - INTERIOR ELEVATION

1 STAINLESS-STEEL TUBE ATTACHED TO BAR
2 STAINLESS-STEEL TUBE
3 MAHOGANY HANDRAIL
4 STAINLESS-STEEL ANGLE
5 MAHOGANY SIDING
6 STAINLESS-STEEL T-SECTION
7 LIGHT FIXTURE
8 STAINLESS-STEEL SUPPORTS BEYOND
9 JUNCTION BOX
10 STAINLESS-STEEL PERFORATED METAL PANEL
11 JOINT BETWEEN PANELS AT 12'-0" O.C.
12 STAINLESS-STEEL BAR

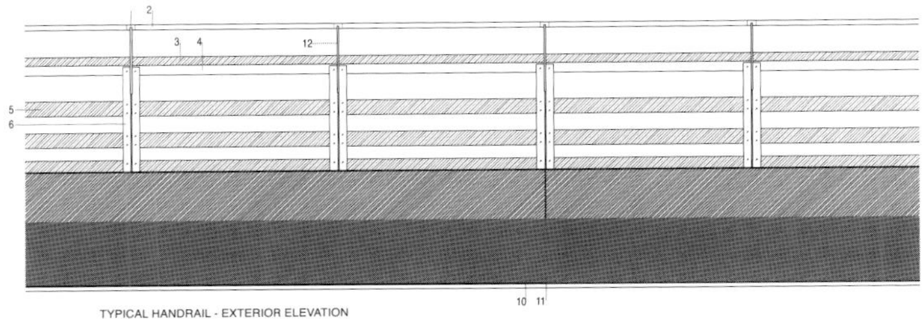

TYPICAL HANDRAIL - EXTERIOR ELEVATION

1 STAINLESS-STEEL TUBE ATTACHED TO BAR
2 STAINLESS-STEEL TUBE
3 MAHOGANY HANDRAIL
4 STAINLESS-STEEL ANGLE
5 MAHOGANY SIDING
6 STAINLESS-STEEL T-SECTION
7 LIGHT FIXTURE
8 STAINLESS-STEEL SUPPORTS BEYOND
9 JUNCTION BOX
10 STAINLESS-STEEL PERFORATED METAL PANEL
11 JOINT BETWEEN PANELS AT 12'-0" O.C.
12 STAINLESS-STEEL BAR

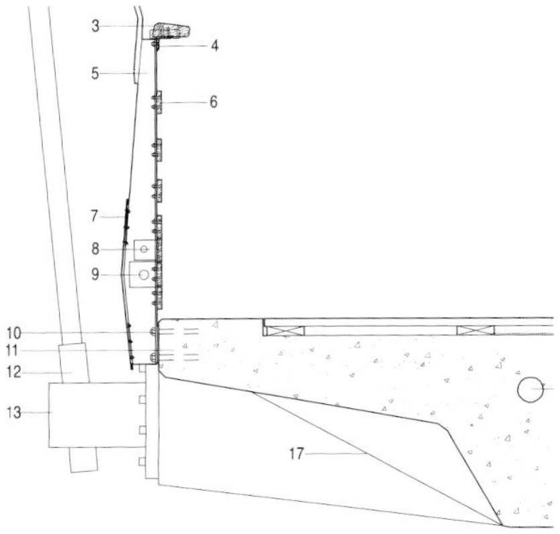

STEEL AND WOOD HANDRAIL SECTION

1 STAINLESS-STEEL TUBE
2 STAINLESS-STEEL BAR
3 MAHOGANY HANDRAIL
4 STAINLESS-STEEL ANGLE
5 STAINLESS-STEEL POST
6 MAHOGANY SIDING
7 STAINLESS-STEEL PERFORATED METAL PANEL
8 JUNCTION BOX
9 LIGHT FIXTURE
10 ANCHOR BOLT
11 POURED CONCRETE SPINE
12 STAINLESS-STEEL CABLE
13 CABLE CONNECTION
14 IRONWOOD DECKING
15 PRESSURE TREATED WOOD SLEEPERS
16 POST TENSIONING DUCT
17 FOLD IN CONCRETE

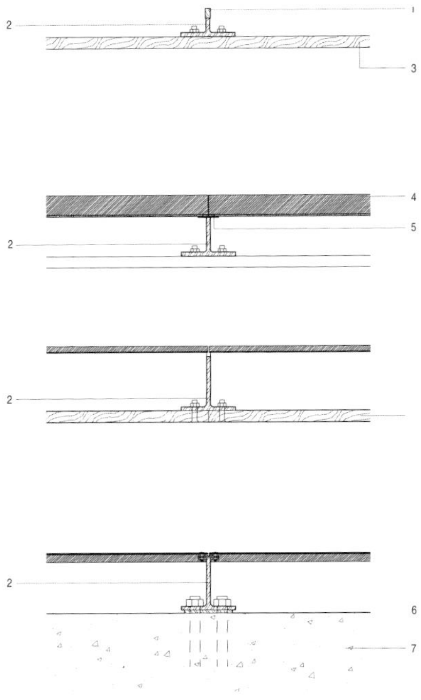

STEEL AND WOOD HANDRAIL - PLAN SECTION

1 STAINLESS-STEEL BAR WELDED TO POST
2 STAINLESS-STEEL T-SECTION POST
3 WOOD RAILING
4 STAINLESS-STEEL PERFORATED METAL PANEL
5 STAINLESS-STEEL ATTACHMENT TAB
6 STAINLESS-STEEL SPACER
7 POUREC CONCRETE BRIDGE DECK

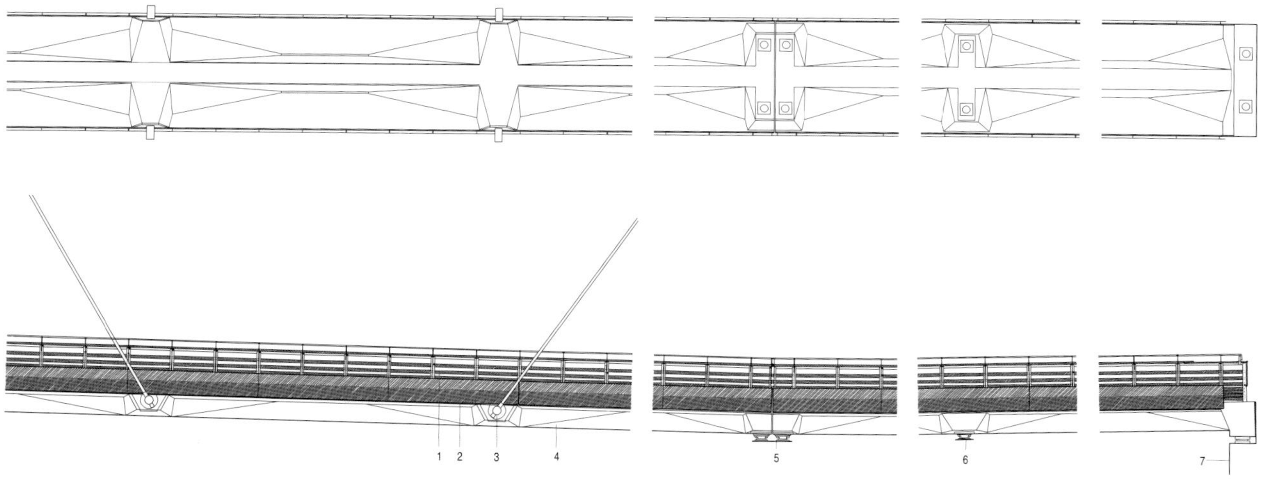

PEDESTRIAN BRIDGE UNDERSIDE AND ELEVATION

1 WOOD INTERIOR RAILING SYSTEM
2 STAINLESS-STEEL PERFORATED METAL PANEL
3 CABLE CONNECTION
4 POURED CONCRETE DECK
5 DOUBLE BEATING POINT AT EXPANSION JOINT
6 SINGLE BEARING POINT
7 POURED CONCRETE ABUTMENT

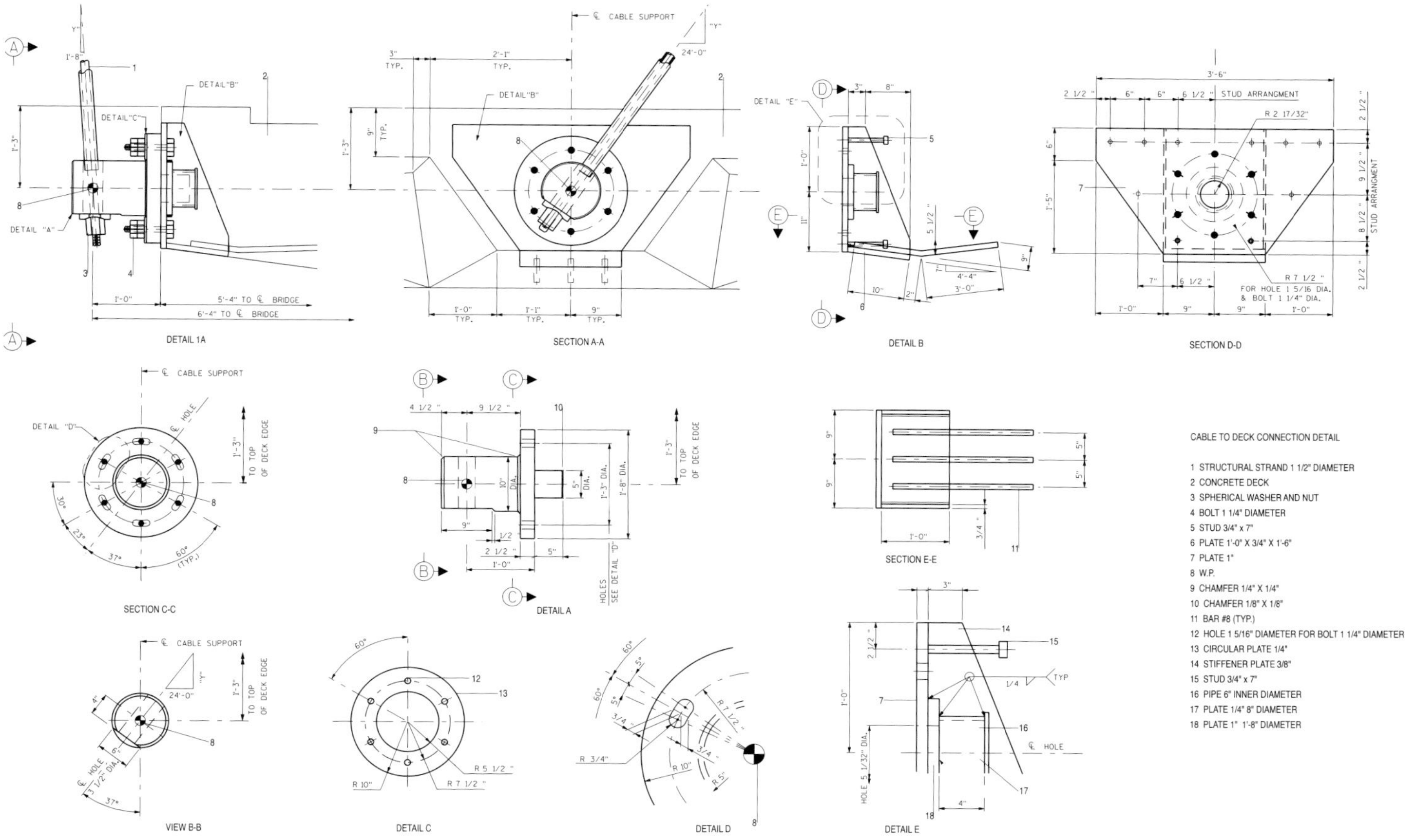

CABLE TO DECK CONNECTION DETAIL

1 STRUCTURAL STRAND 1 1/2" DIAMETER
2 CONCRETE DECK
3 SPHERICAL WASHER AND NUT
4 BOLT 1 1/4" DIAMETER
5 STUD 3/4" x 7"
6 PLATE 1'-0" X 3/4" X 1'-6"
7 PLATE 1"
8 W.P.
9 CHAMFER 1/4" X 1/4"
10 CHAMFER 1/8" X 1/8"
11 BAR #8 (TYP.)
12 HOLE 1 5/16" DIAMETER FOR BOLT 1 1/4" DIAMETER
13 CIRCULAR PLATE 1/4"
14 STIFFENER PLATE 3/8"
15 STUD 3/4" x 7"
16 PIPE 6" INNER DIAMETER
17 PLATE 1/4" 8" DIAMETER
18 PLATE 1" 1'-8" DIAMETER

This page
Top: Bridge-deck soffit
Middle: Elevation
Bottom: Cable-to-deck-connection details

Opposite
Top: Analogous forms
Middle: Bridge soffit (left); cable-to-deck connection
Bottom: Deck detail from above (left); cable-to-deck-connection detail

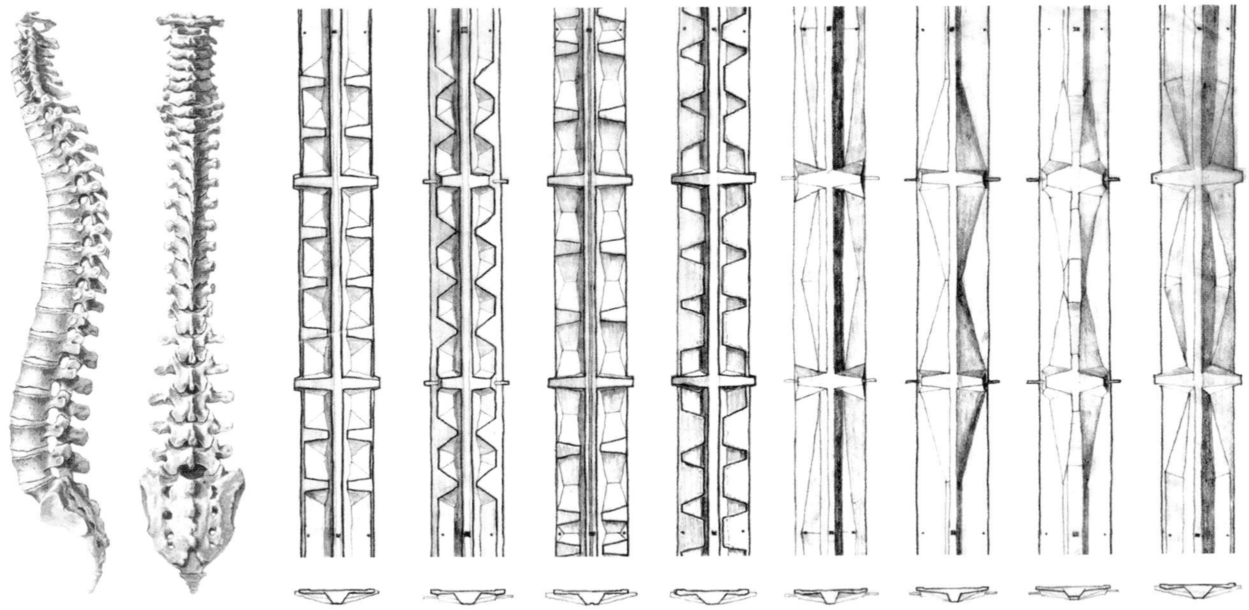

Desert House Prototype, Desert Hot Springs, California
Marmol Radziner Prefab, Los Angeles, California

Located on a hilly 5-acre site in Desert Hot Springs, the Desert House was designed as a prototype for Marmol Radziner Prefab, a company that produces a system of custom-designed houses built with prefabrication technologies. The buildings consist of steel-frame house modules and covered-deck modules, each 12 feet wide, 13 feet high, and up to 55 feet long. The cladding can be metal, wood, or glass (the deck modules have no cladding at all), with options for exterior and interior finishes, appliances, and kitchen and bathroom fixtures. The objective of the Marmol Radziner prefab system is to create finished volumetric modules that can ship to any site, with preinstalled finishes, floors, countertops, appliances, windows, and doors that can be fully installed within a year after an order has been placed and the design and fabrication process has begun.

Desert House comprises four house modules with a total of 4,550 square feet—2,100 interior square feet and six deck modules with 2,450 square feet of covered exterior space—all delivered on specialized trailers and lowered into place with a mobile crane, then bolted together. Both the house modules and covered decks are mounted on a recessed concrete foundation, which creates the illusion that they float above the desert floor; insertion of a rubber membrane between the metal cladding and wood-lined interior creates a thermal barrier.

The hallway from the entry separates the master bedroom from the kitchen-dining-living space, which opens onto a covered terrace and pool. A separate walkway leads to a rectangular unit, perpendicular to the main house, containing the guest bedroom and a detached studio. The L-shaped plan of the house creates a protected exterior environment that includes a pool, fire pit, and detached prefab carport. Large areas of glazing open onto panoramic vistas of desert and mountains.

The Desert House derives 100 percent of its power from solar panels. In colder months, the concrete floor provides a large area of thermal mass that absorbs solar radiation during the day and releases it gradually at night. Sunshade modules on the south and west facades minimize the impact of the harsh summer sun.

Marmol Radziner Prefab occupies its own 60,000-square-foot factory in Vernon, California, with three assembly lines for prefab modules. Cabinet, metal, and window-and-door shops are all located within the factory. Structural steel components for the modules, sheet metal for flashings, roofs, and door frames, plus posts and beams that provide structural support and create rigid structural frames, are all manufactured in the metal shop. For each module, steel floor frames are welded together, then steel columns are added. The roof frame is welded separately and lifted on top of the columns. Once the steel frame is set, the interior wall framing, plumbing, and electrical and mechanical components are completed, and finishes, cabinetry, appliances, and fixtures installed. Finally, the module is shrink-wrapped for delivery.

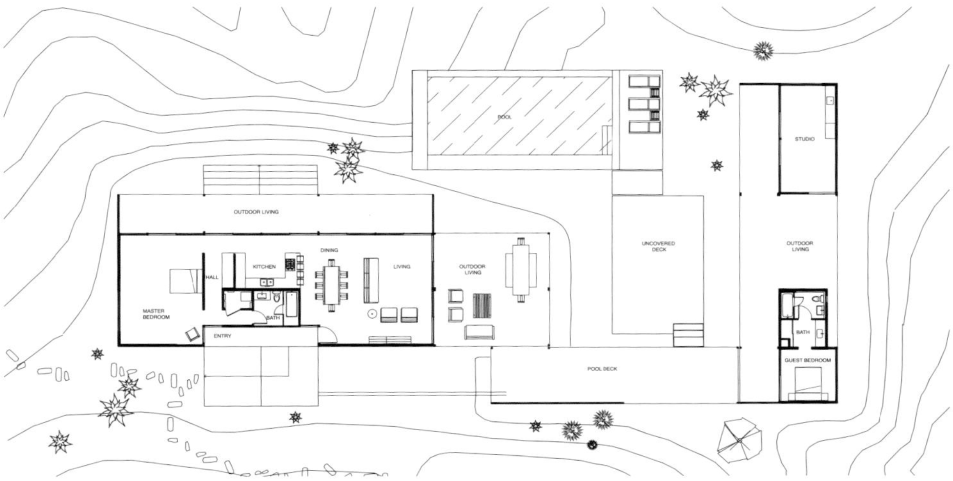

This Page
Plan

Opposite
Top: West elevation
Bottom: Outdoor living modules

This page
Left (top to bottom): Factory; fabrication; structure; transport
Right (top to bottom): assembly; prepared foundation; installation

Opposite
Top: Outdoor living space
Bottom: View north to studio

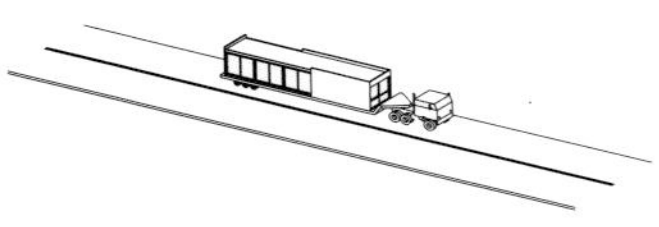
Good truck access to your site makes delivery easy.

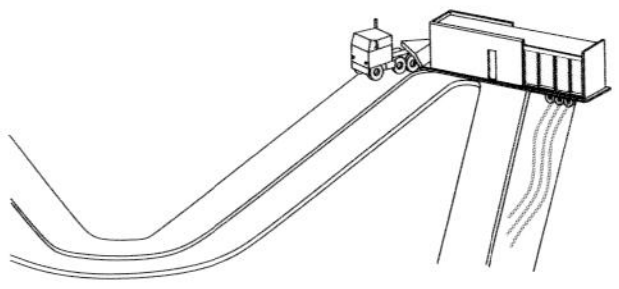
Tight turns and hills can pose delivery problems.

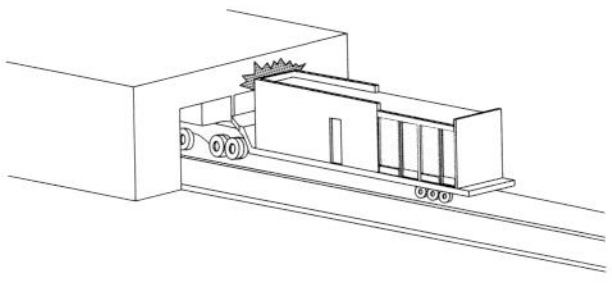
The route to your site must be approved to ensure adequate overhead clearances.

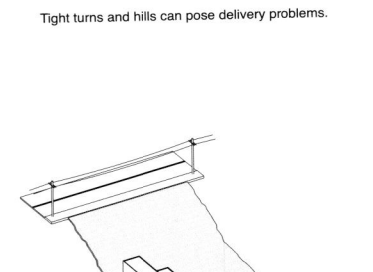

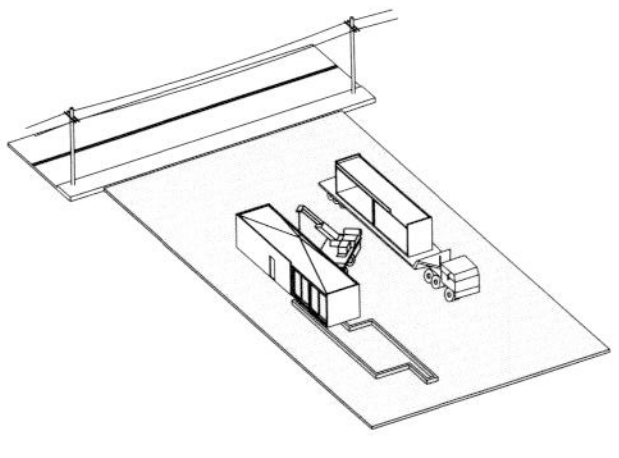
Ideally your site will have a flat lot with a simple foundation and a flat staging area for the crane.

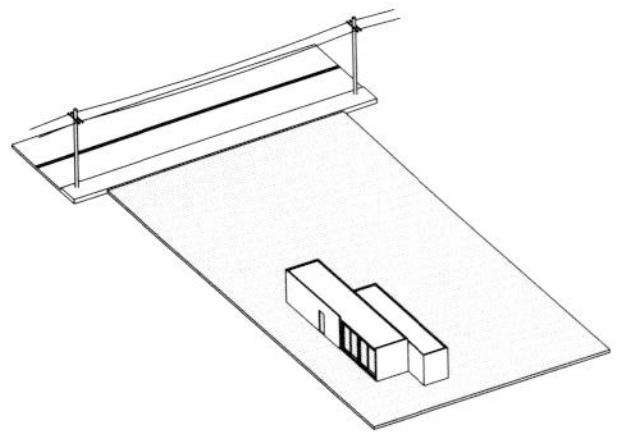
The crane and trucks must be able to fit under any power lines.

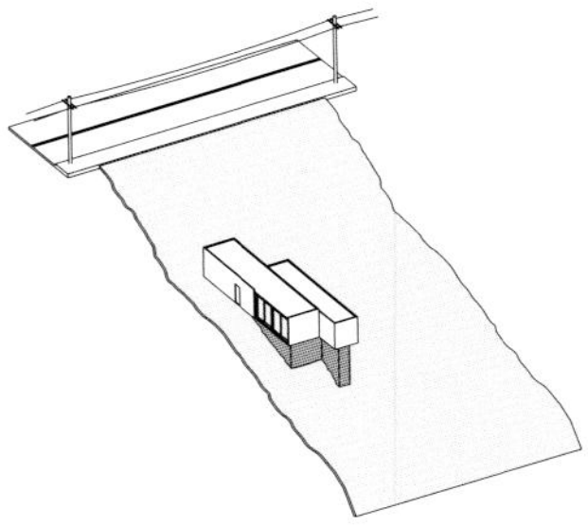
Steep slopes complicate foundation design and construction.

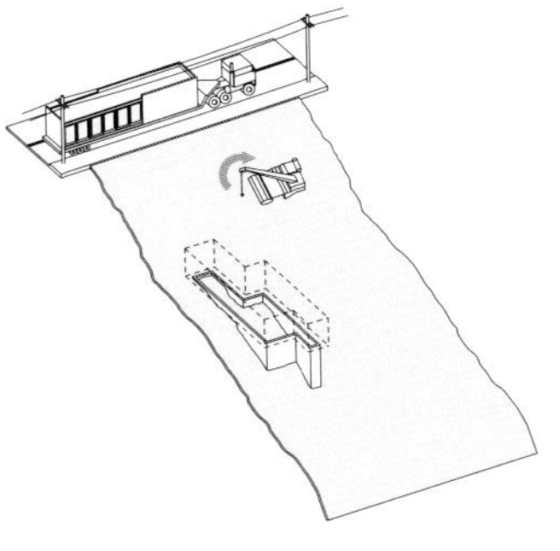
A flat staging area is necessary for the crane to lift the modules off the truck and onto your foundation.

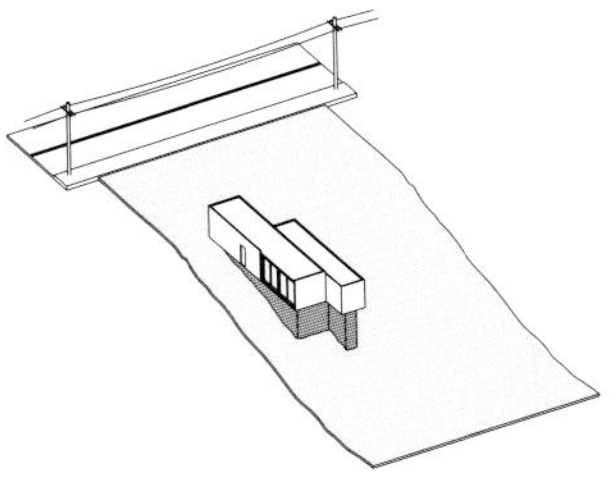
Sloped sites are most manageable if there is a flat area for the crane adjacent to the nearest road.

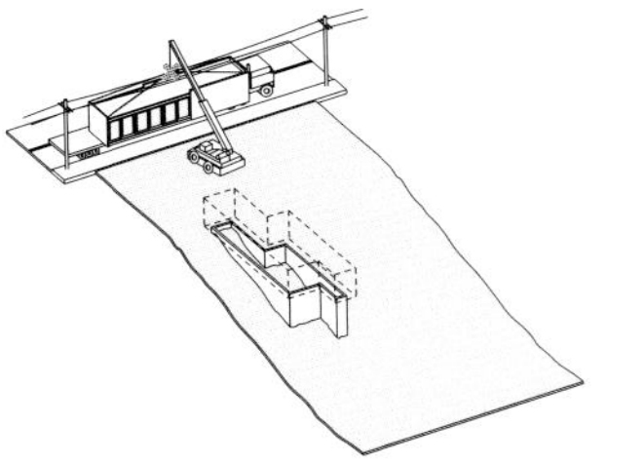
The road can serve as a staging area if power lines will not obstruct the crane's movement.

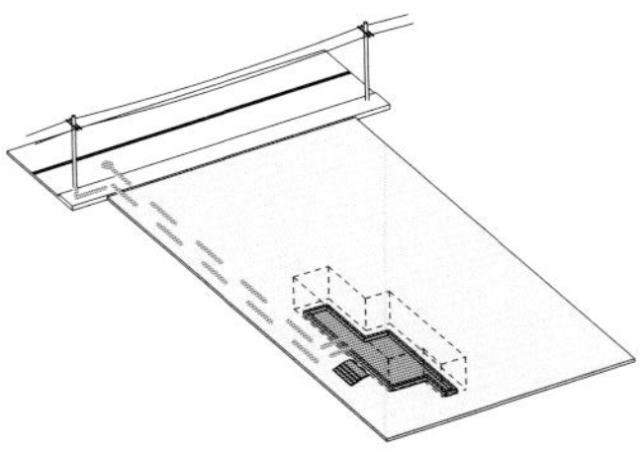
A foundation, utility hook-ups, and entry sequence will need to be designed.

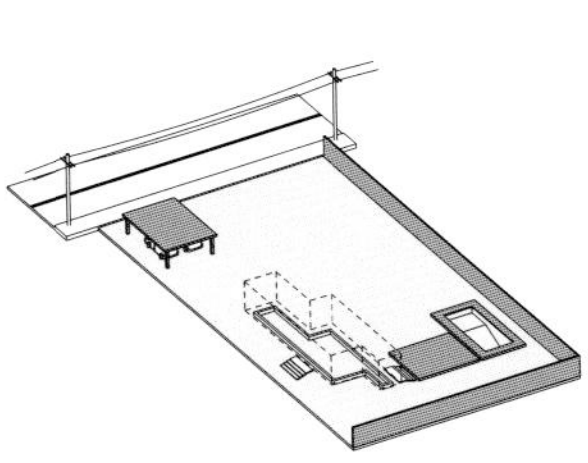
Site features such as a pool, hardscape, fences, walls, landscape, or a carport can be added.

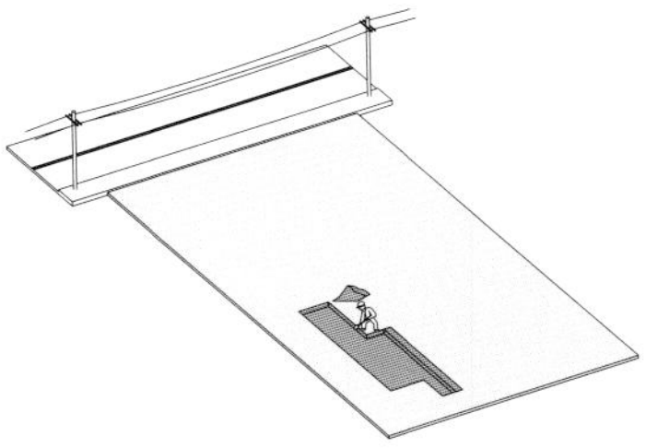
After the foundation is built and the site prepared, the crane and modules can be delivered.

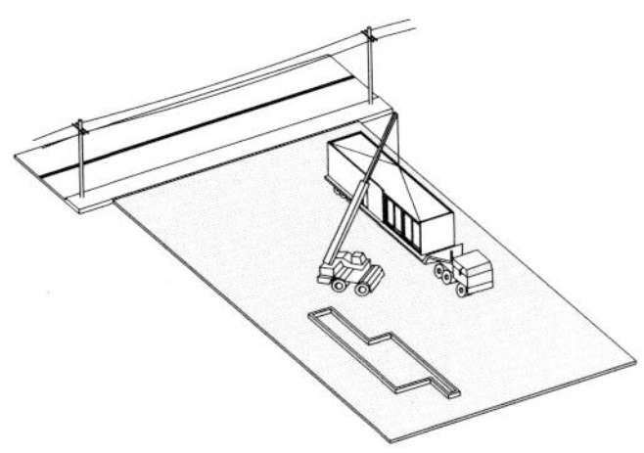
The crane lifts the first module from the delivery truck and places it in its proper location.

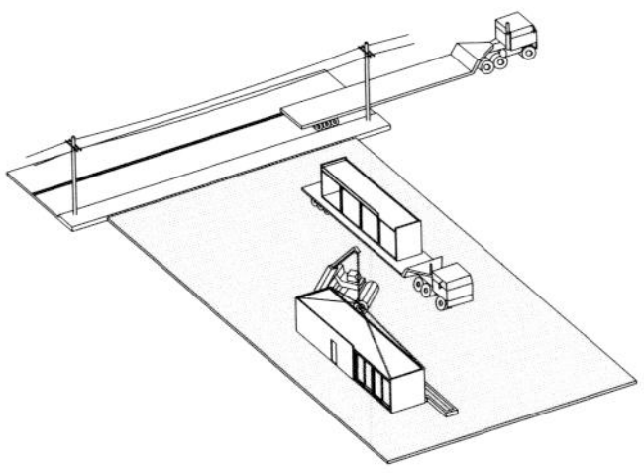
The module is then set and connected to its foundation.

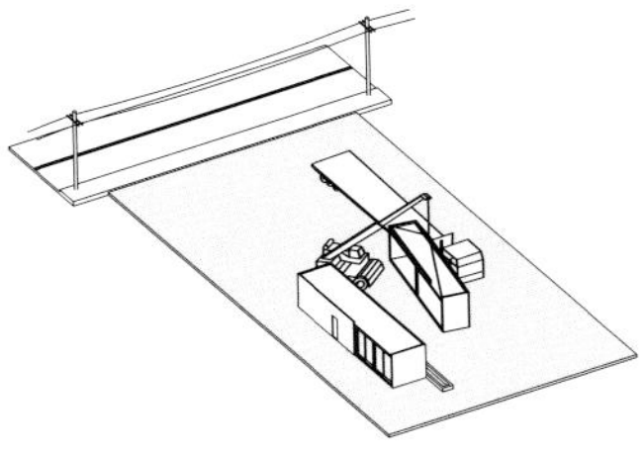
Trucks pull onto the site one at a time for module delivery and placement.

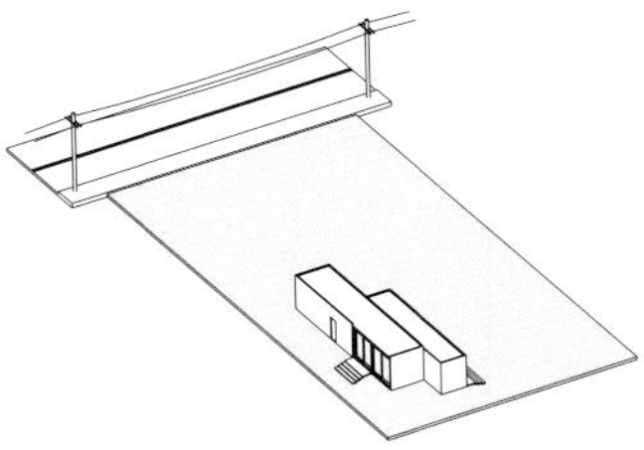
The utilities are then hooked up, and floor, wall, and roof joints sealed where the modules connect.

This page
Building a prefab house

Opposite
Top: View west
Bottom: Outdoor and indoor living space

Pedestrian Bridge, Austin, Texas
Miró Rivera Architects, Austin

Located on a densely vegetated site on Lake Austin, the pedestrian bridge connects the main house on the property with a newly constructed guesthouse surrounded by reed-covered wetlands that provide a stop for migrating egrets, cranes, and swans. The development of the project included a comprehensive analysis of the existing vegetation and wildlife to implement a ten-year plan that will eliminate invasive plants, reintroduce native species, and restore and expand the wetlands.

With a design inspired by the reeds that cover the shores of the lake, with rebar segments that intertwine with the reeds, the footbridge is a light, maintenance-free structure integrated into its wetland setting. The rebar serves as deck and railing material at the abutments and over the length of the bridge, camouflaging it and transforming it into a nearly invisible link.

The bridge is composed of three elements. Superstructure: The arch, which spans 100 feet with a main span of 80 feet, is composed of five nested 5-inch-diameter pipes that diverge between the spring-point of the main span and the abutment at the beginning of the bridge. Decking and railing: The pipes support 1/2-inch-diameter bars, which become both decking and guardrail with a simple field bend from horizontal to vertical. The irregular lengths and close spacing of the bars mimic the native reeds on the site, and the thin profile of the superstructure appears even thinner when viewed through the veil of reeds. The handrail consists of a rope secured with steel-wire rings to a 1-inch horizontal tube welded to the vertical bars. Abutments: Native stone slabs are layered vertically to create ramps at the abutments. Deep raked joints re-create the texture of the deck and railings. To further integrate the bridge with its natural setting, the steel, rope handrails, and stone ramps have been left to weather naturally.

This page
Top: Elevation
Bottom: Plan

Opposite
View east

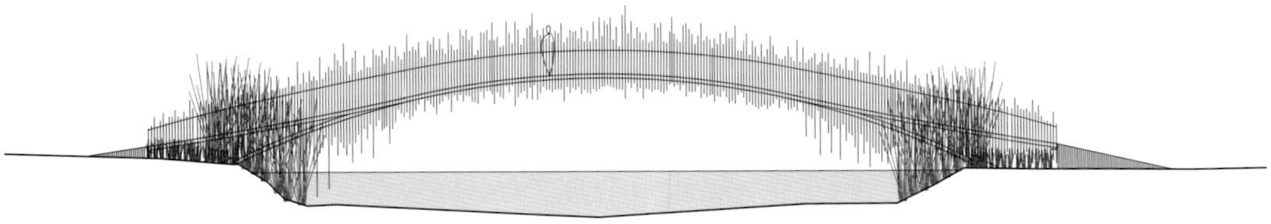

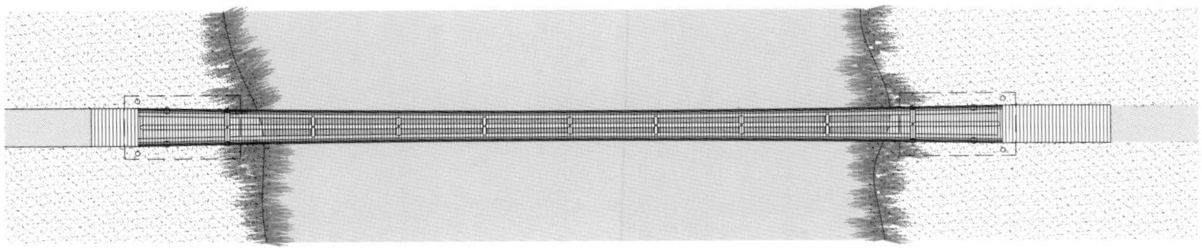

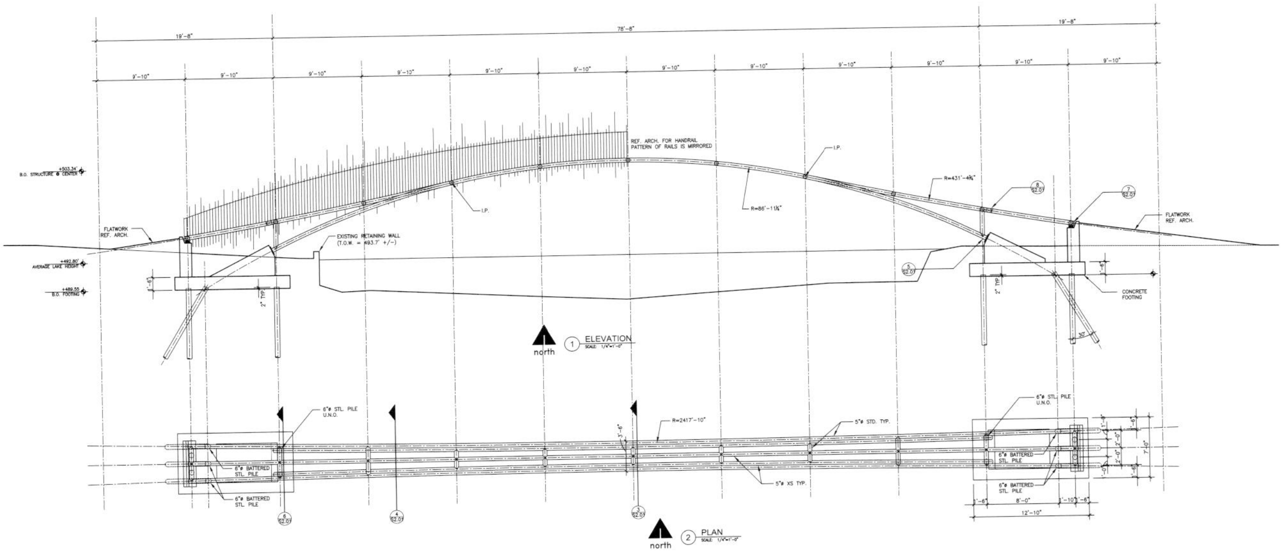
ELEVATION
north
PLAN
north
EXISTING RETAINING WALL
CONCRETE FOOTING
FLATWORK REF. ARCH.
REF. ARCH. FOR HANDRAIL. PATTERN OF RAILS IS MIRRORED

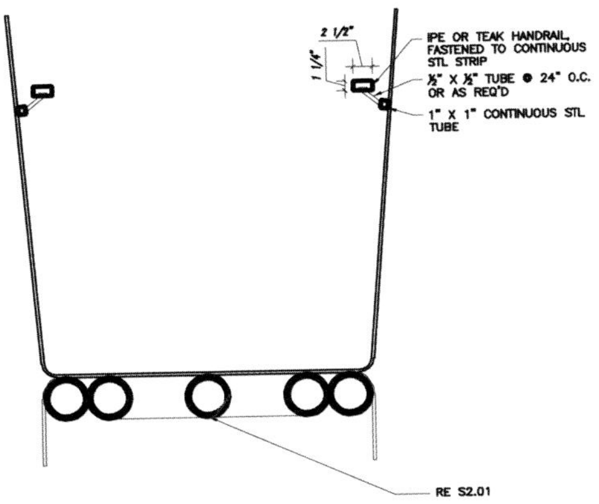
2 1/2"
1 1/4"
IPE OR TEAK HANDRAIL, FASTENED TO CONTINUOUS STL STRIP
½" X ½" TUBE @ 24" O.C. OR AS REQ'D
1" X 1" CONTINUOUS STL TUBE
RE S2.01

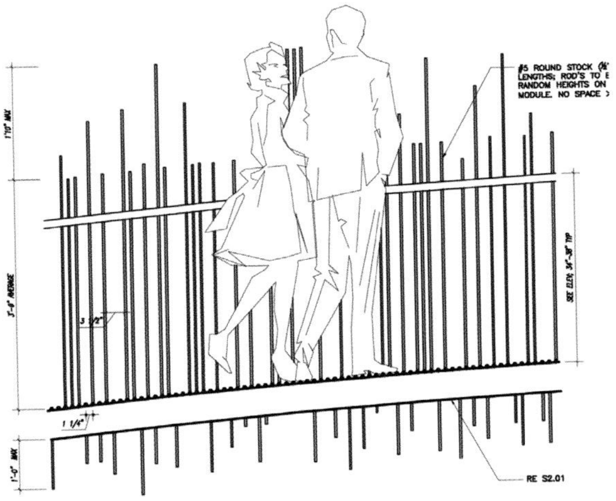
1'10" MAX
3'-6" AVERAGE
1'-0" MAX
3 1/2"
1 1/4"
RE S2.01

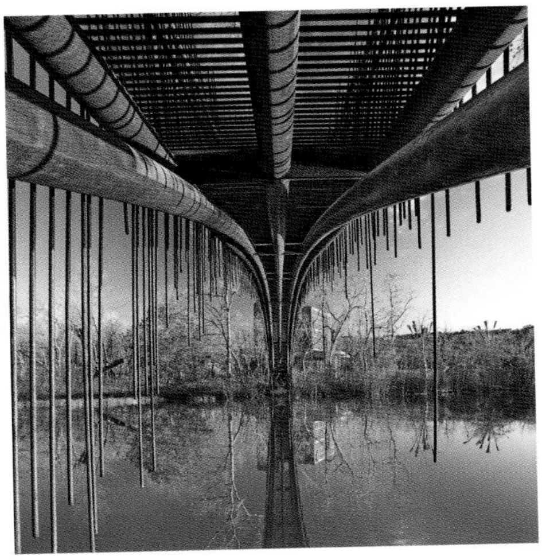

Opposite
Top row: Section mockup and construction
Middle: Structure (above); cross-section detail (below left); longitudinal-section detail
Bottom (left to right): Partial elevation; bridge-deck soffit; detail with existing retaining wall

This page
Top: Structural details
Bottom: Elevation

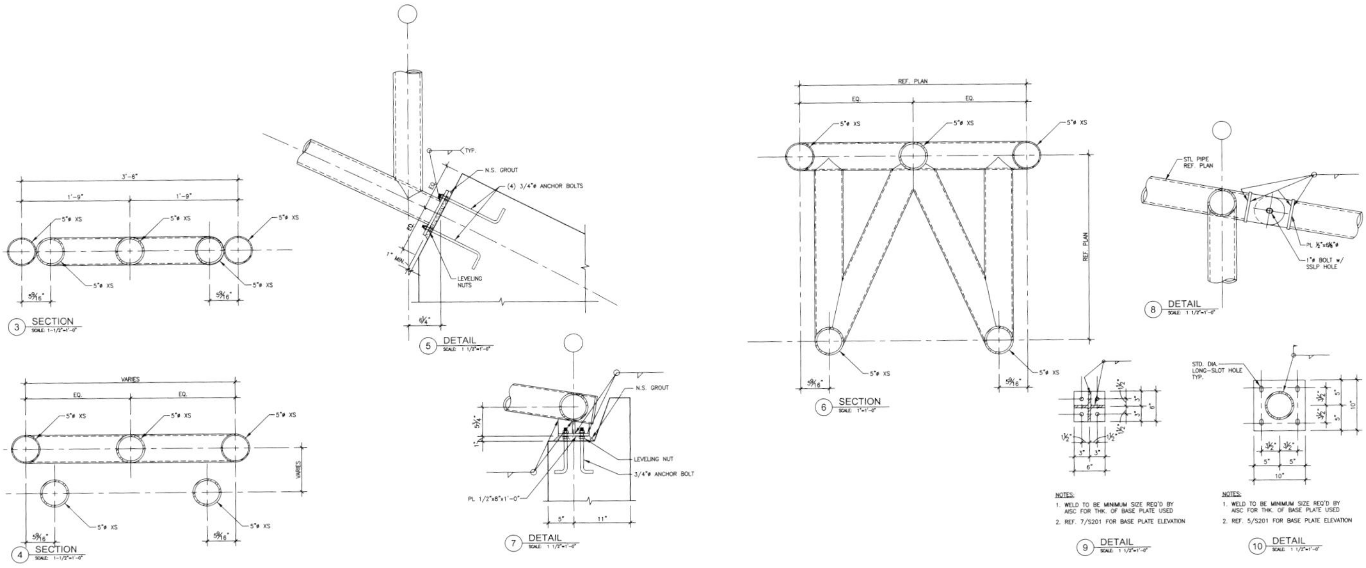

University of Cincinnati Campus Recreation Center, Cincinnati, Ohio

Morphosis, Santa Monica, California
KZF Design, Cincinnati

The original plans for the Campus Recreation Center proposed a single building for student recreation, but both the University of Cincinnati and Morphosis realized that the chosen site presented a larger opportunity. Eventually the size of the project nearly doubled to 350,000 square feet, and the recreation center became a complex of five buildings: a sports center, residence hall, academic building, food hall, and campus store. The architects have described the recreation center as connective tissue composed of background buildings, rather than an object building, woven into the campus fabric by adjacent, overlapping, and overlooking functions and programs. Intertwined strands of pedestrian paths penetrate and wrap around the various buildings—weaving together layers of site and function—before converging at Main Street, the primary pedestrian route through the campus. Many of the activity spaces in the complex are connected by sightlines or separated by walls of glass, emblematic of the transparency and openness intrinsic to university life; the emphasis on visual connections through openings and glazed surfaces promotes the values of communication and free exchange.

In the center of complex, beneath a sloping barrel-vaulted roof, the 200,000-square-foot sports center is built on a dramatically sloping site where it is possible to enter and exit the building at elevations that differ by more than 20 feet. The sports center responds to the various edge conditions of the surrounding site and wraps a variety of program and activity spaces around one another. On the east side of the Marche, or food hall, a 30-foot-high curtain wall overlooks the 36,000-square-foot gymnasium, divided into six spaces, each the size of a basketball court. Around its perimeter, a four-lane 1/8-mile running track, 37 feet above the floor, overlooks the gymnasium. The concrete-slab-on-metal-deck running track is cantilevered from perimeter columns and suspended at the east and west ends from the roof structure, seven three-dimensional box trusses with depths that vary continuously along their spans to fit within the truss volumes that are the principal architectural elements of the gymnasium space. Thirty-five apertures of various shapes and sizes—from large ovals to small circles—are punched through the roof. In areas where the roof extends over an exterior plaza, the apertures are open holes, over interior spaces, skylights.

Morphosis and THP Limited contributed to this text.

Opposite
Lecture hall wing with sunscreen

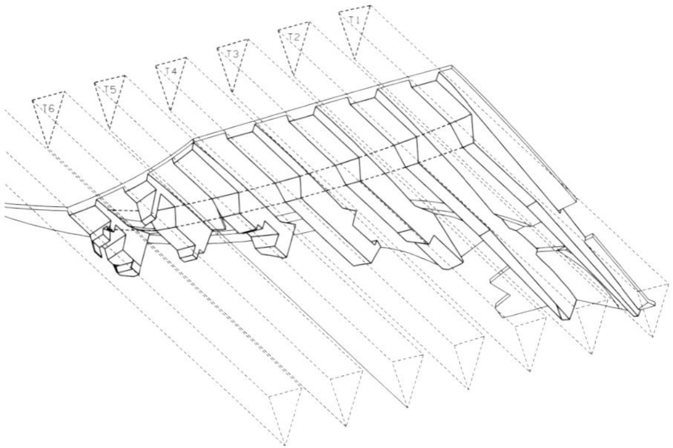
T1
T2
T3
T5
T6

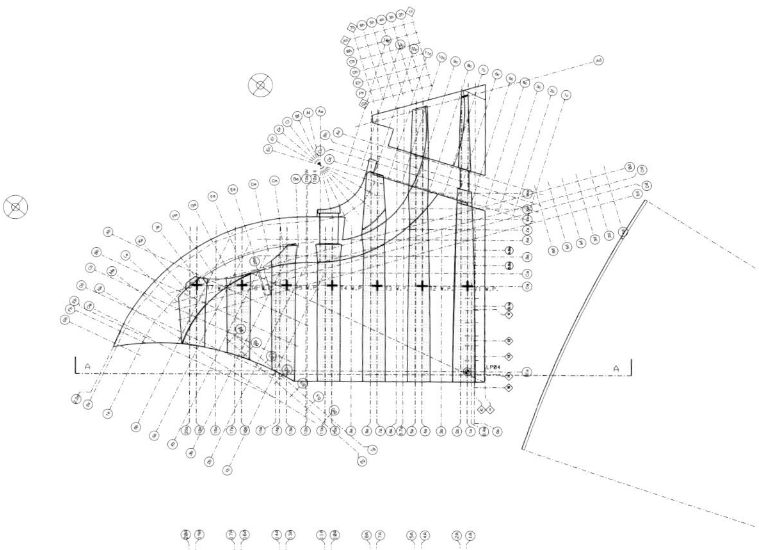
A
A

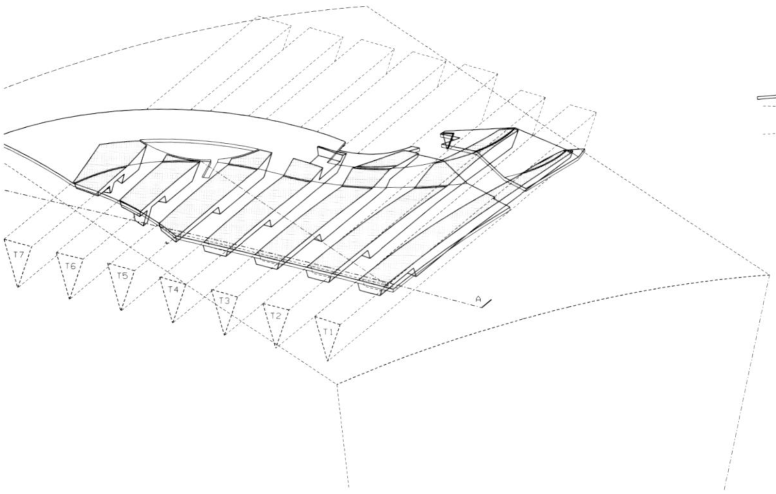
T7
T6
T5
T4
T3
T2
T1
A

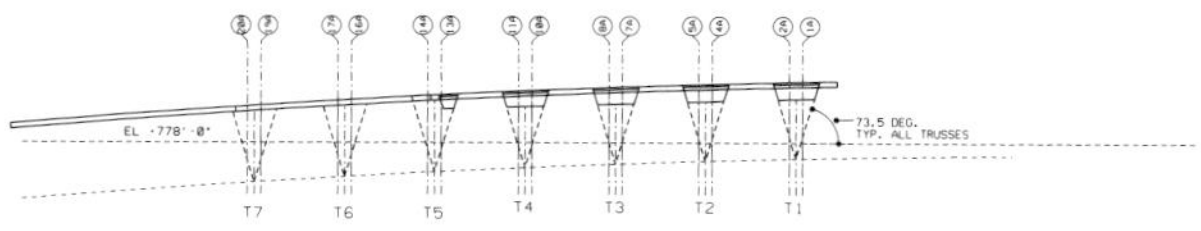
EL -778' 0"
73.5 DEG.
TYP. ALL TRUSSES
T7
T6
T5
T4
T3
T2
T1

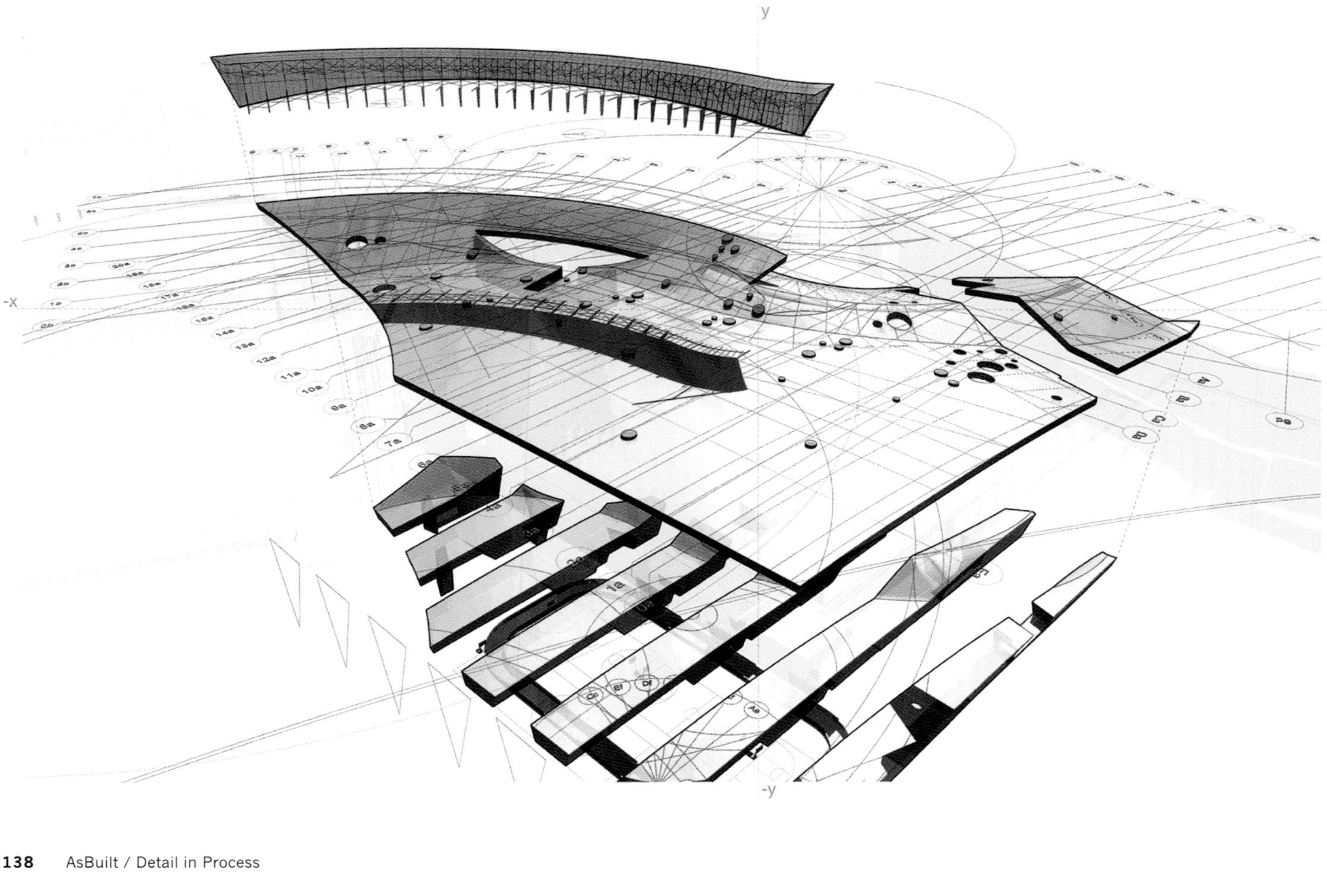
y
-x
x
-y

Opposite
Top: Truss diagrams
Bottom: Components diagram

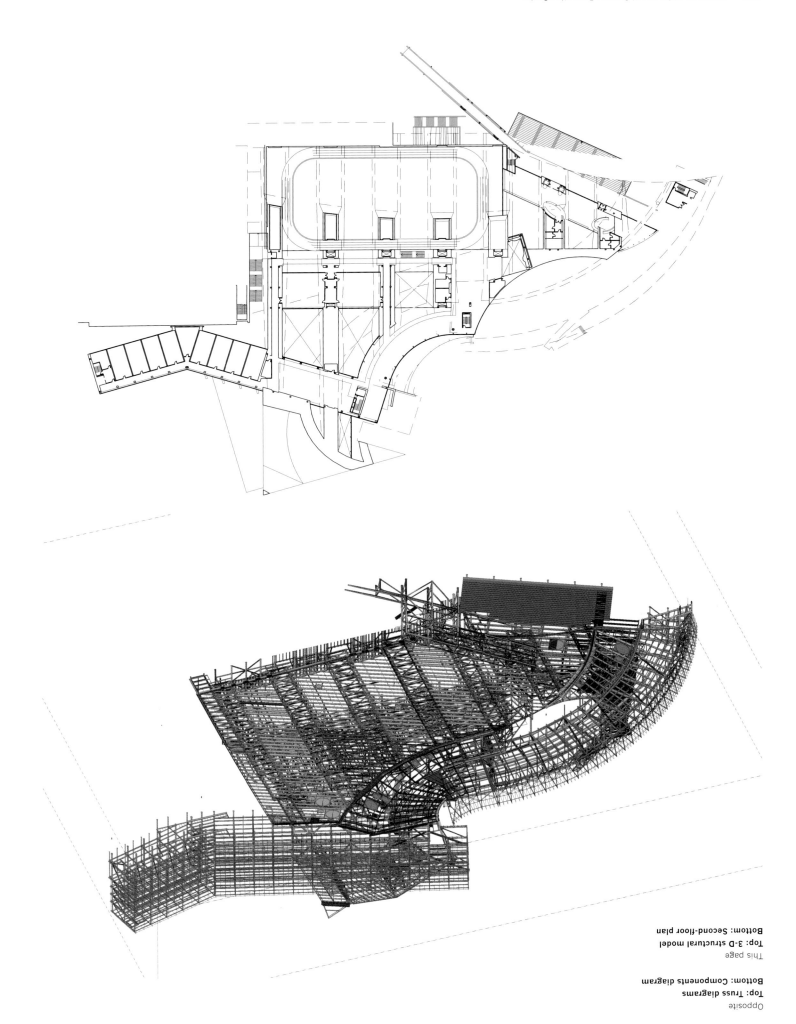

This page
Top: 3-D structural model
Bottom: Second-floor plan

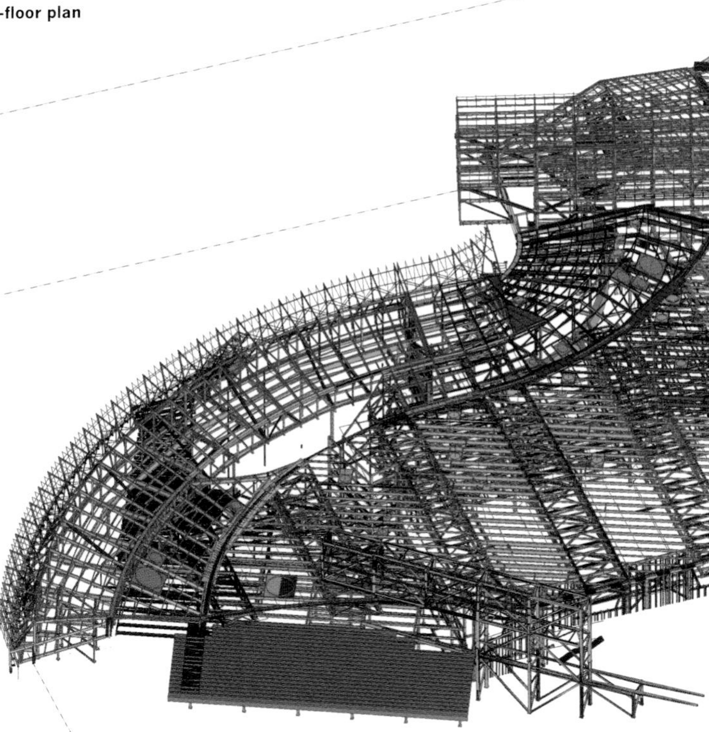

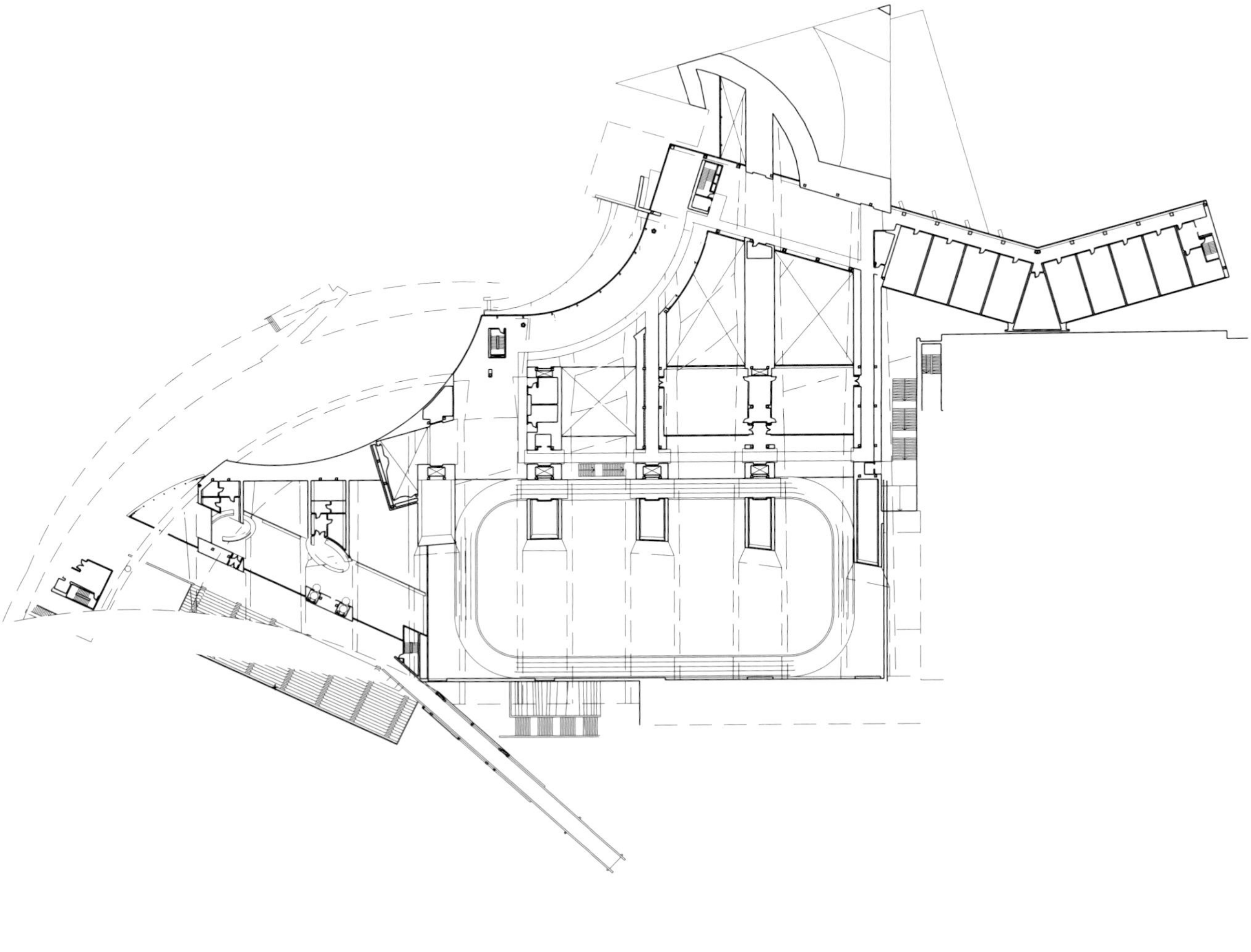

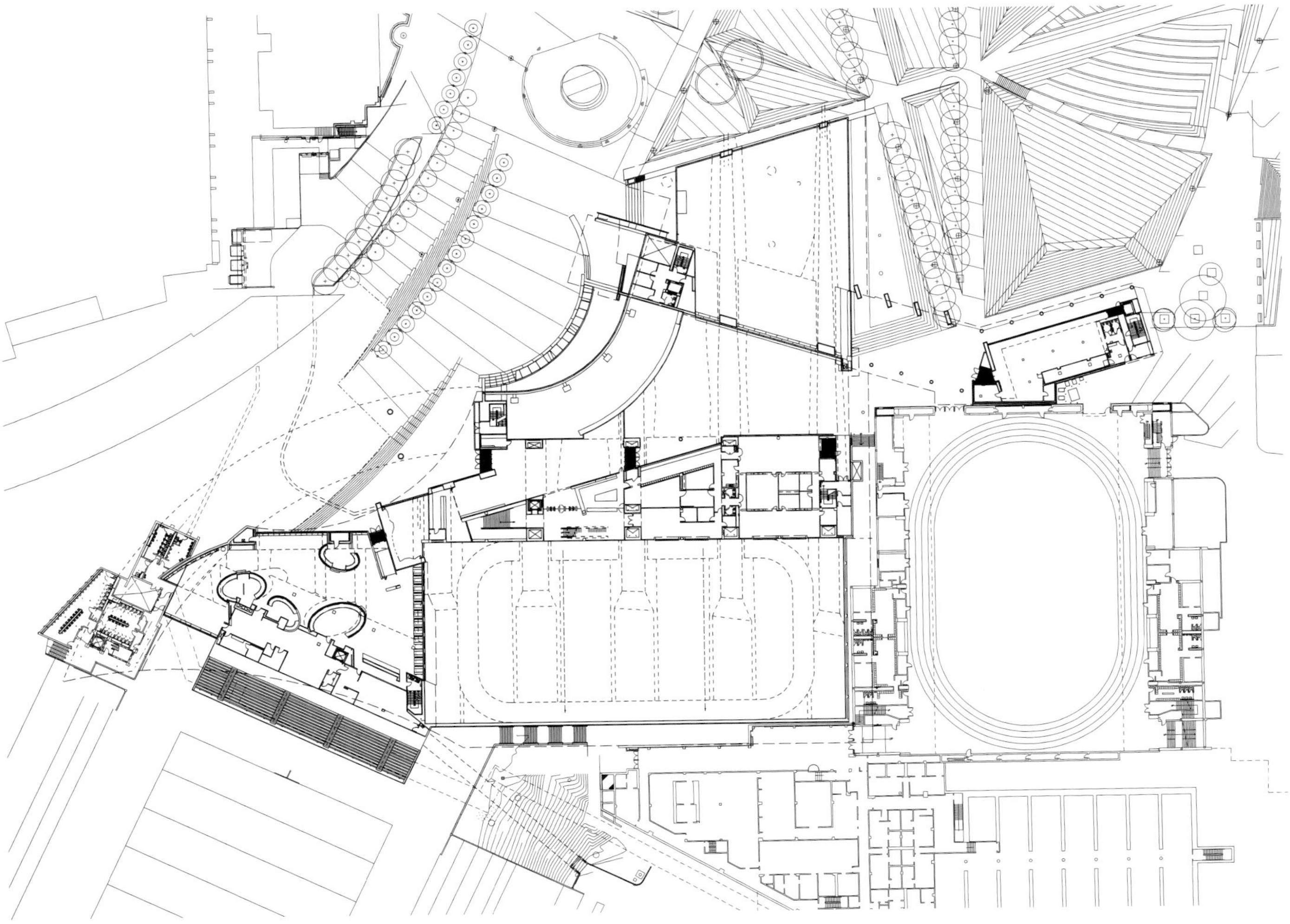

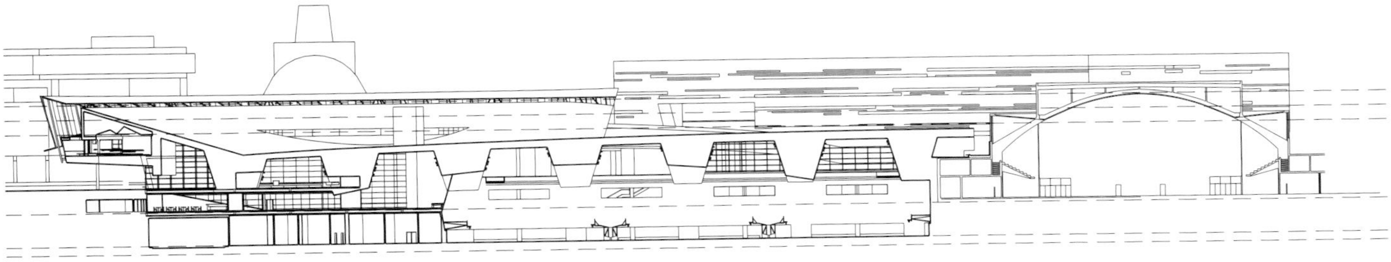

This page
Top: Site plan
Middle: Section
Bottom: Aerial view

Opposite
Entrance

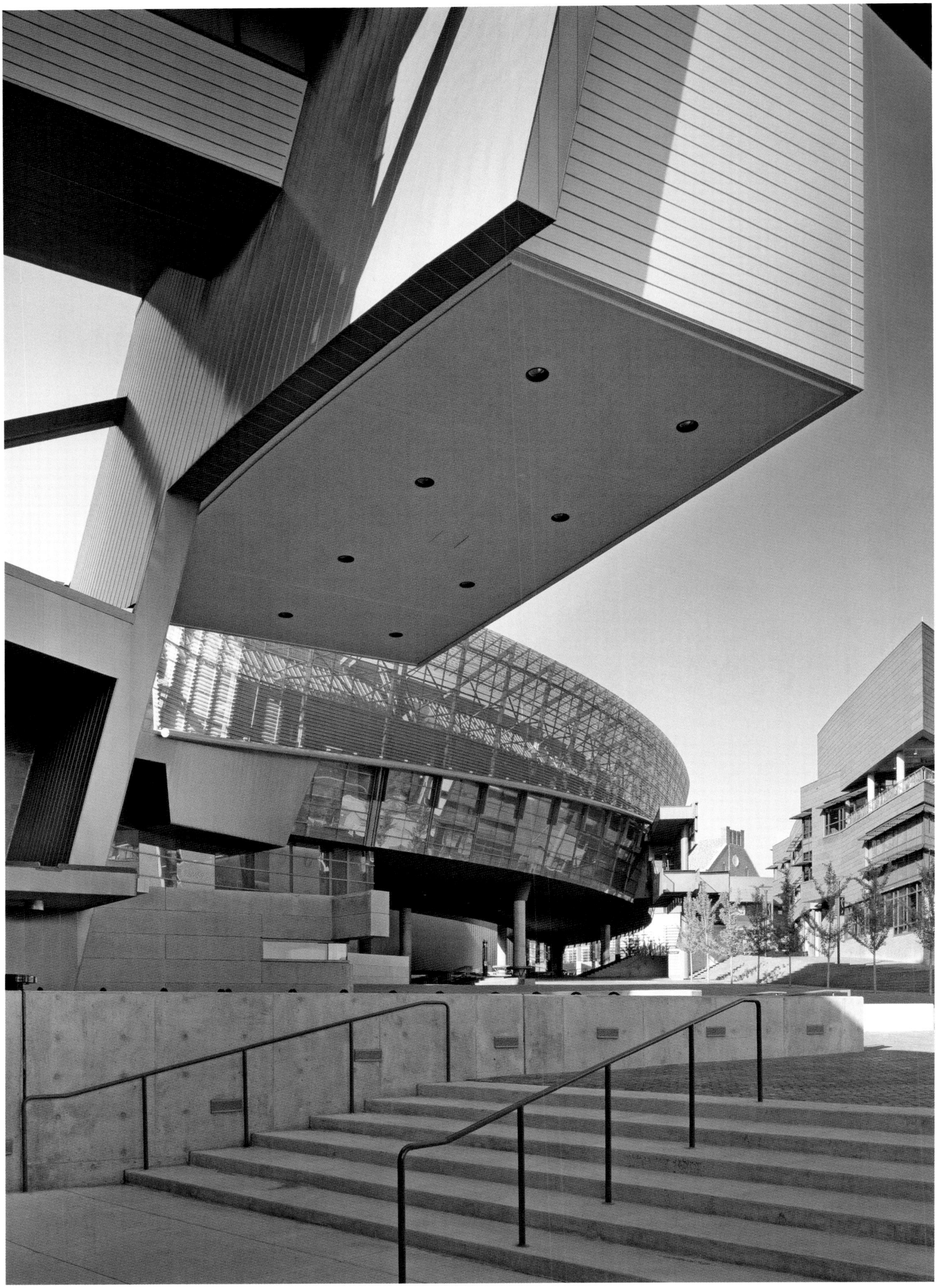

This page
Top: Gym, west-wall section (left); running-track soffit
Bottom: Structural detail

Opposite
Top: West-wall section (left); truss volumes (right); track penetrates truss volumes
Bottom: Steel-hangar-rod track supports

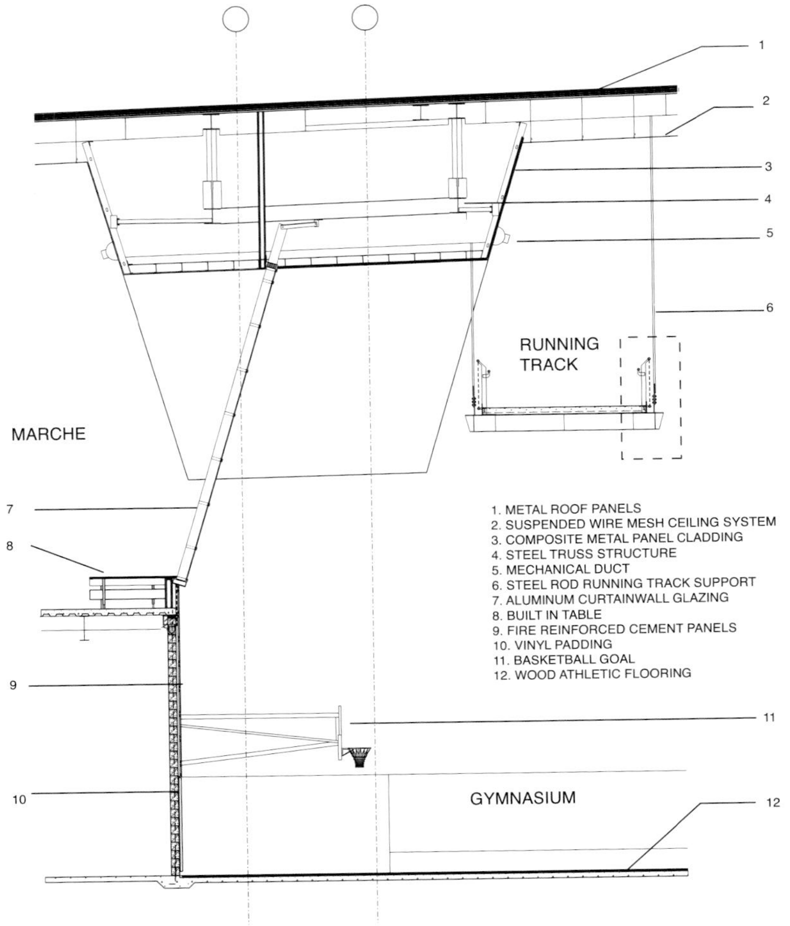

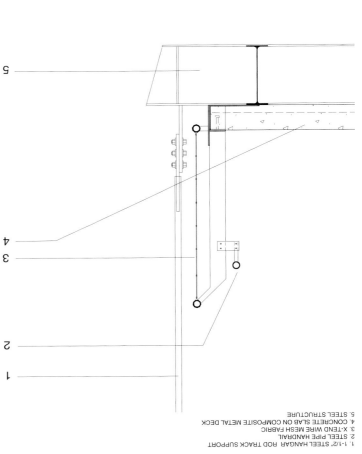

1. 1-1/2" STEEL HANGAR ROD TRACK SUPPORT
2. STEEL PIPE HANDRAIL
3. X-TEND WIRE MESH FABRIC
4. CONCRETE SLAB ON COMPOSITE METAL DECK
5. STEEL STRUCTURE

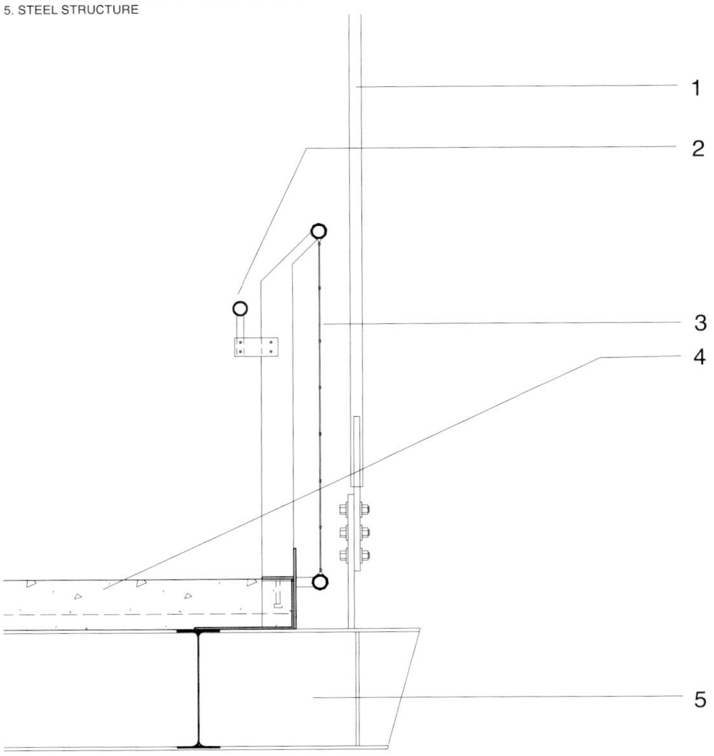

Guthrie Theater, Minneapolis, Minnesota
Ateliers Jean Nouvel, Paris, France
Architectural Alliance, Minneapolis

On the west bank of the Mississippi River, the new Guthrie Theater provides expanded facilities for performance: a classical thrust stage, a proscenium stage for contemporary plays, a studio theater with its adjacent yellow box lobby, and a 35-foot-wide cantilevered lobby known as the Endless Bridge, with windows that frame the many nearby postindustrial landmarks. One of the longest occupied cantilevers in the world, it extends 178 feet from the face of the theater building and 32 feet over the West River Parkway, terminating in an open-air viewing terrace with dramatic views of St. Anthony Falls and the Stone Arch Bridge.

The enclosed portion of the Endless Bridge serves as a continuous ramp to allow visitors to move from the upper lobby to the terrace and the lower lobby; a 2,200-square-foot L-shaped, glass-enclosed "bridge bar" runs underneath the upper-level ramp. A fire-escape catwalk, suspended from the bottom of the bridge and directly connected to fire-exit stairs located on either side of the inside of the bridge, provides egress from the bridge bar, the ramped sections, and the terrace.

The bridge's structural form is that of a cantilevered box truss, its top and bottom chords K-braced, with the apex pointing outward from the building. The aluminum-bar-grating catwalk platform and the K-braced steel angles below provide a miniaturized version of the bracing structure of the bridge itself. A pair of trusses 35 feet apart provides the overall vertical support and continues into the building for 55 feet, where they are terminated at a 55-foot-wide vertical bracing system—the back-span system for the cantilevered portion extends a total of 110 feet into the building. The vertical braces are used to restrain the cantilever from vertical-load effects—downward or uplift—and to provide sway bracing for the elevated cantilever for unbalanced vertical loads.

The vertical trusses are supported at the building face by built-up fulcrum columns 44 feet high, made from W14 x 730 sections and reinforced with plates to form a box. Parallel to the building face, the columns are braced at the bridge truss and at midheight by struts to adjacent vertical braces for stability. The vertical truss-framing members are connected with field-bolted gusset plates fabricated by match-drilling the gusset and the truss pieces in the shop. Floors are framed so as to maximize available dead loads on the vertical brace ballast structure, and the 55-foot-long girders for all levels are framed to the end column of the vertical brace systems to maximize the dead-load ballast. The vertical brace frame columns are supported by reinforced-concrete drilled piers in rock. A pair of 2-foot-wide by 10-foot-deep by 80-foot-long concrete-ballast pads engages each of the three columns in the vertical brace; the column-base plates are oversized and reinforced to engage the mass of the mat against uplift.

The ramp floors are of composite steel framing, beam depths limited by the ceiling height in the bridge bar. The design was made to minimize vibrations so visitors feel at ease on a surface hanging off the face of the building. Floor girders span to posts at the ramp scissors, supported by W40 girders stretching between the bottom chords of the vertical trusses. The bridge bar is supported directly by these girders, the top flange flush with the structural slab; this structural deck supports insulation and a topping slab that is the finished floor of the bar. The girders are unbraced from the edge of the bar floor to the vertical truss as they pass under the steep ramp area. The bottom flanges of the W40s match the bottom chord K-bracing and are covered halfway up the web by a metal-panel soffit. Beyond the point at which the ramps meet, girder trusses of varying depths span the 35 feet to the main vertical trusses. The depth of the top chord of the truss was limited to 8 inches to allow for the required headroom clearances on the egress catwalk. The bottom chord is of the W14 type and integrated with the overall bottom chord K-bracing. The web members of the trusses were configured to include rectangular Vierendeel panels to allow the catwalks to pass through the trusses, which are exposed and can be seen from the bridge bar.

The exterior viewing terrace is framed by tapered, cantilevered trusses perpendicular to the girder trusses. The deck itself is reinforced concrete over galvanized form deck, with precast concrete Ls for the stairs, supporting insulation, waterproofing, and a slab with a snow-melt system. The roof deck for the bridge is a 2 1/2-inch lightweight concrete slab over a 3-inch metal deck that minimizes dead loadings and provides the required one-hour fire rating.

Robert Quinn, P.E., of Ericksen, Roed & Associates contributed to this text.

Opposite
Top: Endless Bridge, night view
Bottom: Endless Bridge, view east

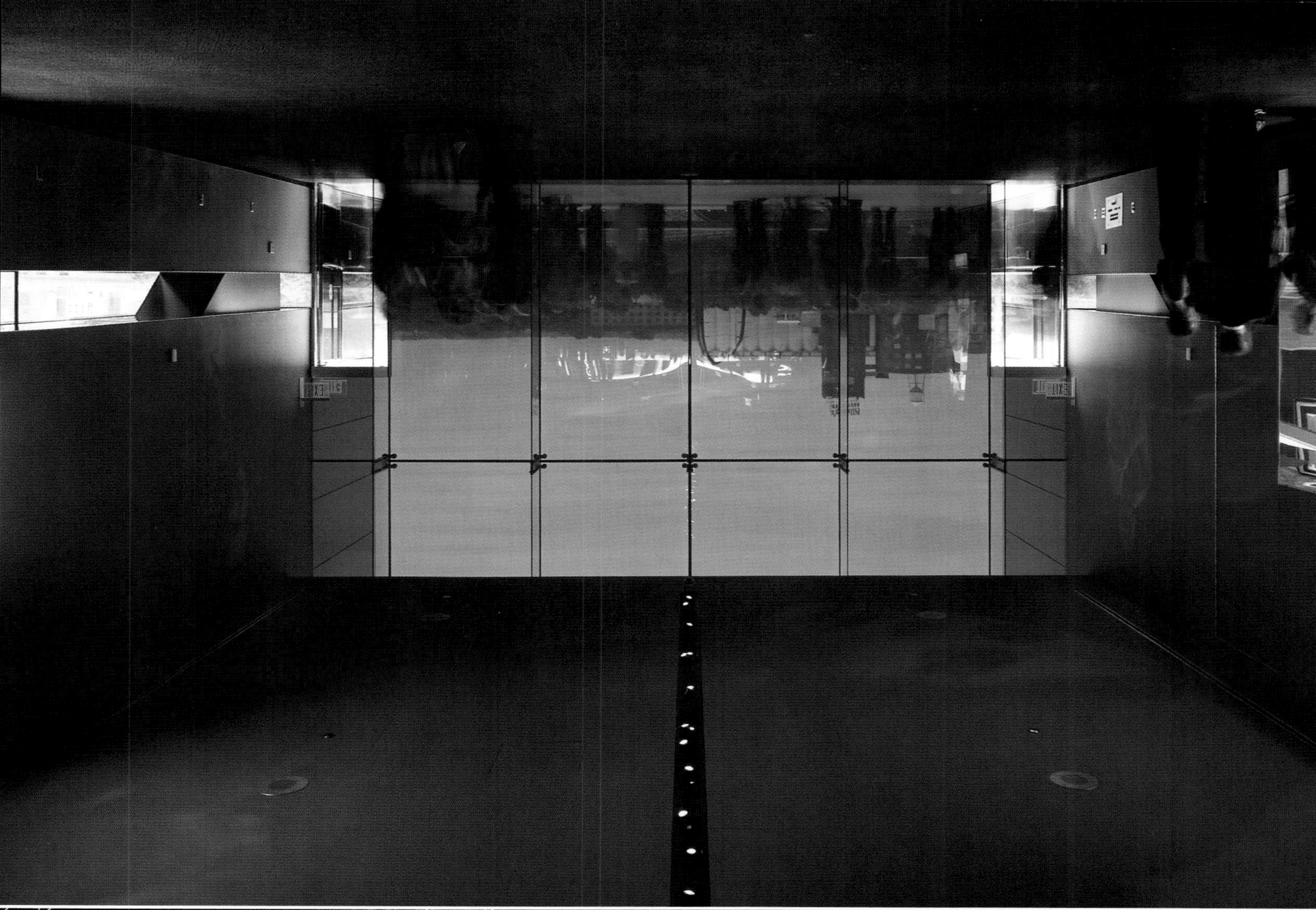

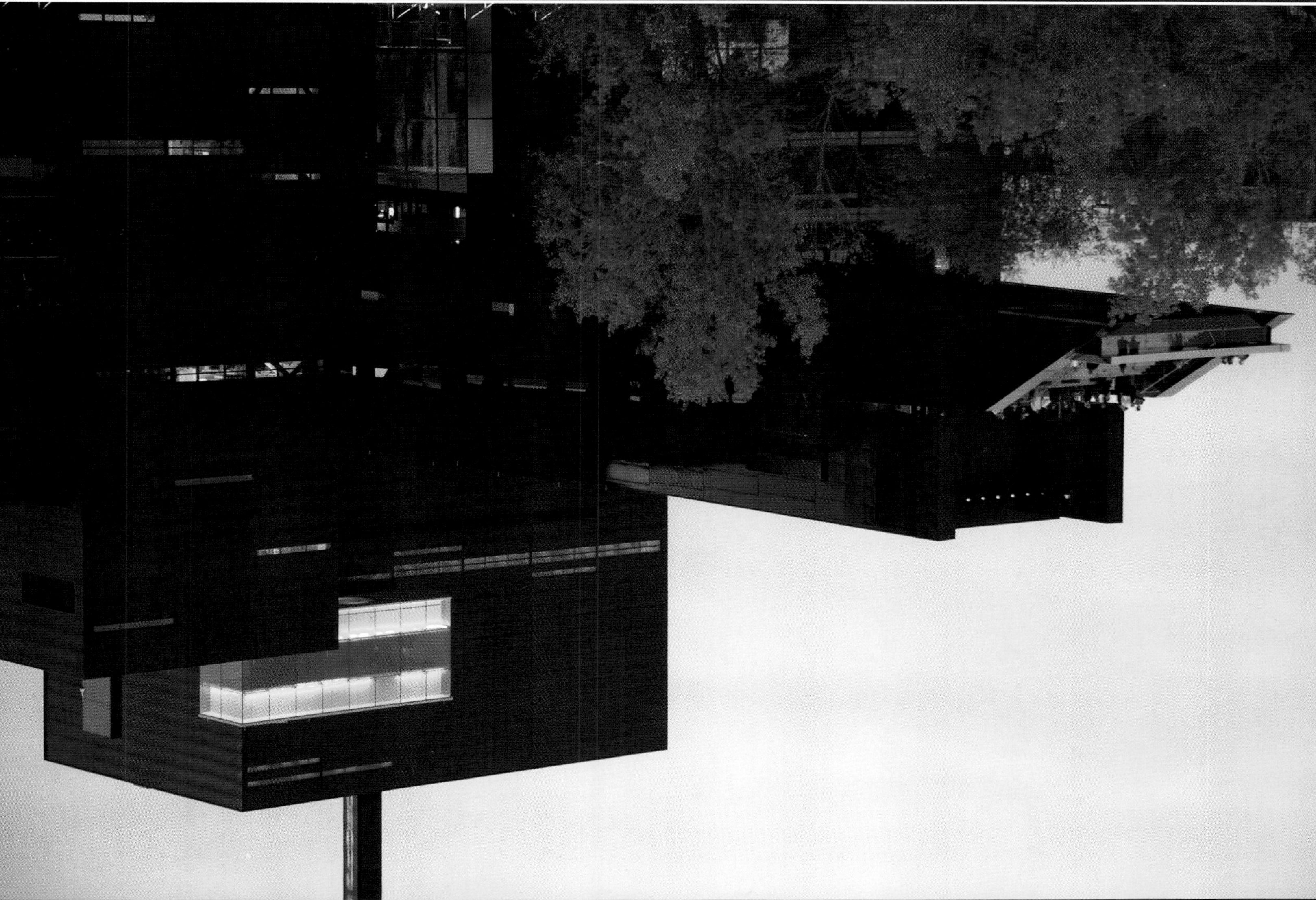

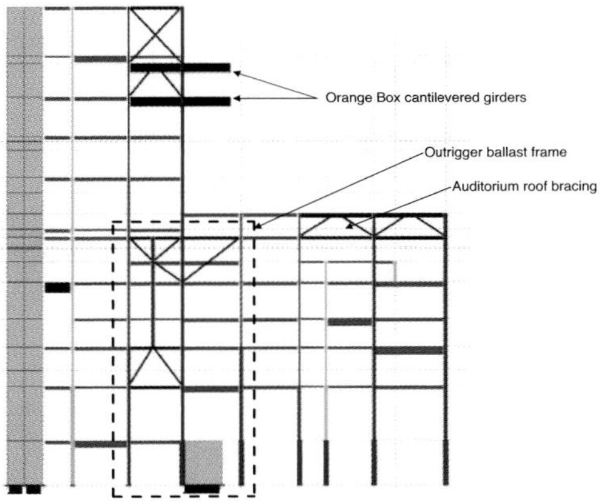

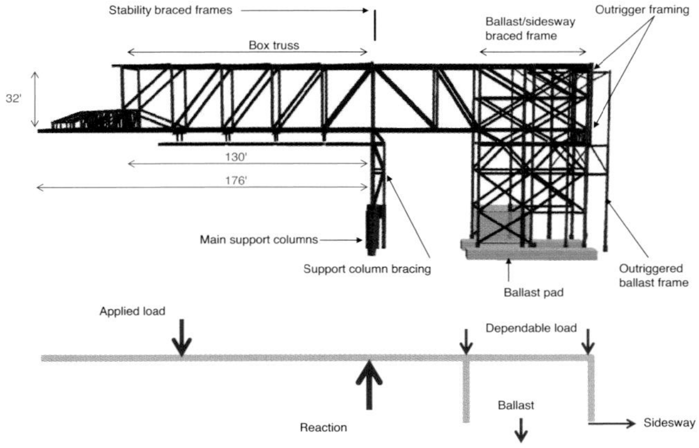

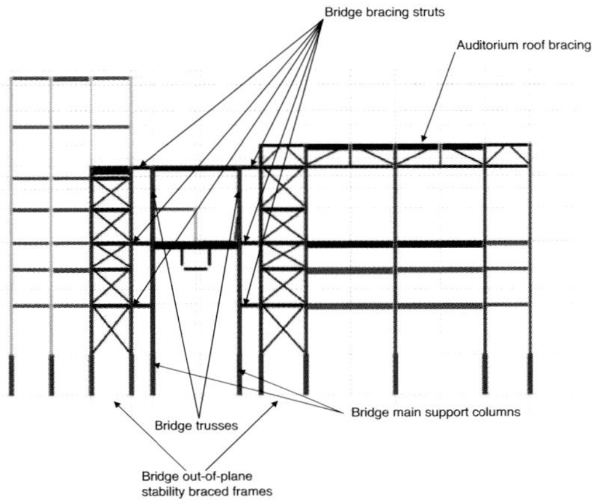

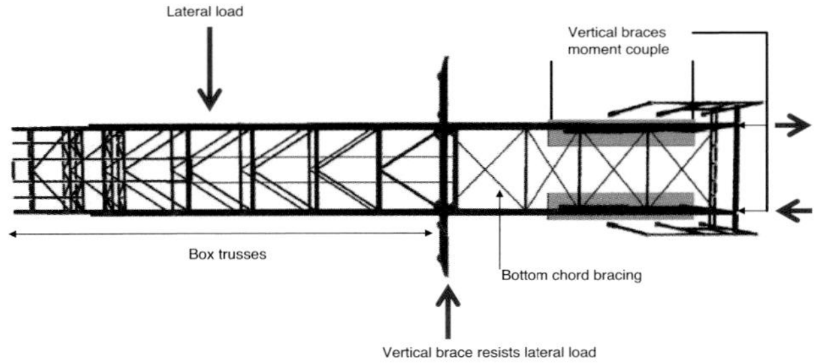

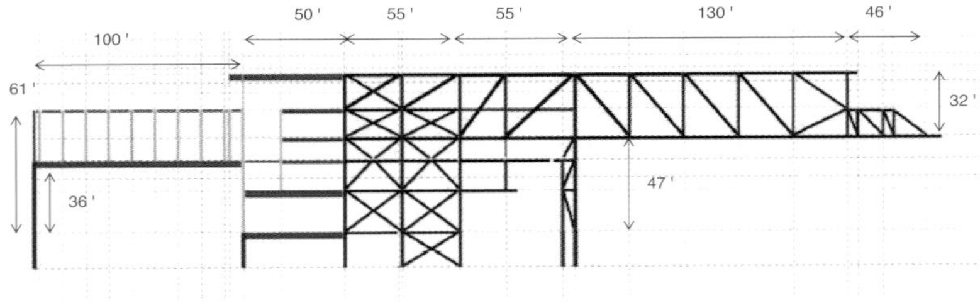

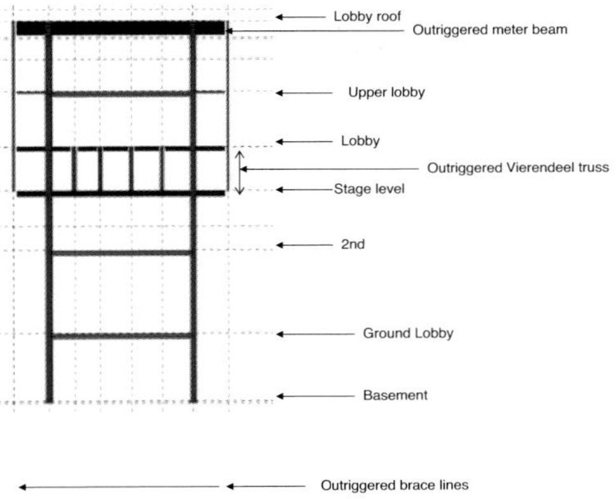

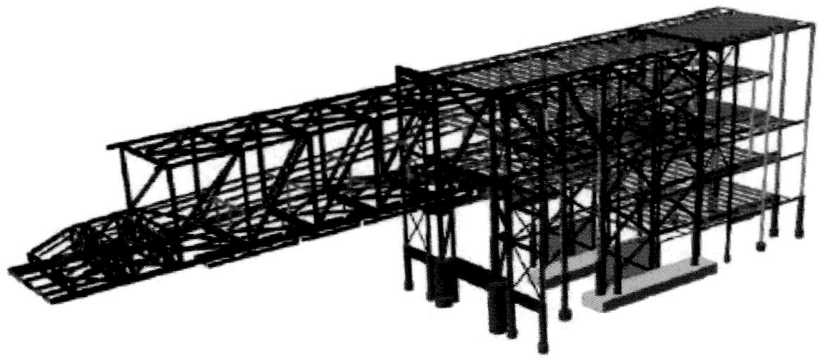

This page

Left (top to bottom): Proscenium theater, west-wall elevation; north-wall bracing section; production link/lobby/bridge elevation; 3-D structural model of northwest elevation
Right (top to bottom): Primary support frame; bridge-framing plan/statics; outrigger ballast frame

Opposite

Top: Longitudinal section
Middle: Endless Bridge, construction view southeast (top left); Endless Bridge, construction view southwest (below left); Endless Bridge, construction view northwest (top right); Endless Bridge, construction view northeast
Bottom: Cantilever over West River Parkway (left); Endless Bridge soffit

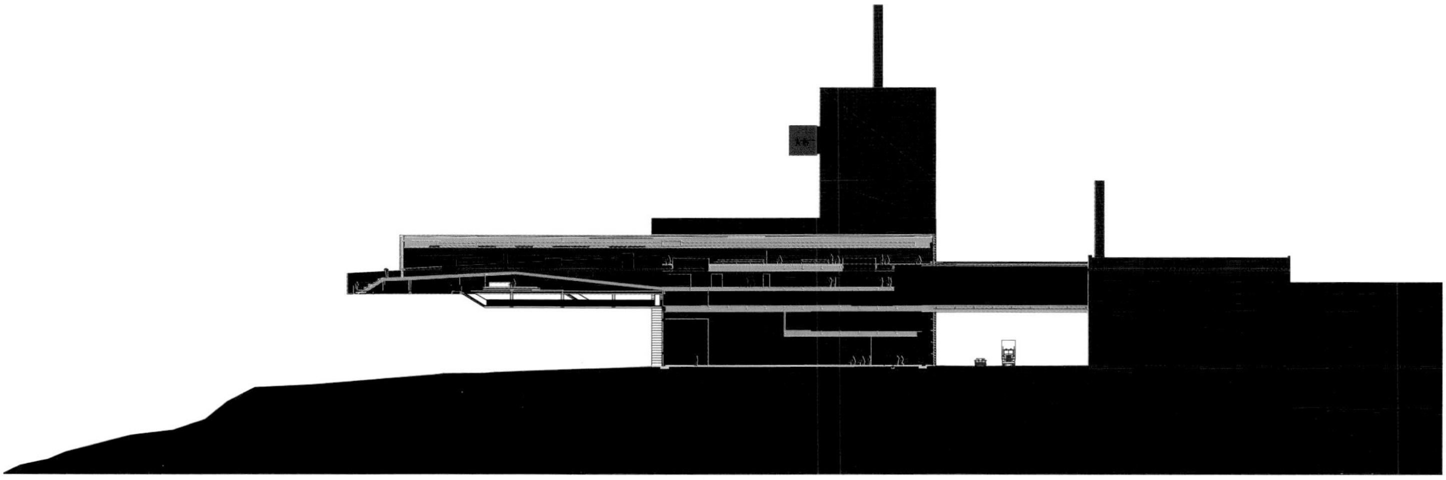

GOLD
MEDAL
FLOUR

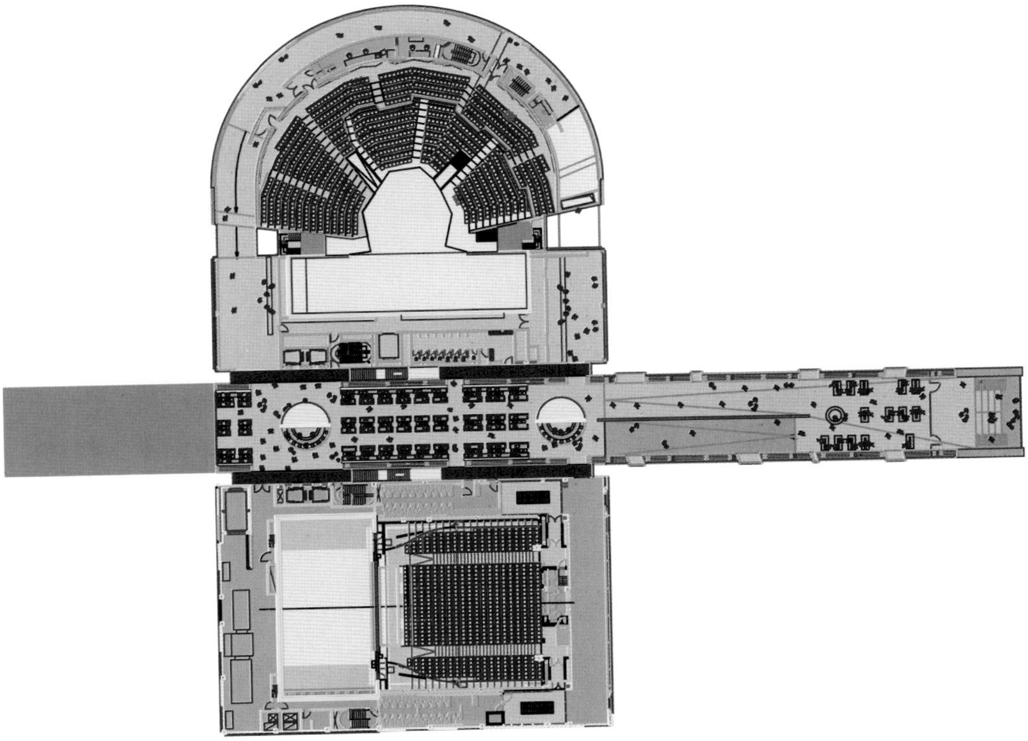

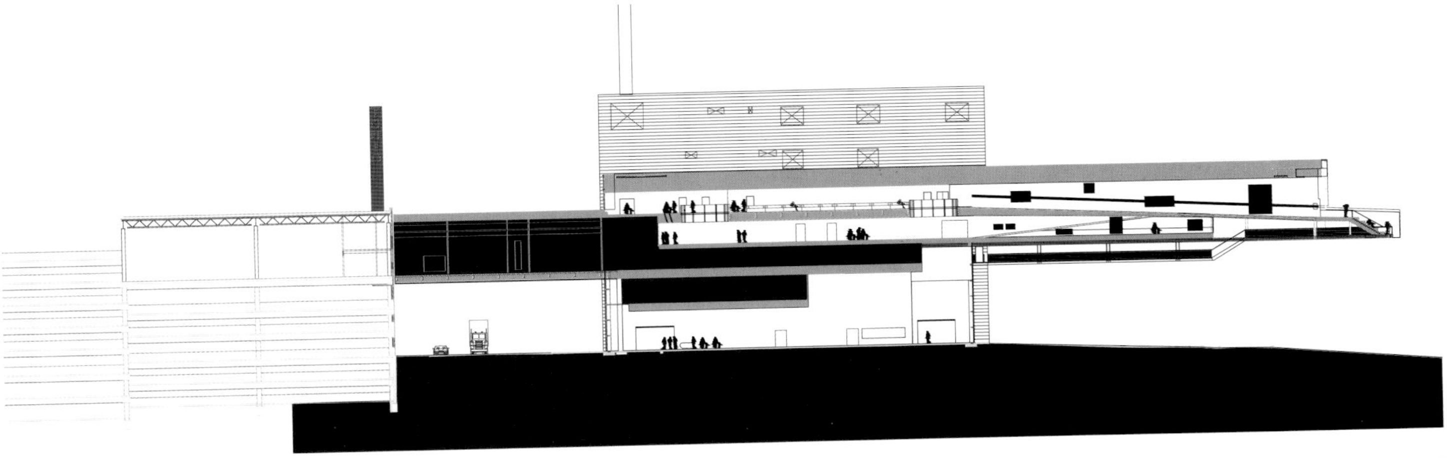

GOLD

Opposite
Top: Level 5
Middle: longitudinal section
Bottom: South elevation, night view

This page
Top: View northeast from Endless Bridge
Middle: Bridge and ramp (left); Endless Bridge, view east
Bottom: Ramp to bridge from level 4

High Museum of Art, Atlanta, Georgia
Renzo Piano Building Workshop, Genoa, Italy
Lord, Aeck & Sargent Architecture, Atlanta

The expansion of the High Museum of Art features naturally lit galleries in an urban setting, a public piazza surrounded by the expanded museum's gallery buildings on the north and west sides, and a restaurant on the south. At ground level, both aluminum-panel-clad gallery buildings incorporate glazed lobbies with expansive views of the city beyond. The glazed areas are protected by large overhangs that shade the interior from direct sunlight and create covered outdoor spaces for the display of art. To maintain maximum transparency, all glazing units, composed of low-iron glass with a low-E coating, extend from floor to ceiling, divided only by vertical support frames. In two locations vertical bands of glazing extend upward beyond the lobby level to the top of the building, where the glass is covered inside and out by motorized translucent shades that allow filtered views while eliminating glare and harmful levels of illumination.

The top gallery levels take full advantage of the roof's potential as a source of illumination, providing optimum conditions for viewing the museum's permanent collection through the controlled admission of natural light from above. One thousand circular skylights, relatively small and evenly distributed across the ceilings, fill both 17 1/4-foot-tall galleries with softly diffused light. Each skylight is composed of three interrelated elements. From the inside looking up, a ceiling coffer formed as an arch at the bottom transitions into a cylindrical tube open at the top to admit light. The coffer elements were fabricated off-site from glass-fiber-reinforced gypsum that was hand formed over a plastic mold, allowed to dry, and then released. At the site, the coffers were set down next to one another in a 4-foot by 4-foot grid that corresponds to their placement in the gallery ceiling vaults. Between each vault is a 4-inch gap containing a track-light system and a return path for conditioned air released at a low velocity from a plenum under the gallery floor. Sprinklers, beam smoke detectors, and security devices are also integrated into the ceiling openings, leaving the coffer light unobstructed. Each coffer is approximately 5 feet high and angled at the top, with the low point facing north to admit indirect north light and block direct south light.

At its upper end, the coffer is inserted inside a second element, a round aluminum double-walled skylight with a glazed aperture comprising two low-iron glass panes with low-E coatings, 2 1/4 feet in diameter and angled parallel with the coffer top opening to the north. This glazing combination maintains the color rendering index at greater than 97, exceeding the ideal for use in art galleries; laminated glass with a 1/10-inch-thick polyvinyl butyral (PBV) interlayer at the interior pane filters out the range of UV radiation most harmful to art objects. The double-walled section is filled with sprayed foam insulation. Anchored to the exterior aluminum shell of the skylight is a third element, named with the Italian word *vela* ("sail"), a sail-shaped 1/8-inch-thick painted aluminum sunshade approximately 6 feet high that curves around the southern portion of the skylight, blocking direct sunlight. The skylights admit reflected light from adjacent velas, an effect that was taken into consideration when calculating illumination levels and evaluating color rendition in the galleries. Approximately 5 percent of the light entering each skylight is reflected from the sunshade to its immediate north, the color of that light warmed by the off-white color of the shade.

The skylight assembly was developed through a process of refinement that included the creation and analysis of hand drawings, physical models, computer models, and a full-scale 16-foot by 40-foot gallery mockup used to verify calculated illumination levels. The focus throughout these studies was to ensure availability of the desired range of properly colored indirect natural light and the exclusion of harmful UV radiation. The resulting levels of natural light, which can be supplemented by artificial light as required—at night or for accenting—are well within the 15- to 30-foot candle range (161 to 323 lux) required by the curators.

Randal Vaughan, AIA, of Lord, Aeck & Sargent Architecture contributed to this text.

Opposite
Top: Velas and transition panels
Bottom: Wieland Pavilion

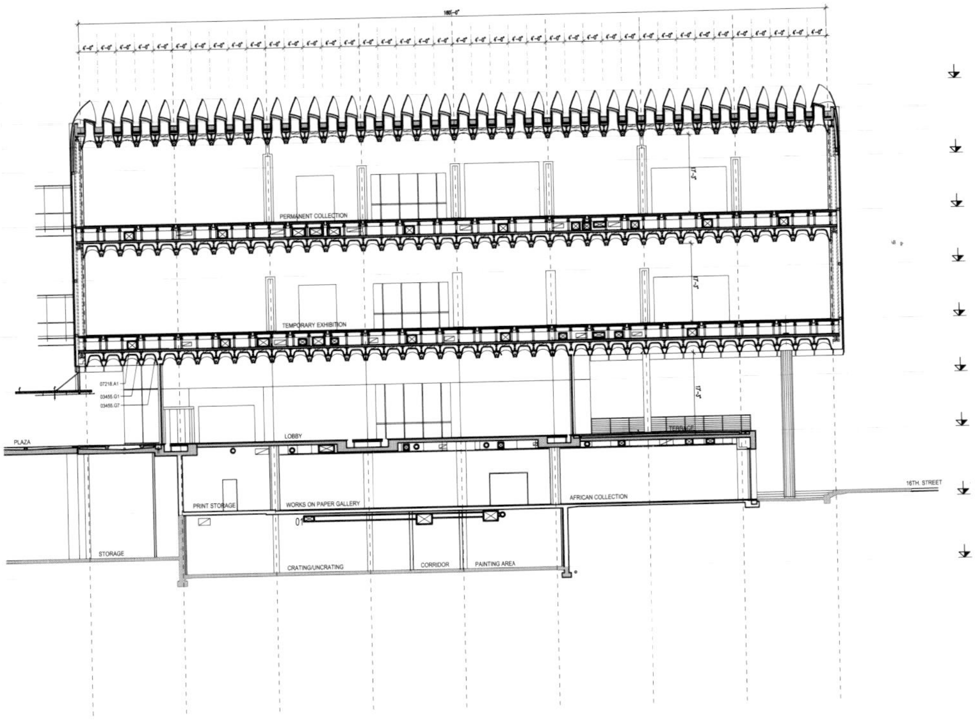

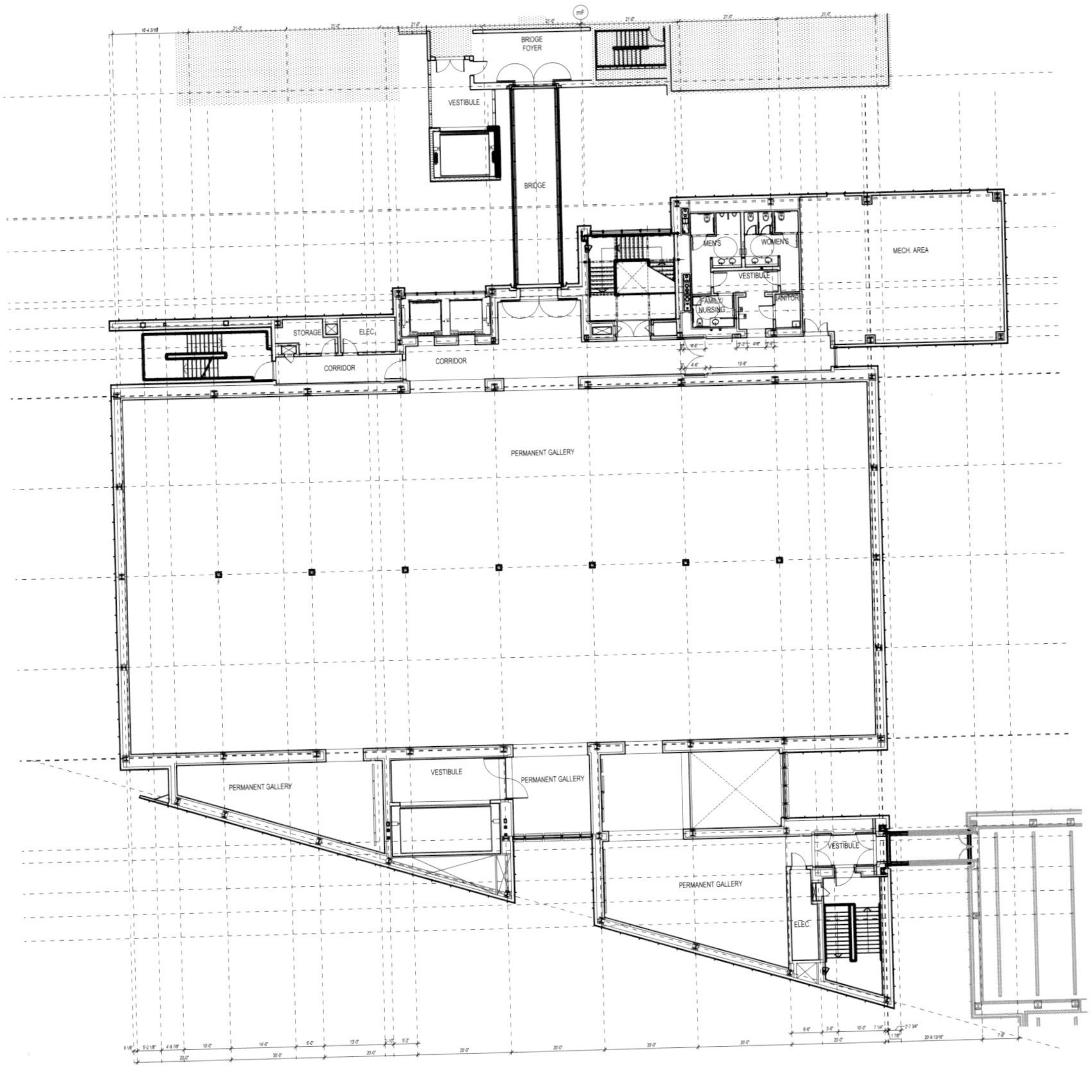

This page
Top: Section
Bottom: Permanent-gallery plan

Opposite
Left (top to bottom): Piazza; cafe
Right (top to bottom): Gallery; Wieland Pavilion; gallery detail

HIGH MUSEUM OF ART

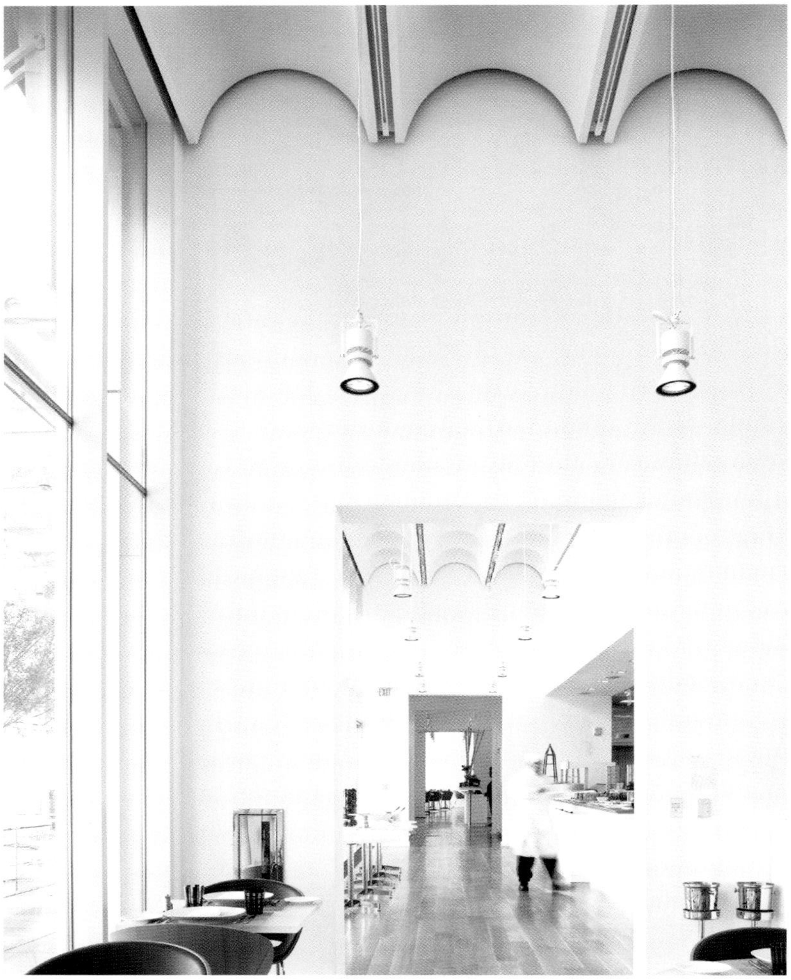

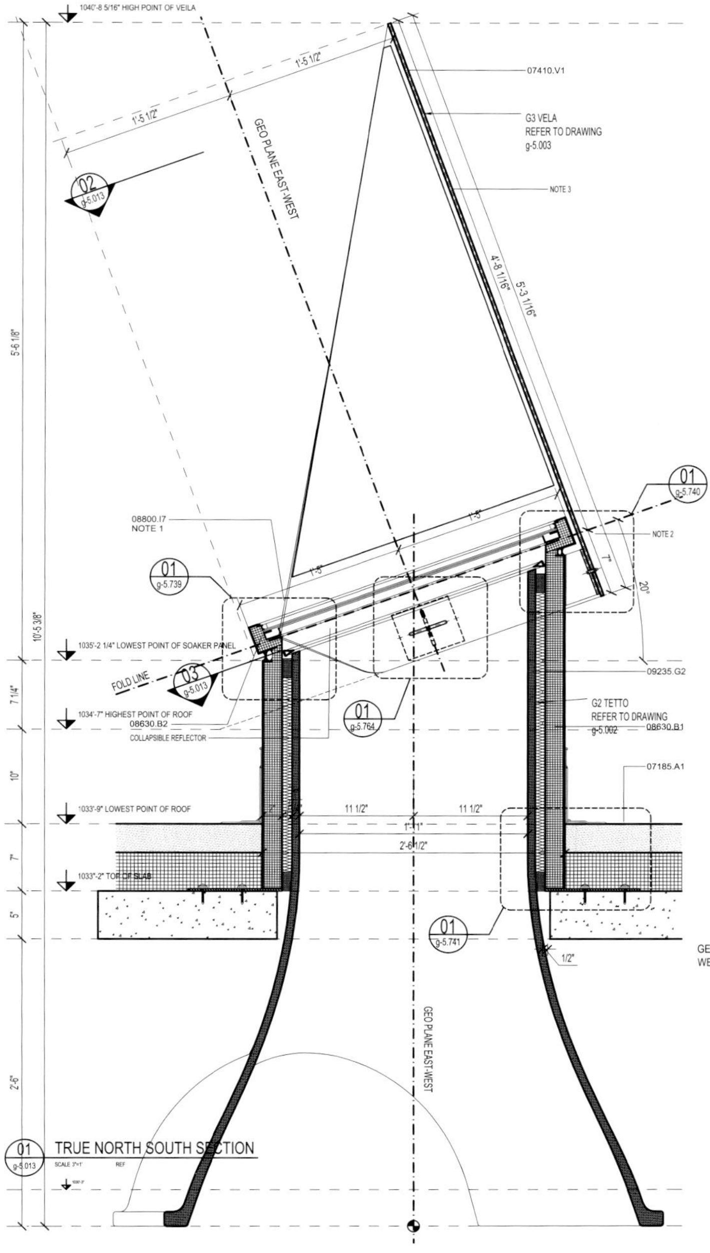
1040'-8 5/16" HIGH POINT OF VEILA
07410.V1
G3 VELA
REFER TO DRAWING
g-5.003
NOTE 3
GEO PLANE EAST-WEST
4'-8 11/16"
5'-3 1/16"
1'-5 1/2"
5'-6 1/8"
10'-5 3/8"
08800.I7
NOTE 1
NOTE 2
1035'-2 1/4" LOWEST POINT OF SOAKER PANEL
FOLD LINE
1034'-7" HIGHEST POINT OF ROOF
08630.B2
COLLAPSIBLE REFLECTOR
09235.G2
G2 TETTO
REFER TO DRAWING
g-5.002
08630.B1
07185.A1
1033'-9" LOWEST POINT OF ROOF
11 1/2"
2'-6 1/2"
1033'-2" TOP OF SLAB
1/2"
TRUE NORTH SOUTH SECTION

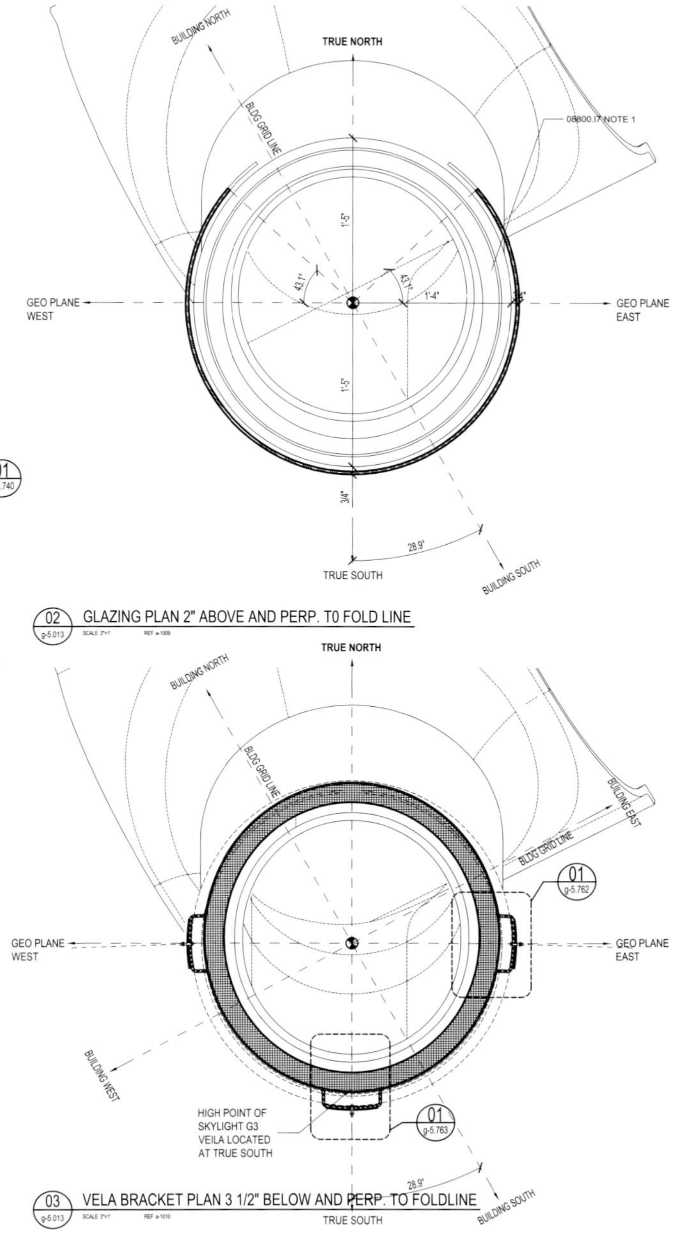
TRUE NORTH
BUILDING NORTH
BLDG GRID LINE
08800.I7 NOTE 1
GEO PLANE WEST
GEO PLANE EAST
1'-5"
1'-4"
43.1°
3/4"
28.9°
TRUE SOUTH
BUILDING SOUTH
GLAZING PLAN 2" ABOVE AND PERP. TO FOLD LINE
BUILDING EAST
BUILDING WEST
HIGH POINT OF
SKYLIGHT G3
VEILA LOCATED
AT TRUE SOUTH
VELA BRACKET PLAN 3 1/2" BELOW AND PERP. TO FOLDLINE

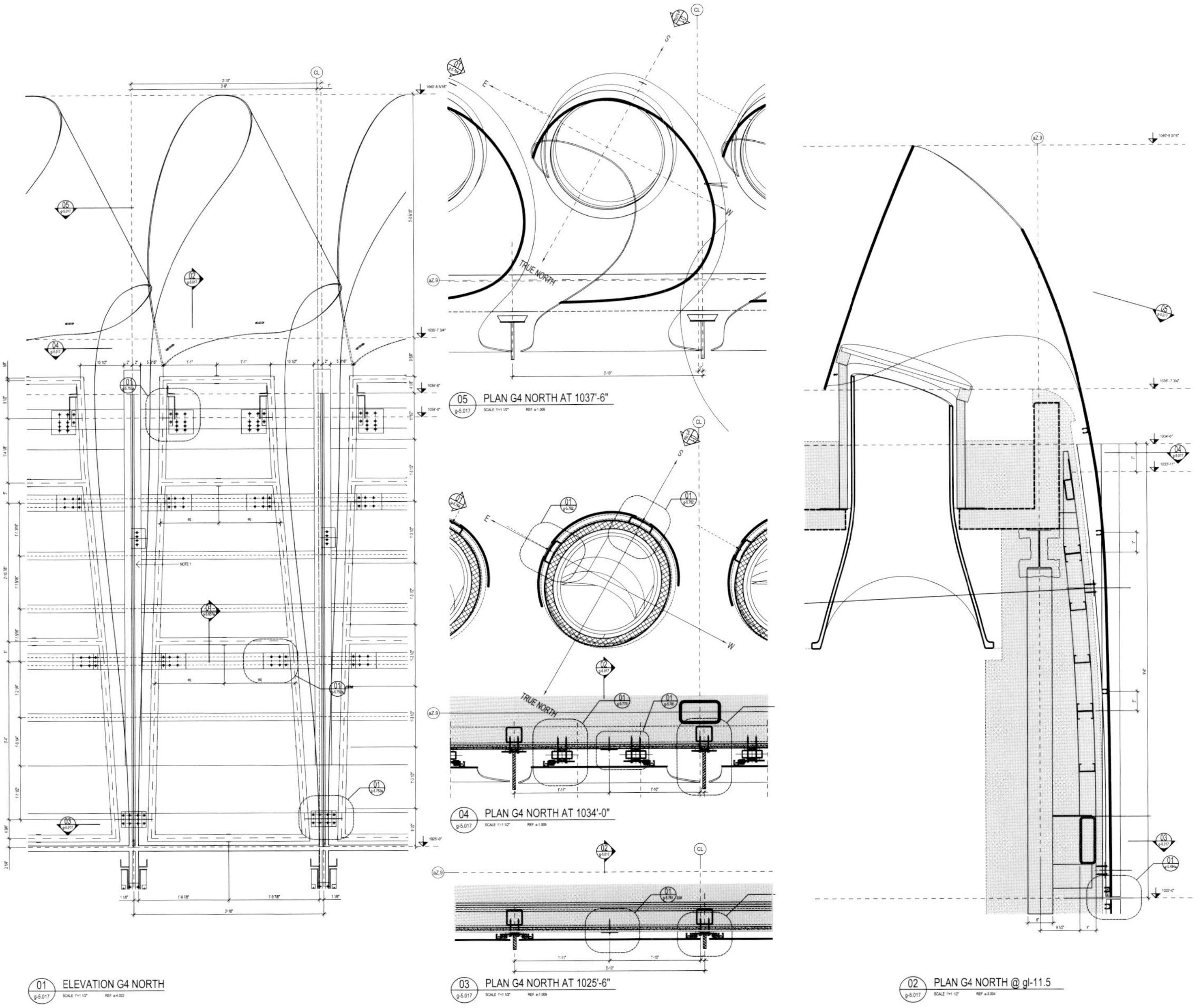

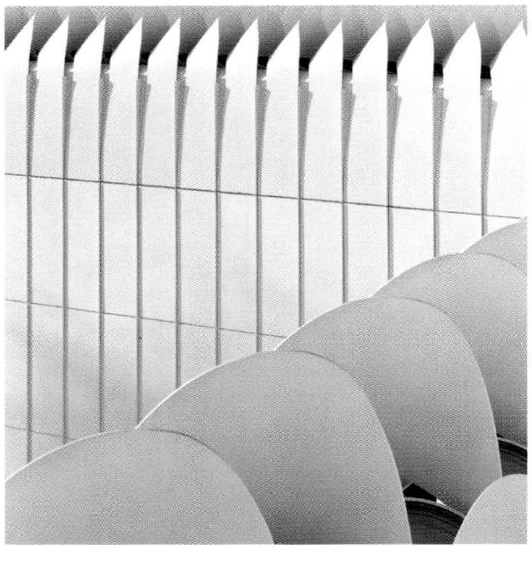

Opposite
Top: Vela assembly
Bottom (left to right): Ceiling coffers on site; ceiling-coffer installation; completed installation

This page
Top: Skylight assembly
Bottom: Velas and skylights

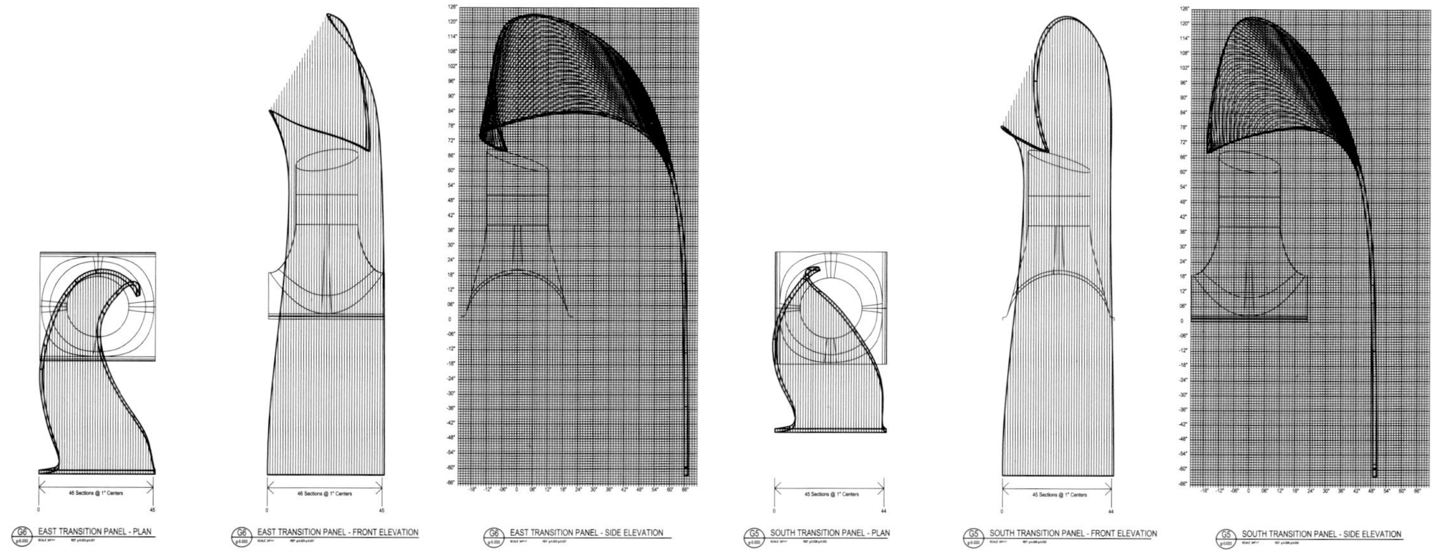
G6 EAST TRANSITION PANEL - PLAN
48 Sections @ 1" Centers
G6 EAST TRANSITION PANEL - FRONT ELEVATION
46 Sections @ 1" Centers
G6 EAST TRANSITION PANEL - SIDE ELEVATION
G5 SOUTH TRANSITION PANEL - PLAN
45 Sections @ 1" Centers
G5 SOUTH TRANSITION PANEL - FRONT ELEVATION
45 Sections @ 1" Centers
G5 SOUTH TRANSITION PANEL - SIDE ELEVATION

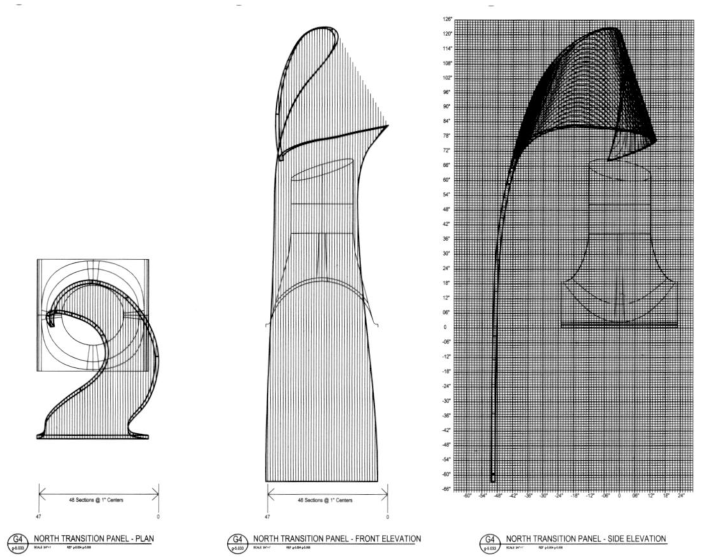
48 Sections @ 1" Centers
G4 NORTH TRANSITION PANEL - PLAN
48 Sections @ 1" Centers
G4 NORTH TRANSITION PANEL - FRONT ELEVATION
G4 NORTH TRANSITION PANEL - SIDE ELEVATION

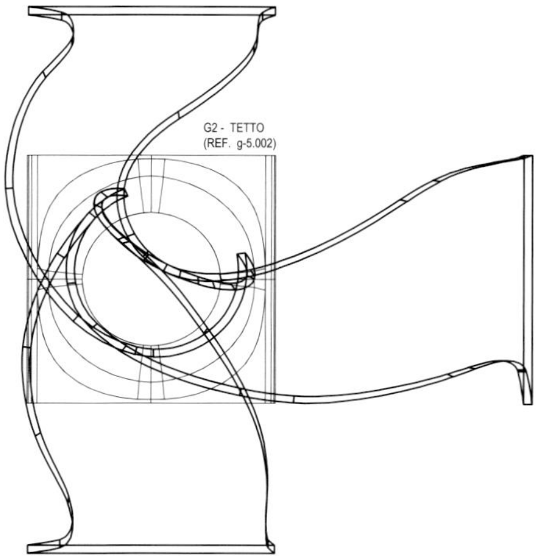
07410.T1
G4 - NORTH TRANSITION PANEL
(REF. g-5.004 g-5.008)
G2 - TETTO
(REF. g-5.002)
07410.T1
G6 - EAST TRANSITION PANEL
(REF. g-5.023 g-5.027)
G5 - SOUTH TRANSITION PANEL
(REF. g-5.028 g-5.032)
07410.T1

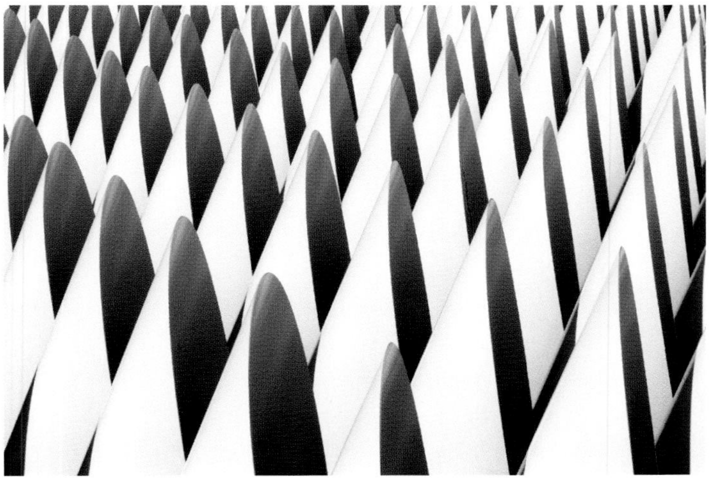

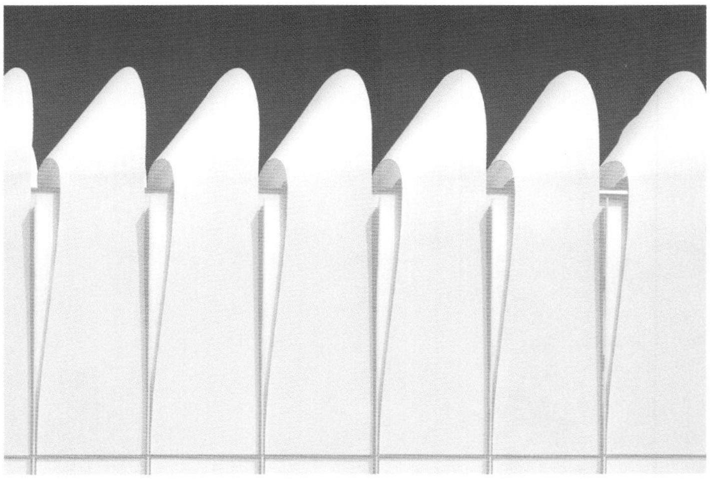

Opposite
Top and middle: Vela transition panels
Bottom: Velas from above (left); transition-panels elevation

This page
Vela variations

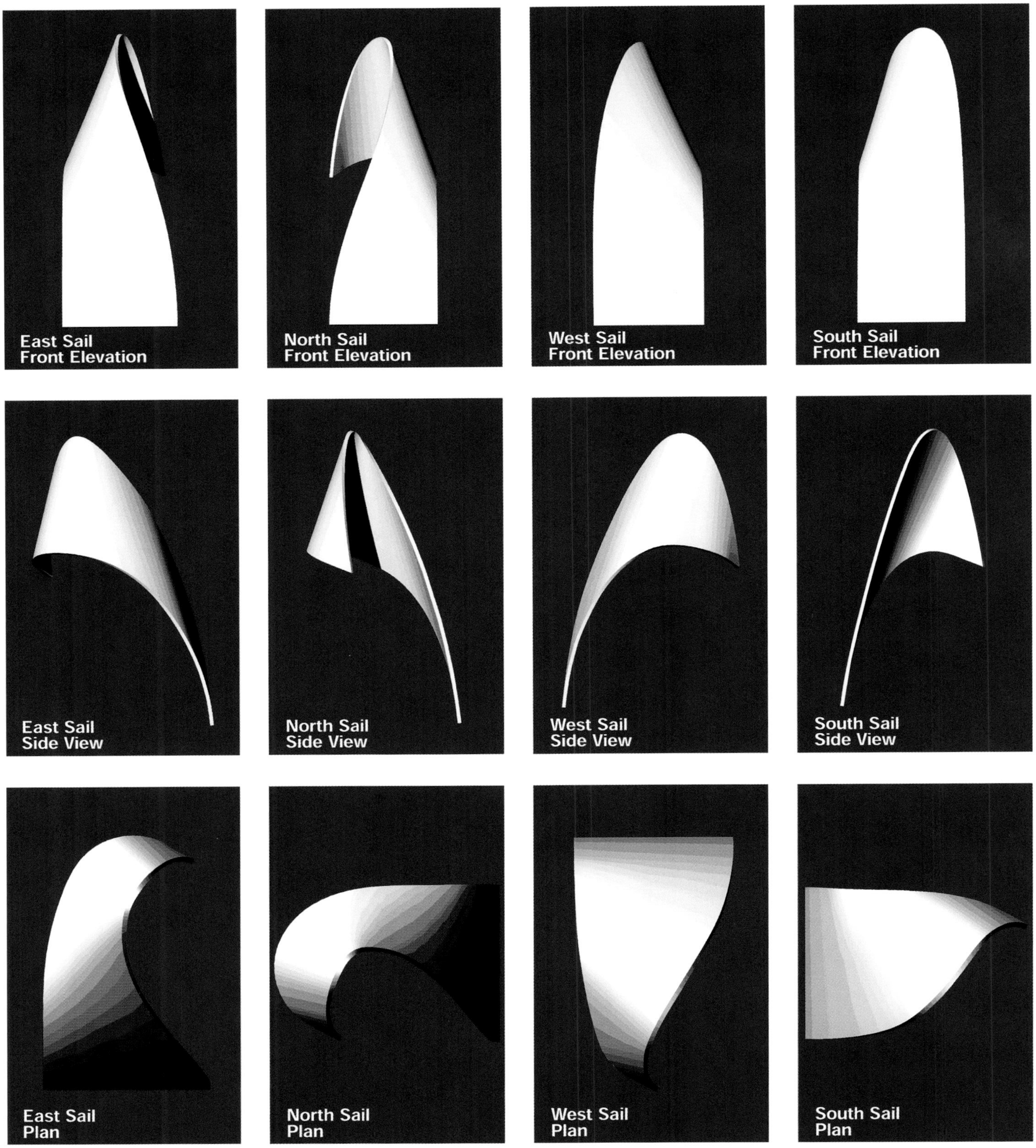

Meinel Optical Sciences Building, Tucson, Arizona
Richärd + Bauer, Phoenix, Arizona

The Meinel Optical Sciences Building is a 47,000-square-foot expansion and partial renovation for the College of Optical Sciences at the University of Arizona in Tucson housing optical research labs, teaching labs, classrooms, interaction areas, and offices for the research program. The project occupies the last open site at one of the most prominent corners on the university mall, but there will be future development on the site south of the expansion.

As the first phase of a relatively high-density site build-out, the new Optical Sciences building establishes the density for the entire site. Its design locates the new facility close to the existing Optical Sciences building; the response to the street edge will be completed during a future expansion.

Vertical-circulation, discussion, and conference spaces in the internal core maximize interaction among researchers and staff. At the lowest level of the building, a two-story lobby space opens to the auditorium and houses displays and exhibits related to optical research. The primary building services and air-handling rooms are at ground level; a large conference room and breakout space are adjacent to the roof terrace at the top level.

The building organization emphasizes the contrast between what the architects describe as "blind" and "seeing" spaces: light-sensitive research functions are organized along the southern side of the building; windowed office and support spaces are open to natural light and views of the university mall and mountains to the north. The building is conceived as an abstraction of a camera obscura, where daylight is introduced and modulated through a series of apertures and three vertical light shafts, each featuring a specific optical effect, that penetrate the building and terminate in a series of two-story interaction spaces. The cast-in-place concrete structure is sheathed in a copper alloy treated to achieve a reddened bronze color, similar to that of the brick buildings on campus, but with a contrasting lightness and luminosity. The skin is designed as a breathable rainscreen, which protects the inner wall membrane from the elements, eliminates the need for surface sealant joints with thermally broken exterior panels that shade the building envelope from the harsh desert sun, and provides a maintenance-free facade for the life of the building.

The northern glass wall, folded as a response to the existing Optical Sciences Building's textured facade, is conceived as an interpretation of the Fresnel lenses used in vehicle headlights and taillights, where many glass prisms focus and intensify rays of light through reflection and refraction, directing them into a narrow beam. The wall's simultaneous use of reflection and transparency creates an apparent mass recalling the rhythm and texture of the existing building's precast facade. By restricting the amount and location of glazing that faces northwest, the facade minimizes solar gain caused by low setting-sun angles while maximizing views from the faculty offices and conference spaces.

Building services are carefully organized to express and convey the technical operation of the building and to provide visual interest for its occupants as well as the surrounding campus. Horizontal utility trays circle each floor and run down the corridors into each of the spaces, permitting easy access and clear order to the building systems. The trays are sheathed in perforated metal panels, allowing a filtered view of the mechanical, electrical, lighting, and data-processing services organized within them.

This page
View southeast from East University Boulevard

Opposite
Northwest elevation

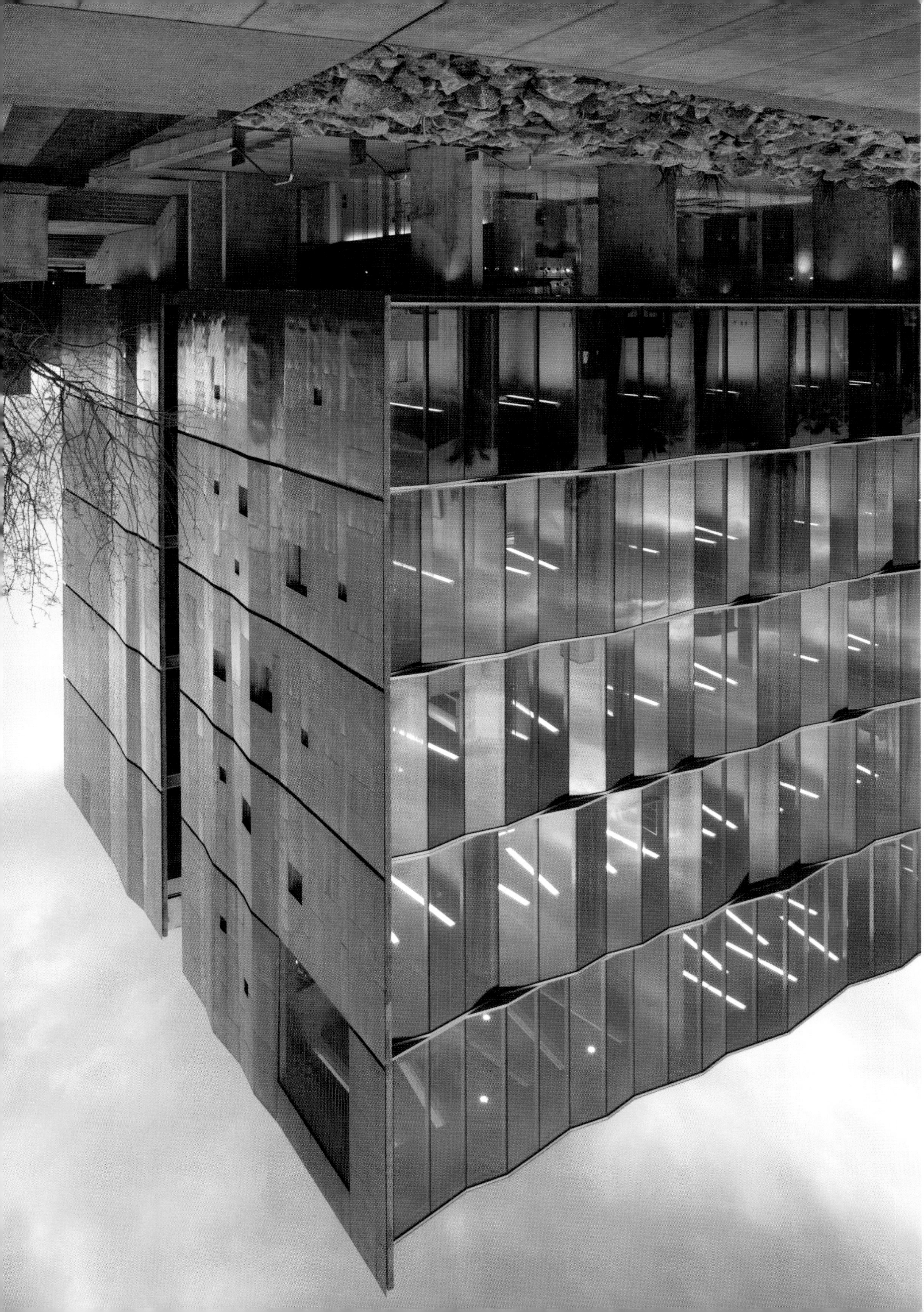

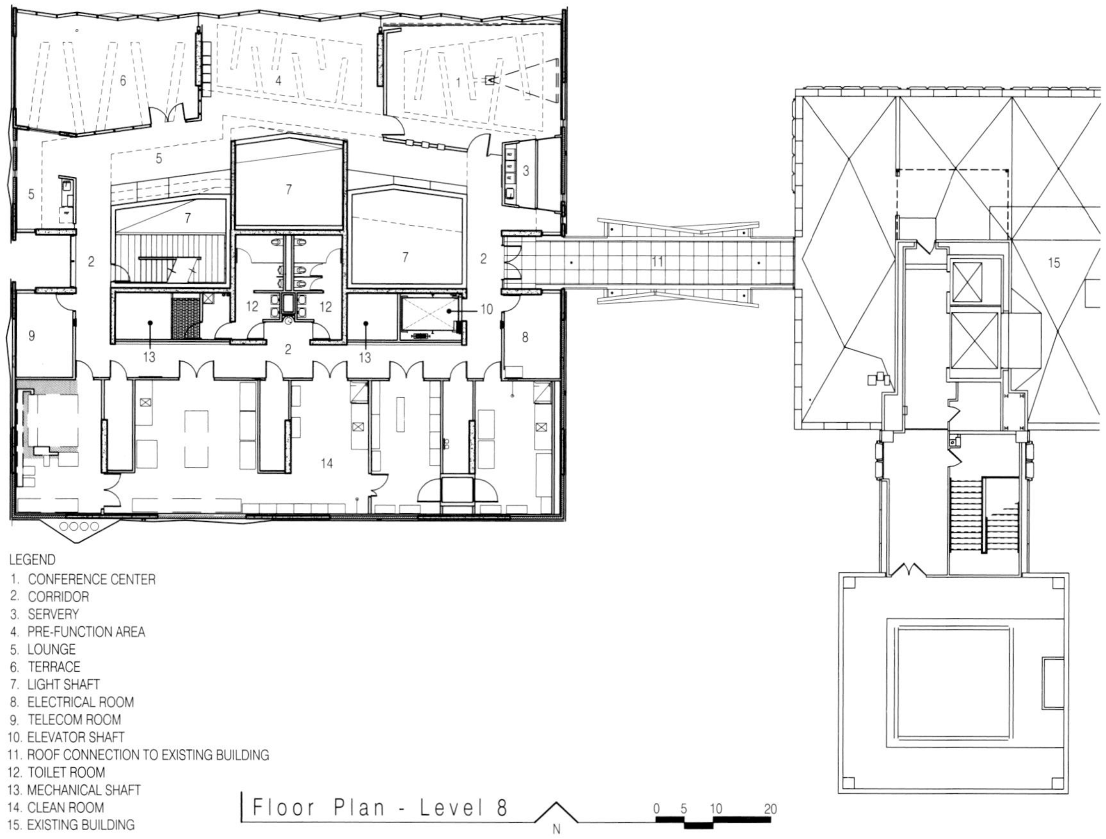

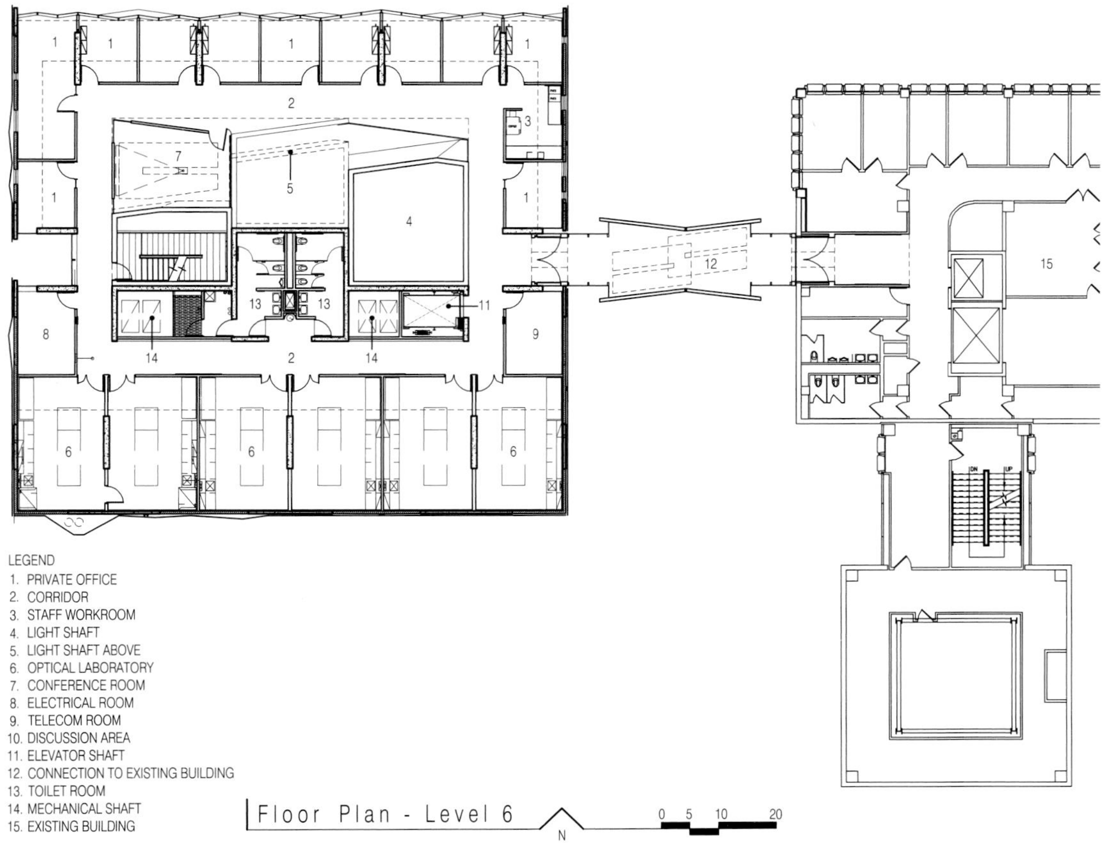

This page
Top: Level-8 plan
Bottom: Level-6 plan

Opposite
Top: Level-3 plan
Bottom: View northeast from Cherry Avenue

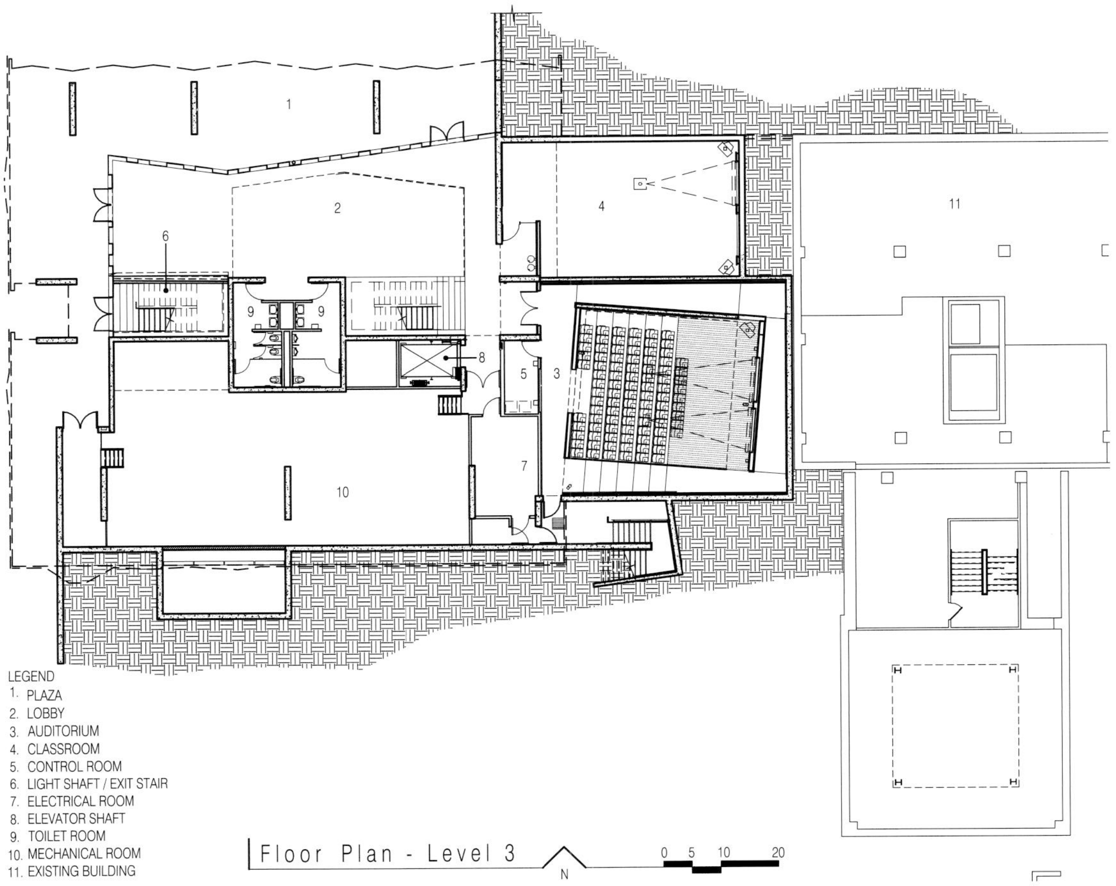

LEGEND
1. PLAZA
2. LOBBY
3. AUDITORIUM
4. CLASSROOM
5. CONTROL ROOM
6. LIGHT SHAFT / EXIT STAIR
7. ELECTRICAL ROOM
8. ELEVATOR SHAFT
9. TOILET ROOM
10. MECHANICAL ROOM
11. EXISTING BUILDING

Floor Plan - Level 3

LEGEND
1. PLAZA
2. BUTT GLAZED GLASS WALL
3. COPPER RAINSCREEN
4. WINDOW
5. ALUMINUM /GLASS SKYLIGHT AT LIGHTSHAFT
6. E.F.I.S. AT EXTERIOR OF LIGHTSHAFT ABOVE ROOF
7. EXISTING BUILDING BEYOND
8. ENTRY
9. CONCRETE STRUCTURE
10. CONCRETE SITE WALL
11. STEEL CABLE GUARDRAIL AT TERRACE
12. LABORATORY EXHAUST EQUIPMENT
13. MECHANICAL EQUIPMENT ENCLOSURE
14. ALUMINUM WINDOW SYSTEM WITH INSULATED GLASS
15. ACCESSIBLE RAMP FROM PARKING AREA

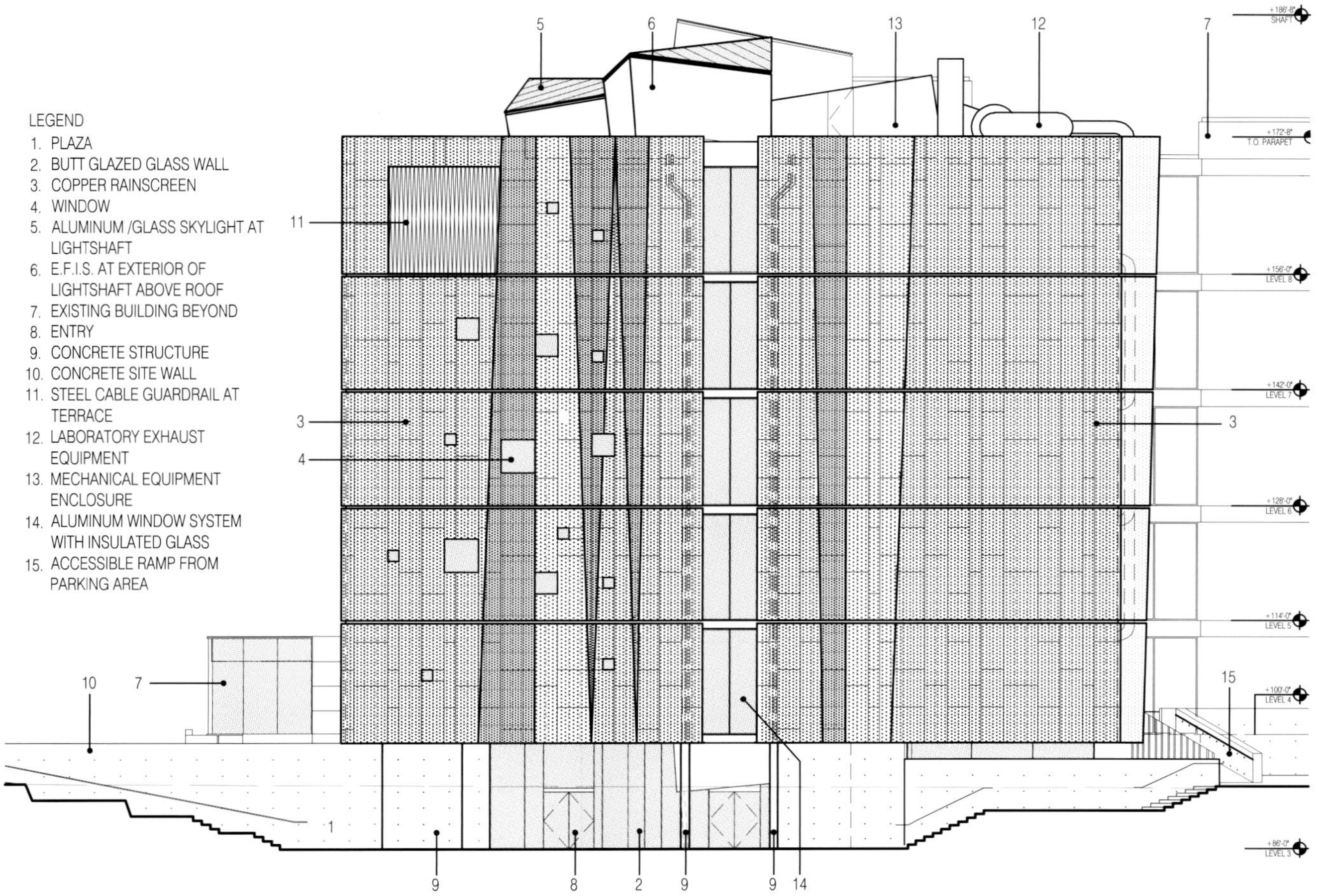

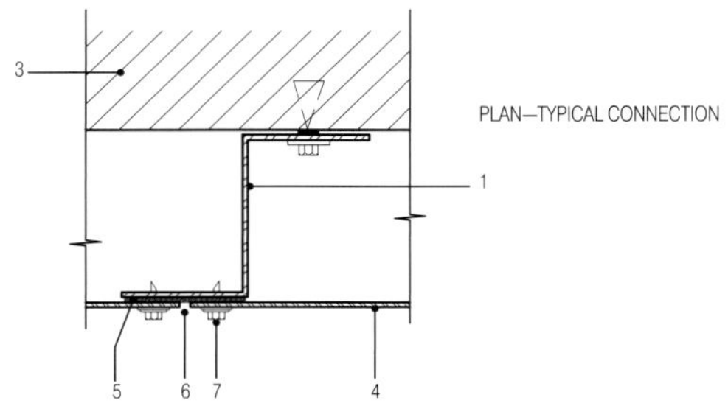

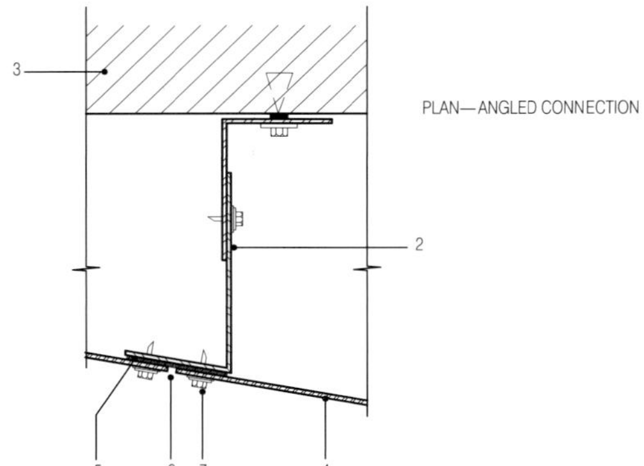

LEGEND
1. 4" GALVANIZED Z-PURLIN ANCHORED TO MASONY
2. GALVANIZED 2 PIECE BREAK METAL Z-PURLIN
3. DAMP PROOFED CMU INFILL WALL
4. 32 oz. COPPER RAINSCREEN PANEL
5. CONTINUOUS ISOLATION TAPE BETWEEN PANEL AND SUPPORT
6. CONTINUOUS 1/4" GAP BETWEEN PANELS
7. STAINLESS STEEL FASTENER

Opposite
Top: West elevation
Bottom: West-elevation detail (left); rainscreen-attachment details

This page
Top: Rainscreen-window detail
Bottom: West elevation

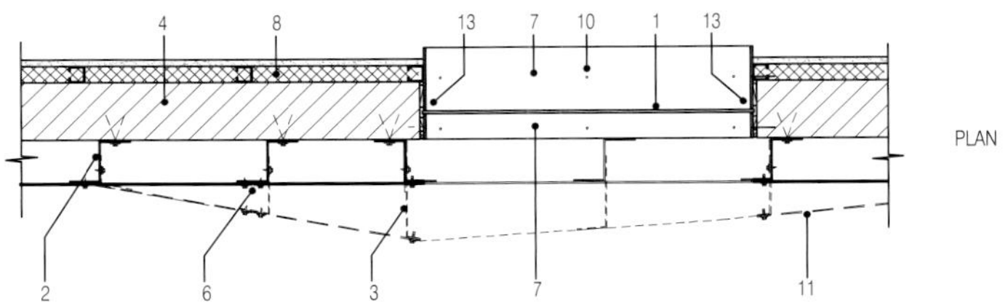

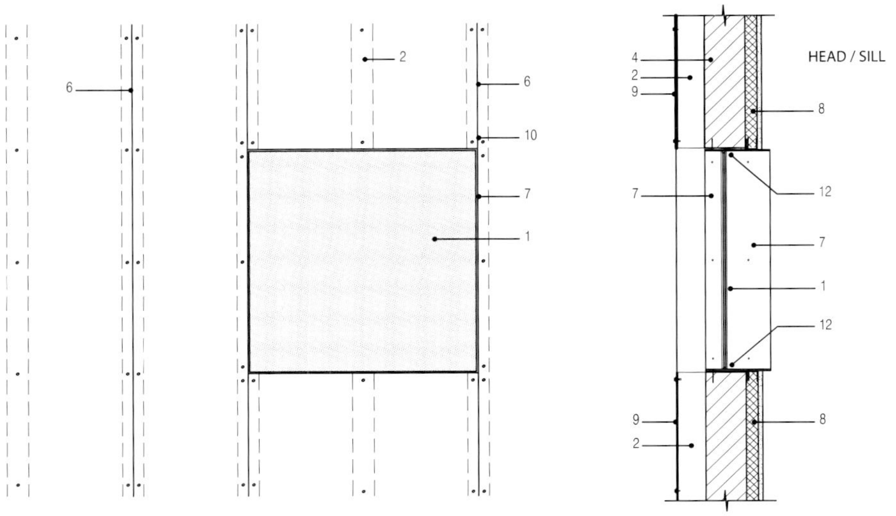

LEGEND
1. GLASS WINDOW- VARIOUS SIZES
2. 4" GALVANIZED Z-PURLIN ANCHORED TO MASONY
3. GALVANIZED 2 PIECE BREAK METAL Z-PURLIN WHERE UNDULATION AT RAINSCREEN OCCURS
4. DAMP PROOFED CMU INFILL WALL
5. 32 oz. COPPER RAINSCREEN PANEL
6. JOINT AT COPPER RAINSCREEN PANELS
7. 1/4" ALUMINUM PLATE WINDOW SURROUND
8. FURRING AT INTERIOR
9. 32 oz. COPPER RAINSCREEN PANEL
10. STAINLESS STEEL FASTENER
11. UNDULATION AT RAINSCREEN WHERE OCCURS
12. SEALANT JOINT
13. GLASS CAPTURED BY WINDOW SURROUND AT JAMB

This page
Top: Interior, view north (left); curtain-wall detail
Bottom: Entrance (left); curtain-wall-section detail

Opposite
Top: North elevation
Bottom: North-elevation detail (left); north elevation

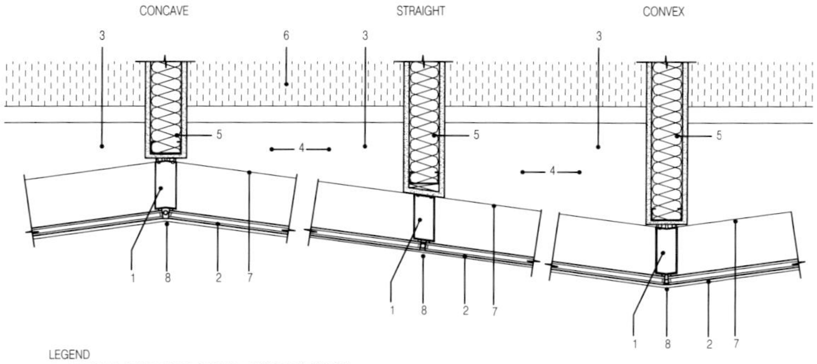

LEGEND
1. ALUMINUM CURTAIN WALL SYSTEM - CUSTOM EXTRUSION
2. INSULATED GLAZING
3. CAST IN PLACE CONCRETE SLAB
4. FLOOR SLAB CAST AS SPLIT SLAB PROFILE OF CURTAIN WALL SAWCUT AT EDGE
5. PARTITION WALL
6. CARPET
7. EDGE OF CONCRETE SLAB
8. BUTT GLAZED VERTICAL JOINT

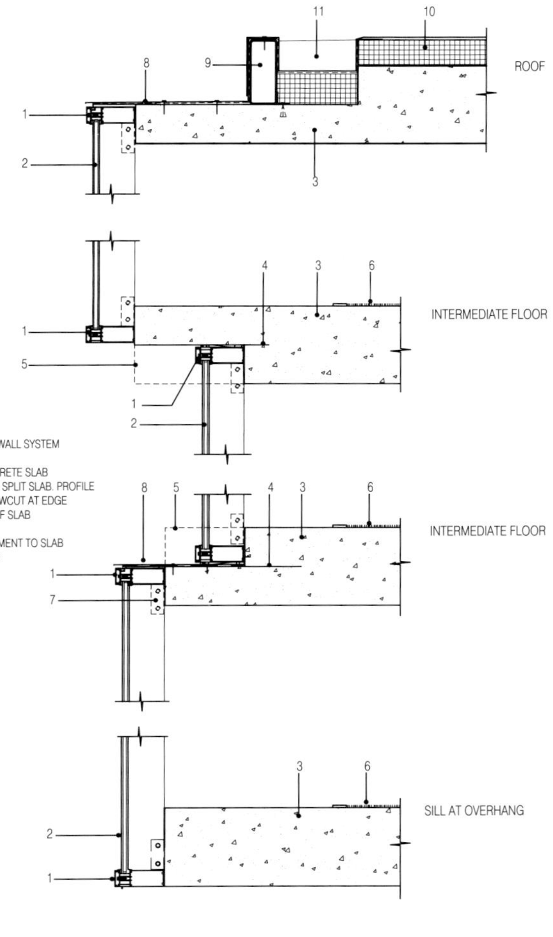

LEGEND
1. ALUMINUM CURTAIN WALL SYSTEM
2. INSULATED GLAZING
3. CAST IN PLACE CONCRETE SLAB
4. FLOOR SLAB CAST AS SPLIT SLAB. PROFILE OF CURTAIN WALL SAWCUT AT EDGE
5. REMOVED SECTION OF SLAB
6. CARPET
7. CONCEALED ATTACHMENT TO SLAB
8. ALUMINUM FLASHING
9. STEEL TUBE
10. ROOFING SYSTEM
11. GUTTER

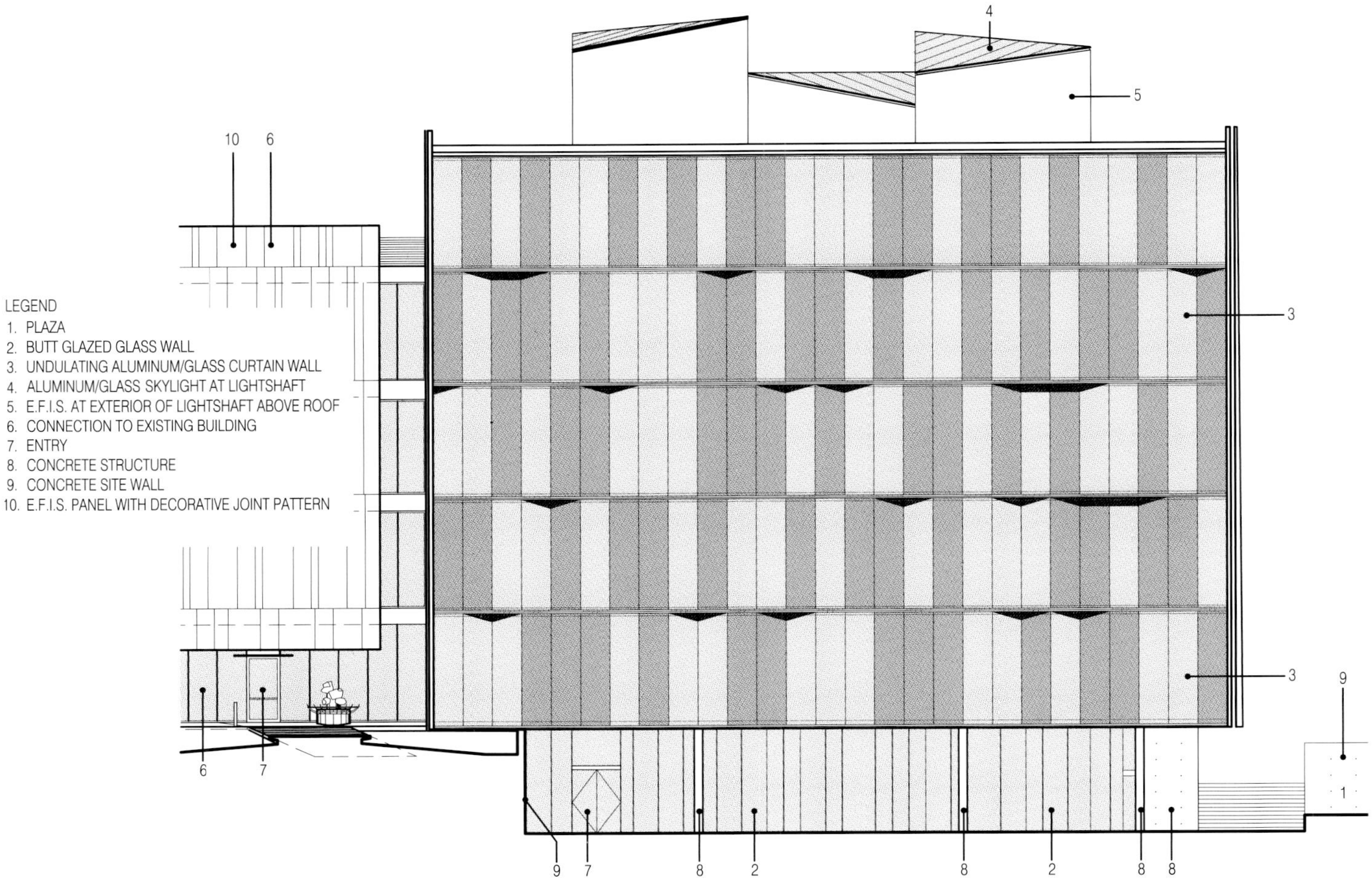
LEGEND
1. PLAZA
2. BUTT GLAZED GLASS WALL
3. UNDULATING ALUMINUM/GLASS CURTAIN WALL
4. ALUMINUM/GLASS SKYLIGHT AT LIGHTSHAFT
5. E.F.I.S. AT EXTERIOR OF LIGHTSHAFT ABOVE ROOF
6. CONNECTION TO EXISTING BUILDING
7. ENTRY
8. CONCRETE STRUCTURE
9. CONCRETE SITE WALL
10. E.F.I.S. PANEL WITH DECORATIVE JOINT PATTERN

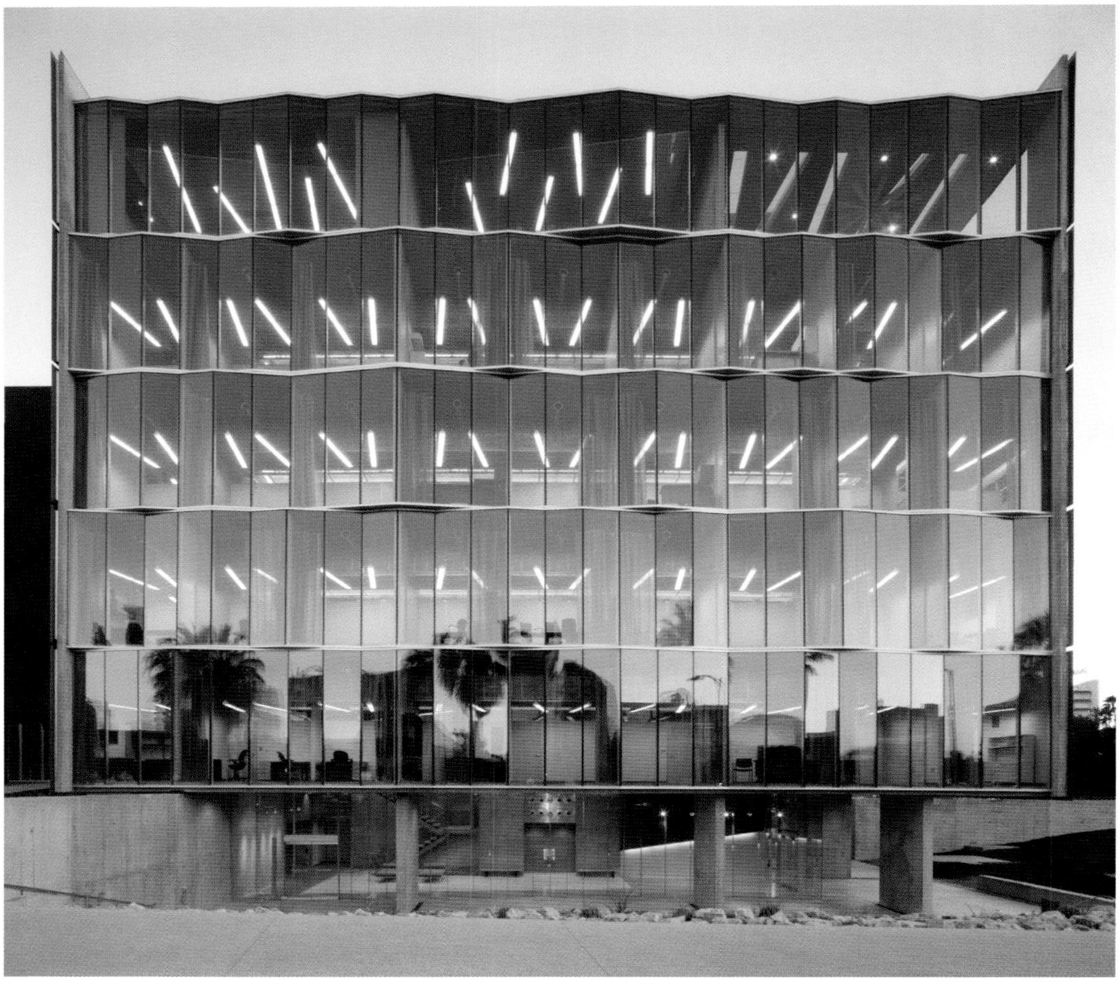

This page
Top: Section at center light shaft
Middle: Section at east light shaft (left); section at west light shaft
Bottom: Light shafts model (left); center light shaft

Opposite
Top: Section detail at light shaft (left); west light shaft, view looking up
Bottom: East light shaft (left); west light shaft, view looking down

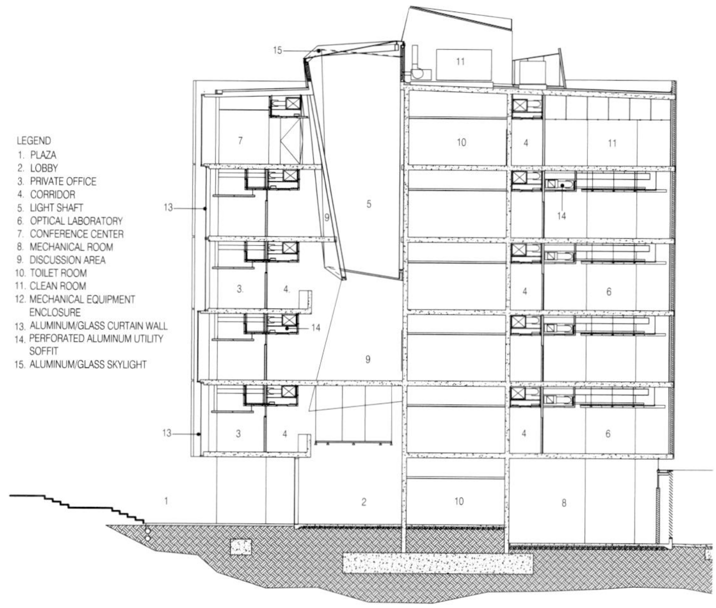

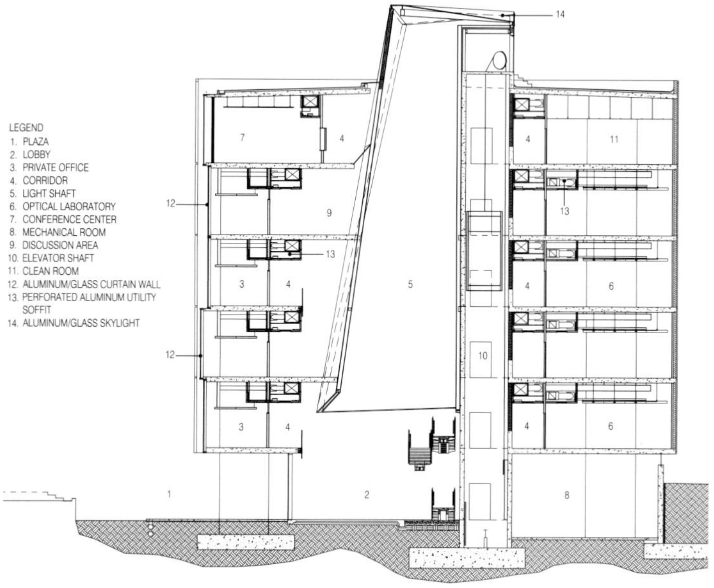

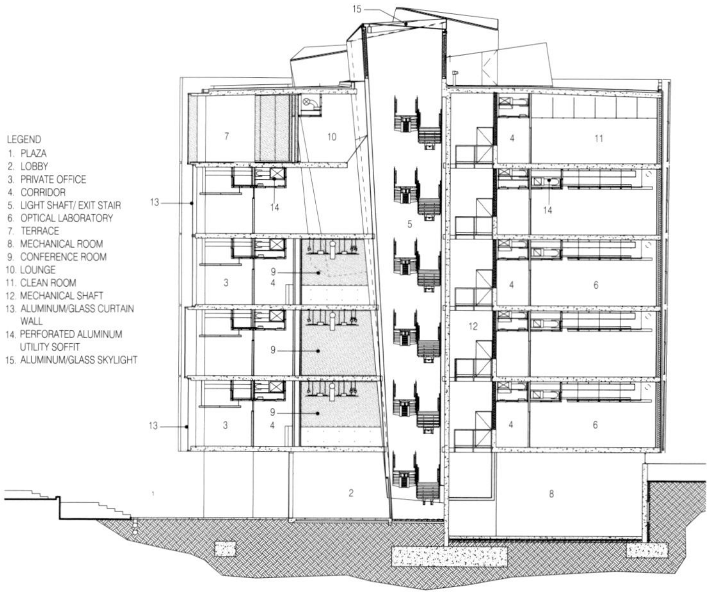

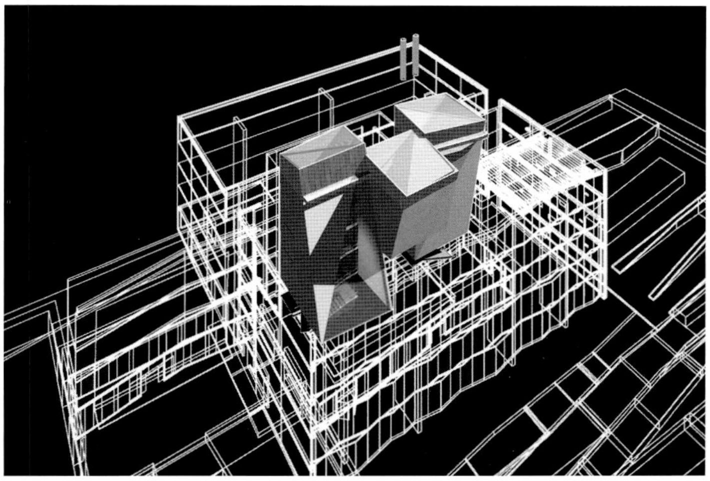

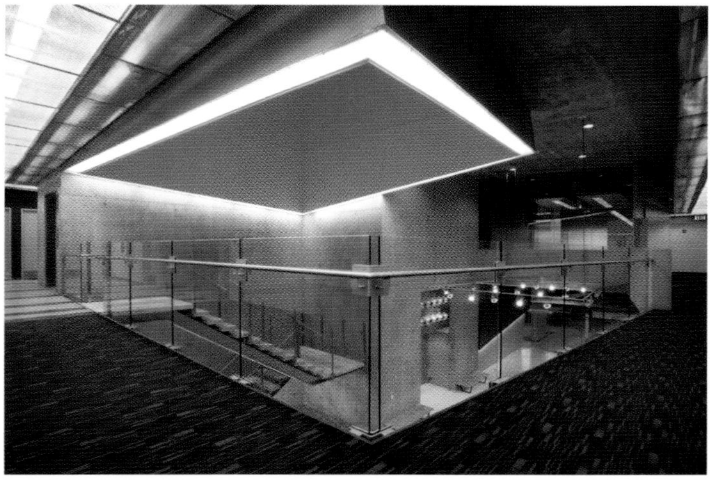

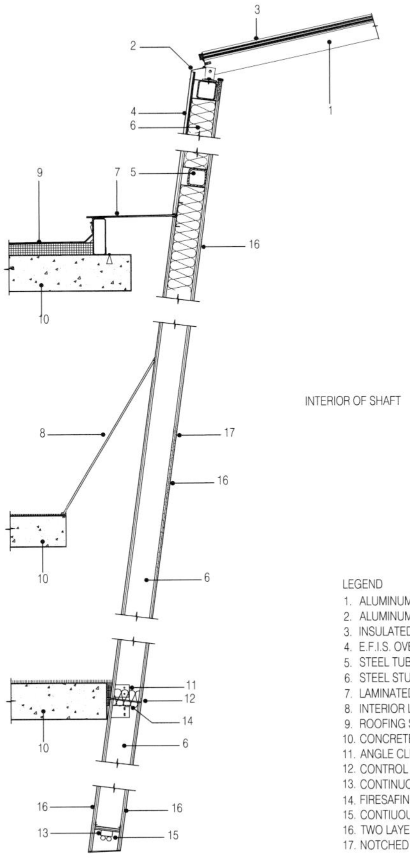

LEGEND

1. ALUMINUM FRAMED SYLIGHT
2. ALUMINUM FLASHING
3. INSULATED LAMINATED GLASS
4. E.F.I.S. OVER PLYWOOD SHEATHING
5. STEEL TUBE FRAME
6. STEEL STUD INFILL FRAMING
7. LAMINATED GLASS SKYLIGHT
8. INTERIOR LAMINATED GLASS SKYLIGHT
9. ROOFING SYSTEM
10. CONCRETE SLAB
11. ANGLE CLIP AT EDGE OF SLAB
12. CONTROL JOINT AT FLOOR LEVEL
13. CONTINUOUS LIGHT FIXTURE
14. FIRESAFING
15. CONTIUOUS ACYLIC LENS
16. TWO LAYERS 5/8" GYPSUM BOARD
17. NOTCHED TROWEL PLASTER FINISH

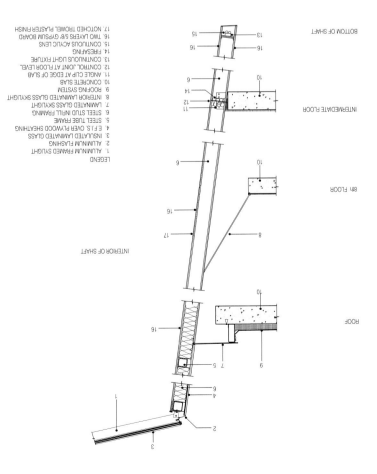

Gary Comer Youth Center, Chicago, Illinois

John Ronan Architect, Chicago

Located on Chicago's South Side, the Gary Comer Youth Center provides a place for area youth to spend after-school hours engaged in educational and recreational programs and also supports the activities of the South Shore Drill Team and Performing Arts Ensemble, a three-hundred-member dance group for children aged eight to eighteen that performs on stage and in parades about fifty times per year. The cafeteria, which serves as a daily practice area for the drill team, overlooks the dynamic center of the building, an adaptable gymnasium that converts to a six-hundred-seat performance venue with a deployable theater seating system, motorized curtains, and an 80-foot by 30-foot performance space behind stage doors.

Programmatically adaptable areas wrapped around the main practice and performance area support educational and recreational activities. An arts-and-crafts room, computer lab, dance room, recording studio, costume-design shop, stage shop, tutoring and study spaces, classrooms, offices, and an exhibition gallery are organized into flexible bars of space that can be modified over time as the youth center's programs evolve. These bar volumes terminate in the dance and art rooms, important spaces on the building's perimeter that advertise the center's activities to the community. Extensive use of glazing within the building to divide the various program spaces allows visual communication between them and fosters a sense of community and security. Classrooms, offices, and exhibition spaces on the third floor overlook a roof garden with a 24-inch soil depth punctuated by skylights to bring daylight into the gymnasium/theater and cafeteria below. The roof garden serves as an outdoor classroom, supports the center's horticultural programs, and serves to reduce the urban-heat-island effect caused by accumulated solar gain from large areas of exposed roofing. Collection and recycling of rainwater and porous paving surfaces that reduce pressure on storm water management systems reinforce the community environmental education mission of the youth center.

On the exterior of the building, a rainscreen cladding system of brightly colored fiber cement panels emphasizes the center's youthful orientation, and an 80-foot-tall mesh tower surmounted by an LED sign announces programs and events, serving as a visual marker for the community. The cement-board panels, arranged in a random pattern to animate the facade, can easily be replaced if damaged without drawing attention to the replacement.

Security concerns posed a challenge in designing the facade's exterior glazing. Bulletproof glass is used at the building's perimeter, and natural daylight brought in from above creates a light and airy interior, while maintaining a secure but inviting exterior. The parking lot, which doubles as a practice parade ground, is surrounded by a perforated-metal-screen fence, providing a secure but visible outdoor practice environment for the drill team. Raised planters along the heavily trafficked street provide an extra measure of safety for visitors as they arrive and depart.

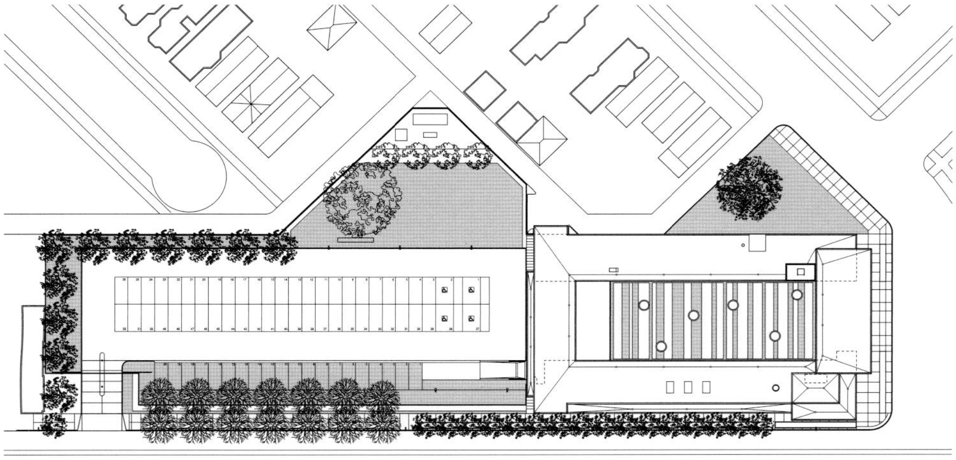

This page
Site plan

Opposite
Top: South Chicago Avenue at South Ingleside Avenue
Bottom: South Chicago Avenue elevation, view southeast

SOUTH SHORE DRILL

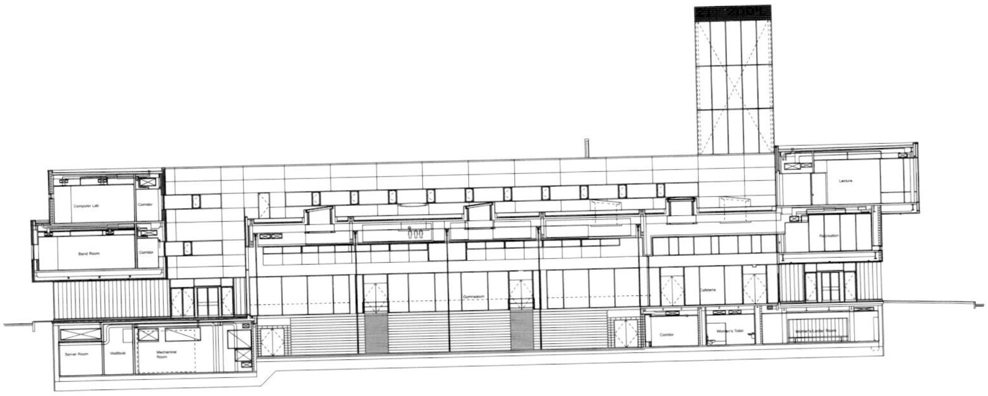

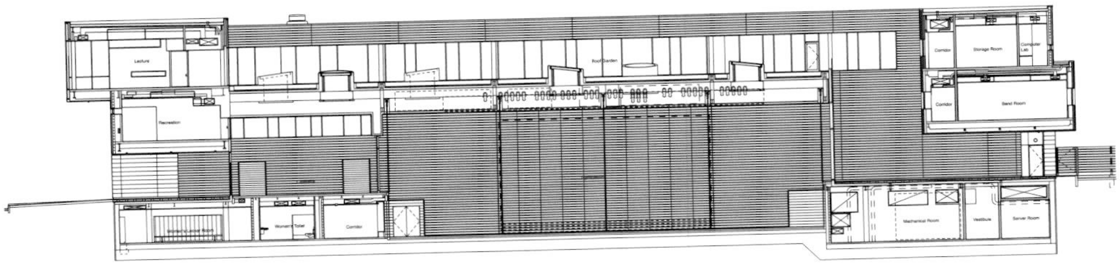

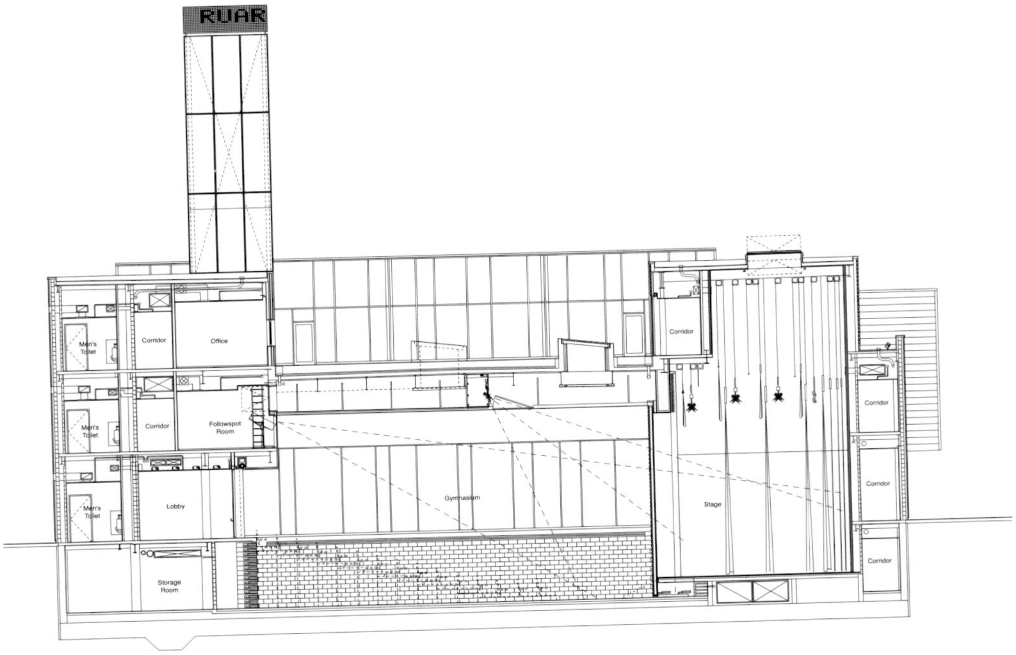

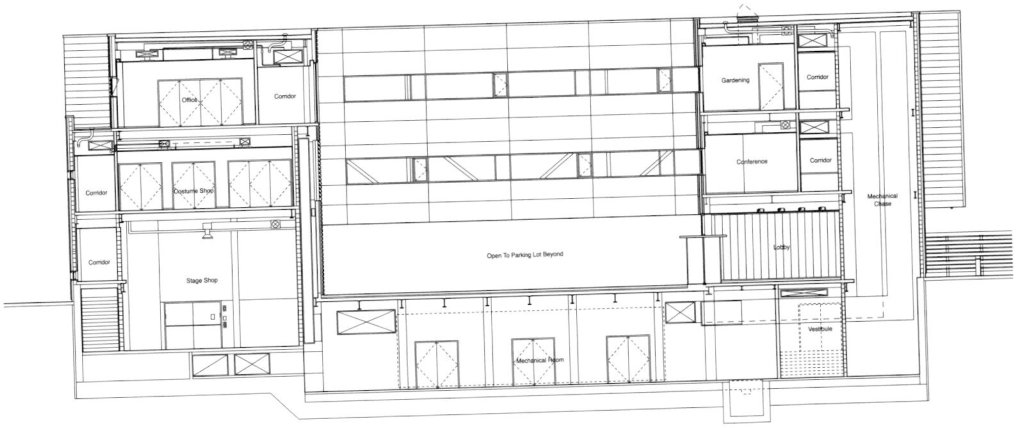

This page
Top to bottom: Longitudinal section, view northeast; longitudinal section, view southwest; cross section, view southeast; cross section, view northwest

Opposite
Top: South Ingleside Avenue entrance
Middle: Northwest elevation and parking lot
Bottom: Gymnasium (left); dance room

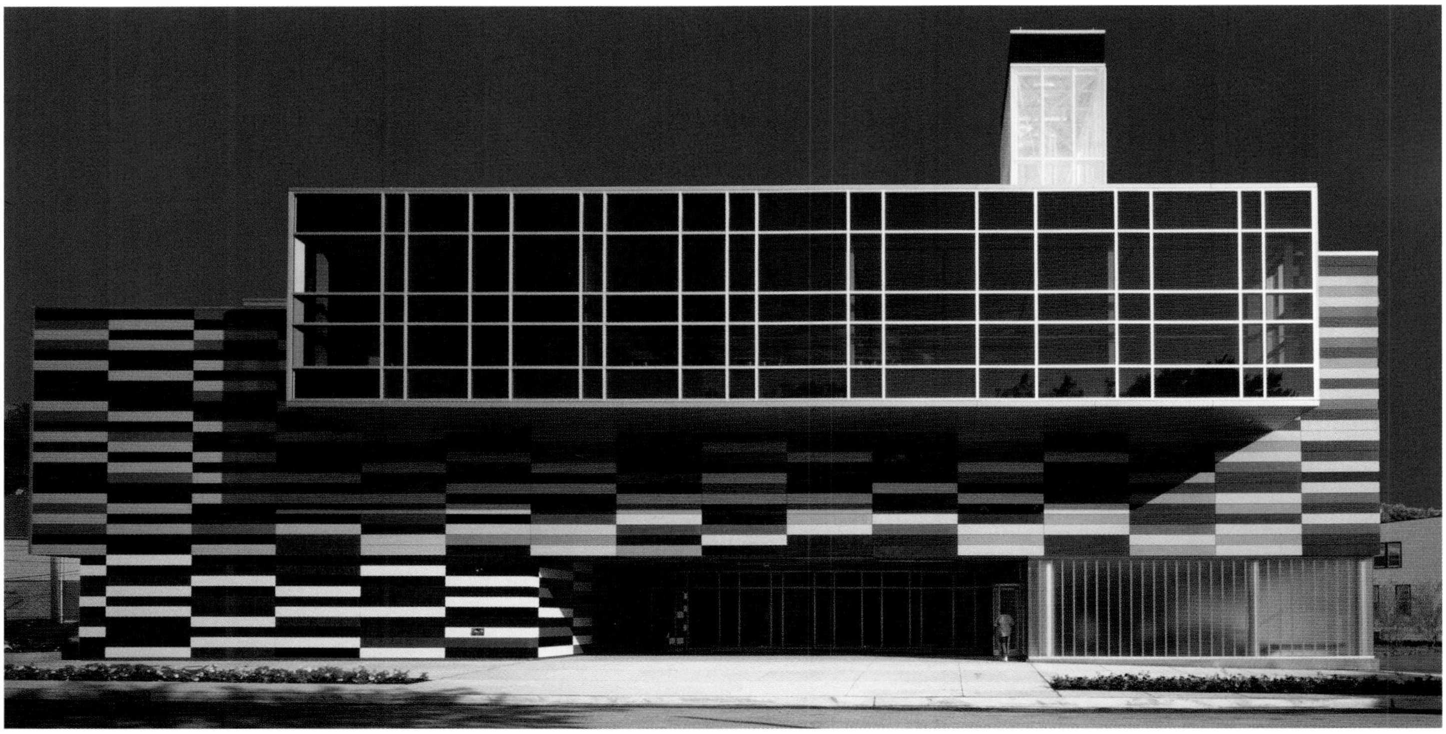

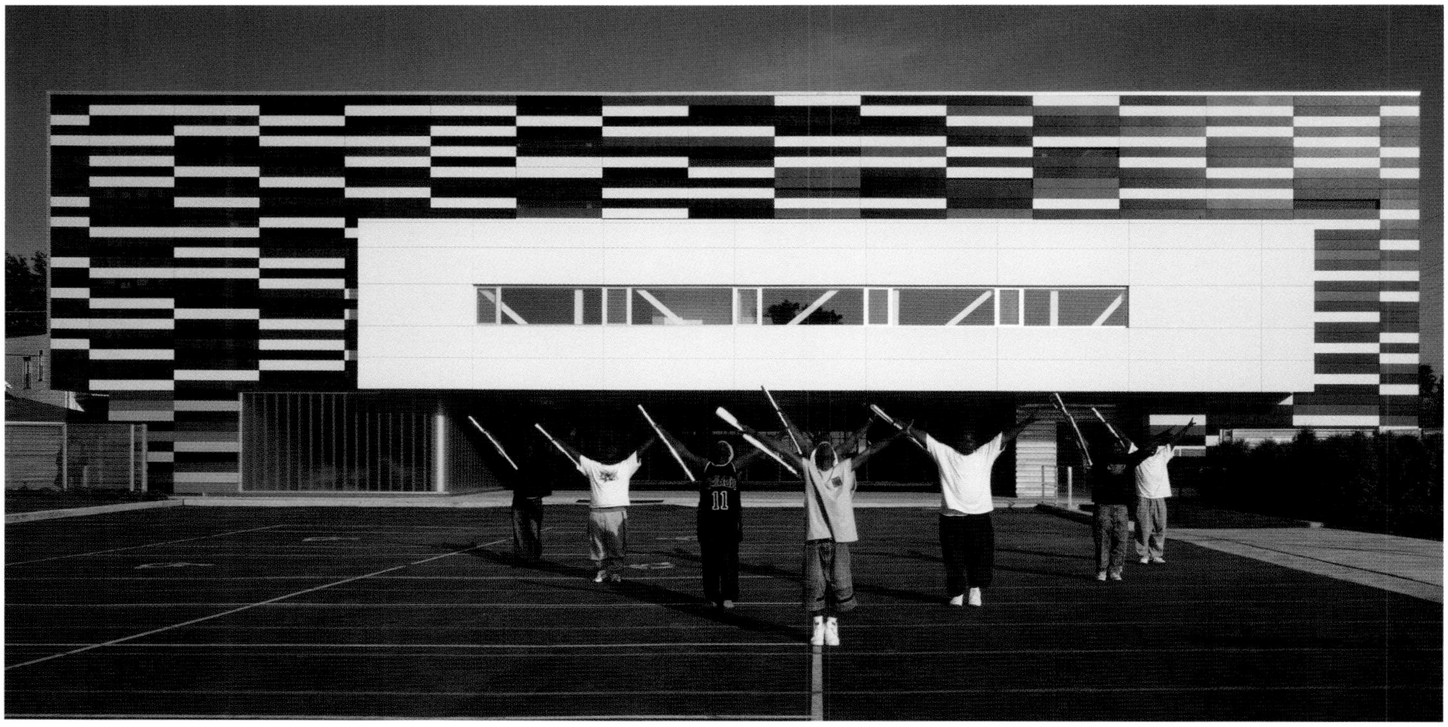

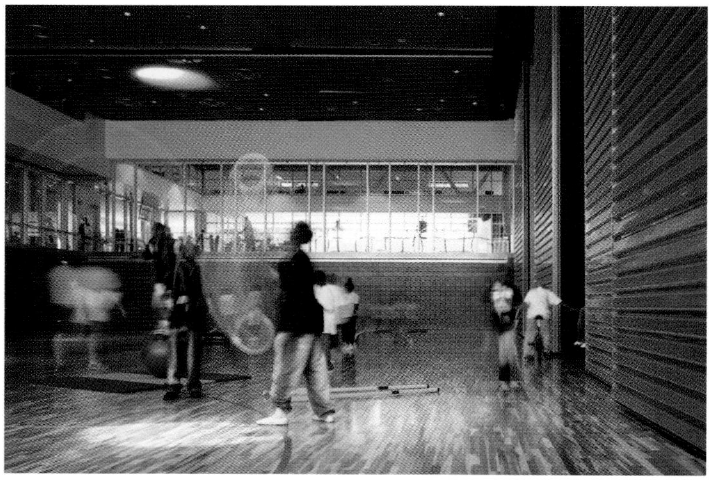

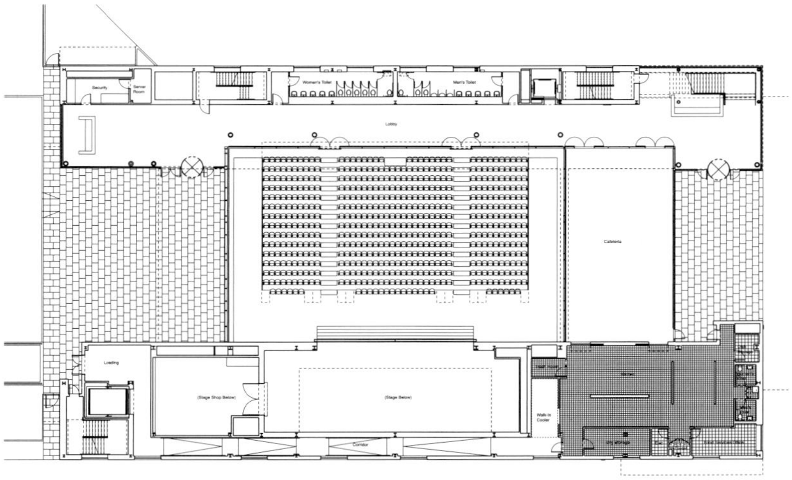

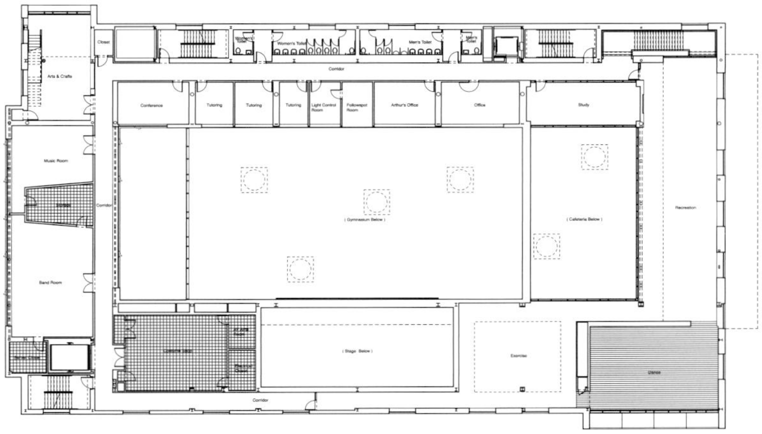

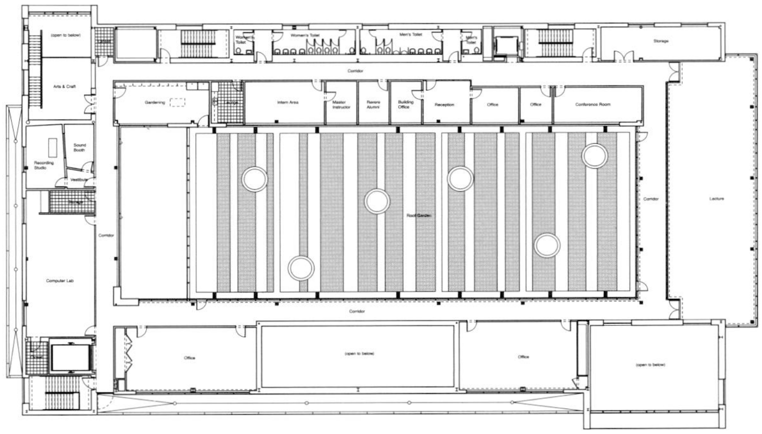

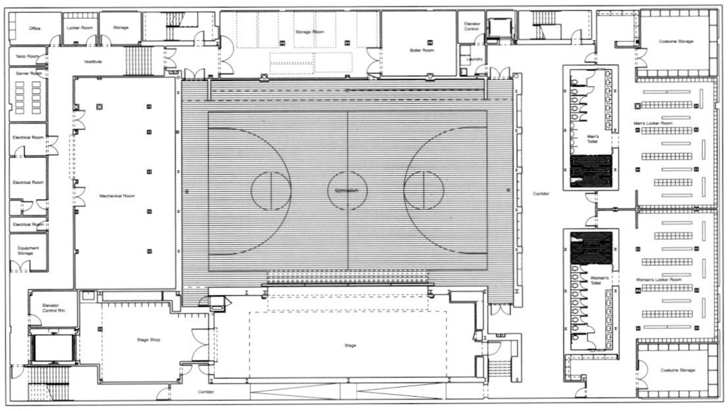

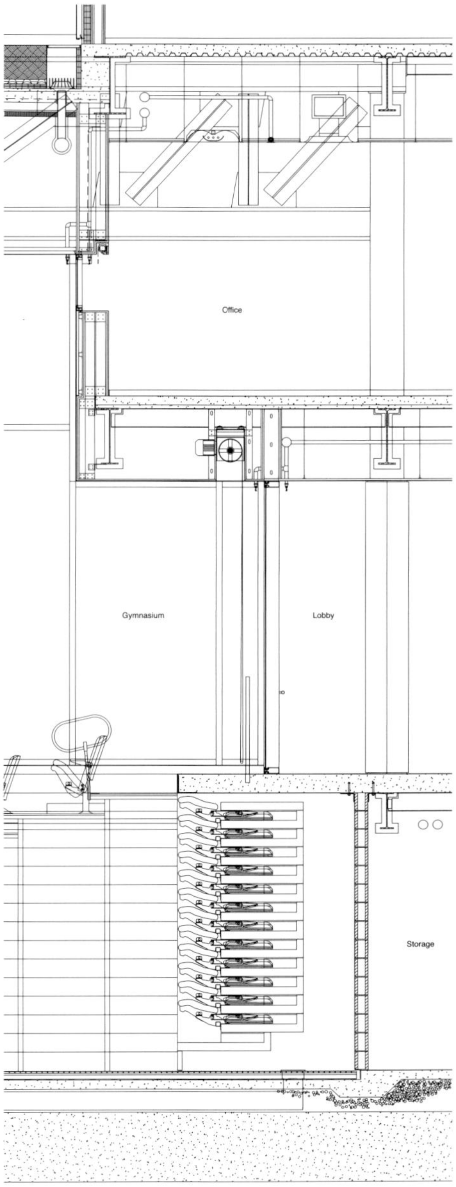

This page

Left (top to bottom): Third-floor plan; second-floor plan; first-floor plan; lower-level plan

Right: Interior-wall section with demountable seating

Opposite

Top (left to right): Exterior-wall section and concrete-panel detail; exterior wall section with window cross-section detail; exterior-wall section with modular concrete panels

Bottom: Main elevations, night view (left); South Chicago Avenue elevation detail

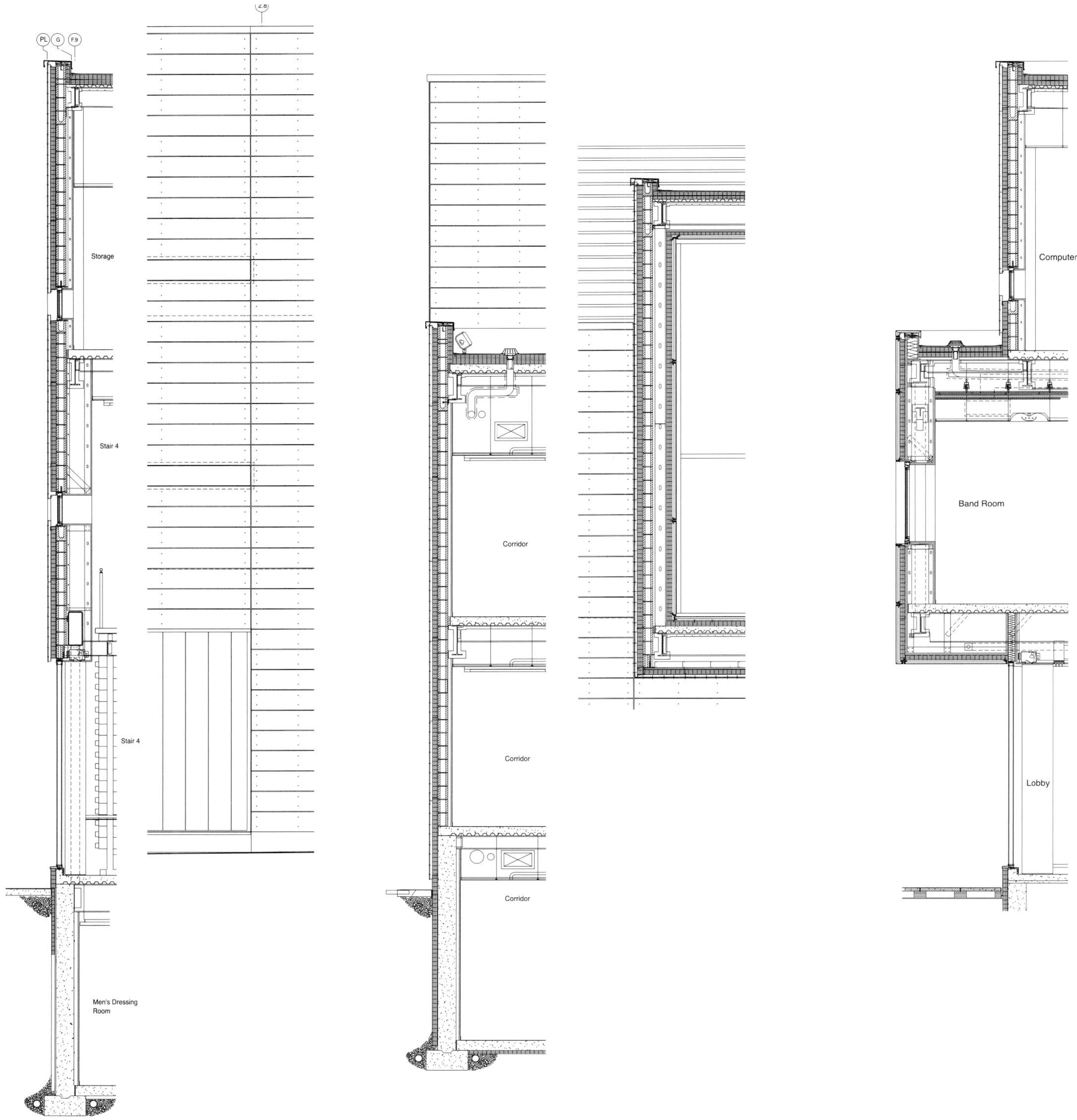
PL
G
F9
2.8
Storage
Stair 4
Stair 4
Men's Dressing Room
Corridor
Corridor
Corridor
Computer Lab
Band Room
Lobby

SOUTH SHORE DRILL

Toledo Museum of Art Glass Pavilion, Toledo, Ohio
Kazuyo Sejima + Ryue Nishizawa / SANAA, Tokyo, Japan
Kendall/Heaton Associates, Inc., Houston, Texas

The Glass Pavilion at the Toledo Museum of Art houses and displays the museum's significant collection of glass objects, provides a place for exhibitions in the art of glass making, and offers studio space for artists in residence. The 76,000-square-foot pavilion dissolves the visual barrier between interior space and the outside environment and gives visitors the feeling of walking under the trees in the parklike setting, through light, transparent spaces uncluttered by structural support elements and building services.

The formal arrangement of the main level—thirteen discrete, vitrinelike glass volumes within a glass envelope—was inspired by its programmatic elements. Spaces with very different environmental requirements, such as exhibition galleries, two glass-making studios or "hot shops"—with glassblowing furnaces that can reach 2,400 degrees Fahrenheit—a black box gallery, and a cafe are located within separate glass volumes in close proximity to one another.

The structure devised for the 15-foot-high main level of the Glass Pavilion combines unorthodox solutions for steel framing in the roof and the concrete framing in the floor to reduce circulation space for services to the narrowest possible profile. The steel roof consists of a horizontal moment-connected beam-and-girder grid. Comparable to a flat plate, the system has a maximum structural depth of 12 inches for spans of up to 50 feet. The roof is supported by thirty-five steel round bar columns, nine of them hollow and twenty-six solid, which support pin connections at the top. Although the roof appears to be flat, it is actually a series of inverted pyramids, each connected to a drainpipe that channels water into the main drainage system.

The exterior and interior glass panels were manufactured in Germany, of Pilkington low-iron Optiwhite glass to maximize their colorless transparency, and shipped to China to be heated over flat and curved molds of various sizes before being laminated together for added strength. Most of the glass panels are 8 feet wide and 13 feet 2 1/2 inches high. The exterior has 122 1-inch-thick panels, made of two layers of 1/2-inch glass, 30 of them curved; there are 91 flat interior panels and 129 curved, all 3/4 inches thick, made of two 3/8-inch panels laminated together and set into embedded floor and ceiling tracks. In response to shifting stresses and loads on the building, a rocking stainless-steel damper mechanism embedded in the bottom tracks allows the panels to move up and down slightly without breaking. Gaps between the glass panels are filled with clear silicone sealant.

Wiring and HVAC ducts in the Glass Pavilion are routed through the floors and ceiling of the building, as well as within the opaque dry-walled sections of the main level. The concrete floor contains shallow, wide band beams, with one-way slabs to allow for numerous linear slots to feed HVAC conduits through from below. To provide for the different temperature and humidity conditions needed for various rooms—cool and dry with precise temperature control for display of the glass pieces, superheated for the glass-making areas—the Glass Pavilion has three separate heating and air-conditioning systems. Interstitial spaces between most volumes act as insulating pockets, further regulating the interior conditions of the galleries. The mechanical system uses these interstitial spaces between the glass volumes as a temperature buffer, recycling the cooled air from the galleries to the hot shops. Recirculated air in the voids between the outer and inner glass walls also acts as insulation to moderate temperatures within the building. A hood around each of the furnaces in the hot shops exhausts most of the heat through the roof of the building; the radiant heating system, with recovery coils embedded in the floors, returns the rest of the heat from the furnaces to the voids between the glass volumes and cavities elsewhere in the building.

Special translucent sunlight-reflecting curtains installed in the spaces surrounding many of the galleries are adjusted according to seasonal sun angles to regulate the amount of daylight entering the building.

SANAA, Transsolar, and Guy Nordenson & Associates contributed to this text.

Opposite
Interior

This page
Top: Exterior elevation at Hot Shop, view southeast
Middle: East and north elevations
Bottom: Exterior elevation at Hot Shop, view southwest

Opposite
Top: Interior court without curtains (left); curtain-wall detail
Bottom: Interior court with curtains closed

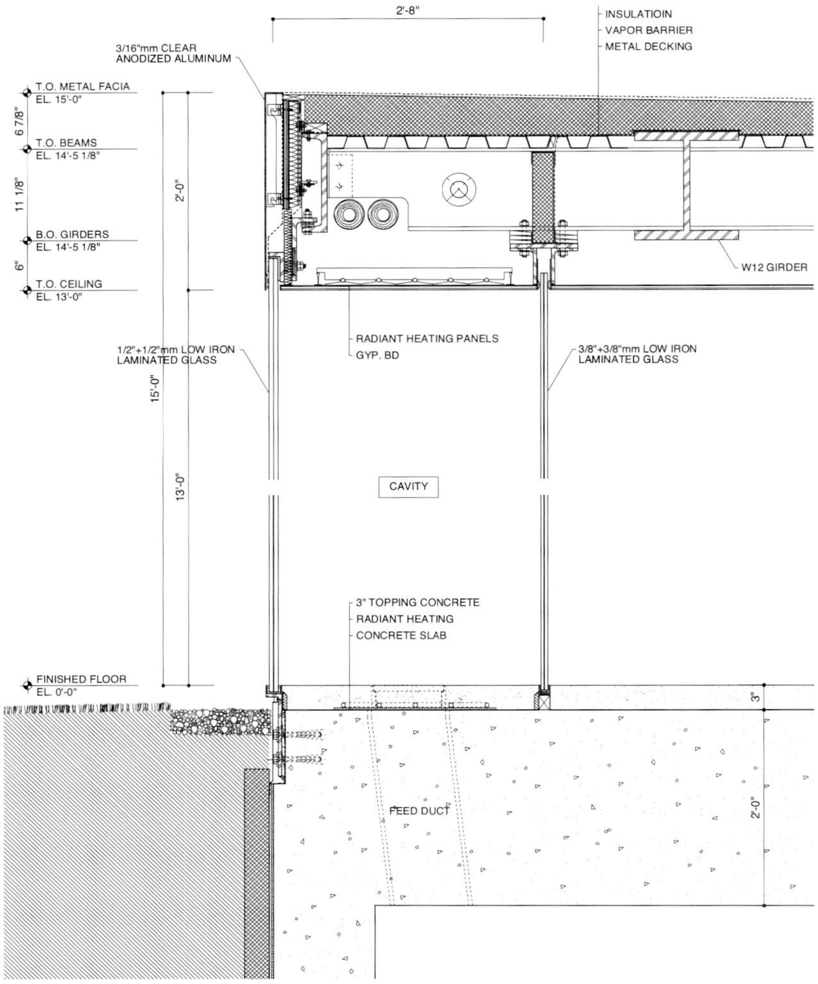
2'-8"
INSULATIOIN
VAPOR BARRIER
METAL DECKING
3/16"mm CLEAR
ANODIZED ALUMINUM
T.O. METAL FACIA
EL. 15'-0"
6 7/8"
T.O. BEAMS
EL. 14'-5 1/8"
11 1/8"
2'-0"
B.O. GIRDERS
EL. 14'-5 1/8"
6"
T.O. CEILING
EL. 13'-0"
W12 GIRDER
RADIANT HEATING PANELS
GYP. BD
1/2"+1/2"mm LOW IRON
LAMINATED GLASS
3/8"+3/8"mm LOW IRON
LAMINATED GLASS
15'-0"
13'-0"
CAVITY
3" TOPPING CONCRETE
RADIANT HEATING
CONCRETE SLAB
FINISHED FLOOR
EL. 0'-0"
3"
FEED DUCT
2'-0"

This page
Top: Section
Middle: Interior view to exterior courtyard (left); glass cavity-wall detail
Bottom: Exterior courtyard

Opposite
Top: Glass-panel-layout plan
Bottom: Exhibition space (left); exterior view to exhibtion space

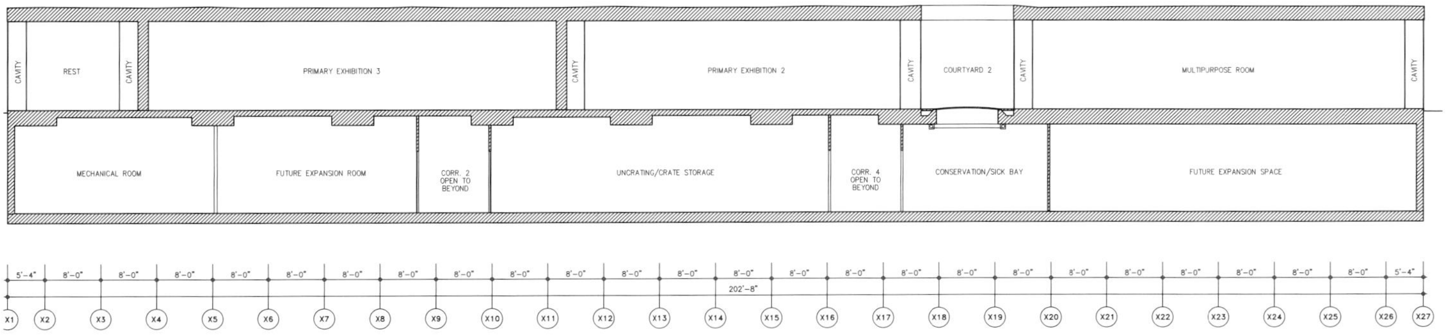

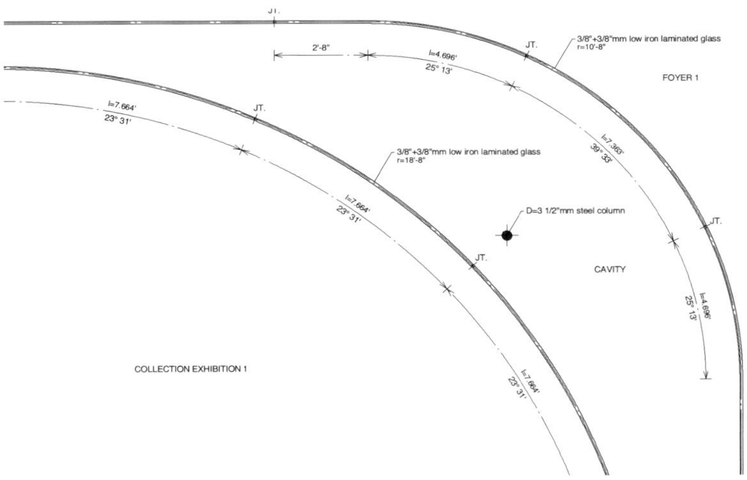

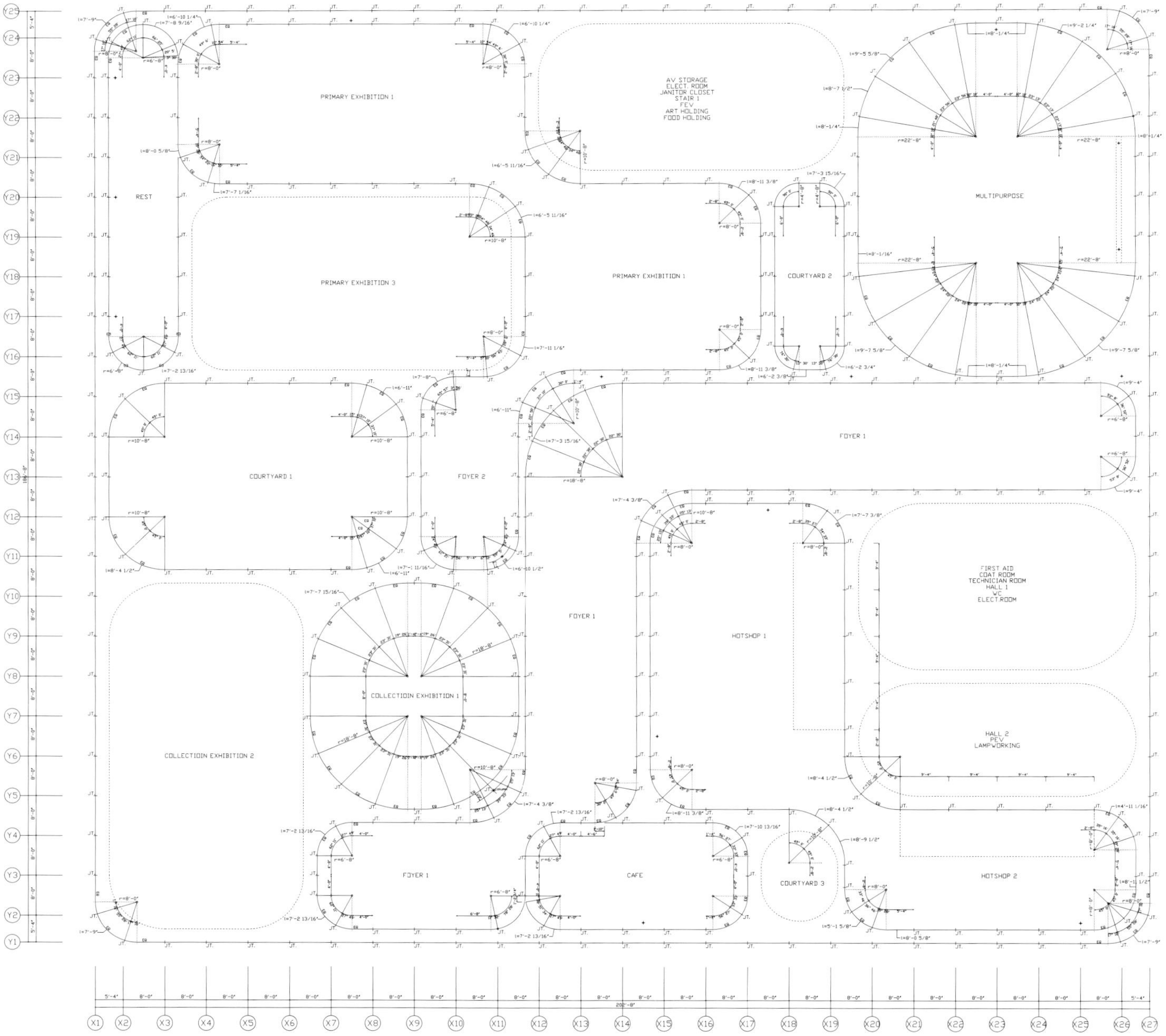
PRIMARY EXHIBITION 1
AV STORAGE
ELECT. ROOM
JANITOR CLOSET
STAIR 1
FEV
ART HOLDING
FOOD HOLDING
REST
MULTIPURPOSE
PRIMARY EXHIBITION 3
PRIMARY EXHIBITION 1
COURTYARD 2
FOYER 1
COURTYARD 1
FOYER 2
FIRST AID
COAT ROOM
TECHNICIAN ROOM
HALL 1
WC
ELECT.ROOM
FOYER 1
HOTSHOP 1
COLLECTIOIN EXHIBITION 1
COLLECTIOIN EXHIBITION 2
HALL 2
FEV
LAMPWORKING
FOYER 1
CAFE
COURTYARD 3
HOTSHOP 2

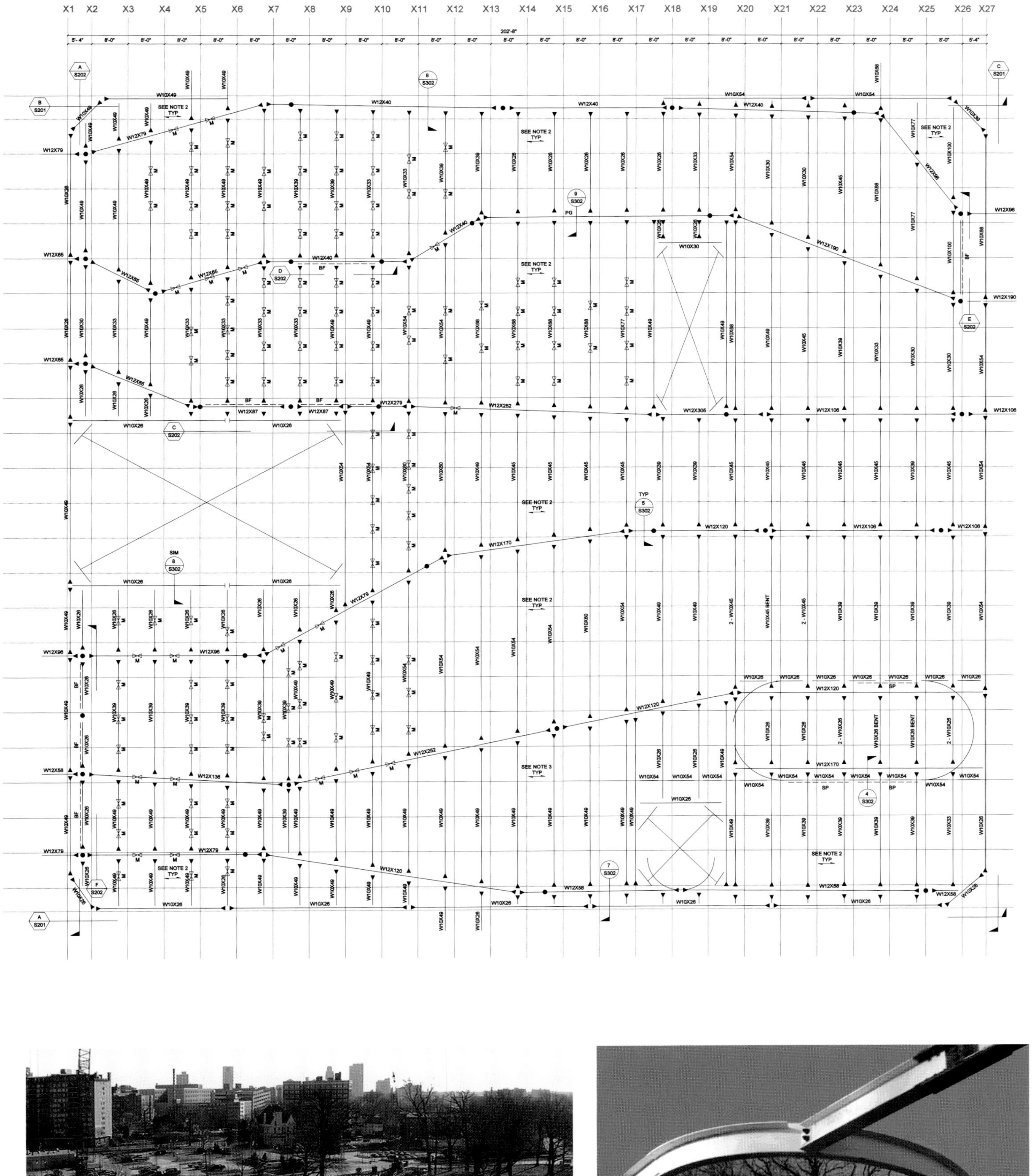
X1 X2 X3 X4 X5 X6 X7 X8 X9 X10 X11 X12 X13 X14 X15 X16 X17 X18 X19 X20 X21 X22 X23 X24 X25 X26 X27
202'-8"

Opposite
Top: Roof-framing plan
Bottom: Framing construction (left); framing detail

This page
Top: Steel structural model
Middle: Steel structural model, deflection (left); ground-floor beams and basement-column moments
Bottom: CATIA roof, isometric

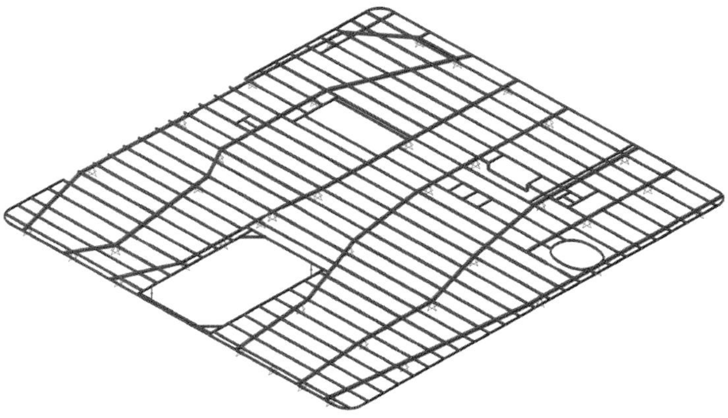

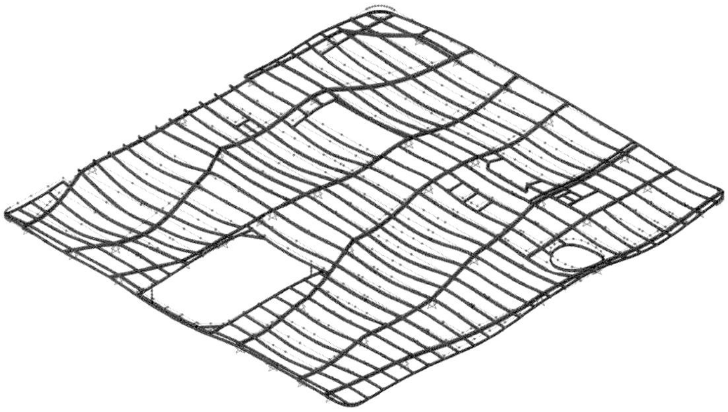

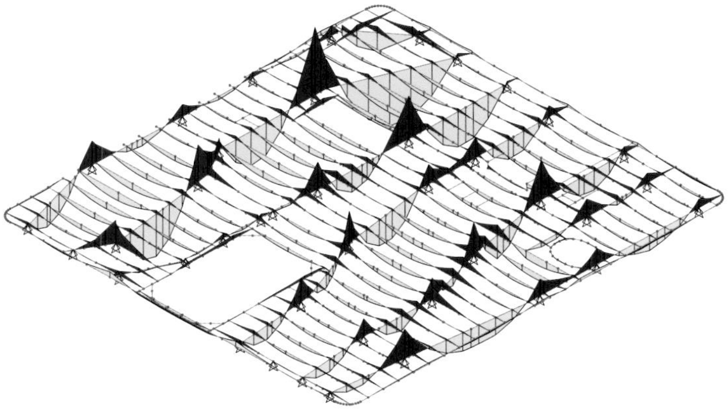

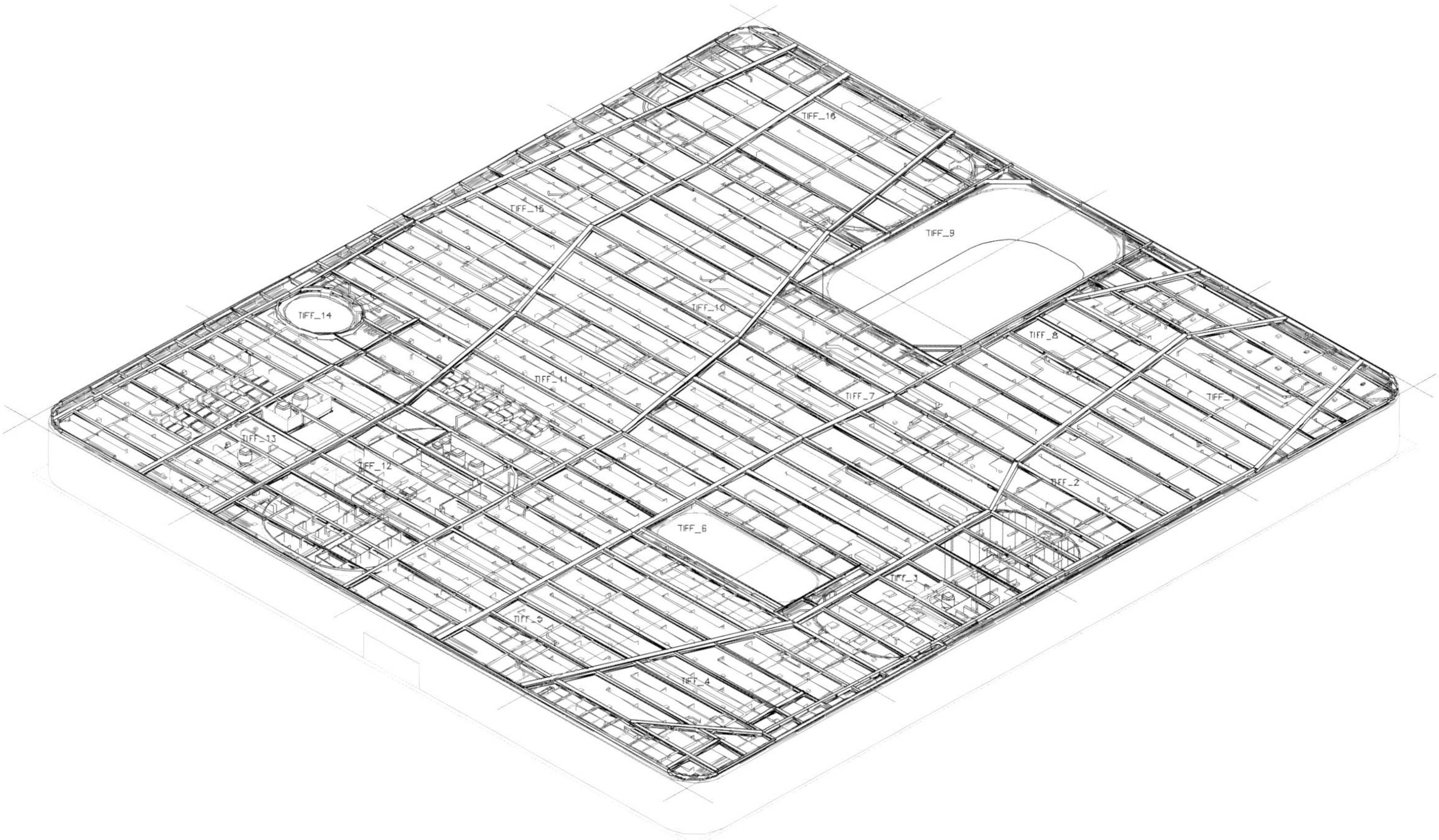

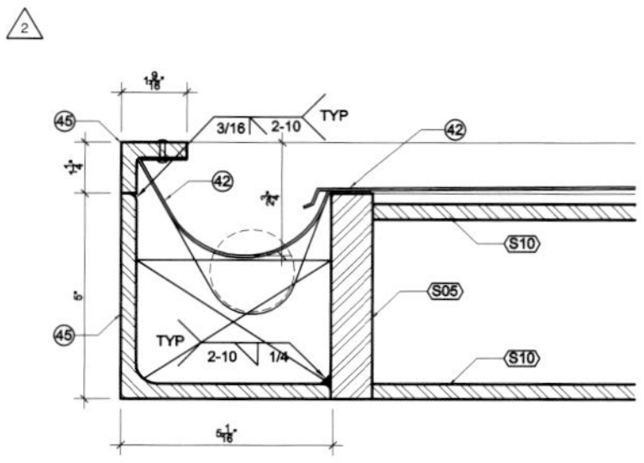

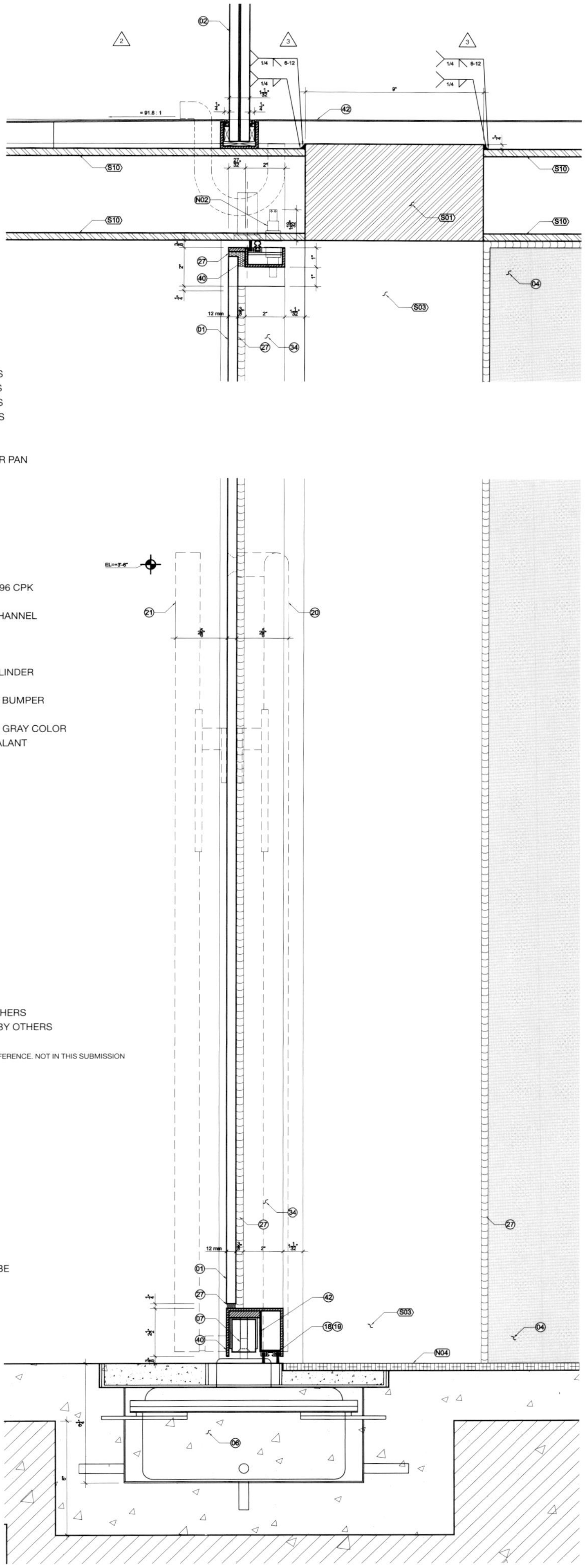

MATERIAL LIST AND NOTATIONS

01 12 mm TEMPERED GLASS
02 12 mm + 12 mm TEMPERED LAMINATED GLASS
03 12 mm + 12 mm ANNEALED LAMINATED GLASS
04 10 mm + 10 mm TEMPERED LAMINATED GLASS
05 10 mm + 10 mm ANNEALED LAMINATED GLASS
06 SAINO TN OPERATOR WITH COVER PAN
07 SAINO DOOR SHOE
08 RIXSON H28 FLOOR CLOSER WITH 7/8" COVER PAN
09 RIXSON 587 CLOSER ARM
10 RIXSON H28 CLOSER ARM
11 RIXSON 6-526 DOORS TOP/HOLD
12 RIXSON 370 FLOORBEARING BOTTOM PIVOT
13 RIXSON 3/4" H345 TOP PIVOT
14 RIXSON H345 TOP PIVOT RECEIVER
15 RIXSON SL 102 TOP PIVOT RECEIVER
16 RIXSON 340 TOP PIVOT
17 PEMKO BRUSH 5041P AND PEMKO GASKET 296 CPK
18 PEMKO BRUSH 5041AP WITH DOUBLE LAYER
19 CUSTOM ALUMINUM WEATHER STRIPPING CHANNEL
20 CRL PA 110 PANIC DEVICE
21 CRL KS EXTERIOR HANDLE
22 CRL SURFACE MOUNT STRIKE
23 CRL DB140 DEADBOLT HANDLE WITH KEY CYLINDER
24 CRL N EXTERIOR HANDLE
25 MCMAS TERCARR MALE-THREADED RUBBER BUMPER
26 LCN ACTUATOR 7918
27 DOW CORNING STRUCTURAL SILICONE WITH GRAY COLOR
28 DOW CORNING TRANSLUCENT WEATHER SEALANT
29 ø 5/8" X 6" LARGE EXPANSION ANCHOR BOLT
30 ø 3/8" X 6" LARGE EXPANSION ANCHOR BOLT
31 NONSHRINK GROUT
32 5" X 2-1/2" S/S BAR
33 5" X 1-5/8" S/S BAR
34 1" X 2" S/S BAR
35 7/8" X 2-1/4" S/S BAR
36 1" X 2-1/4" S/S BAR
37 3/8" THICK S/S PLATE
38 1/4" THICK S/S PLATE
39 1/8" THICK S/S SHEET POURSTOP AND CASE
40 1/8" THICK S/S BUILT-UP RAIL
41 5 GA S/S PLATE
42 16 GA S/S SHEET
43 3/8" STEEL ANGLE
44 ø 7/8" BENT CONDUIT TUBE
45 3/8" THICK STEEL ANGLE
N01 7/16" X 1/2" CONDUIT
N02 3/4" GE RECESSED SECURITY SENSOR BY OTHERS
N03 SECURITRON IMXD-12 MAGNET AND STRIKE BY OTHERS
N04 3/8" THICK MATTING BY OTHERS
N05 EXTERIOR ALUMINUM GLASS SILL ONLY FOR REFERENCE. NOT IN THIS SUBMISSION
N06 3" THICK PAVER BY OTHERS
N07 3" THICK CONCRETE TOPPING BY OTHERS
N08 STRUCTURAL CONCRETE SLAB BY OTHERS

STRUCTURAL MEMBER LIST

S01 5" X 9" HOT ROLLED STEEL BEAM
S02 2" X 5" STEEL BAR
S03 1-7/8" X 9" STEEL BAR
S04 1-7/8" X 5" STEEL BAR
S05 1" X 5" STEEL BAR
S06 1" X 4" STEEL BAR
S07 3/4" X 4" STEEL BAR
S08 1-5/8" X 1-7/8" X 3/16" FABRICATED STEEL TUBE
S09 1-7/8" X 2" X 3/16" FABRICATED STEEL TUBE
S10 3/8" THICK STEEL PLATE
S11 5/8" X 8" X 8" THICK STEEL BASEPLATE
S12 5/8" X 9" X 9" THICK STEEL BASEPLATE

This page
Right: Entrance-canopy-detail section
Left: Entrance-door detail (top); entrance-ceiling detail

Opposite
Left (top to bottom): Foyer model; velocity vectors, colored by velocity magnitude; radiant-floor-room model; air-storm-room model
Right (top to bottom): Foyer; foyer with curtains closed

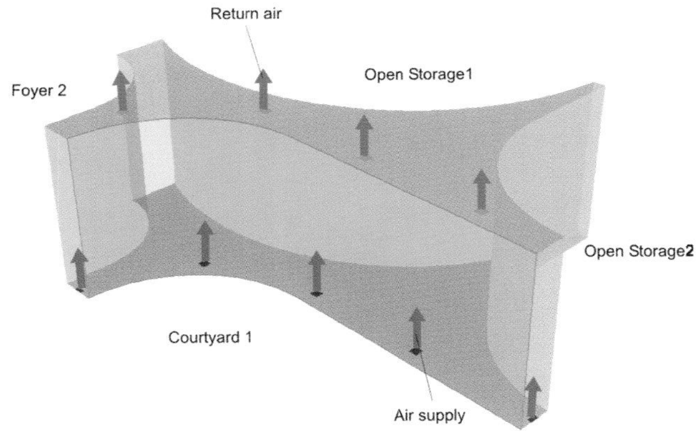
Return air
Foyer 2
Open Storage1
Open Storage2
Courtyard 1
Air supply

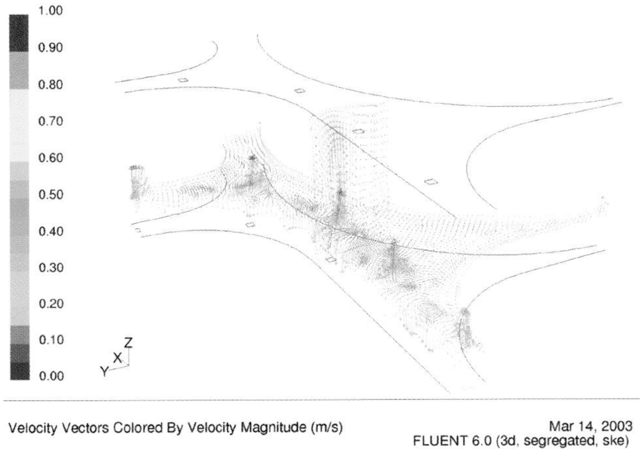
1.00
0.90
0.80
0.70
0.60
0.50
0.40
0.30
0.20
0.10
0.00
Z
X
Y
Velocity Vectors Colored By Velocity Magnitude (m/s)
Mar 14, 2003
FLUENT 6.0 (3d, segregated, ske)

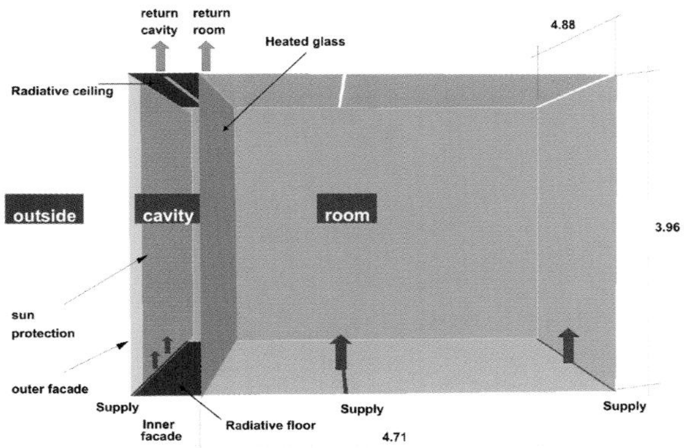
return cavity
return room
Heated glass
4.88
Radiative ceiling
outside
cavity
room
3.96
sun protection
outer facade
Supply
Inner facade
Radiative floor
Supply
Supply
4.71

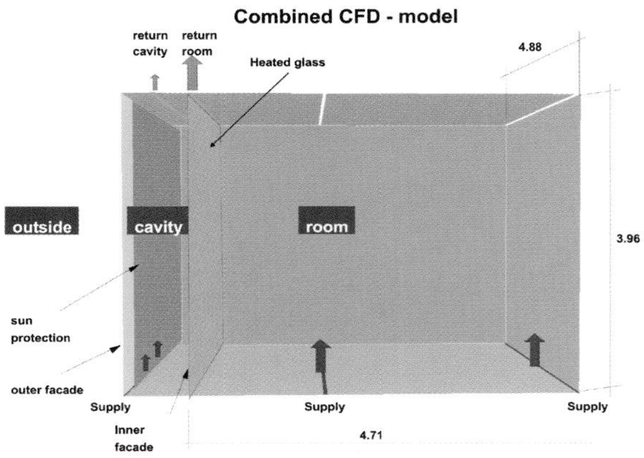
Combined CFD - model
return cavity
return room
Heated glass
4.88
outside
cavity
room
3.96
sun protection
outer facade
Supply
Inner facade
Supply
Supply
4.71

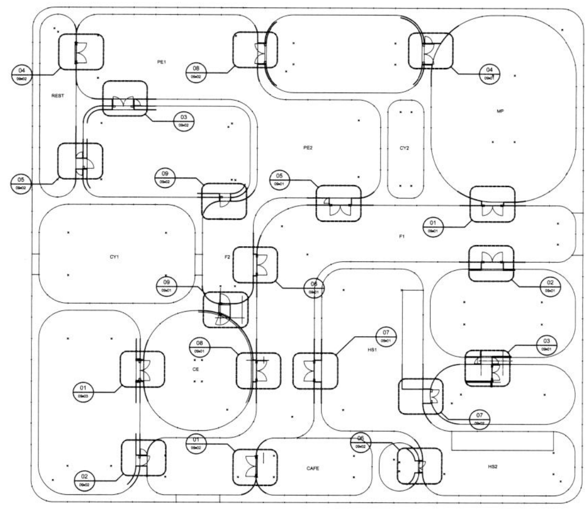

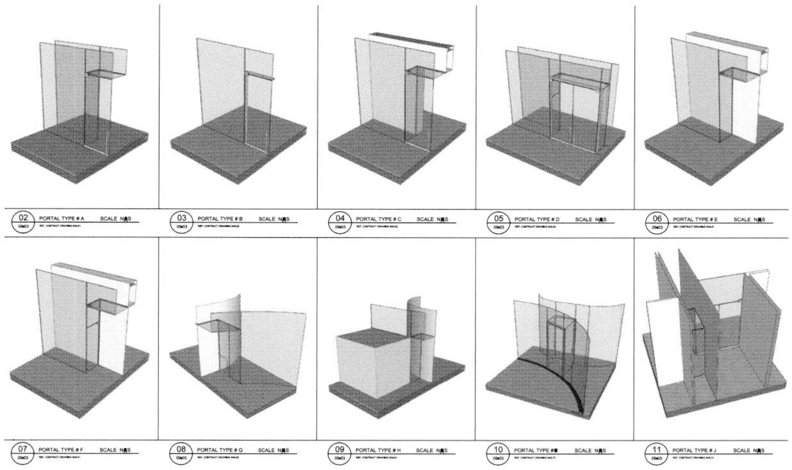

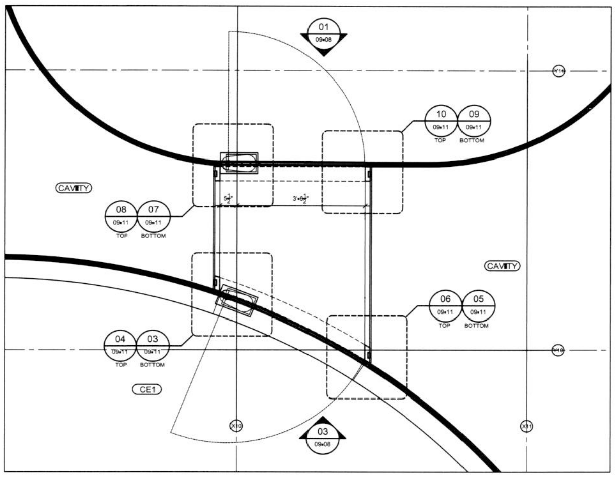

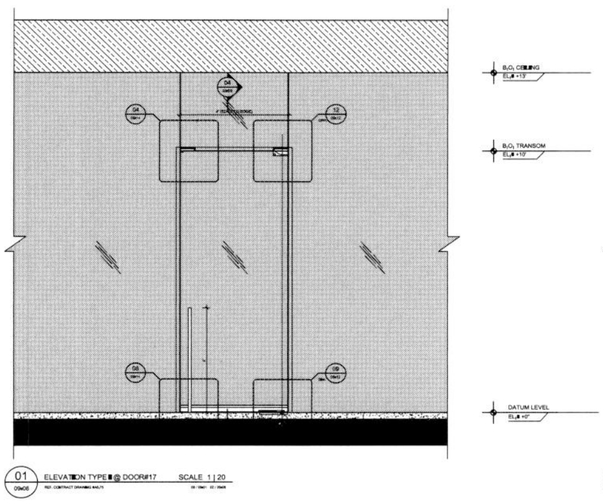

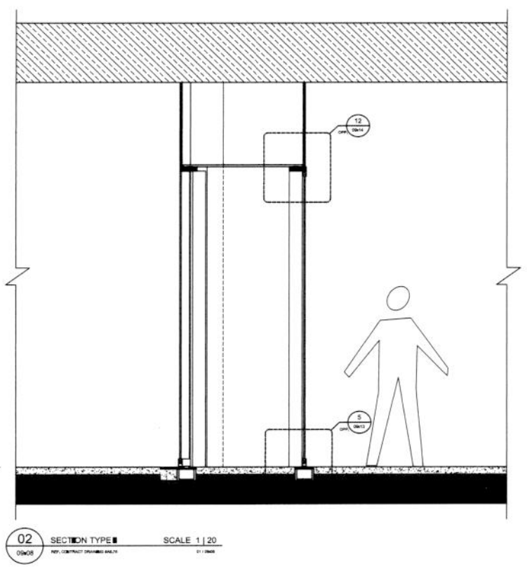

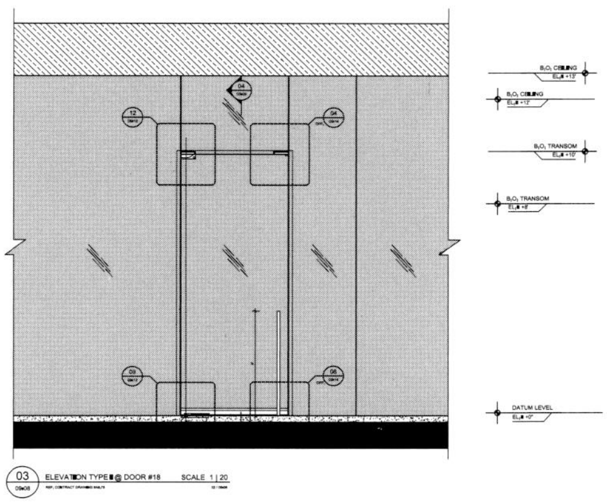

This page
Top: Portal-key plan
Middle top: Portal types (left);
Portal-I plan
Middle bottom: Portal-I elevations
Bottom: Portal-I (left);
Portal-I detail

Opposite
Portal details

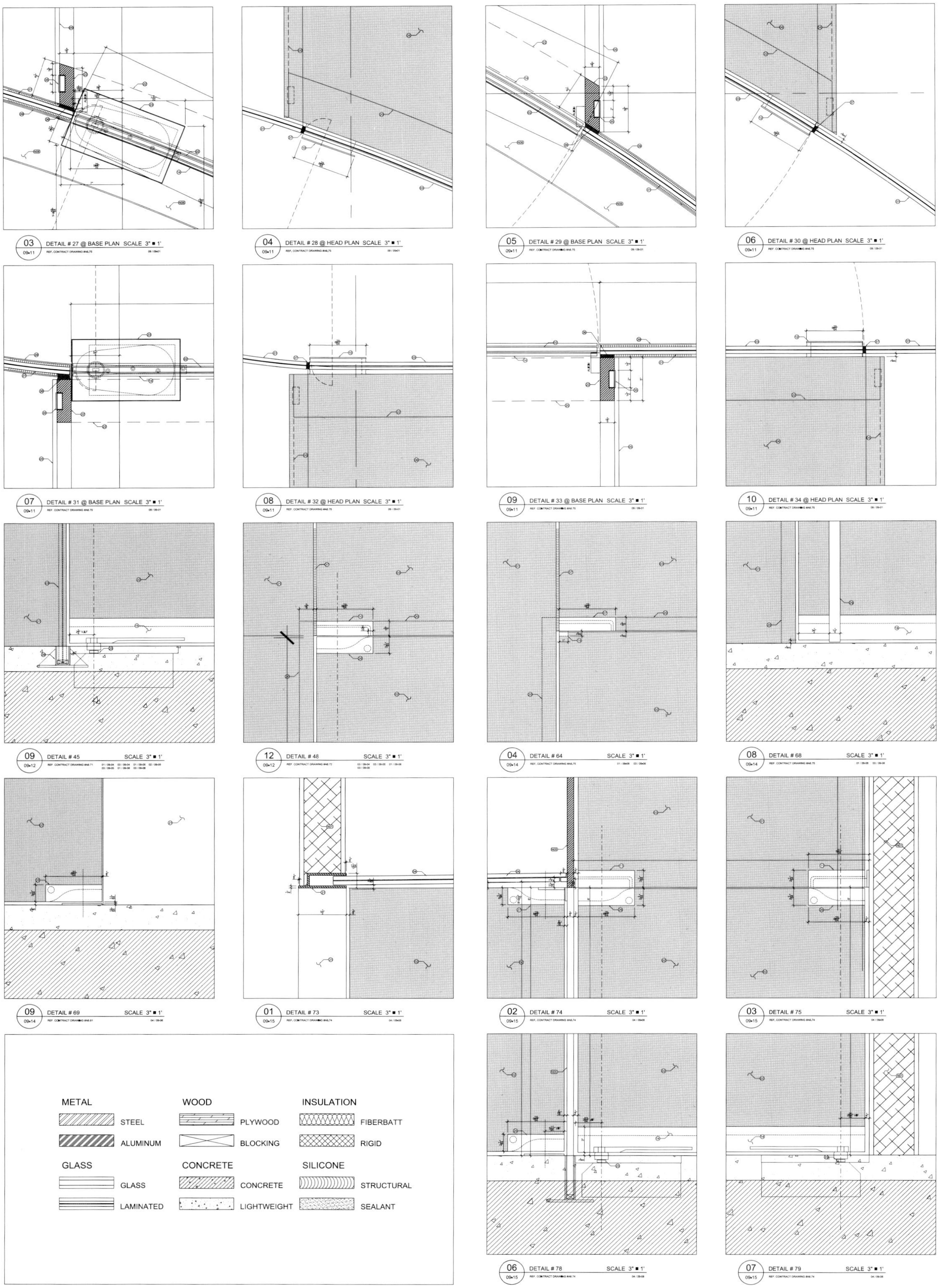
03 09•11 DETAIL # 27 @ BASE PLAN SCALE 3" ■ 1'
04 09•11 DETAIL # 28 @ HEAD PLAN SCALE 3" ■ 1'
05 09•11 DETAIL # 29 @ BASE PLAN SCALE 3" ■ 1'
06 09•11 DETAIL # 30 @ HEAD PLAN SCALE 3" ■ 1'
07 09•11 DETAIL # 31 @ BASE PLAN SCALE 3" ■ 1'
08 09•11 DETAIL # 32 @ HEAD PLAN SCALE 3" ■ 1'
09 09•11 DETAIL # 33 @ BASE PLAN SCALE 3" ■ 1'
10 09•11 DETAIL # 34 @ HEAD PLAN SCALE 3" ■ 1'
09 09•12 DETAIL # 45 SCALE 3" ■ 1'
12 09•12 DETAIL # 48 SCALE 3" ■ 1'
04 09•14 DETAIL # 64 SCALE 3" ■ 1'
08 09•14 DETAIL # 68 SCALE 3" ■ 1'
09 09•14 DETAIL # 69 SCALE 3" ■ 1'
01 09•15 DETAIL # 73 SCALE 3" ■ 1'
02 09•15 DETAIL # 74 SCALE 3" ■ 1'
03 09•15 DETAIL # 75 SCALE 3" ■ 1'
METAL
STEEL
ALUMINUM
WOOD
PLYWOOD
BLOCKING
INSULATION
FIBERBATT
RIGID
GLASS
GLASS
LAMINATED
CONCRETE
CONCRETE
LIGHTWEIGHT
SILICONE
STRUCTURAL
SEALANT
06 09•15 DETAIL # 78 SCALE 3" ■ 1'
07 09•15 DETAIL # 79 SCALE 3" ■ 1'

7 World Trade Center, New York, New York
Skidmore, Owings & Merrill LLP, New York

The 740-foot-tall 7 World Trade Center tower (7 WTC) marks the northern entrance to the World Trade Center complex, where Greenwich Street now passes through the site, to establish a new visual connection between TriBeCa and the Financial District. The original 7 WTC, completed in 1987, was constructed above a service node to the World Trade Center containing a Con Edison substation with ten active transformer vaults. Design work on the new 7 WTC began shortly after September 11, 2001, because of the urgent need to restore these vaults to the Manhattan power grid. The office tower had to be designed and constructed above a substation, creating two independent yet connected structures in one building.

One of the main objectives in the design of 7 WTC was the creation of a porous podium wrapper that would accommodate the intense airflow requirements of the substation's transformers, be animated and interesting at street level to passing pedestrians, and have the visual strength to support the crystalline tower above. An industrial filtration product, made for use in hydroelectric dams, was appropriated for the stainless-steel screen created with James Carpenter Design Associates. Through manipulation of metal rods in profile, orientation, finish, and density, the screen's surface became both reflective and porous, providing depth, textural variation, and visual ambiguity in a relatively shallow construction space. An internally radiant volume, or "locking block," that gradually changes from white to cobalt blue after dusk was introduced to fuse the stainless-steel screen surrounding the podium visually and conceptually with the glass volume of the forty-two-story tower into a single continuous form.

An 8-inch space between the two layers of the screen accommodates an interactive lighting program. Motion sensors embedded in the wall signal strips of blue and white LED fixtures inserted in the cavity to illuminate as pedestrians pass by, creating a moiré effect that corresponds directly to their movements. The highly specular prismatic wires at the front of the screen all have 1/2-inch cross-sectional faces, and the back-screen prismatic wires, glass bead blasted to diffuse and scatter light, have 1/4-inch cross-sectional faces. The two wire sizes produce complementary patterns of light reflection to modulate the moiré effect created by two layers of parallel lines. The material qualities, size, spacing, and orientation of the wires fulfill the practical and aesthetic requirements of the installation, providing a screen to ventilate the transformers and an animated backdrop for pedestrian traffic. The scrim of stainless-steel prisms both reflects and re-projects the variable light conditions of the urban site.

The LED fixtures programmed to create a range of scenes using varying compositions of blue and white light are linked to a video-camera recognition system, with eight cameras mounted 60 feet above street level on the north and south elevations to track pedestrian movement on the sidewalk below. This system can be programmed to detect the movements of individual pedestrians and represent them as 80-foot-high vertical bars of colored light inside the podium skin.

A 40-foot-tall by 110-foot-long glass wall, inserted between two rows of transformer vaults, serves as the street-level entry to the building. The use of a cable-net wall, which tolerates movement, allowed the expanse of glass at the lobby entrance to be maximized without compromising security and provides effective protection against blasts. An innovative method of mechanically capturing the interlayer of the laminated glass allows the glass to be held in place even after structural failure of the wall itself.

SOM and James Carpenter Design Associates contributed to this text.

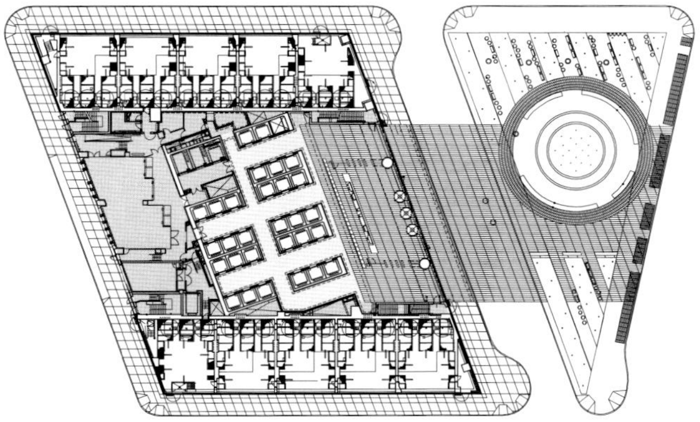

This page
Site plan

Opposite
Top: View southeast
Bottom: Podium detail

This page
Top: Curtain-wall mockup
Middle: Curtain-wall installation (left); exterior-wall construction
Bottom: Typical-floor curtain-wall section and elevation detail (left and middle); curtain-wall detail

Opposite
Top: Typical panel at podium wall (left); podium corner, axonometric
Bottom: Podium wall, exploded axonometric

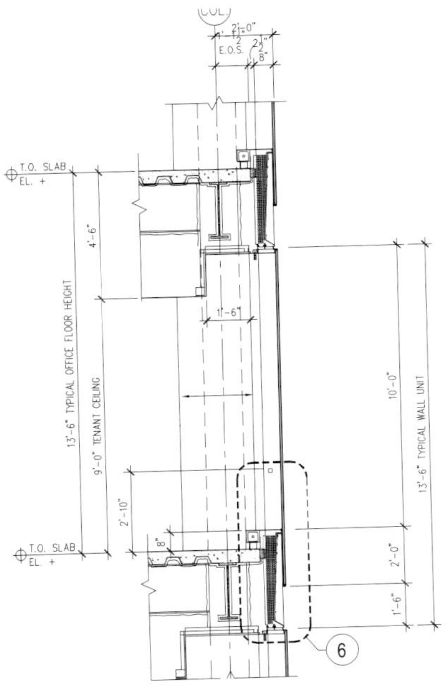

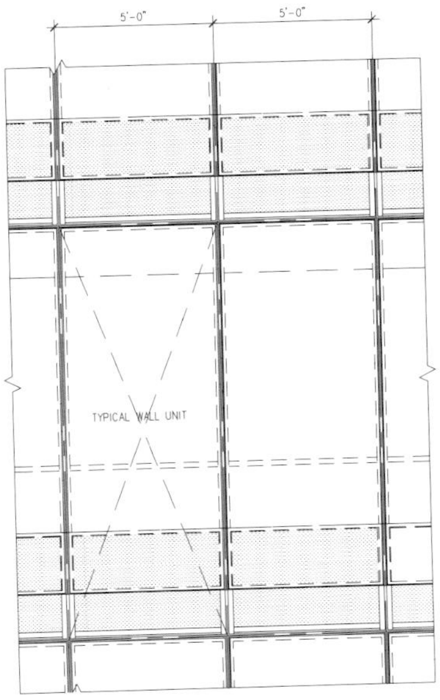

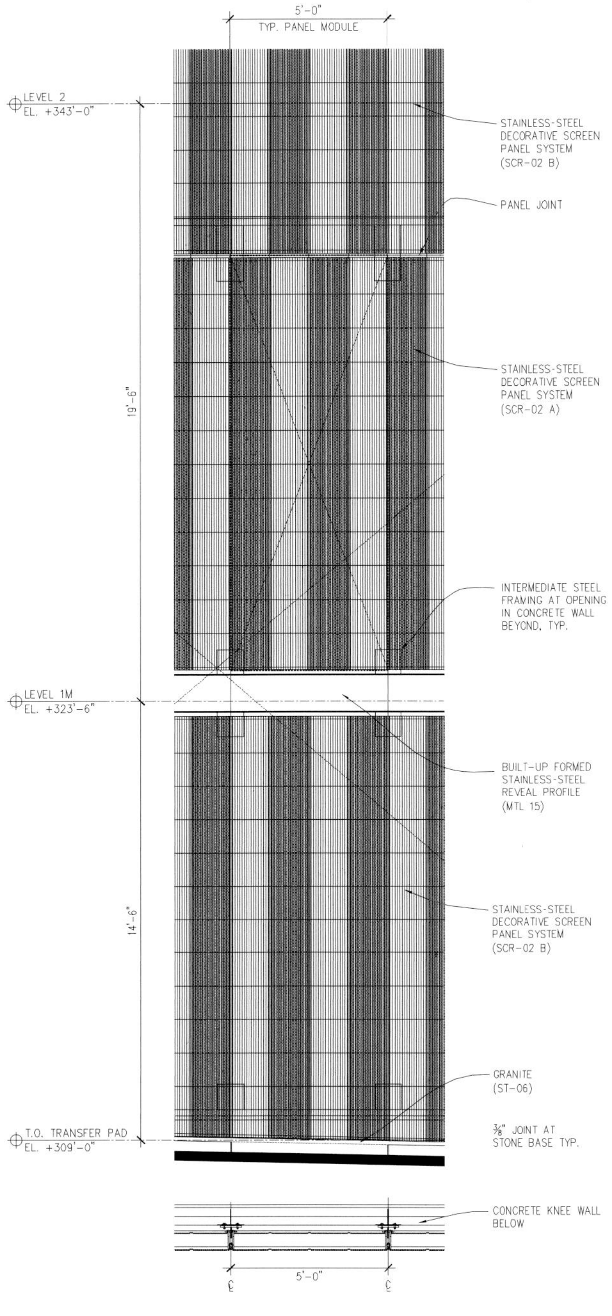
5'-0"
TYP. PANEL MODULE
LEVEL 2
EL. +343'-0"
STAINLESS-STEEL
DECORATIVE SCREEN
PANEL SYSTEM
(SCR-02 B)
PANEL JOINT
19'-6"
STAINLESS-STEEL
DECORATIVE SCREEN
PANEL SYSTEM
(SCR-02 A)
INTERMEDIATE STEEL
FRAMING AT OPENING
IN CONCRETE WALL
BEYOND, TYP.
LEVEL 1M
EL. +323'-6"
BUILT-UP FORMED
STAINLESS-STEEL
REVEAL PROFILE
(MTL 15)
14'-6"
STAINLESS-STEEL
DECORATIVE SCREEN
PANEL SYSTEM
(SCR-02 B)
GRANITE
(ST-06)
T.O. TRANSFER PAD
EL. +309'-0"
3/8" JOINT AT
STONE BASE TYP.
CONCRETE KNEE WALL
BELOW
5'-0"

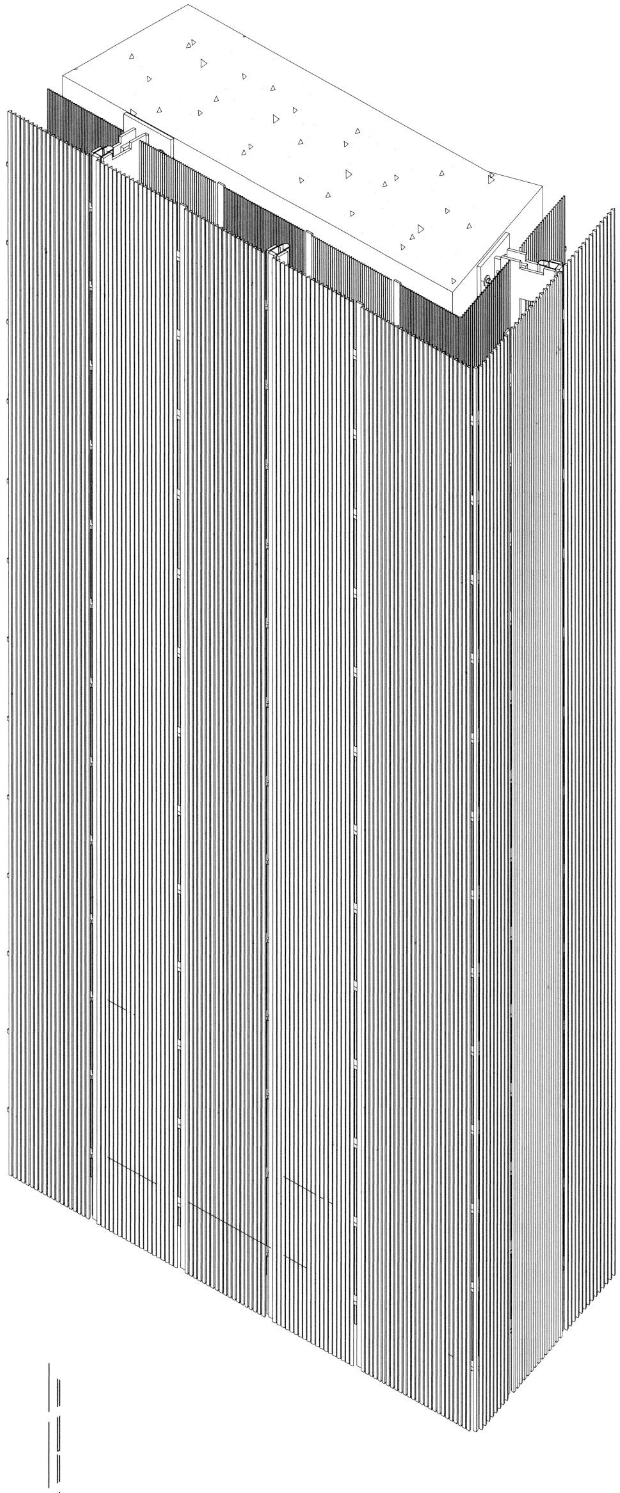

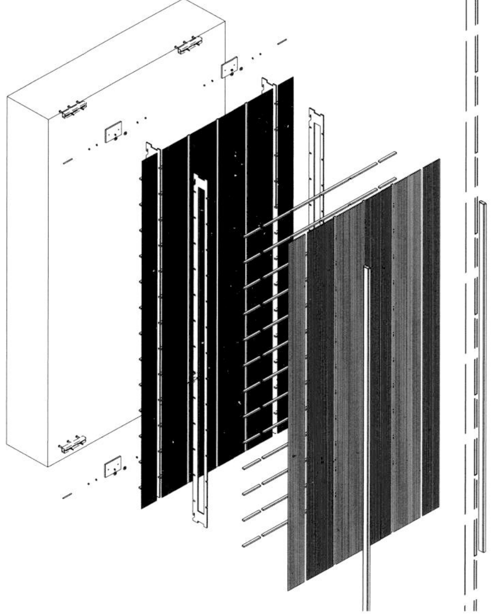

This page
Top: Installation detail
Middle: Panel installation on podium wall
Bottom: Acute-corner detail at exterior podium wall (left); eight-inch space between podium screens

Opposite
Left (top to bottom): Podium-panels detail; panel mockup
Right: Partial section at Greenwich Street

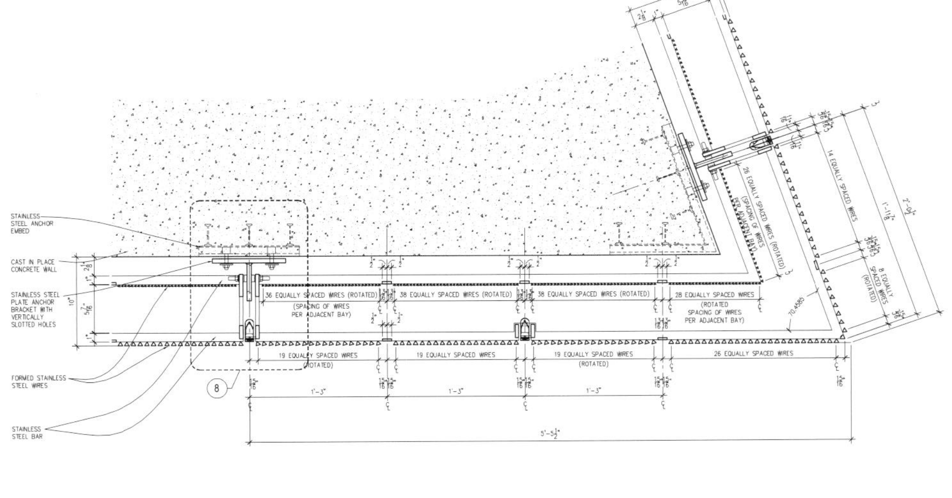

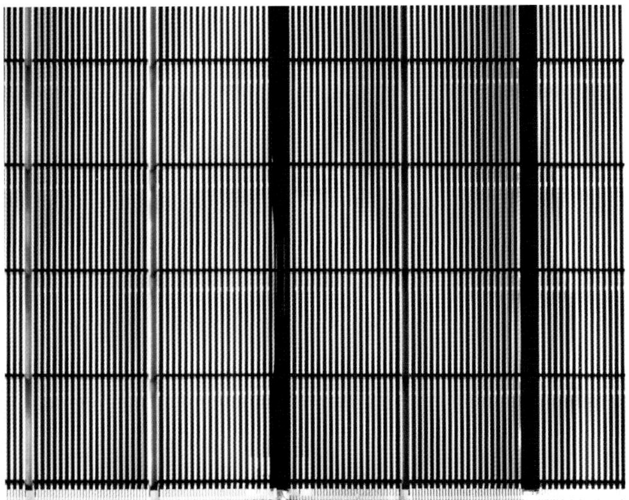

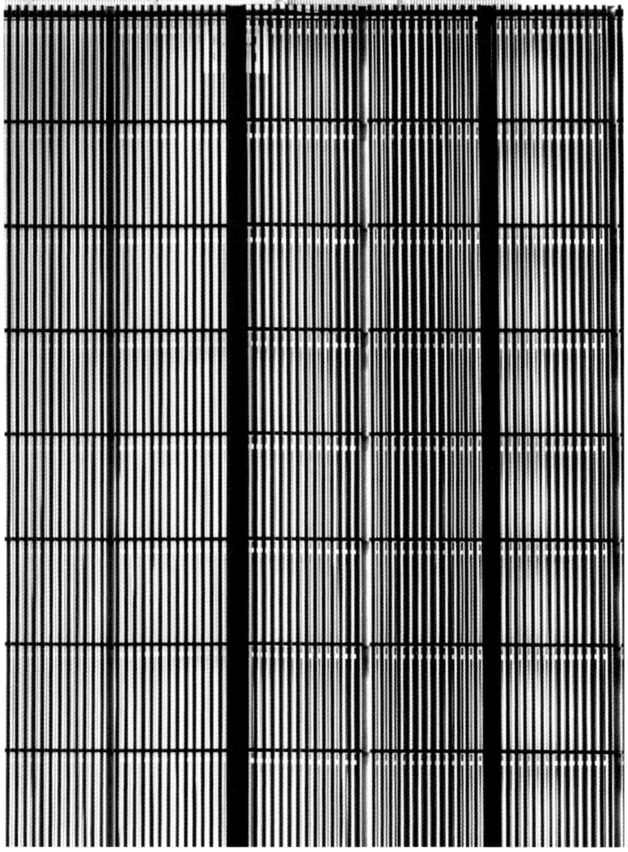

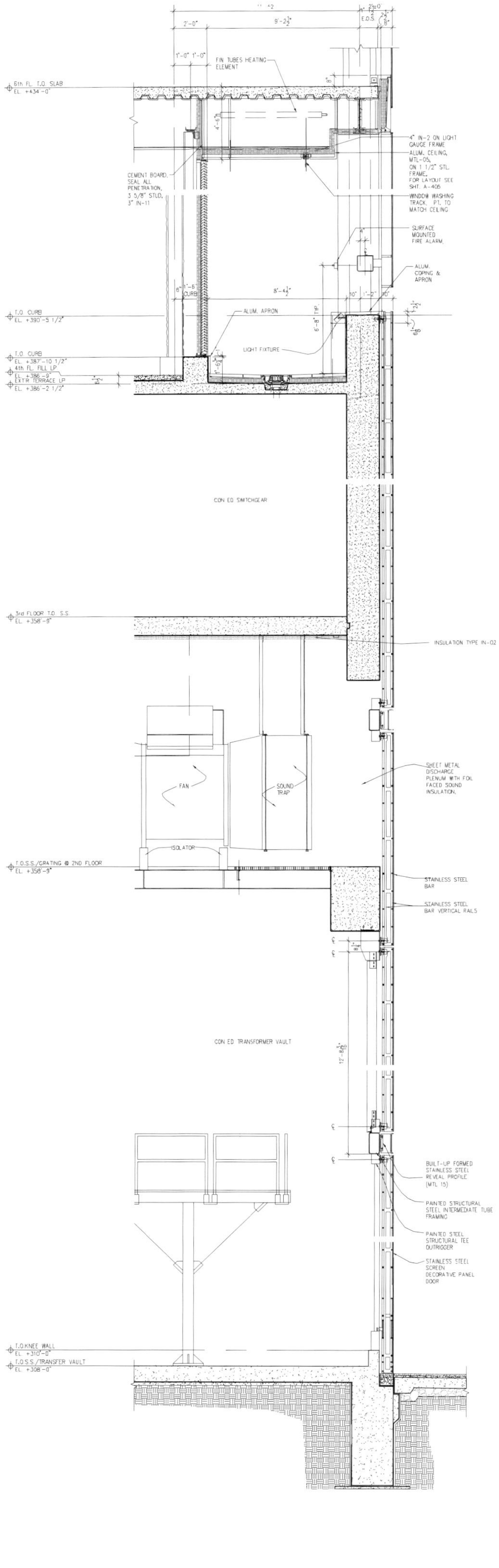
6th FL. T.O SLAB
EL. +434'-0"
FIN TUBES HEATING ELEMENT
4" IN-2 ON LIGHT GAUGE FRAME
ALUM. CEILING, MTL-05, ON 1 1/2" STL. FRAME, FOR LAYOUT SEE SHT. A-405
CEMENT BOARD, SEAL ALL PENETRATION, 3 5/8" STUD, 3" IN-11
WINDOW WASHING TRACK, PT. TO MATCH CEILING
SURFACE MOUNTED FIRE ALARM
ALUM. COPING & APRON
T.O CURB
EL. +390'-5 1/2"
ALUM. APRON
LIGHT FIXTURE
T.O CURB
EL. +387'-10 1/2"
4th FL. FILL LP
EL. +386'-9"
EXT'R TERRACE LP
EL. +386'-2 1/2"
CON ED SWITCHGEAR
3rd FLOOR T.O. S.S.
EL. +358'-9"
INSULATION TYPE IN-02
SHEET METAL DISCHARGE PLENUM WITH FOIL FACED SOUND INSULATION
FAN
SOUND TRAP
ISOLATOR
T.O.S.S./GRATING @ 2ND FLOOR
EL. +358'-9"
STAINLESS STEEL BAR
STAINLESS STEEL BAR VERTICAL RAILS
CON ED TRANSFORMER VAULT
BUILT-UP FORMED STAINLESS STEEL REVEAL PROFILE (MTL 15)
PAINTED STRUCTURAL STEEL INTERMEDIATE TUBE FRAMING
PAINTED STEEL STRUCTURAL TEE OUTRIGGER
STAINLESS STEEL SCREEN DECORATIVE PANEL DOOR
T.O.KNEE WALL
EL. +310'-0"
T.O.S.S./TRANSFER VAULT
EL. +308'-0"

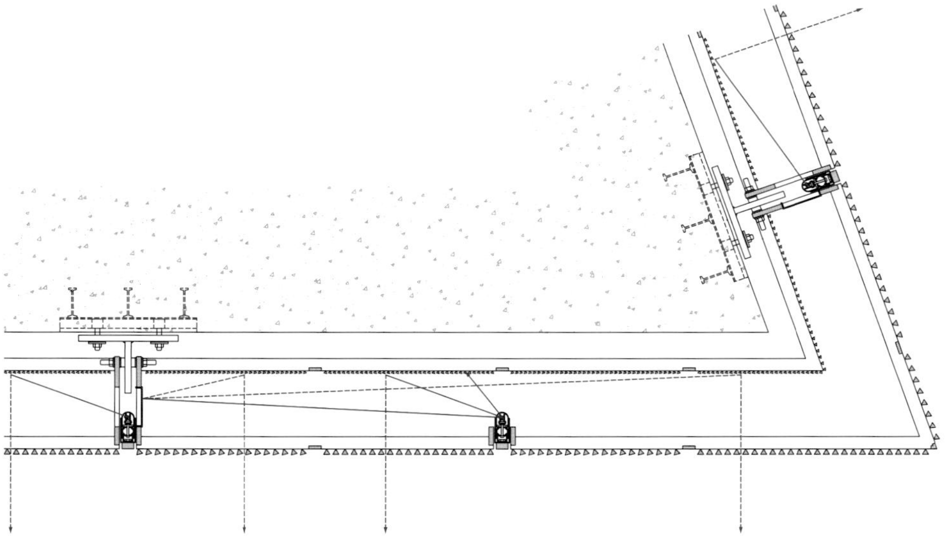

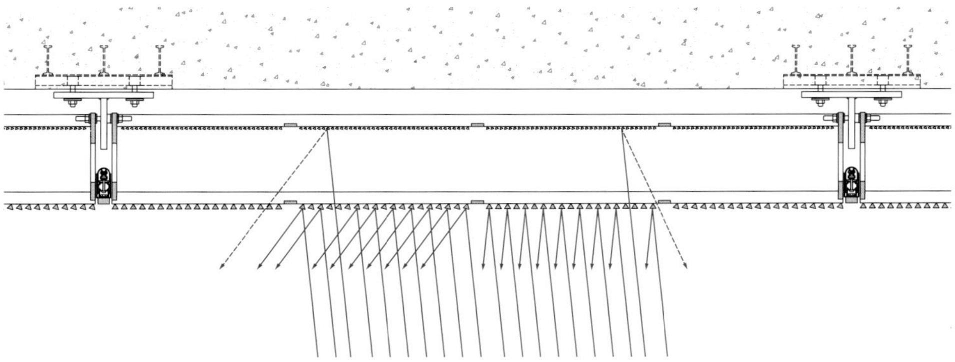

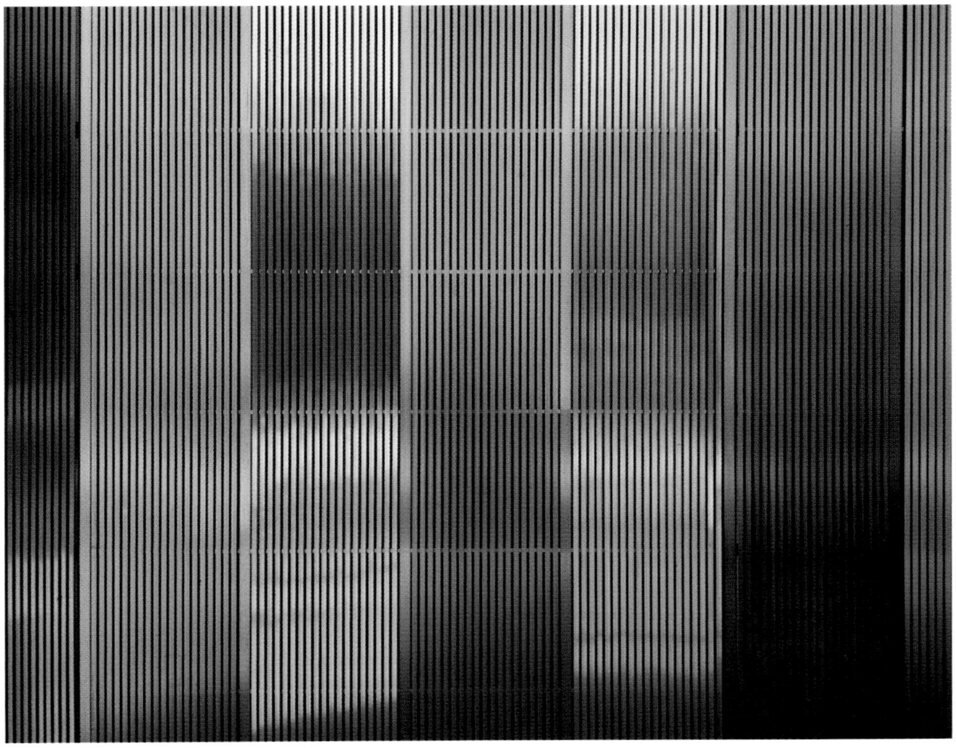

This page
Top: Podium, LED ray trace corner
Middle: Podium, sun ray trace
Bottom: Podium wall, view looking up (left); concept models (top right); podium-wall detail

Opposite
Podium north wall, night view

Library for Manuscripts, Wellesley, Massachusetts
vir.mueller Architects, New Delhi, India

Adjacent to an existing residence, the 900-square-foot Library for Manuscripts houses a collection of primarily Persian manuscripts and paintings for a young family. The owners of the house required a library for their collection that did not attempt to disguise its provenance as a twenty-first-century addition to an existing colonial house. The architects scaled the front of the library to connect with the massing and elevations of the house. The back opens up with a double-height space and window-wall views of the south-facing garden; the library is a large sunny space where the family can work and read together.

Materials include a polished concrete floor with a radiant heating system, bamboo plywood shelves and stairs, and insulated plate-glass windows. A standing-seam metal roof and industrial zinc-coated board-and-batten siding envelop the laminated-timber column-and-beam structure. The roof profile has been designed to channel rainwater and snowmelt into a cistern located at the rear of the building.

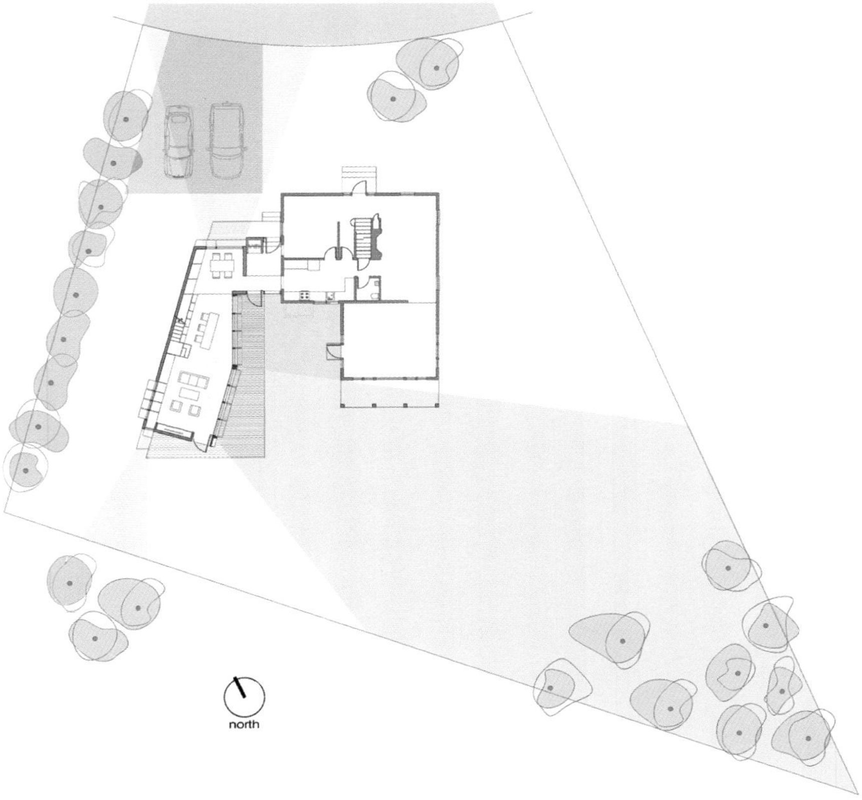

This page
Top: Plan
Bottom: North elevation (left); section

Opposite
Top: South elevation
Bottom: North elevation

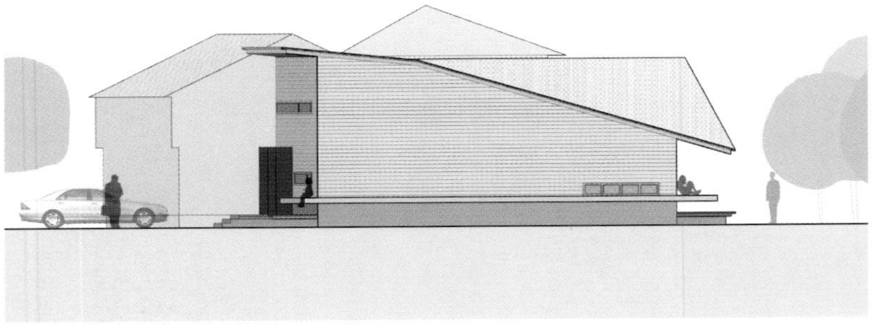

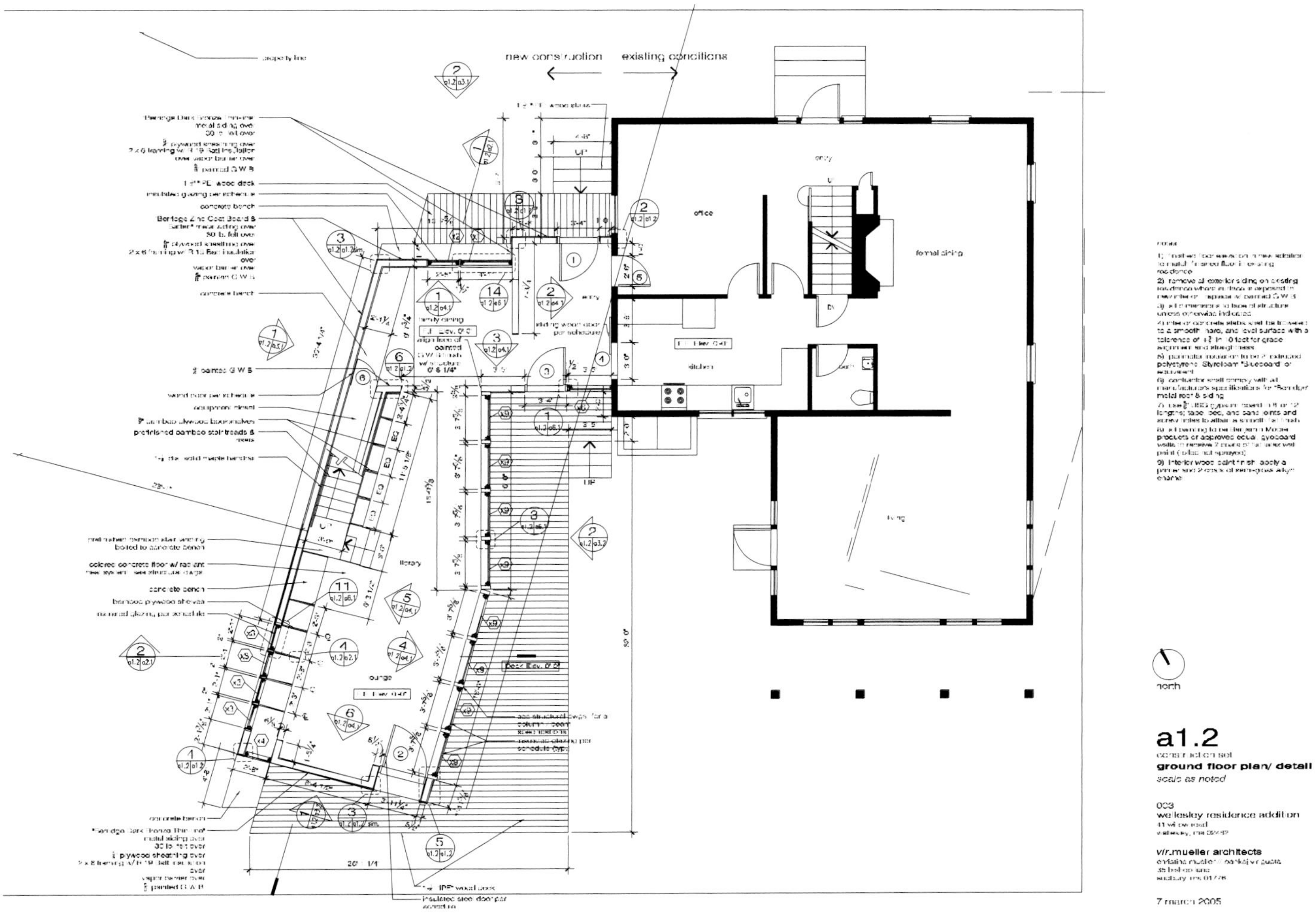

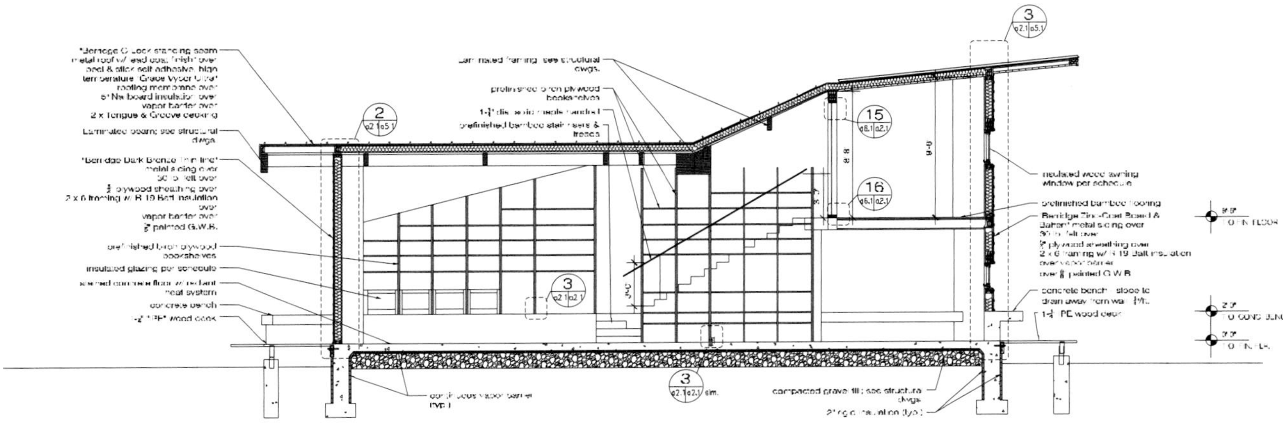

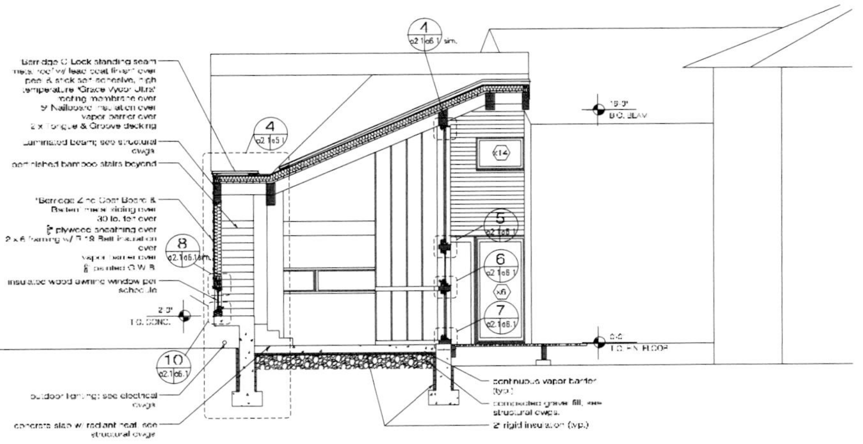

This page
Top: Ground-floor plan
Middle: Longitudinal section
Bottom: Cross section

Opposite
Left: Plan details
Right: Library entrance (top); interior

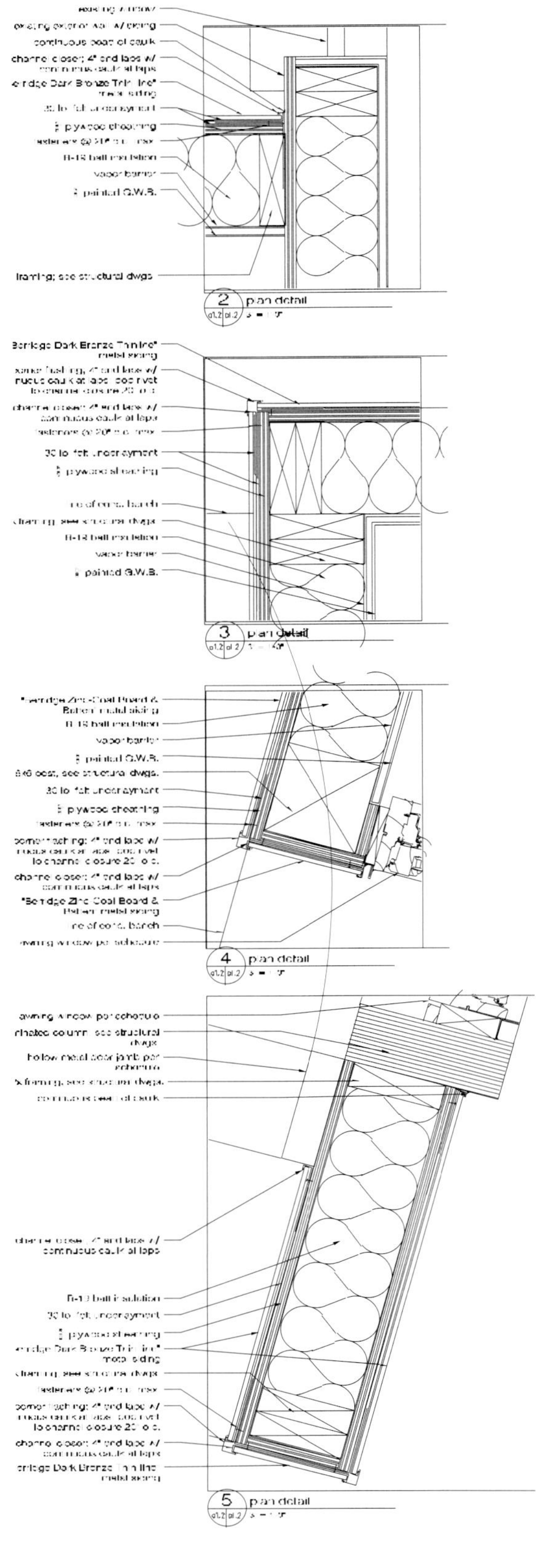

continuous bead of caulk
¾ plywood sheathing
R-19 batt insulation
vapor barrier
½ painted G.W.B.
framing; see structural dwgs
2 plan detail
a1.2 a1.2
Bendige Dark Bronze Trim Inc®
metal siding
30 lb felt underlayment
¾ plywood sheathing
R-19 batt insulation
vapor barrier
½ painted G.W.B.
3 plan detail
a1.2 a1.2
R-19 batt insulation
vapor barrier
½ painted G.W.B.
30 lb felt underlayment
¾ plywood sheathing
*Bendige Zinc Coat Board &
Batten metal siding
4 plan detail
a1.2 a1.2
hollow metal door jamb; per
R-19 batt insulation
30 lb felt underlayment
¾ plywood sheathing
5 plan detail
a1.2 a1.2

House of Sweden (Swedish Embassy), Washington, D.C.
Wingårdh Arkitektkontor AB, Göteborg, Sweden
VOA Associates, Washington, D.C.

The 70,000-square-foot building for the Swedish Embassy is set on a narrow peninsula at the confluence of Rock Creek and the Potomac River. Surrounded by water on three sides, the peninsula faces south and commands spectacular views up and down the Potomac. The prominent site called for an emblematic building through which the essence of Swedish culture, technology, design sensibility, and governance would be expressed.

The House of Sweden redefines the conventional typology of the embassy as fortified bunker by combining spaces for public and commercial activities with official functions behind broad glass facades. The building consists of five floors and a rooftop terrace overlooking the river. The public areas on the first two floors include a lobby, exhibit hall, and a fully equipped event center with conference and meeting rooms. The Swedish Embassy is housed on levels 2 and 3, and there are apartments on levels 4 and 5.

The architecture of the embassy emphasizes transparency rather than barriers, but it is also intended as a response to a new type of diplomacy that includes a commercial component. In addition to the traditional affairs of a diplomatic mission, the Event Center is designed to accommodate public and commercial functions such as conferences and exhibitions. The expanded agenda of the chancellery is reflected in the variety of spaces: the exhibition space on the first floor, with sliding doors that open it to the outside in suitable weather; the lower-level auditorium; and nineteen corporate apartments on the upper floors for lease by Swedish firms, several with balconies overlooking the Potomac. The exterior glazed balconies provide an extra layer of privacy and shade for the apartments and offices. Translucent wood veneer was the architects' first choice for the balconies, but because of concerns about the effects of high humidity on thin layers of wood, a computer-generated wood texture was printed on film and laminated between sheets of glass. When backlit at night, it creates the low-light effect of the setting sun in northern latitudes.

Blond maple veneer is used extensively throughout the interior, as is etched glass with a scrim of mistlike white dots that shifts from opaque to transparent according to the density of the gradient in the dot screen and the application—it disappears almost entirely around stair balustrades. This shift from presence to absence reinforces the building's formal theme of openness and transparency as the basis of Swedish politics and culture, the more solid upper levels supported by a semi-transparent base.

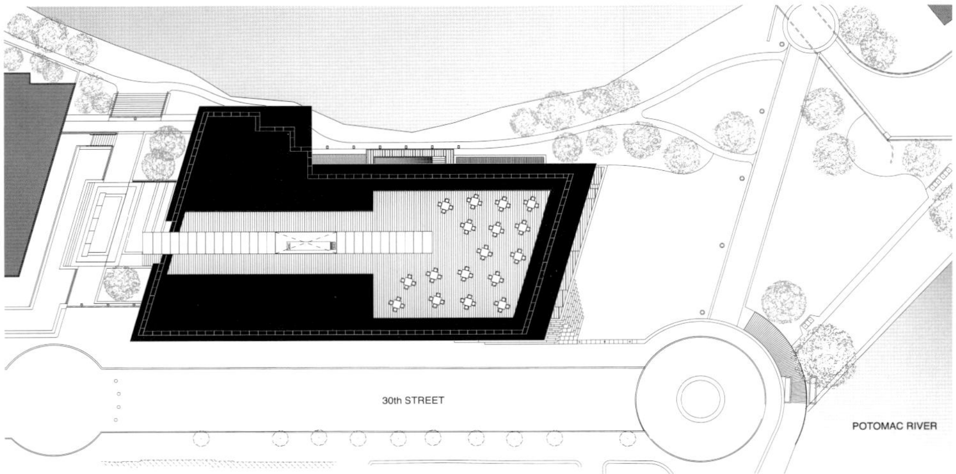

This page
Site plan

Opposite
Top: 30th Street elevation
Bottom: Terrace elevation

This page
Top: Cross section
Middle: Level-2 plan
Bottom: Residential terrace

Opposite
Top: Ceiling detail (left); glass-railing detail
Middle: Terrace elevation (left); soffit detail
Bottom: Interior

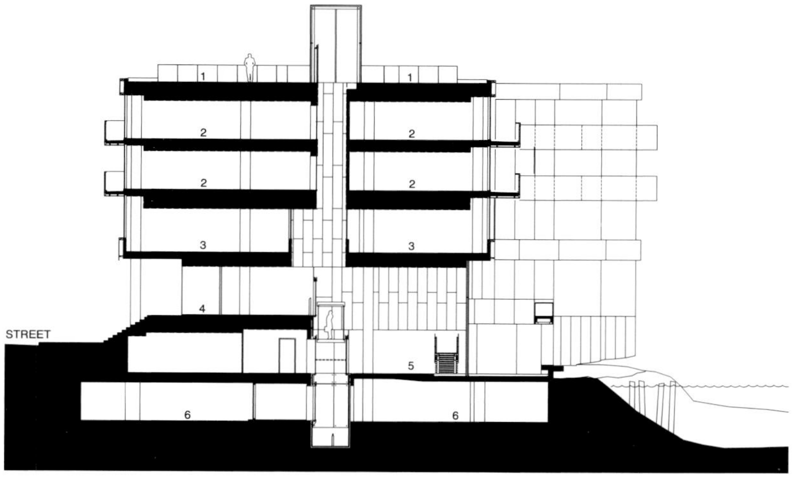

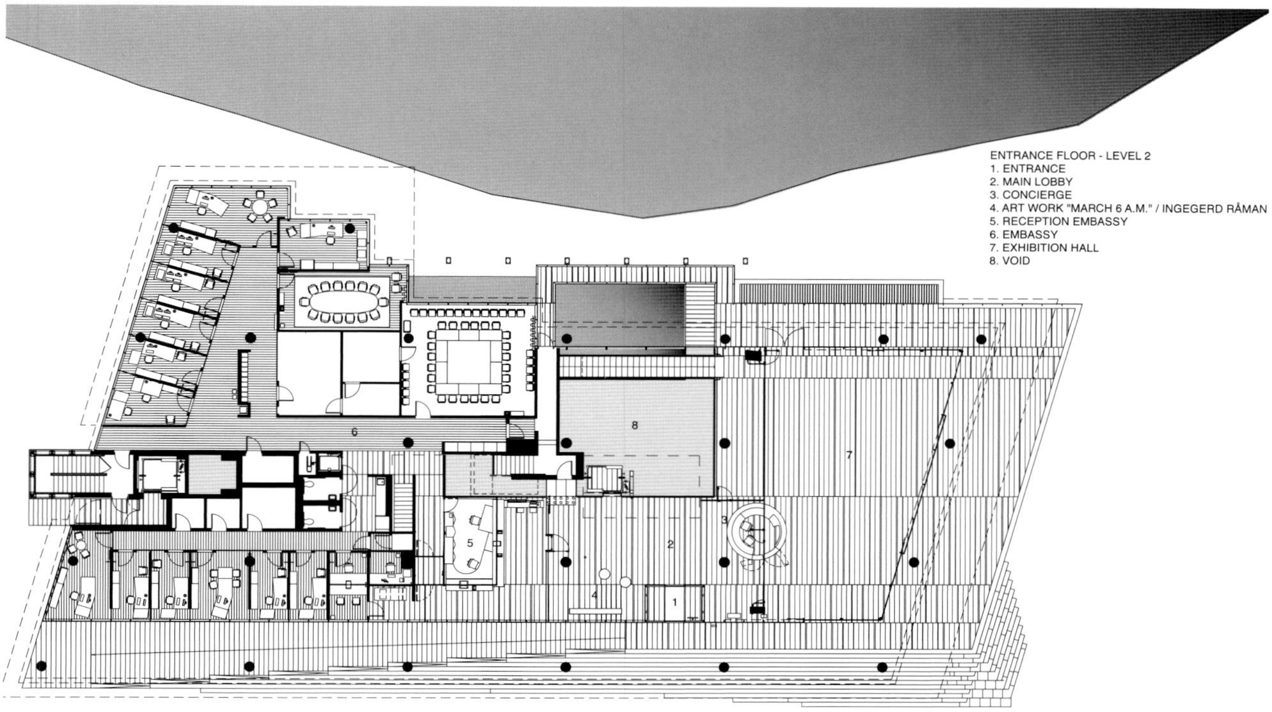

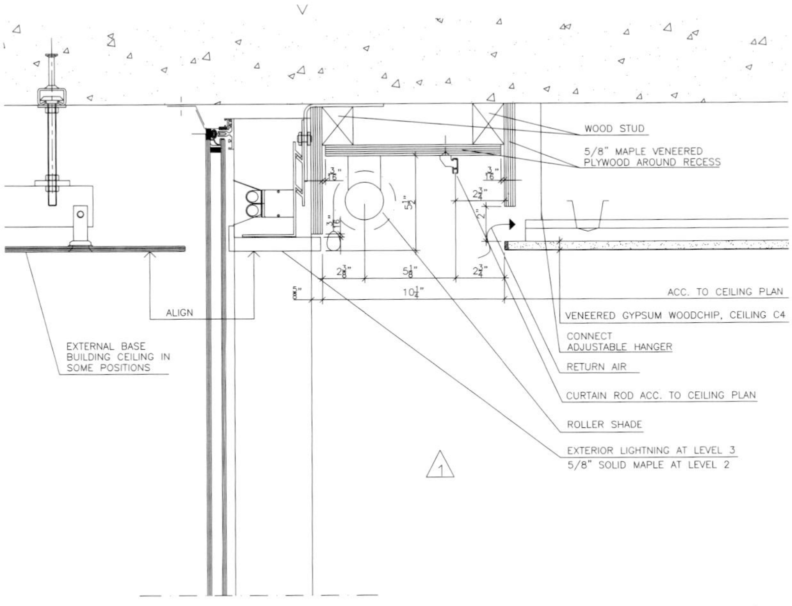

CSD4
OFFICE AND LARGE OFFICE ROOMS
– RAISED CEILING, TYPICAL

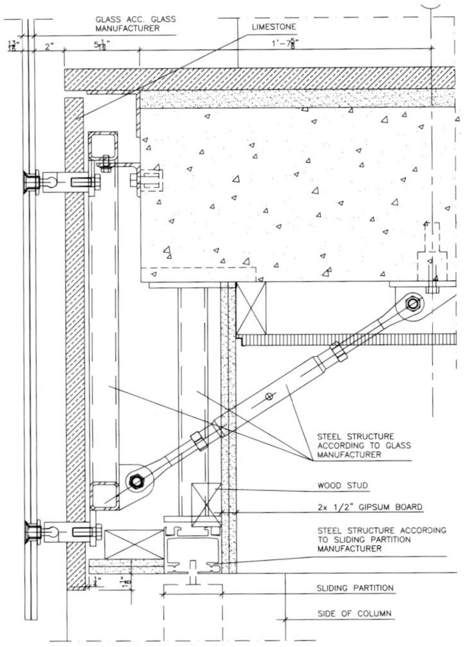

ISD1
GLASS RAILING
/SLIDING PARTITION

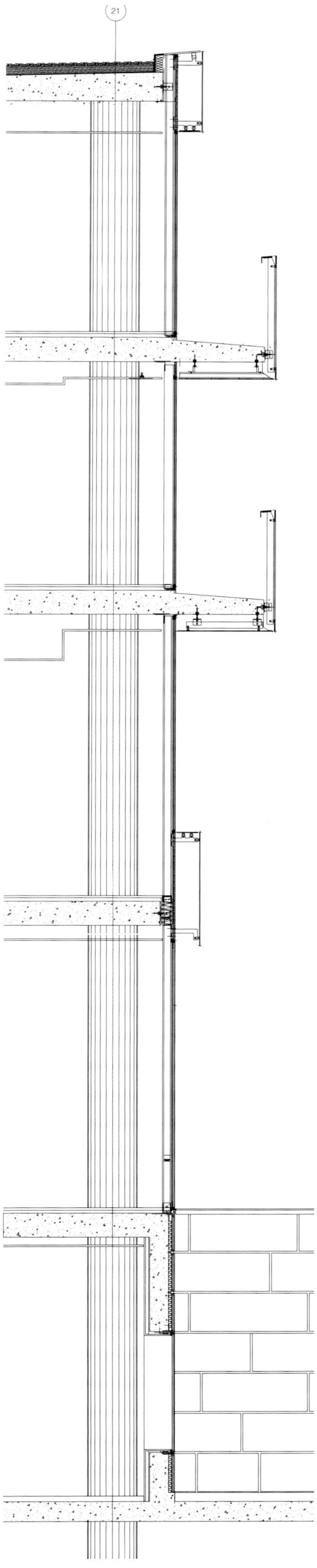
21

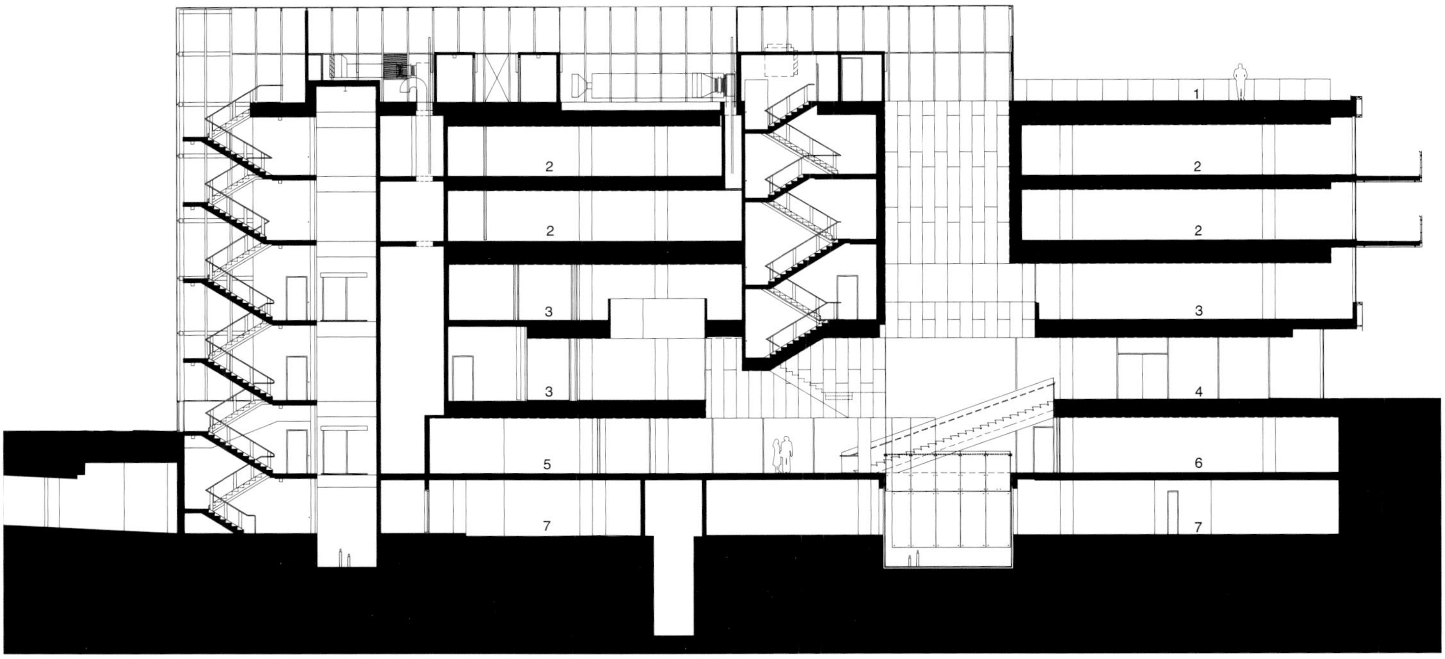

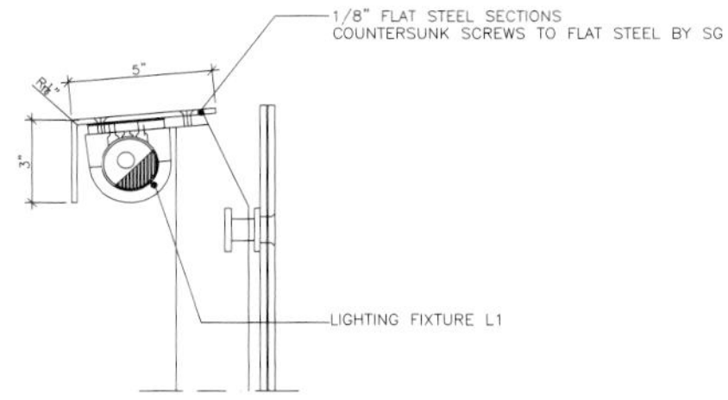

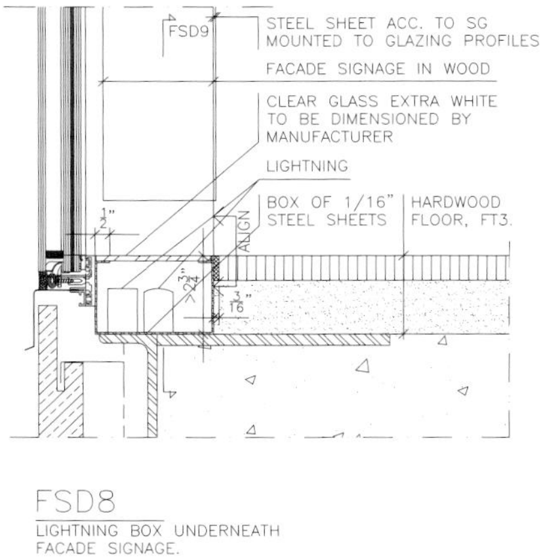

Opposite
Left (top to bottom): Balcony and roof soffits; translucent glass balcony panels
Right: Section detail

This page
Top: Longitudinal section
Middle: Balcony-light detail (left); facade light-box detail
Bottom: Balcony elevation (left); balcony soffit

Acknowledgments

The editors would like to thank the architects, engineers, consultants, manufacturers, and fabricators, as well as their technical and administrative staffs, who have provided drawings, images, and written material for the second volume of AsBuilt; the many excellent architectural photographers who have consented to publication of their work; the Graham Foundation for Advanced Studies in the Fine Arts and Harrison Fraker, FAIA, Dean of the College of Environmental Design at the University of California, Berkeley, for start-up grants; and Jennifer Thompson, Linda Lee, Paul Wagner, Becca Casbon, and Princeton Architectural Press for their continuing support of the AsBuilt series.

Project Credits

7 World Trade Center
Client: Silverstein Properties, Inc.
Architect: Skidmore, Owings & Merrill LLP
Structural Engineers: WSP Cantor Seinuk
Mechanical, Electrical, Plumbing / Vertical Transportation Engineer: Jaros Baum & Bolles
Civil and Transportation Engineer: Philip Habib & Associates
Acoustical Engineer: Cerami & Associates, Inc.
Geotechnical Engineer: Mueser Rutledge Consulting Engineers
Landscape Architect: Ken Smith Landscape Architect
Design Consultant: James Carpenter Design Associates

Biodesign Institute Building B
Client: Arizona State University
Architects: Gould Evans Associates; Lord, Aeck & Sargent Architecture
Structural Engineer: Paragon Structural Design
Mechanical, Electrical, Plumbing, Fire Protection/Alarm, Telecom/Data, and Security Engineer: Newcomb & Boyd
Civil Engineer: Evans, Kuhn & Associates
Vibration and Acoustical Engineer/Design for Technical Spaces: Colin Gordon & Associates
Landscape Architect: Ten Eyck Landscape Architects, Inc.
Lighting Design: Horton Lees Brogden Lighting Design
Acoustical Design: Media Associates, Inc.
Irrigation Design: Aqua Engineering, Inc.

BRIDGES Center
Client: BRIDGES, Inc.
Architect: buildingstudio
Structural Engineer: Guy Nordenson and Associates
Mechanical, Electrical, Plumbing, and Fire Protection Design Engineer: Arup
Civil Engineer and Landscape Architect: ETI Corporation

Children's Museum of Pittsburgh
Client: Children's Museum of Pittsburgh
Design Architect: Koning Eizenberg Architecture
Architect of Record: Perkins Eastman
Structural Engineer: Arup
Mechanical Engineer: IBE Consulting Engineers
Landscape Architect: LaQuantra Bonci Associates
Environmental Artist: Ned Kahn Studios
Consultant: CTG Energetics
Lighting Consultant: Vortex Lighting

de Young Museum
Client: Corporation of the Fine Arts Museums of San Francisco
Design Architect: Herzog & de Meuron Architekten
Principal Architect: Fong & Chan Architects
Structural Engineer: Rutherford & Chekene
Mechanical, Services, and Lighting Engineer: Arup
Design-build Facade Fabricator: A. Zahner Company, Architectural Metals
Landscape Architect: Hood Design

Des Moines Public Library
Client: City of Des Moines
Design Architect: David Chipperfield Architects
Associate Architect: Herbert Lewis Kruse Blunck Architecture
Project Construction Manager: The Weitz Company
Structural Engineer: Jane Wernick Associates
Landscape Architect: ZGF Partnership

Desert House Prototype
All design, engineering, and fabrication by Marmol Radziner Prefab

Floating Box House
Client: Alexa and Blaine Wesner
Architect: Peter L. Gluck & Partners, Architects
Contractor: AR/CS (Architectural Construction Services), Inc.
Structural Engineer: Robert Silman Associates
Mechanical Engineer: S. Berkowitz & Associates

Gary Comer Youth Center
Client: Comer Science and Education Foundation
Architect: John Ronan Architect
Structural Engineer: Arup
Mechanical, Electrical, and Plumbing Engineer: CCJM Engineers Ltd.
Acoustical Engineer: Kirkegaard Associates
Landscape Architect: Peter Lindsay Schaudt Landscape Architecture
Lighting Consultant: Charter Sills & Associates
A/V Consultant: db Integrated Systems

Guthrie Theater
Client: The Guthrie Theater
Design Architect: Ateliers Jean Nouvel
Architect of Record: Architectural Alliance
Structural Engineer: Ericksen, Roed & Associates
Mechanical and Electrical Engineer: Michaud Cooley Erickson
Acoustical Engineer: The Talaske Group, Inc., Kahle Acoustics
Civil Engineer: Van Sickle, Allen & Associates
Geotechnical/Environmental Engineering Consultant: Braun Intertec Corporation

Project Credits

Landscape Architect: oslund.and.assoc.
Theater Consultant: Fisher Dachs Associates

Hearst Tower
Client: The Hearst Corporation
Design Architect: Foster + Partners
Associate Architect: Adamson Associates Architects
Structure: WSP Cantor Seinuk
Mechanical, Electrical, and Plumbing Engineer: Flack + Kurtz
Vertical Transportation: VDA
Lighting: George Sexton Associates
Construction Manager: Turner Construction Company
Design Consultants for Ice Falls Water Feature: James Carpenter Design Associates; Fluidity Design Consultants; Foster + Partners

High Museum of Art
Client: High Museum of Art
Architect: Renzo Piano Building Workshop, in collaboration with Lord, Aeck & Sargent Architecture
Engineers: Arup, in collaboration with Uzun & Case Engineers and Jordan & Skala Engineers
Civil Engineer: HDR
Acoustical, Facade, and Lighting Engineer: Arup

House of Sweden
Client: National Property Board of Sweden
Design Architect: Wingårdh Arkitektkontor AB
Architect of Record: VOA Associates
Structural Engineer: Flygfältsbyrån AB
Mechanical, Electrical, and Plumbing Engineer (USA): Joseph R. Loring & Associates, Inc.
Electrical Engineer (Sweden): MIAB (Mikaelssons Ingenjörsbyrå AB)
Mechanical, Electrical, and Plumbing (Sweden): L.E.B Consult AB
Lighting Design: Ljusarkitektur P & Ö AB

La Maison Unique
Client: Longchamp
Design Architect: Heatherwick Studio
Associate Architect: Atmosphere Design Group LLC
Structural Engineer: Building Structural Engineering Services
Engineering Services: Gilsanz Murray Steficek

Leslie Dan Pharmacy Building
Client: University of Toronto
Design Architect: Foster + Partners
Architect of Record: Cannon Design / Moffat Kinoshita Architects
Quantity Surveyor: Vermeulens Cost Consultants
Structural Engineer: Halcrow Yolles
Electrical and Mechanical Engineer: H. H. Angus & Associates Ltd.
Laboratory Consultant: Levine Lauzon Architects
Landscape Architect: Diana Gerard Landscape Architecture
Lighting Design: Claude R. Engle Lighting Consultants

Library for Manuscripts
Client: Parinaz Eleish
Architect: vir.mueller Architects
Structural Engineer: Simpson Gumpertz & Heger Inc.
Mechanical and Electrical Engineer: Ibrahim & Ibrahim Consulting Engineers

Marsupial Bridge and Urban Plaza
Client: City of Milwaukee Department of Public Works
Architect: La Dallman Architects, Inc.
Structural Engineer: Bloom Consultants, LLC
Electrical Engineer: Powrtek Engineering, Inc.
Lighting Design: Noele Stollmack Lighting Design

Meinel Optical Sciences Building
Client: University of Arizona
Architect: Richärd + Bauer
Structural, Mechanical, Electrical, and Lighting Engineer: Arup
Civil Engineers: KPFF Consulting Engineers
Landscape Architect: Sage Landscape
Architecture IT Consultants: Arup
Lab Consultants: Earl Walls Associates

Morimoto New York
Client: Starr Restaurant Organization
Design Architect: Tadao Ando Architect & Associates
Project Architect: Gotodesigngroup LLC
Architect of Record: Guggenheimer Architects
Furniture Design: Ross Lovegrove
Structural: Leslie E. Robertson Associates
Mechanical, Electrical, and Plumbing Engineer: Thomas Polise Consulting Engineers
Geotechnical Engineer: Langan
Lighting Consultant: Isometrix Lighting + Design
Concrete Consultant: Reginald D. Hough, FAIA

Pedestrian Bridge
Client: Name Withheld
Architect: Miró Rivera Architects
Structural Engineer: Chuck Naeve, Architectural Engineers Collaborative
Landscape Architect: David Mahler, Environmental Survey Consulting
Contractor: Don Crowell, Inc.

Picower Institute for Learning and Memory
Client: Massachusetts Institute of Technology
Design Architect: Charles Correa Associates
Architect of Record and Laboratory Architect: Goody Clancy
Facade Engineer and Vibration Consultant: Arup
Building Structural Engineer: LeMessurier Consultants
Geotechnical Engineer: Haley & Aldrich
Mechanical and Electrical Engineer: BR+A Consulting Engineers

Terrence Donnelly Centre for Cellular and Biomolecular Research
Client: University of Toronto
Design Architect: Behnisch Architekten
Architect of Record: architectsAlliance
Structural Engineer: Halcrow Yolles
Mechanical and Electrical Engineer: H. H. Angus & Associates Ltd.
Landscape Architect: Diana Gerrard Landscape Architecture

Toledo Museum of Art Glass Pavilion
Client: Toledo Museum of Art
Design Architect: Kazuyo Sejima + Ryue Nishizawa / SANAA
Architect of Record: Kendall / Heaton Associates, Inc.
Structural Engineer: SAPS / Sasaki and Partners
Engineer of Record: Guy Nordenson and Associates
Mechanical, Electrical, and Plumbing Engineer: Cosentini Associates
Civil Engineer: The Mannik & Smith Group, Inc.
Geotechnical Engineer: Bowser Morner Environmental Design
Climate Engineer: Transsolar Klima Engineering
Acoustical Consultant: Harvey Marshall Berling Associates
Facade / Glass Consultant: Front Inc.
Project Manager: Paratus Group

University of Cincinnati Campus Recreation Center
Client: University of Cincinnati
Design Architect: Morphosis
Executive Architect: KZF Design
Interior Designer: Morphosis
Structural Engineer: THP Limited, Inc.
Structural System Schematic Design: Arup
Mechanical, Electrical, and Plumbing Engineer: Heapy Engineering
Mechanical, Electrical, and Plumbing Schematic Design: IBE Consulting Engineers
Landscape Architect: Hargreaves Associates

University of Phoenix Stadium
Client: Arizona Cardinals; Arizona Sports & Tourism Authority
Design Architect: Eisenman Architects
Facility Architect: HOK Sport
Structural Roof Engineer: Walter P. Moore
Structural Frame Engineer: TLCP
Mechanical and Electrical Engineer: M-E Engineers
Roof & Field Mechanization: Uni-Systems
Geotechnical Engineer: GEC
Playing Field: CMX Sports Engineers
Civil Engineer: Evans, Kuhn & Associates
Electrical Engineer: CR Engineers
Civil Engineer: MX Sports Engineers, Inc.
Bridge Engineer: Stanley Consultants

Illustration Credits

7 World Trade Center
James Carpenter Design Associates 189, 191BL, 192 left column, 192TR
Skidmore, Owings & Merrill LLP 186, 188T, 188CR, 188BL, 188BC, 190BL, 190BR, 191R
David Sundberg/Esto 187B, 188CL, 183BR, 190T, 190C, 191TL, 192BR, 193
Ruggero Vanni 187T

Biodesign Institute Building B
Mark Boisclair 85, 86B, 87 left column, 88B, 89B
Gould Evans Associates 84, 86T, 87T, 87BR, 88T, 89TL, 89TR

BRIDGES Center
buildingstudio 28, 30, 32TL, 32 bottom row, 33, 34T, 36T
Guy Nordenson and Associates 32TR, 32CR
Timothy Hursley 29, 31, 36B, 37
Anastasia Laurenzi 34B, 35

Children's Museum of Pittsburgh
Ned Kahn 113, 114, 115B, 116BL, 117
Koning Eizenberg Architecture 112, 115R, 116T
Roderick Villafranca 116BR

de Young Museum
A. Zahner Company 104C, 104CR, 104 bottom row, 106, 107, 108TL, 108CL, 110, 111TL, 111TR
Corporation of the Fine Arts Museums of San Francisco 101, 103CB, 103B, 104CL, 105BL, 105BR, 108B, 109B, 111B
Herzog & de Meuron Architekten 102, 103T, 103CT, 104TL, 104TR, 105 top & center rows, 108TR, 109TL, 109TR

Des Moines Public Library
Farshid Assassi 39, 41, 43B
David Chipperfield Architects 38, 40, 42T
Des Moines Public Library 42BL, 42BR
Okalux GmbH 43 top row

Desert House Prototype
Benny Chan/Photoworks 127, 129, 131
Marmol Radziner Prefab 126, 128, 130

Floating Box House
Peter Gluck and Partners 78, 80 left column, 80TR, 81T, 81CT, 81CB, 82TL, 82TR, 83TL, 83TR, 83CR
Paul Warchol 79, 80B, 81B, 82BL, 82BR, 83B

Gary Comer Youth Center
Steve Hall/Hedrich Blessing 169, 171, 173BL, 173BR
John Ronan Architect 168, 170, 172, 173 top row

Guthrie Theater
Ateliers Jean Nouvel 145B, 146T, 148T, 148C, 149
Ericksen Roed & Associates, Inc. 146

Roland Halbe 147BL, 148B
Kveberg Photo & Electronics, Inc. 145T, 147CTL, 147CBL, 147CTR, 147CBR, 147BR

Hearst Tower
Chuck Choi 61, 63T
Fluidity Design Consultants 64B, 66, 67TL, 67TR
Foster + Partners 60, 62T, 65T
James Carpenter Design Associates 62B, 63B, 64T, 64CL, 64CR, 65B, 67B

High Museum of Art
Michel Denance 151B, 153BL, 153TR, 153BR, 155BL, 155BR, 156BR
Georgia-Pacific Building Products 154 bottom row
High Museum of Art 151T, 156BL
Lord, Aeck & Sargent Architecture 152, 154TL, 154TR, 154CR, 155 top row, 156 top & center rows
Renzo Piano Building Workshop 157
Randal Vaughan, AIA 153TL, 153CR

House of Sweden
Ake E:son Lindman 199, 200B, 201CL, 201CR, 201B, 202TL, 202TR, 203BL, 203BR
Wingårdh Arkitektkontor 198, 200T, 200C, 201TL, 20TR, 202R, 203T, 203CL, 203CR

La Maison Unique
Atmosphere Design Group LLC 95 left column, 95TR, 96, 98
Heatherwick Studio 90, 92T, 93T, 94T
Nic Lehoux 91
Adrian Wilson 92BL, 92BR, 93BL, 93BR, 94BL, 94BR, 95CR, 95BR, 97, 99

Leslie Dan Pharmacy Building
Foster + Partners 68, 74, 75TL, 75TR, 75CR, 76T, 76C, 77T
Gokche Erkan 75BL, 75BR, 76BL, 76BR, 77B
Walters, Inc., 70, 71, 72
Nigel Young/Foster + Partners 69, 73

Library for Manuscripts
John Horner 195, 197TR, 197BR
vir.mueller Architects 194, 196, 197L

Marsupial Bridge and Urban Plaza
Bloom Consultants, LLC 119T, 122TL, 122CT, 122CB
La Dallman Architects, Inc. 118, 119B, 120, 121, 122TR, 122BL, 122BR, 123, 124, 125

Meinel Optical Sciences Building
Richärd + Bauer Architects 160, 161T, 162T, 162BR, 163T, 164TL, 164BL, 165T, 166T, 166CL, 166CR, 167TL
Bill Timmerman 158, 159, 161B, 162BL, 163B, 164TR, 164BR, 165B, 166BL, 166BR, 167TR, 167BL, 167BR

Morimoto New York
Baltz & Company 12, 13, 15, 16BL, 16BR, 17BL, 17BR, 19T, 19BC, 19BR
Front, Inc. 18BR, 19BL
Gotodesigngroup 14, 18BL
Guggenheimer Architects 16TL, 16TR, 16C, 17TL, 17TR, 18TL, 18TR, 18CL, 18CR

Pedestrian Bridge
Miro Rivera Architects 132–35

Picower Institute for Learning and Memory
Arup 49TL, 49TR
Goody Clancy 44, 46, 47TL, 47TR, 47C, 48T, 48C, 48BL, 49BR
Patrick S. McCafferty 48BR, 49BL
Andy Ryan 45, 47BL, 47BR

Terrence Donnelly Centre for Cellular and Biomolecular Research
Tom Arban 21, 22R, 23BL, 23BR, 25
Behnisch Architekten 20, 22L, 23T, 24, 27
Commercial Vision—Window Blinds & Shading Systems 26

Toledo Museum of Art Glass Pavilion
Guy Nordenson and Associates 180T, 180BR, 181
Christian Richter 175, 176, 177B, 178CL, 178B, 179BL, 179BR, 183TR, 183BR, 184BL, 184BR
SANAA 177TR, 178T, 178CR, 179T, 180BL
Toledo Museum of Art 177TL, 182CL, 182BL
Transsolar Energietechnik GmbH 183 left column
UAD Group 182BR, 184T, 184 center top & center bottom rows, 185

University of Phoenix Stadium
Arizona Cardinals 51, 53B, 54B, 55C, 55BL, 55BR, 57B, 58BL, 59B
Eisenman Architects 52, 53T, 53C, 56T, 58T
Roland Halbe 58BR, 59T
Walter P. Moore 55TL, 55TR, 57CL
Uni-Systems 54TL, 54TR, 56CL, 56CR, 56BL, 56BR, 57T, 57CR

University of Cincinnati Campus Recreation Center
Detailed Design Drafting Services 139T
Roland Halbe 137, 141, 142TR, 142B, 143TR, 143CR, 143B
McKenrick-Lee Photography, LLC 140B
Morphosis 138, 139B, 140T, 140C, 142TL, 143TL